CARING FOR
School-Age Children

SECOND CANADIAN EDITION

Phyllis M. Click

Jennifer Parker
Moorpark College

Deborah Stone-Zukowski
Conestoga College Institute of
Technology and Advanced Learning

NELSON

NELSON

Caring for School-Age Children
Second Canadian Edition

by Phyllis M. Click, Jennifer Parker,
Deborah Stone-Zukowski

COPYRIGHT © 2013, 2010 by
Nelson Education Ltd.

Adapted from *Caring for
School-Age Children,* Third Edition,
by Phyllis M. Click and Jennifer
Parker, published by Delmar,
a division of Nelson Education Ltd.,
Copyright © 2002.

Printed and bound in Canada
29 30 31 32 22 21 20 19

For more information contact
Nelson Education Ltd.,
1120 Birchmount Road,
Toronto, Ontario M1K 5G4.
Or you can visit our Internet
site at nelson.com.

ISBN-13: 978-0-17-664921-0
ISBN-10: 0-17-664921-2

Cover Image:
© Anatoliy Samara/Shutterstock

In memory of Noel Young

Noel Young was involved in out-of-school programs for 25 years. He was a practitioner, program supervisor, consultant, advocate, and trainer. He was instrumental in setting up a school-age child care association in Ontario and the Exploring Environments newsletter. He was involved in planning an annual school-age child care conference for a number of years and taught in the Early Childhood Education Department at George Brown College. His influence in promoting quality child care and services for children across Canada continues.

BRIEF TABLE OF CONTENTS

TABLE OF CONTENTS

SECTION 3   BACKGROUND

PREFACE

This Second Canadian Edition of *Caring for School-Age Children* is an easy-to-use course of study for those who are preparing for a career in early childhood education and recreation leadership. It is also a valuable resource for those working with school-age children in full-day learning kindergarten programs, extended-day school-age programs, and recreation programs before and after school, and on PD days and holidays. It will also help those in administrative positions, such as directors, principals, managers, or supervisors. In addition, parents of school-age children will find useful information for understanding their youngsters and for participating in the operation of their children's school-age child care program. The text can be used as the basis for a college or university course or for a series of in-service training sessions sponsored by boards of education or community agencies. It will also be useful for administrators of out-of-school programs who wish to upgrade the skills of staff members through in-service training sessions.

Rationale

When the first edition of this book was written, there was little information for those interested in before- and after-school programs. The First Canadian Edition of *Caring for School-Age Children* reflected on a growing international interest in providing quality programs for the large numbers of children who were spending their out-of-school time in a group setting. The authors continue to strongly believe that school-age child care professionals should be able to obtain the education and training they need to provide an optimum environment for young children. Therefore, the Second Edition of this book is based on the most recent information concerning child care and early learning, policies and standards, developmentally responsive practice with kindergarten and school-age children, and the adult role as a professional. The authors have many years of experience teaching both adult and child learners. They have brought their knowledge to this edition to help others achieve quality programs for children through the education of professionals in the fields of full-day early learning–kindergarten, school-age care, and recreation.

Highlights of the Second Canadian Edition

Section 1 New to the first section is an introduction to full-day early learning–kindergarten programs and the extended-day operations of before- and after-school care. ***Chapter 1*** discusses the role of the early childhood educator in early learning and care programs for kindergarten children. ***Chapter 2*** introduces new research about the importance of children's ability to regulate their emotions in prosocial ways, which helps them with later success in school and in life. ***Chapter 3*** provides an update of research on the configuration of families in Canada, outlining current initiatives to combat poverty in Aboriginal communities.

Section 2 ***Chapter 4*** continues to explore ways to assist children in maintaining their physical development and overall well-being. Some new statistics have been added on obesity in school-age children. In ***Chapter 5***, the constructivist learning theory is added, bringing forth a fresh perspective on how children learn and the role that school-age child care professionals take in promoting discovery, inquiry, and investigative learning in programs for children from ages 3.8–12 years of age.

Chapter 6 talks about the benefits of risk taking as a means of developing strong emotional and social capabilities as children meet everyday challenges. Self-regulation skills are discussed in *Chapter 7* under the topic of developing social competence. Ways of supporting children as they learn to manage their own emotions, behaviour, and attention in socially acceptable ways are expanded on. Programs such as Reaching In … Reaching Out, Roots of Empathy, and other resources about anti-bullying have been added.

Section 3   Chapter 8 expands on how to apply constructivist theories of learning to program planning. It talks about the processes of observation, child-to-staff interactions, and documentation as a means of developing children's interests and making their learning meaningful and relevant to them. High/Scope, Waldorf, and Montessori programs have been added, with particular emphasis on out-of-school options that they offer. Full-day early learning–kindergarten programs are also explored in more detail here. In *Chapter 9*, some more current perspectives on the aesthetics, multipurpose, and flexible arrangements of indoor space and the use of natural play spaces outdoors is discussed.

Section 4   This section looks in more detail at the practices of incorporating inquiry learning, investigation, and exploration throughout the curriculum of the program through the children's ongoing interests and experiences. *Chapter 10* explains how games can help children develop self-regulation skills by learning to take turns, work together, and problem solve. *Chapter 11* brings more focus to inquiry learning through the arts in various ways. *Chapter 12* provides a greater examination of how children can find more meaning in their learning through exploration and investigation of interests in mathematics, science, and technology. *Chapter 13* has some new updated resources added. *Chapter 14* continues to support the benefits of active play and the importance of staying fit in lots of fun and meaningful ways, both indoors and outdoors. Research on the benefits of spending time outdoors for children's overall well-being has been added.

Section 5   Chapter 15 continues to recognize the importance of community and provides a number of ways that this can be facilitated within a school-age program. *Chapter 16* contains some new trends that are added in the field of early learning–kindergarten programs, the extended day, and school-age child care across Canada. The College of Early Childhood Educators in Ontario is a new professional organization that registers those working in the field and provides standards of professional practice. Some discussion of the reconceptualist movement in early childhood education is introduced.

Features

Profiles of school-age programs, full-day learning–kindergarten programs, school-age child care professionals, and resources for families across Canada are a special feature throughout the book. These vignettes allow the reader to get a glimpse of the different types of early learning kindergarten and school-age programs across Canada and the people who are involved with them. They also allow the reader to relate the stories to the content of each chapter. One program featured is in a community-based facility at Parkdale Public School in Toronto, where a number of out-of-school options are available for parents, including a full-day learning "seamless day" for junior and senior kindergarten children and an extended-day program. Another profile is about the Boys and Girls Clubs of Canada, which have been offering out-of-school programs for children for over 100 years. The Clubs also support children from immigrant and refugee families, helping them to feel comfortable in their new country. Another chapter introduces a Discovery Asthma camp outside Regina, Saskatchewan, that provides children who have asthma with a safe place to actively explore and play all kinds of games and activities. Awareness of diversity in curriculum planning and the celebration of community and culture are introduced in the profile of Bkejwanong Children's Centre on Walpole Island, Ontario.

There is a list of key terms at the end of each chapter and a glossary at the end of the book defining those terms. Students will be able to test their knowledge by answering the review questions and considering the questions following a case study at the end of each chapter. All chapters have references to websites where additional information, ideas, and activities can be found.

Finally, the text's appendices provide an "All About Me" questionnaire, a summary chart about the inquiry learning process, guidelines for planning a field trip, parent permission forms, a list of possible causes of conflict, a sample individual contract, a sample patent registration form, and a list of children's books.

How to Use This Text

The sequence of chapters provides the reader with a logical progression of topics that has been field-tested by many instructors using the text. The order can be adopted as is or changed to suit the needs of a particular setting. Review questions and activities at the end of each chapter also make it applicable to a self-study plan by individual students.

Ancillaries

Internet Disclaimer

The authors and Nelson affirm that the website URLs referenced herein were accurate at the time of printing. However, due to the fluid nature of the Internet, we cannot guarantee their accuracy for the life of the edition.

About the Authors

Phyllis Click obtained her bachelor's and master's degrees from the University of California at Berkeley in psychology and child development. Throughout a long career, her interest in providing the best possible environment for young children led her to work in a variety of settings, from preschools to summer camps for older children as well as programs for children with special needs. For several years she developed and taught in a preschool for children diagnosed with autism. Later, she began working with adults, teaching college students, administering grant programs, and designing a curriculum for a private college for prospective teachers.

She is currently an instructor at Moorpark College, Moorpark, California, and has published extensively. Her publications include another textbook for administrators of child care programs, articles in professional journals, and ancillary materials for other authors' texts. She has participated in research studies that are written up in anthologies. She belongs to the National Association for the Education of Young Children, the California School-Age Consortium, and the Association for Childhood Education International.

Jennifer Parker is currently a professor of Early Childhood Education Studies at Moorpark College, Moorpark, California. She recently was instrumental in adding a school-age component to the child development degree program there. Her classes include students with diverse backgrounds and experience, ranging from entry level to those who are currently teaching in early childhood programs. Her course load also includes supervision of student teachers in their field placements.

She received her Master's Degree from California State University, Northridge, and has had extensive experience working with children, families, and adults. She founded a parent-support program for infants and toddlers in a developmentally appropriate environment and has been a lead kindergarten teacher in an on-campus demonstration school. She is currently a member of an evaluation team using the School Age Environmental Rating Scale to evaluate a multi-site before-and-after-school child care program. She also coordinates a mentor teacher program in which she selects and trains school-age child care professionals to mentor student teachers.

Deborah Stone-Zukowski is a professor and coordinator in the Early Childhood Education Program at Conestoga College, Institute of Technology and Advanced Learning, in Kitchener, Ontario. She developed the School Age Programs course and has been teaching it to second-year ECE students for 24 years. She also developed competencies for the school-age component of field placement. She works closely with community school-age programs to promote and support quality. Colleagues and students at Conestoga College have awarded the Aubrey Hagar Award to her for teaching excellence in 1995. She has acquired a certificate of participation in SACERS (School-Age Child Care Environmental Rating Scale. Taking part in workshops and presentations on topics related to quality school-age care and as a school-age network leader with the Conestoga College Resource Centre are important parts of her professional work in the field of Early Learning and Care.

She holds a Masters of Education from the Ontario Institute for Studies in Education at the University of Toronto and has had a variety of experiences with different age groups. She has written a number of articles for early childhood journals on effective school-age programs, helping school-age children cope with stress, the benefits of risk taking and the influence of the media on school-age children. She is a great advocate for promoting diversity and the acceptance of differences and was instrumental in bringing awareness to Intergenerational Programs across Ontario.

Acknowledgments: Second Canadian Edition

Thank you to people at Conestoga College: my great team of friends and colleagues in ECE who have been helpful with information, pictures, and support. My students, from whom I am always learning, have brought a multitude of ideas and experiences to the School-Age Programs course, some of which are in this book.

Thanks to people from the lab schools and professional resource centre at Conestoga College, such as Joyce Chapman, and Samantha Burns for their photo contributions and shared learning experiences about programming for school-age children. Thanks to Jan Sherman for her contribution of photos and the profile on her program, called Spirit Connections, in Guelph. Thanks also to Barb McKee from Wellington Early Learning Centre school-age program in Guelph for photos of the documentation process of various curriculum topics.

Thanks to my husband for his ever-present support of my endeavours; to my children Natalie and Jason, and my daughter-in-law Lisa, for their talents and everything they have taught me; and to my Mom and Dad (now deceased) for their interest in my work.

Last but not least, thank you to the publishing team of James Kean, Susan Calvert, and Vicki Gould at Nelson, and freelance editor Karen Rolfe, for their hard work and efforts to see this Second Canadian Edition through to its final production.

—Deborah Stone-Zukowski

The People in School-Age Child Care

Chapter 1

School-Age Child Care Professionals: Who Are They?

Objectives

After studying this chapter, the student should be able to:

- Describe the characteristics of an effective school-age child care professional
- State education and experience requirements of a school-age child care professional
- Relate children's needs to a school-age child care professional's role

 ## Profile

Sierra is 32 and she is a lone parent with two children, 5 and 8 years of age. She worked part-time in a department store for 10 years and she did some volunteer work in her children's kindergarten and after-school program, which were in the same school that her children attended. Recently she went back to college and graduated with a diploma in Early Childhood Education. She learned a great deal about the importance of early brain development; how to facilitate an emergent curriculum; and about how to be an advocate for the importance of early learning and care. As a student, she worked in a variety of placements that incorporated a variety of curriculum approaches, such as Reggio, High Scope, and Play to Learn. She was introduced to the new seamless day, full-day early learning and care programs in schools for children 3.8- to 8-year-olds. She enjoyed working with the many age groups, but she knew that her favourite age group was the 5- to 10-year-olds. Her dream was to have a job in a full-day kindergarten extended-day program where she could work with the kindergarten children part of the day and with the school-age children after school.

Sierra's professional values and beliefs led to her present job at a school in the Waterloo Public School Board in an FDELK and extended day program. She works alongside the kindergarten teacher, providing an exciting play-based learning process of learning that encourages children to explore, inquire, and investigate. Her shift begins at 7:00 a.m. when she is with the 3.8- to 8-year-old children before school and then she works from 9:00 to 3:00 with the kindergarten children.

Sierra would like to continue working in a full-day kindergarten program for a few years and perhaps return to postsecondary education to work on her Bachelor's of Art degree.

She would like to expand her knowledge about early leaning and care in order to become a consultant or work in other related fields of family and children's services.

What Do Children Really Need from School-Age Child Care Professionals?

The term used to refer to experiences offered to children and their families before and after school differs across the country. It may be called a school-age program, extended day program, or "out of school child care." Children have many unique needs at these times of the day. They can be tiring, frustrating, and demanding as well as humorous, marvellously exciting, and fun. This chapter should help you determine how to support children's continued learning experiences and facilitate their daily routines. First, try to answer the question "What do children need from school-age child care professionals?" What did you want from the adults in your life? Children need security—a feeling they can trust adults and be trusted. They want freedom to be independent, while at the same time they like clear limits that define what they can or cannot do. They like adults who are flexible and can respond to new situations and interests with enthusiasm. They need affection, caring, and acceptance of their individual differences. They want to solve their own problems but have an adult's help available when needed. They want to be challenged to use their skills and abilities. Probably, most of all, they want to feel competent and successful.

What Are People Who Work with Children Called?

Many different titles are used to designate the adults who spend time with children in school programs. There is still no universally accepted designation that indicates the importance of this type of work. Some adults prefer to be called **early childhood educators** (ECE) or teachers. Others emphasize their caring role and therefore prefer to be called **child care practitioners** (CCP) or **school-age child care professionals** (SACCP). Those who emphasize the recreational aspect of after-school programs use **recreation leader** or supervisor. Others use the title of child care worker (CCW) or **school-age care worker** (SACW). The Canadian Child Care Federation (CCCF) supports the term **early childhood education and care** (ECEC). Efforts have been made over the years to bring higher recognition and value to both care and education of

early childhood educator
trained professional who works with children primarily from birth to age 8 and up to age 12

child care practitioner
an individual whose profession is working in child care

school-age child care professional
individual working in a licensed school-age program in child care or with a recreational focus

recreation leader
adult in a school-age program where the emphasis is on recreational aspects

school-age care worker
adult working in child care or recreation-oriented school-age program

early childhood education and care
term that denotes higher recognition and value for both care and education of children in formal schooling and in child care

early learning and care professional
registered early childhood educator working in a full-day early learning and care and extended day program in an elementary school

children in formal schooling and in child care. The Association of Early Childhood Educators in Ontario has coined the saying, "Good education cares and good care educates." More recently, with the incorporation of full-day kindergarten and extended day programs, the term **early learning and care professional** has been introduced. The term "school-age child care professional" (SACCP) will be used to describe those who are working in a school-age program in the following chapters.

Characteristics of the Effective School-Age Child Care Professional

If you want to work with school-age children, you need certain characteristics. Do not be discouraged if you do not have every single quality in the following list; you will acquire some of these attributes as you gain more experience.

Someone Who Really Likes School-Age Children

Liking school-age children should certainly be the first important characteristic for a school-age child care professional, since few of us relate well to children of all ages. "Liking" school-age children means many things: it means being interested in these children, enjoying conversations with them and being with them, appreciating each child's unique qualities, and accepting their differences.

Someone Who Encourages Children to Be Independent

School-age children are striving to be autonomous. They want to do things for themselves and to solve their own problems. Often adults want children to be compliant and obedient. They may feel threatened when children say, "I want to do it my way." Others feel frightened by what might happen when children are allowed to do what they want. It is important that children develop a sense that they can do things for themselves and that they be given the opportunity to increase their independence.

Figure 1-1 ■ Children are encouraged to work independently, but an adult is available to help when needed.

Someone Who Understands Child Development

You should have a good knowledge of how children develop during middle childhood. You need to know what children are like at each stage of development throughout the elementary years. What are their physical abilities? What are they capable of learning? What do these children need? How do they form their identity and acquire moral values? It is important to be aware of the causes of behaviour so you can better understand why a particular child responds the way he does. Why does one child go along willingly with the group and another want to be alone? Why are the eight-year-olds in your group suddenly rebelling against your ideas or directions? Why are some children easy to get along with some days, but impossible on others? To understand the "whys" of behaviour, you need to know the emotional stresses most children go through at various stages of childhood. When you do understand, it is easier to realize that often just the passage of time will change behaviour. In other words, children may just be going through an expected phase in their development. Soon it will change as they move into the next stage. Beyond that, what behaviours may create problems for children themselves? What are the things that make it difficult for them to have friends or to accomplish what they want to do? Then—and this is the hard part—how can you help each child change his behaviour for more mature actions? A knowledge of development will help you find the answers.

You need knowledge of child development to understand how to provide guidance of behaviour in positive ways. How you guide the behaviour of a five-year-old is very different from directing a nine-year-old. The five-year-old needs clear, firm expectations to assist him with learning how to interact with others. The nine-year-old needs more guidance

Figure 1-2 ■ **Both boys and girls need male role models.**

about learning to control her own behaviour. Therefore, you allow as much freedom as possible while helping her to set her own limits. It is a subtle kind of guidance that respects the child's desire to be competent.

Understanding development is basic to planning any activities in school-age child care. You need to know what children are capable of doing or learning. With that knowledge, you can plan age-appropriate activities at which children are likely to succeed. Sometimes the children themselves have ideas for projects that are far beyond their capabilities. You must guide them to choose things they can do.

Someone Who Is a Good Role Model

Although parents still continue to be important, school-age children will be looking to you as a model. They watch what you do and listen to your words. They sometimes imitate you as they develop their own standards for behaviour. Therefore, you should have the characteristics you want children to have. Honesty, dependability, fairness, and trustworthiness are some of the qualities you should possess. You could add flexibility, caring, tolerance, and patience. You could also include a happy disposition and optimistic outlook.

Whenever possible, programs should have both male and female leaders. The majority of elementary school teachers are female, and boys spend a large part of their day without a male role model. These children also may be being raised in lone-parent families, often by the mother. A male staff member in a school-age program can help to fill the gap. Girls, too, need male school-age child care professionals to help them develop their own identities in relation to males. Both girls and boys need both sexes to help them learn to trust adults outside their own home.

Someone Who Has Lots of Interests

You should know a lot about many things. Your own curiosity and interests should have led you to seek out information you can share with children. They will be fascinated by what you know about stars, electricity, dinosaurs, or many other topics. Know also where to look for answers to their questions. Know how to find information in your local library. Have some ideas about what is available in your community. When you share children's excitement about learning, you encourage rather than discourage their own desire to discover.

You should be able to do a lot of things. Any skills you have can be shared. If you are adept at woodworking, you can teach children how to use tools. If you know how to knit or crochet, children can learn as well. If you do not have many skills, find out how you can develop some. You can read about how to do some things in books; there are many "how-to" books that will help you. You can also learn from someone who already has a particular skill.

You should be willing to learn from children as well. Often there is more than one way of doing things. A child may show you a way you would not have thought of yourself. But you have to be willing to consider alternatives rather than feeling there is one absolute right way. Many children have information and skills they can share with the group. Be willing to listen to children yourself and provide opportunities for others to listen as well.

Someone Who Allows Freedom While Setting Limits

School-age children are trying to move from dependence upon adults to independence. Consequently, they need the freedom to make their own decisions and to set their own rules. This bolsters their self-esteem. You have to be willing to give up or share control when it is appropriate. For instance, you may want to set rules that involve safety but allow them to write their own code of conduct and rules in the group.

On the other hand, when limits are needed, such as in a situation of bullying, you have to be able to follow through firmly and consistently. Children will test how far they can go before you will stop them, but they want to feel secure in the knowledge that you will not let them go too far. You should be clear about what is expected in terms of appropriate behaviour in the program—for example, respect and peaceful resolution of conflict. Explain why the rule is necessary and follow up with consequences. You will gain their respect and trust.

Sometimes you have to balance individual freedoms with group rights. One child cannot be allowed to work at a noisy project alone when the group is listening to a story. If a group of children wants to play with blocks, one child cannot be allowed to take all the blocks. However, there are times when individual rights must be considered. Some children need to have exclusive use of materials or space for a period of time. Others want to be able to choose another child as a partner for an activity. You will need a great deal of sensitivity to children to decide when to meet individual or group needs.

Someone Who Has Good Communication Skills

Communication includes both the ability to convey messages and to listen. You should be able to do both well. When you give children directions, they should be stated clearly. There should be no ambiguity about your meaning. "You have five minutes to finish what you are doing before snack time" is a clear statement. "It will be snack time in a few minutes" leaves room for confusion. What is a few minutes? Five? Three? Ten? You should also be able to express your feelings honestly. "I don't like it when you call me names" lets a child know exactly how you feel. In addition, good communication skills involve the ability to write in an organized, concise manner. You may need to write information for children, parents, or other staff members.

The other side of communication is the willingness to listen. Children often need to talk about school, their families, or their friends. You should be willing to listen and be interested in what they have to say. Children are not the only ones who appreciate a good listener; parents and other staff members occasionally need a "friendly ear." Share conversations about daily happenings with other professionals such as teachers, librarians, custodians, and principals if your program is within the school.

There is one last reminder about communication: It is important when you work with children not to talk down to them; use language that is appropriate for their level of understanding.

Figure 1-3 ■ Effective school-age child care professionals are willing to listen to children.

Someone Who Can Guide Children in Social Problem Solving

Children without social skills do not have friends, and that often leads to either aggressive or passive behaviours. These are the children who become bullies or sit quietly in the background alone. They need help to change their behaviours so they can make and keep friends. A sensitive adult can help these children understand what is preventing them from achieving their goals or making friends.

The most effective ways to help children learn the techniques that allow them to have friends include discussing strategies in small groups and modelling friendships among the adults. Individual children can be coached. You can review the behaviours that led to the child being excluded and then suggest alternative behaviours. Encourage the child to practise the behaviours, and then evaluate the results. Sometimes it even helps to set up a private signal system, such as a hand sign, word, or phrase. If aggressive behaviour has prevented the child from being part of a group, signal him to remind him to try an alternate method. Problem solving is discussed further in Chapter 7.

Someone Who Enjoys Physical Activity

You should like to play active games and sports with children. Children who attend elementary school spend a large part of their day sitting down. When they come to the program, they need to be involved in activities that allow them to move around. They want to be able to play games outdoors, climb, run, jump, skate, or do whatever else is available. Both you and the children will get a great deal of pleasure doing some of these together. That takes a lot of energy and good health on your part.

Someone Who Cares about Families

All children you work with are part of a family. As described in Chapter 3, these families will vary; they may be like your own family or very different. It is up to you to get to know family members. Find out what they are like and what they want for their children. Try to understand their cultural values and the standards they set for their

Figure 1-4 ■ **School-age child care professionals should have a good relationship with parents.**

family, then be supportive and avoid criticizing them. Find ways to strengthen their role as parents. You should see child care as a family service, not just a place for children.

You should be the kind of person parents can talk to. If you are young and have not had children yourself, you may find this difficult. But remember what parents probably want most is an indication that you know their children and care about them. They want to hear what their children did during the day and how their children are getting along. Sometimes they may want to talk about their children's problems. Do not feel you have to have solutions but just be willing to listen. Often it is enough to listen to a parent talk about the difficulties of working and having time for children. They do not always want advice, just understanding.

Someone Who Understands the Role of a School-Age Child Care Professional

You are filling the roles of both a parent and a teacher when you work in a school-age program. When children arrive at the program, they may need someone to talk to about their day. At times you have to listen to their problems. Sometimes you have to set limits or administer appropriate consequences when limits are overstepped. You have to see that they get their homework done. These are things a parent does. At other times you become an instructor. In the course of a day's activities, you will often teach them some of the same things they learn in school. They need help with math concepts when they work on projects. They may need help reading a recipe while cooking a snack. You may encourage them to pursue their interest in astronomy, then praise their accomplishments. You may explain instructions when they play a game. Your role, therefore, is a combination of teacher and parent but is also different. Your primary role is to see that children are well cared for while their parents are at work.

Figure 1-5 ■ **School-age child care professionals can teach children new skills.**

Someone Who Is Able to Work as Part of a Team

You should be able to get along with other adults as well as you do with children. Other staff members within your centre will depend upon you or will have to coordinate their activities with yours. Therefore, you have to be willing to share responsibilities, space, and materials. Sometimes you have to be ready to do more than is expected of you. You should see working with children as a profession, not just a job. When you do, you will respect fellow workers and be respected by them.

Being part of a team may also mean working with elementary school personnel. This can be difficult because school-age child care professionals often seem to be invisible, not seen as part of the school. Whether your program is located within a school facility, on the school grounds or off-site in a facility such as a recreation centre, boys and girls club, or church, it is important that you have a positive relationship with the school and the school board it serves (Howe, Neufeld & Anderson, 2003). When your program is within a school or housed on the school grounds you will need to be familiar with the lease/operating agreement. You will have to work out the arrangements for sharing indoor and outdoor space. Share policies and procedures for emergency procedures, arrival and departure, behaviour guidance, and confidentiality practices between school, child care centre, and children and their families. You should discuss the coordination of resources, equipment, and materials. In order to foster a good working relationship, initiate ways to inform school personnel about your program's curriculum and philosophy. Let the principal know about any special events such as open houses, parent nights, and annual general meetings that the school staff would be invited to. Submit information about the program to the school newsletter. Offer to put up a display of children's artwork or school-age child care posters in the school. Attend Parent Advisory Council meetings, and ask if you can take part in Professional Development days. A healthy relationship with school personnel will be worth the effort it takes to establish and maintain.

Education and Experience

Each child care centre will have its own requirements for school-age child care professionals. Criteria for employment are usually based on guidelines mandated by local or provincial/territorial licensing regulations as well as by the funding sources that support the program. In addition, each situation will have demands based on the needs of the program or the children to be served. In general, there are two broad areas of education and experience that are usually required in school-age child care.

Some centre directors look for personnel who have strong backgrounds in early childhood education. School-age child care professionals must be knowledgeable in the development of young children. Directors also want people who have expertise and experience in planning a curriculum for "school-agers." Many people who fit these requirements have completed courses in early childhood education and have worked in preschool programs. In addition, they may have had the opportunity to work with five- or six-year-olds. Some are able to find courses in school-age programs at colleges and universities.

Other directors seek personnel who have strong backgrounds in recreation. These staff members should know a lot of games suitable for this age level. Staff members should be aware of activities that are safe for young children. Professionals with this kind of background will probably have taken courses in physical education and recreation. They may have had experience supervising playground situations or working in summer camps.

As you look at these two areas of background and experience, it probably occurs to you that a good school-age child care professional needs both. You are absolutely right. It would certainly be ideal if that were so. In most school-age programs, however, the problem is resolved by hiring school-age child care professionals who have skills that complement one another. In each group there may be one person who has an early childhood education background and one who comes from recreation programs.

To further achieve an ideal staff balance in a program, it would be beneficial to have school-age child care professionals from a variety of different cultural backgrounds or those who are comparable ethnically to the surrounding community. It also helps to have people of different ages. Those who have their own children will bring a different perspective to the care of the children. As well, recent graduates will bring new experience and fresh ideas to the curriculum of the program.

By now you should have a picture of the kind of person who would work well with school-age children. Let us take one last look at the role of a school-age child care professional in children's development.

The School-Age Child Care Professional's Role in Meeting Children's Specific Needs

In general terms, your role as a school-age child care professional is to foster all aspects of children's development through a play-based learning environment. The ways in which you do that are implied by the description of characteristics needed for the job. However, look at it in another way. Children have specific needs; your job is to provide opportunities to facilitate their development.

- Children need security; you provide a secure environment.
- Children need to trust themselves and others; you show you can be trusted and that you trust them.
- Children need to be independent; you allow freedom within limits.
- Children need to develop interests; you encourage and foster those interests.
- Children need a positive self-image; you appreciate their similarities and differences.
- Children need to feel competent; you provide opportunities for them to be successful.
- Children need to acquire values; you offer a positive role model for them to imitate.
- Children need to belong to a group; you include each child and encourage friendships.
- Children need to develop critical thinking skills and to solve problems; you facilitate opportunities for them to solve their own problems.
- Children need experiences that encourage them to explore, investigate, and inquire throughout the teaching and learning process

As you can see, having a part in the development of young children is an awesome task. Should you choose this as a career, you will find that it is never boring, for you are constantly challenged. You will find that children will force you to grow in order to keep up with their demands. It is certainly a job that will keep you learning for many years into the future.

Ethical Considerations

As a school-age child care professional, whether you are experienced or just starting out, you will be faced with situations that call for a difficult decision. For example, you may suspect that a child in your class is being exposed to sexually explicit experiences. Or you may see a fellow staff member taking home paper and paint to use with her own child. How do you decide the right way to respond to either of these situations or even whether to do anything at all? Your own personality or personal attributes will affect the solution. These are the ways you react to situations, how you think, and what you feel. Those who are working with children in child care tend to be caring, empathetic people who try to be fair. The trouble is that these are not always enough to guide you when you are faced with ethical dilemmas. Your values also play a part in helping to decide what to do. **Values** are the qualities that we believe to be intrinsically desirable and that we strive to achieve in ourselves. Our own personal values are the basis for our professional values. However, not everyone has the same values, and the choice you

values

the qualities we believe to be intrinsically desirable and that we strive to achieve in ourselves make may not be acceptable to or understood by others. A good example is the dilemma you face when a parent asks you to discipline her child in a way that is counter to your values. You may truly believe your way is the right way, but the parent may have just as strong a conviction. Often these values arise out of the cultural background and expectations that the parent is from. It is important to listen to the values of the family's culture, bringing a sense of understanding and caring to the situation.

Our own sense of morality also affects our decisions. **Morality** is our perception of what is good or right. Morality also includes beliefs about how people should behave and the kind of obligations we have to one another. During the early years, children are taught by their parents or their religion that it is wrong to lie or to steal and that it is right to be truthful and to treat others kindly. This becomes the core of our moral sense as adults.

morality
our perception of what is good or right

However, as professionals we need another standard by which to decide how to resolve problems. We need a code of **ethics** that outlines our responsibilities in ways that we can agree upon. Ethics is the study of right, wrong, duty, and obligation. Ethics and morality are closely related and in fact are often used interchangeably, but ethics implies a conscious deliberation regarding moral choices.

ethics
a study of right, wrong, duty, and obligation

The Canadian Child Care Federation (CCCF) has developed a *Code of Ethical Conduct* (n.d.) that "focuses on the daily interactions with children from birth through age 12 and their families in child care programs." The code consists of eight ethical principles that address particular areas of professional responsibilities and relationships. The intent is to portray exemplary professional practice and define practices that are required and permitted.

Eight Ethical Principles

Child care practitioners:

1. promote the health and well-being of all children
2. enable children to participate to their full potential in environments carefully planned to serve individual needs and to facilitate the child's progress in the social, emotional, physical and cognitive areas of development
3. demonstrate caring for all children in all aspects of their practice
4. work in partnership with parents, recognizing that parents have primary responsibility for the care of their children, valuing their commitment to the children and supporting them in meeting their responsibilities to the children
5. work in partnership with colleagues and other service providers in the community to support the well-being of children and their families
6. work in ways that enhance human dignity in trusting, caring and cooperative relationships that respect the worth and uniqueness of the individual
7. pursue, on an ongoing basis, the knowledge, skills and self-awareness needed to be professionally competent
8. demonstrate integrity in all of their professional relationships.

© Canadian Childcare Federation. Reprinted with permission.

National and provincial/territorial organizations in child care and recreation have their own codes of ethics that can be accessed through their websites. For example, the Occupational Standards for Early Childhood Educators was developed by the Canadian Child Care Human Resources Sector Council and the College of Early

Childhood Educators in Ontario has established a Code of Ethics and Standards of Practices. You can access national and provincial/territorial organization through the Canadian Child Care Federation website and other websites listed at the end of this chapter.

> The Canadian Child Care Federation
> 700 Industrial Ave., Suite 600
> Ottawa, ON
> K1G 0Y9

Summary

School-age children have specific needs, which include to be trusted, to be independent, to have challenges, to be accepted for who they are, and to be successful.

Many different titles are used to designate the adults who spend time with children in school-age programs: early childhood educator, teacher, child care practitioner, school-age child care professional, recreation leader, and school-age care worker. All should be acceptable, in recognition of ECEC, early childhood education and care. Current practices in full-day kindergarten and extended day programs in most provinces use the term "early learning and care professional" to refer to the Registered Early Childhood Educators working with the kindergarten teachers in a school setting. The term chosen for this book for those working in school-age programs of all kinds is "school-age child care professional."

Those who care for school-age children should be people who

- like school-age children
- understand child development
- are good role models
- have a lot of interests
- allow freedom while setting limits
- have good communication skills
- can guide children in critical thinking and problem-solving skills
- facilitate investigation, exploration, and inquiry-based learning processes
- enjoy physical activity
- care about families
- understand the role of a school-age child care professional
- are able to work as part of a team

School-age programs may require personnel who have a background in either early childhood education or recreation. Both are helpful. All school-age child care professionals should have knowledge of what is developmentally appropriate for children.

In general, the role of professionals working with school-age children is to foster all aspects of children's development. They should be familiar with and put into practice the code of ethics as outlined by their provincial/territorial and/or national professional association.

Key Terms

early childhood educator

child care practitioner

school-age child care
    professional

recreation leader

school-age care worker

early childhood
    education and care

early learning and care
    professional

values

morality

ethics

Student Activities

1. Visit two different kinds of school-age extended day programs. Choose, for instance, one that is operated within an elementary school setting and one that is part of a child care organization. In what ways are the children's activities the same or different in these two programs?
2. Observe several school-age child care professionals as they interact with children. How do their styles differ? Describe the one you would use as your own model for interactions with children.
3. Interview the director of a school-age program. What are the qualities she looks for when hiring new school-age child care professionals?
4. In class, write a short description and be prepared to share it with classmates when finished. Spend one minute responding to "One teacher was my favourite because _____." List three main characteristics to complete the sentence and then prioritize them. State why your first priority item is the most important.
5. Write an advertisement for the perfect school-age child care professional.

Review Questions

1. List the reasons school-age child care professionals need a knowledge of child development.
2. Describe the qualities of a good role model for school-age children.
3. This chapter suggests a school-age child care professional should have a lot of interests. Explain why.
4. Effective communication has two parts. What are they?
5. Describe ways to foster your relationship with parents.
6. Why is it important that school-age child care professionals work together as a team in a full-day early learning and care kindergarten and extended day program?
7. What kinds of education and experience should be required to qualify as a school-age child care professional?

Case Study

As a new early childhood educator in a full-day early learning kindergarten program, you are excited about working in an elementary school and to have the opportunity to put your learning about inquiry learning to work. You spend hours at home going through all the resources you compiled while you were an ECE student. You start to do some observations of the children in the program and develop lots of ideas to extend children's abilities and interests. The kindergarten teacher is still learning about emergent curriculum and has been used to doing themes but he knows a lot about inquiry learning.

You want to develop a cooperative partnership with the teacher when it comes to facilitating the program for the kindergarten children.

1. How would you work together to facilitate a dynamic inquiry-based curriculum?
2. How would you introduce the concepts of emergent curriculum?
3. List other people in the school who would be part of this partnership.

References

Code of Ethical Conduct, Canadian Child Care Federation. (n.d). Retrieved March 29, 2005, from the Canadian Child Care Federation website: http://www.cccf-fcsge.ca/practice/ethical%20dilemmas/codeofethics_en.htm

Howe, A., Neufeld, T., & Anderson, C. (2003). *Building relationships with schools and school boards.* Retrieved April 19, 2005, from http://www.cccf-fcsge.ca/practice/policy/relatn_en.html

Selected Further Reading

Bumgarner, M. A. (1999). *Working with school-age children.* Mountain View, CA: Mayfield Publishing Company.

Ferguson, E. (2004). *What's in a name?* Discussion Paper. Retrieved March 29, 2005, from http://www.cccf-fcsge.ca/images/whatsinaname_en.pdf

Koralek, D. G., Newman, R., & Colker, L. J. (1995). *Caring for children in school-age programs, Volume I & II.* Washington, DC: Teaching Strategies.

Musson, S. (1999). *School-age care, theory and practice* (2nd ed). Don Mills, ON: Addison-Wesley Publishers.

Newman, R. L. (2002). *Training new after-school staff.* Nashville, TN: School-Age Notes.

Websites

Canadian Child Care Federation and affiliates (provincial associations, early childhood education, child care, family day care, aboriginal care, early childhood development, francophone education, home child care, day care operators)
http://www.cccf-fcsge.ca/affiliates_en.html

Canadian Parks and Recreation Association (CPRA)
http://www.cpra.ca

School-Age NOTES
http://www.afterschoolcatalog.com

Parks and Recreation Ontario (PRO)
http://216.13.76.142/PROntario

Westcoast Child Care Resource Centre
http://www.wstcoast.org

College of Early Childhood Educators: Code of Ethics and Standards of Practice
http://collegeofece.on.ca/en/Documents/CECE%20Code%20of%20Ethics%20and%20Standards%20of%20Practice%20Feb%202011.pdf

Occupational Standards for Early Childhood Educators
http://www.allthedaze.com/files/OccupationalStand_2010_EN_march164.pdf

Child and Youth Care Association of Alberta (CYCAA)
http://www.cycaa.com

Chapter 2

The Children

Objectives

After completing this chapter, the student should be able to:

- State the factors that are important to children's sense of self
- Discuss the ways in which children develop friendships
- State the ways school-age child care professionals can help children develop a healthy sense of self and form friendships

 ## Profile

The Boys and Girls Clubs of Canada have been in operation for over 100 years. The program began as a boys club or playground, providing recreational activities for boys in the new industrial town of Saint John, New Brunswick, in 1900. The organization now has over 105 Boys and Girls Clubs (girls were allowed membership in 1976) serving 150 communities across Canada. Most of the clubs have after-school programs, providing safe and secure places for children age six and up. As the children interact with each other and engage in a variety of activities, they develop a sense of self in relation to others.

Toronto, Ontario's Davencourt club helps children of immigrant families adjust to their new community, orienting them to a new culture and new language. Children from different cultures have an opportunity to take part in activities together, developing an appreciation and understanding about how they are the same and different from each other. Some programs offer a one-on-one help-with-homework program through the assistance of volunteer tutors from high schools, colleges, and universities. This helps children to develop competence, feeling more able to be successful in their school work.

The East Scarborough, Ontario, club has eight computers that have been supplied by Microsoft Canada, plus Internet connections and a library of software. Many of the children do not have computers at home, which places them at a disadvantage. When children have access to computers at the Boys and Girls Club, it gives them a sense of competence and the necessary skills they will need for their future schooling and work.

Physical development occurs through sports and recreational activities, such as games and crafts in which children can take part. They learn new skills and develop the ability to grow and do things that they never thought they could do before. These physical activities help children develop positive self-esteem, which then reduces behavioural problems and assists with improving school grades. Children also learn how to handle their emotions and think through problems.

Programs operate in a variety of community settings, depending on the particular needs of families in each community. Families continue to be a central part of school-age children's daily lives. Boys and Girls Clubs in Calgary, Alberta, offer a program called FANS (food and nutrition at school), serving breakfast and lunch to school children. The Boys and Girls Club of Peel, Ontario, provides programs for 800 members in schools, housing developments, and even individual homes. The clubs' emphasis is on bringing the program to the children and families rather than the children coming to a central physical space.

National Post, September 9, 2000, pp. E1–E6.

Development of Self

self-esteem

children's view of themselves in relation to their ability to accomplish their goals and expand their skills

Middle childhood is an important period when children develop a sense of who they are, what they can do, and how others perceive them. It is a time when the focus of their daily lives is on school, and their **self-esteem** is closely tied to school success. Most children enter kindergarten eager to learn and are optimistic in their evaluation of self and their expectations for academic success (Stipek & MacIver, 1989). When they first begin reading and writing, they have little idea of how successful they will be and cannot accurately assess their own competence. Young children assume they are successful because they put a lot of effort into their activities. As they get older and more experienced, they become more realistic. They learn that different people have different abilities, enabling them to achieve at varying levels. They may find they are good at reading but not so capable at math.

Emerging research on early schooling suggests that the relationships that children build with their peers and their ability to regulate their emotions in prosocial ways help children's chances of doing well academically (Ladd, Birch & Buhs, 1999 in Raver, 2002). School-age children may feel uncomfortable with the fact that they go to child care when they are not in school. This is especially the case as they get older, when their need for more autonomy and independence emerges. They may see their other friends going home after school and not understand why they cannot do the same.

A second way children develop a sense of self is through their feelings of power. One source of power is their status with their peers. They measure and compare themselves to others. Are they liked and looked up to? Are they similar to their peers in appearance, dress, and abilities? If they answer in the affirmative, they feel more powerful. Another source of power is inner control over their own behaviour; in other words, being able to behave in ways that their parents and society look upon favourably. Children also have good self-esteem if they are accomplishing their goals and expanding their skills.

Acceptance by peers is a third way children refine their sense of self. At times school-age children can be cruel to their peers. Teasing and hostility are ways of testing feelings of power and learning just how much aggression will be tolerated. The ups and downs of childhood friendships are part of growing up, but children who are persistently exposed to cruelty or rejection have a difficult time. Rejected children are likely to develop negative attitudes about themselves, leading them to further unacceptable behaviours that bring derision and exclusion.

A final standard by which school-age children evaluate themselves is in terms of good or bad behaviour. In Chapter 6 you will read that Lawrence Kohlberg describes moral behaviour in middle childhood as being nice to others, behaving in ways that others approve of, and obeying rules or laws. Peers and sometimes staff inappropriately use these standards to label children as good/nice or bad/not nice. Reputations acquired during middle childhood may affect an individual's behaviour into adolescence and adulthood.

Children's **self-concept** or perception of themselves and others is often based on making sense of diversity and inequality among people. Concepts of race and ethnicity play a part in how children perceive themselves and others. Holmes (1995) studied kindergarten children in several schools in southern California. She found that the content of children's self-concepts and the way children perceive themselves and convey information about themselves is linked to their cognitive maturation. At the kindergarten level children concentrated on specific, observable characteristics: gender, skin colour, eye colour, hair type, shape of facial features, and language. The children described themselves by saying, "I have brown skin" or "My eyes are brown." According to Holmes, older children at a higher cognitive level will portray themselves as having personal preferences or personality traits—"I'm pretty good at sports and have a lot of friends." They pay more attention to character dispositions and make finer distinctions between people. They develop the capacity to classify their social world in multiple ways, allowing them to understand that people can be both "the same" and "different"—that those who look different do not necessarily think, feel, or act differently (Bigler & Liben, 2003; Doyle & Aboud, 2003).

Holmes found that socialization experiences were important factors affecting children's subjective feelings about themselves. Children often pick up information about particular group status from implicit messages in their environment. In one

Figure 2-1 ■ **"Mom, me, Dad, and Rascal, my dog." Carissa, age 6**

Figure 2-2 ■ **"This is me." Sarah, age 6**

self-concept
perception of one's self and perceptions conveyed by others

Figure 2-3 ▨ Snack time can be an opportunity for socializing.

study of 7- to 12-year-olds in a summer school-age program, children were assigned to two social groups, denoted by yellow or blue T-shirts. When staff gave preference and praise to the higher status yellow-group members, those children viewed themselves more favourably than the other group. Children in the lower status group of blue T-shirts viewed their own group less favourably. No prejudice emerged when teachers gave equal recognition of both groups (Bigler, Brown, & Markell, 2003). These findings indicate that children do not necessarily form stereotypes when some basis for difference exists. Only when an authority figure places some higher status or recognition to one group over another do the children develop biased attitudes.

Children do not always adopt their attitudes and values toward race, ethnicity, gender, and social status from their parents and friends. A Canadian study found that there were few similarities between white school-age children's racial attitudes and those of their parents. Perhaps Caucasian parents were reluctant to discuss their racial views with their children and when children have limited or ambiguous information, children may fill in the gaps or rely on their own attitudes toward differences (Aboud & Doyle, 2003).

Implications for School-Age Child Care Professionals

Children's feelings about themselves develop not in a vacuum but rather within the context of their daily experiences and their contacts with others. The development of self-esteem and social competence is influenced by many factors. According to Katz and McClellan (1997), these are "the children's attachments to their primary caregivers within the family; the modeling, guidance, and support of parents and teachers; the opportunity to observe peers and interact with them; and children's relationships with non-family adults involved in their care and education and those involved in the neighbourhood and community in which they spend a large proportion of their time." School-age child care professionals can encourage children's positive feelings about themselves by

- providing authentic feedback to children rather than empty praise. Help them evaluate their own skills realistically and to set feasible goals for themselves. "You were having a hard time learning to use the saw, but you figured out how to do it. Look how well you were able to cut a straight line for the side of your birdhouse."

- providing supportive intervention to children who have been rejected or are having difficulty gaining acceptance by their peers. Offer help to upgrade skills that will bring acceptance in the classroom or playground. Teach children how to be successful. "I can see that you were hurt you weren't chosen for their team. Suppose I help you practise so that you will be able to play better." Or "Not everyone can be a good basketball player. Remember how great you are when we put on plays." Or encourage children who are good at certain skills, such as dribbling the ball, to show others how to do it.

- encouraging children to feel positive about their experience in the school-age program. Help them to feel that they are part of a special community of friends and celebrate each child's own unique contributions. Talk to the children about giving their program a special "club" name. This would give them a sense of greater ownership and pride. Give them more responsibility, independence, and freedom in the program as they get older.

- accepting children's feelings rather than denying or belittling their importance. Be a sensitive listener. "I can see you're pretty mad about something today. If you feel like talking about it, I'm ready to listen."

- providing positive encounters with individuals from different races, ethnic/cultural backgrounds, social classes, ages, abilities, and genders. Invite the children and adult visitors to come and talk about their culture or experiences.

- encouraging children to work together in groups on activities that require cooperation and compromise. Invite children to talk about similarities and differences that they notice about each other, in terms of physical characteristics, beliefs, and opinions. Promote the premise that it is okay to be different, that all people are unique and have something to offer.

Peer Groups, "The Society of Children"

Beginning in the preschool period, when children first understand the meaning of the word "friend," the need to have friends becomes increasingly important. As children's cognitive abilities change, so does their concept of friendship and its purpose. At first there is a mutual dependence upon friends to share activities, carry on conversations, and provide support for attempts at independence from parents. Young school-age children often choose friends who are the same gender, have similar interests, and share similar values. There is very little cross-gender fraternization and, in fact, even some antagonism toward members of the opposite sex. Girls pal around with girls, tell each other secrets, watch movies, and talk on the telephone. The leader of a group of girls is chosen for her managerial skills; for having new ideas; and for being thoughtful, friendly, and organized (Edwards, 1994). Boys get together to skateboard, play video games, or compete in organized sports. Boys and girls in middle childhood will play together at times where there are more "open-ended" materials such as with blocks, building structures, musical experiences, dramatics, cooperative games, and sports.

The most popular children are prosocial (i.e., caring, sharing, and helpful). They have strong verbal skills and know how to keep aggressive impulses in control. Popular children have good interpersonal skills, are empathetic, can take on other viewpoints, and know the difference between right and wrong (Slaughter et. al 2002; Dkovic and Gerris, 1994 in Dewar, 2009).

Older school-age children rely upon friends for intimate conversations about problems, dreams, and expectations. Friends are seen as people who will remain loyal and can be relied upon when life is difficult. The circle of friends gradually becomes

Figure 2-4 ■ **School-age children choose friends who have the same interests.**

smaller as children become more selective about the qualities of a friend. Often, by age 10 both boys and girls have a single best friend, although this exclusivity tends to occur more frequently with girls. By the end of middle childhood, many girls have only one best friend upon whom they depend for all their social needs (Gilligan, Murphy, & Tappan, 1990). Around the fourth or fifth grades, children begin to change their perceptions of the opposite gender, and intergender interactions are more frequent (Adler, Kless, & Adler, 1992). Often by age nine, everyone knows who is best friends with whom and they would be less likely to think of trying to disrupt the pair. This fraternity of friend relationships makes it difficult for children who have not found a companion. It is also heart wrenching when one of a pair becomes more mature than the other and moves on to other alliances. The deserted partner may experience difficulty in finding a new companion.

Middle childhood is also a period when children form cliques, clubs, or gangs with the primary purpose of gaining independence from adults. Each group has its own vocabulary, dress code, rules, and activities (Opie & Opie, 1959). The group provides a mutual support system and a sense of solidarity as children learn to sharpen their social skills. Those who belong build self-esteem, but those who are excluded have difficulties socially and often academically as well.

Adler and Adler (1998) have been following 200 elementary-age children in their community. They found that children are very aware of the importance of **cliques** and the power they give the members who belong. Some of the influence is positive, helping children learn appropriate social behaviour and the consequences of misbehaviour. Clique members tend to have similar characteristics. During middle childhood they have similar interests or come from similar backgrounds. Cliques can provide children with a social identity and a sense of belonging.

Adler and Adler (1998) found that cliques can be extremely limiting, prescribing very specific ways of behaving, dressing, or associating with others outside the group. Those outside the group can be derided for wearing the wrong clothes, being of a different race or religion, or being too studious. Members of the clique may even carry on "negative campaigns" against chosen targets, heaping verbal abuse and humiliation on them. In order to stay in the group and be accepted, as well as gain the feelings of power that result, members go along with this behaviour. The consequence is that bigotry and racism become part of children's value system as well as increase their need to conform to standards that may conflict with values they have been taught at home.

In the case of **gangs**, the purpose may be even more negative. Not only are they outside the realm of adults, but also they may even be antisocial. The result is that members engage in vandalism or criminal activities that put them in legal jeopardy.

The need to form groups may be observed in the school-age program as well as in the community. The number of individuals involved is usually smaller than in school or in the neighbourhood, but the same dynamics can be seen. Friendships form and break up. Groups congregate and then change. But the need to belong remains strong in all children, with those who are not included feeling left out and unhappy.

clique

a group of children who have similar characteristics and interests

gang

a group of children who gather together to be out of the realm of adults but also to be antisocial

Figure 2-5 ■ Five- to seven-year-olds have one or two best friends.

Some children seem to make friends easily and are sought out while others find it extremely difficult. Certain social skills are necessary and may be in the formative stage during middle childhood. The first is the ability to understand that others may have views different from their own. Younger children are egocentric, believing that they are the centre of the universe and that friends are there to satisfy them. "He's my friend because he plays with me" or "He's my friend because he shares his toys with me." Older children begin to realize that others have needs and feelings too. In order to make and maintain a friendship, they must make compromises to accommodate the other's needs or feelings. They may have to negotiate whether they want to go to a party or just hang out at the mall if they want to be together.

A second essential skill for making friends is the ability to recognize that others have separate identities and feelings of their own. Although children tend to choose friends who are like themselves, each has different characteristics and ways of reacting. It is a difficult lesson to learn that sometimes a best friend can be cross and want to be alone.

Finally, children have to understand that each encounter with others is part of a relationship. They tend to isolate incidents and fail to see the importance of their behaviour in specific situations. If they lash out at another child in anger, they do not immediately recognize that that will have consequences for their ability to form a friendship with that person. They must learn that in order to have friends they must curb certain behaviours.

Stages in Children's Concept of Friendship

Stage	Name	Approximate Age	Comments
0	Momentary physical interaction	3–6	Someone who they play with nearby Someone who has similar toys Egocentric view
1	One-way assistance	5–9	Friends have different thoughts and feelings Friend is someone who does what they want ... places own desires first
2	Fairweather cooperation	7–12	Friends do things for each other (reciprocal) Self-interest
3	Intimate and mutual sharing	10–15	Mutual support over a long period of time Focus on the relationship rather than individuals
4	Autonomous independence	12 & older	Friendship grows and changes as people change Different friends satisfy different personal and social needs

(Selman, 1980)

Implications for School-Age Child Care Professionals

People working in school-age programs can have a significant impact on children's ability to make friends and be part of a group.

- Allow children opportunities to spend time with a friend without the pressure of having to engage in an activity. Let them "just hang out" in a corner of the room or an outdoor area.

- Encourage children to take another's point of view. Ask "How do you think he feels when you call him that name?"

- Help children recognize their own psychological characteristics and that others can accept those qualities. An adult who says "Thanks for helping me understand that sometimes you just want to be alone" does that.

- Foster children's ability to examine the basis for friendships. Lead discussions about what makes a good friend and how to maintain friendships.

- Help individual children develop a plan to change behaviours that interfere with friendships. Discuss alternative ways of behaving, encourage the child to test out the behaviour, and then evaluate the results. Give honest appraisal and rewards for positive outcomes. "When you asked how you could help rather than just pushing into his activity, he made a place for you."

- Foster empathy and sympathetic concern for others.

- Help children become aware of and accept differences.

- Discourage attempts to exclude individual children from activities. Suggest ways each can contribute.

Overview of Developmental Stages

Boxes 2-1, 2-2, and 2-3, which summarize typical developmental characteristics of children during middle childhood, should provide further help in understanding the children in your program. With an understanding of developmental expectations within each age group, you can better understand individual behaviours and interactions among children. This will also help in knowing what goals to set for individual children and what kinds of tools, materials, and activities are appropriate. However, the boxed lists are merely a prediction of when these behaviours will occur. There will be wide variations from child to child, with some behaviours happening earlier in some children and later in others. Children should be seen as individuals in terms of their stage of development.

Box 2-1 ■ Overview of Developmental Stages: Five- to Seven-Year-Olds

Family Relationships

- are more independent of parents, but still need rules

- need assurance of being loved

- have a sense of duty and take on family responsibilities

- develop a conscience

Peers

- begin to see others' points of view

- rely upon their peer group for self-esteem

- criticize differences in others

- have two or three best friends

- exhibit little interaction between boys and girls

- learn to share and take turns

- can participate in organized games

School

- want approval from teacher for achievement
- are eager to learn and be successful in school
- are influenced by teacher's attitudes and values

Emotions

- begin to inhibit aggression and resolve problems with words
- use humour, often expressed in riddles, practical jokes, or nonsense
- learn to postpone immediate rewards for delayed gratification
- become sensitive to what others think
- become concerned with issues of right and wrong or fair and unfair

Thinking

- are usually clear about differences between fantasy and reality
- can sustain interest for long periods of time
- give more thought and judgment to decisions
- have a good memory for concrete ideas and can remember two things for short periods of time
- can understand and abide by rules
- have a natural curiosity and often ask "why" questions

Language

- learn that words and pictures represent real objects
- can remember and relate past and present events
- sometimes use language aggressively
- understand more language than they use in their communication
- may tease others whose language is different from their own

Physical Development

- Girls are developing faster than boys.
- Children have good small-muscle and eye–hand coordination.
- Children are able to handle simple tools and materials.
- Children have a high energy level.

Box 2-2 ■ Overview of Developmental Stages: 8- to 10-Year-Olds

Family Relationships

- need parental guidance and support for school achievements
- rely on parents for help in assuming personal and social responsibilities

Peers

- overly concerned about conforming to peer-imposed rules

- competition is common

- teasing or quarrels result from antagonism between boys and girls

- develop pronounced gender differences in interests

- form cliques of same gender

- spend a lot of energy in physical game playing

School

- greater competition in school activities may lead to problems handling failure

- need teacher approval and attention

- academic achievement important

Emotions

- react to feelings of others and are sensitive to criticism

- look for friendly relationships with adults

- make value judgments about own behaviour and set standards for self

- are aware of the importance of belonging

- exhibit strong conformation to gender role

- are independent and self-sufficient

- begin to develop moral values

Thinking

- are capable of sustained interest; can make plans, then carry them out

- can begin to think logically about practical problems

- begin to understand cause and effect

- understand abstract concepts such as time and the value of money

Language

- exhibit abilities to use language or to read widely

- use language to communicate ideas, spend a lot of time in discussion

- can use more abstract words

- often resort to slang and profanity

Physical Development

- Physical skills are becoming important in determining status and self-concept.

- Girls are taller, stronger, and more skilful in small-muscle activities.

- Children have a high energy level.

- Girls begin adolescent growth spurt toward end of this period.

- Children take responsibility for their own personal hygiene.

Box 2-3 ■ Overview of Developmental Stages: 11- to 13-Year-Olds

Family Relationships

- ready to make own decisions outside the family
- aware that parental influence is decreasing
- sometimes rebellious but still need input on family values

Peers

- peer-group model sets standards for behaviour
- choice of friends based on common interests
- seek information about appropriate gender roles from peers
- may conform rigidly to role assigned by peer group
- team games increasingly important
- boys' and girls' interests more divergent
- may develop crushes and hero worship
- are often self-conscious and may become boisterous to cover anxiety
- interested in opposite gender; girls are more interested than boys
- faced with decisions regarding behaviour: sex, drugs, and alcohol

School

- worry when in a new school setting
- begin to question adult authority, particularly in school
- often focus on school for social experience
- are reluctant to attend child care; are bored or think they can care for themselves

Emotions

- may lack self-confidence, be shy, or be introspective
- worry about what others think, especially peers
- may be moody
- may experience great stress caused by physical changes heralding puberty
- develop own value systems, although influenced by peers
- seek self-identity, may result in rebellious behaviour

Thinking

- can now move from dependence on concrete thinking to abstract concepts
- can apply logic and solve problems
- can consider more than one solution to problems
- enjoy problem-solving games and puzzles

Language

- have a good command of spoken and written language

- can use language to discuss feelings, thus bringing about self-understanding

- are often argumentative and contradict adults

Physical Development

- Boys begin adolescent growth spurt.

- Adolescent growth peaks in girls, who experience changes in body proportions.

- In girls, secondary gender characteristics develop: breasts, menstruation.

- Early maturing is related to positive self-image.

- Boys have improved motor development and coordination and can excel at sports.

- Girls and boys master physical skills that are necessary for playing games.

Summary

Middle childhood is an important period when children develop a sense of who they are, what they can do, and how others perceive them. Since the focus of their daily lives is school, their self-esteem is closely tied to school success.

A second way children develop a sense of self is in terms of feelings of power. One source of power is their status with their peers. Another is an inner control over their own behaviour.

Acceptance by their peers is a third way children refine their sense of self. School-age children can be cruel to their peers as they test their own power. Children who are often the target of teasing have a difficult time, further eroding their self-esteem.

The final standard by which school-age children evaluate themselves is in terms of good or bad behaviour. Often reputations acquired during middle childhood may affect the individual's behaviour into adolescence and adulthood.

Race, ethnicity, and social economic status also play a part in how children perceive themselves and others. Children first describe themselves in terms of observable characteristics. Socialization experiences are important factors affecting children's subjective feelings about group members.

Positive encounters with individuals of different cultural or socioeconomic backgrounds can lead to a belief that all people are unique and have something to offer their community. This is the basis for promoting diversity and bringing recognition to prejudice and stereotypes.

Beginning in the preschool period, when children first learn the meaning of the word "friend," the need to have a friend becomes increasingly important. Young school-age children choose friends of the same gender and age who have similar interests and values. Older children rely upon friends for intimate conversations about problems, dreams, and expectations.

Children usually have one best friend and by age nine everyone knows who is best friends with whom. Later in middle childhood, children form cliques, clubs, or gangs with the main purpose of gaining independence from adults.

Cliques provide children with a sense of belonging and a feeling of power. Cliques can be limiting in that they prescribe specific ways of dressing or behaving. In the case of gangs, the purpose may be to not only operate outside the realm of adult supervision but also be antisocial. Gangs may engage in illegal activities.

However, the need to form friendships and to belong is strong. In order to make friends, certain skills are necessary: the ability to understand that others have different points of view, the ability to recognize that others have separate identities, and the ability to understand that each encounter is part of a relationship.

Key Terms

self-esteem   clique   gang

self-concept

Student Activities

1. Observe children on a school playground or in a park. Notice how they group themselves. Are there mixed-gender or single-gender groups? How many children are in each group? What are they playing? Write a short report describing your observation, relating what you saw to the information in this chapter. Compare your findings with those of your classmates.
2. In small groups, discuss your own perceptions of the following:
   a. Aboriginal people
   b. Homeless people
   c. People whose second language is English
   Describe the experiences that have led you to your perceptions. Were some of your perceptions based on prejudices? If so, what can you do to change your beliefs?
3. Ask the children in your school-age group to draw a picture of themselves. Bring the pictures to class. Choose two to share with classmates. Show the pictures and tell what you think the pictures say about the children's self-esteem.

Review Questions

1. Describe the changes that take place in children's assessment of their school achievement.
2. This chapter stated that children derive some of their sense of self through feelings of power. What are the sources of that power?
3. Explain the importance of peers in determining children's sense of self.
4. State three ways in which school-age child care professionals can help children increase their self-esteem.
5. Compare the criteria for choosing friends among young school-age children with those of older children.
6. What is the primary purpose of groups, clubs, and gangs? Are there other purposes?
7. What are the positive aspects of belonging to a clique or group? What are the negatives?
8. List and explain the three skills children need in order to make friends.
9. This chapter suggested that school-age child care professionals allow children opportunities to "just hang out" with a friend. Why is that important?
10. What would you say to children to achieve the following:
    a. encourage them to take another person's point of view
    b. help them recognize their own personality characteristics
    c. evaluate their attempts to change behaviours that interfere with friendships

Case Study

Justin is an eight-year-old boy from Vietnam who was adopted by his Caucasian parents when he was only three months old. His two older siblings had been born into the family before he was chosen. The siblings are both boys and much larger than Justin, and they are both very involved in school sports. Justin wants to follow in their footsteps but finds it difficult to match their success. In his after-school program, Justin loves to paint and creates some beautiful watercolour paintings that the school-age child care professional displays on the bulletin board. However, Justin still longs to join in when the other children are playing baseball. He is usually the last one to be chosen for a team and is booed or called names when he strikes out. When this happens, he goes back to the bench and looks like he can hardly keep from crying. He doesn't cry but tries again when it is his turn at bat.

1. What do you think are the causes of Justin's lack of confidence in his own abilities?
2. What are some things the school-age child care professional can do to help him feel better about himself?
3. Are there ways Justin's parents can help?
4. What group games could school-age child care professionals facilitate that would encourage teamwork and ultimately help Justin feel a valued part of the team?

References

Aboud, F. E. & Doyle, A. (1996). Parental and peer influences on children's racial attitudes. *International Journal of Intercultural Relations, 20,* 371–383.

Adler, P. A. & Adler, P. (1998). *Peer power: Preadolescent culture and identity.* Piscataway, NJ: Rutgers University Press.

Adler, P., Kless, S., & Adler, P. (1992). Socialization to gender roles: Popularity among elementary school boys and girls, *Sociology of Education,* 65, (July) 169–187. Retrieved April 19, 2005, from http://www.findarticles.com/p/articles/mi_m1249/is_n2_v66/ai_14715579

Bigler, R. S., Brown, C. S., & Markell, M. (2001). When groups are not created equal: Effects of group status on the formation of inter-group attitudes in children. *Child Development, 72,* 1151–1162.

Bigler R. S. & Liben, L. S. (1993). A cognitive development approach to racial stereotyping and reconstructive memory in Euro-American children. *Child Development, 64,* 1507–1518.

Dewer, G. (2009). How to help kids make friends: Evidence-based tips. www.parentingscience.com/kids-make-friends.html

Doyle, A. B. & Aboud, F. E. (1995). A longitudinal study of white children's racial prejudice as a social cognitive development. *Merrill-Palmer Quarterly,* 41, 209–228.

Edwards, C. P. (1994). Leadership in groups of school-age girls. *Developmental Psychology, 30*(6), 920–927.

Gilligan, C., Murphy, J. M., & Tappan, M. B. (1990). Moral development beyond adolescence. In C. N. Alexander & E. J. Langer (Eds.), *Higher stages of human development.* New York: Oxford University Press.

Holmes, R. N. (1995). *How young children perceive race.* Thousand Oaks, CA: Sage Publications.

Katz, L. G. & McClellan, D. E. (1997). *Fostering children's social competence.* Washington DC: NAEYC.

Opie, I. & Opie, P. (1959). *The lore and language of children.* New York: Clarendon Press.

Raver, C. (2002). Emotions matter: Making the case for the role of young children's emotional development for early school readiness. *Giving child and youth development knowledge away.* Vol. XVI, #2. University of Chicago: Society for Research in Child Development.

Selman, R. (1980). *The growth of interpersonal understanding: Developmental and clinical analysis.* New York: Academic Press.

Stipek, D. J. & MacIver, D. (1989). Developmental change in children's assessment of intellectual competence. *Child Development, 60,* 521–538.

Chapter 3

Families: Where Children Are Nurtured

Objectives

After studying this chapter, the student should be able to:

- State changing definitions of a family
- Describe family types
- Discuss the effects of each family composition on children
- Review the role of school-age child care professionals in relation to parents

 Profile

In a school-age program, staff are working not only with the children, but also with families. When children and families are in crisis, such as in situations where children are dealing with the separation or divorce of their parents, staff need to give support and understanding. Sometimes staff and parents can seek support from various sources together to assist themselves and the children.

Reaching In ... Reaching Out (RIRO) is a research-based program that began at the University of Pennsylvania. In it, children learn resiliency skills by watching adults model them.

Resilience is the ability to "bounce back" from life's hard times. It helps individuals cope with stress, overcome adversities, recover from trauma, and become open to grow and learn with new opportunities (Masten & Coatsworth, 1998 in Reaching In ... Reaching Out—The Child and Family Partnership, 2011).

Adults are taught skills needed to handle life's challenges with resilience and how to pass those skills along to children. These skills promote children's strengths and resilience, which helps them build the confidence they may need to deal with helplessness, violence, and risk of depression.

"Road of Life" Travel List

Outside Supports

- Caring relationships
- Positive role models
- Community supports

Inner Strengths

- Self-control
- Thinking skills
- Confidence
- Positive outlook
- Responsibility and participation

"This training is important for self-growth, self-evaluation, and understanding of our own behaviours. It gives us tools to understand the behaviours of others and assists them in developing their resiliency." HT (manager, child care program)

"The resiliency skills have affected every aspect of my life, both in personal relationships and as a manager of a daycare centre. I've just become more effective in my relationships with other adults." LD (manager, child care program)

(Reaching In ... Reaching Out—Promoting Resilience in Young Children: http://www.reachinginreachingout.com)

The Changing Family

Historically, humans have always grouped themselves together in tribes, clans, networks, or families. In her book *Families,* Howard (1978) writes, "The trouble we take to arrange ourselves in some semblance of families is one of the imperishable habits of the human race." Although we continue to group together, as society changes, the definition of family changes. The meaning most widely used by scholars in the past was one that signified parents and their biological children who were dwelling together or not. Legal experts have also stressed the biological relationships but broadened the definition to include any individuals related by blood. This definition is becoming less meaningful in today's surrogate parenting situations. Another definition would include a group of kin and others living together day by day. Some contemporary researchers broaden the definition even further. They state that a family is an attitude, identification with and among a group of individuals who support and nurture one another. Kevin and Elizabeth, whose family portraits appear in this chapter, even included their pets as important members of their families. Families can also be defined by their function. A well-functioning family supports its members in developing their full potential. The family nurtures children in the following five ways (Berger, 2000, p. 367):

- meeting basic needs for food, clothes, and shelter
- encouraging learning through guidance and motivation
- developing self-esteem by helping children to feel competent
- nurturing friendships with peers
- creating an atmosphere of harmony and stability in the home

Eighty-four percent of the population in Canada live in families. This encompasses a married or common-law couple with or without children, or a lone parent living with at least one child in the same dwelling (Statistics Canada, 2007). Families tend to be smaller, with one or two children, and individuals often postpone having children until they are well established in their careers, sometimes well into their 30s.

The configurations of families in North America continue to change. There are many different types of families: two-parent married couples or common-law families, often called "nuclear families"; lone-parent families; stepfamilies; blended families, and same-sex parent families.

Married-couple families still constitute the large majority of families in Canada. The 2006 census reported that married-couple families with children made up 62.9 percent of all families in Canada (Statistics Canada, 2007). Married-couple families or "traditional families" include a mother and father who have registered a legal marriage with the province/territory and who have one or more children.

In Canada, **common-law** partners are defined as two persons of opposite sex who are not legally married to each other, but live together as husband and wife in the same dwelling. Common-law families with children compose 11.3 percent of families, with a larger percentage living in Quebec (Statistics Canada, 2007).

A **lone-parent family** is one that is headed by either the father or mother. In Canada, as of the 2006 census, 25.8 percent of families with children are lone-parent families. Lone-parent families headed by women continue to outnumber those headed by men by more than four to one. One must be aware of negative stereotypes associated with lone-parent families, especially that of the lone "never-married" mother. Being labelled with a negative stereotype is nonproductive in terms of accessing the needs of lone mothers in determining the future success of their children (Vanier Institute of the Family, 1999).

Stepfamilies comprise 12 percent of all couple families in Canada (Vanier Institute, 2010). **Stepfamilies** are two-parent families where one parent is not the biological or adoptive parent of the children (Vanier Institute of the Family, 1999). In the creation of a new family, these children often have fears about what their new family will be like. Their biggest fear is losing touch with their original parent or that the new stepparent will not like them (South Cochrane Child and Youth Services, 2004).

One half of stepfamilies are **blended families**. These are families where there is at least one child from one or both previous relationship plus one child from the current union (Vanier Institute, 2010). Children in blended families need to adjust not only to a new stepparent but also to changing roles that arise as a result of new stepsiblings. These families face added financial pressures along with difficulties in coparenting steprelations and in dealing with the legacy of an earlier marriage. Couples in blended families are often more prone to breakup depending on how well they meet these challenges. Sometimes a new "invisible" type of family, the binuclear family, emerges, in which the children of divorce continue to have two parents but in separate households (Eichler, 1988).

married-couple family
family led by a mother and father who have registered a legal marriage and who have one or more children

common-law family
two individuals of the opposite sex who are not legally married to each other but live together as husband and wife in the same dwelling and have one or more children

lone-parent family
family led by a father or mother with one or more children

stepfamily
two-parent family where one parent is not the biological or adoptive parent of the child(ren)

blended family
These are families where there is at least one child from one or both previous relationships plus one child from the current union

Figure 3-1 ■ **Many children grow up in a household with either their father or their mother.**

same-sex-parent family
composed of lesbian couples, gay male partners, or singles from this group with one or more children

Same-sex-parent families are composed of lesbian couples, homosexual male partners, or singles of this group. A 2006 census revealed that 16 percent of households headed by lesbian couples had children versus 3 percent among male same-sex households (Statistics Canada, 2009). Some of the children in these relationships are the result of previous marriages to heterosexual partners. Adoption laws across Canada—particularly in British Columbia, Alberta, Saskatchewan, Ontario, Quebec, Nova Scotia, and Newfoundland—allow children to be adopted into gay or lesbian families on the same basis as heterosexuals (Review Panel on Common Law Relationships, 2001.) Some children have been produced through artificial insemination or by a surrogate parent. Lesbian mothers and gay fathers continually deal with negative stereotypes that are related to a homophobic ideology that separates family and homosexuality and perpetuates the view that gay men and lesbians should not be responsible for children (Mandell & Duffy, 1995).

In addition to understanding family forms, it is important to note that existing families change as the members grow and develop, or as their circumstances shift. The first child may have grown up in a nuclear family, but her sibling may be reared by a lone parent. A child whose divorced mother remarries may suddenly find herself with several new siblings. Whatever the form, the family is the first and therefore the most important determinant in children's development.

Program Options for Working Parents and the Effect of the Home Environment on Children

Over the decades there has been an increase in dual-income families. In 2001, 61.9 percent of couples worked outside the home. The percentage of women in the workforce went from 45.7 percent in 1976 to 61.8 percent in 2005. The hours worked require parents to find programs for their school-age children, well past school hours and on school holidays. As a result, the need for quality school-age care continues to increase across the country (Canadians in Context, 2011).

Parents have many options when choosing an out-of-school program for their children while they are at work. Some families employ a <u>nanny</u> or someone who can come into their own home. This is convenient when there are younger children who are at home and need care on a daily basis. <u>Advantages</u> for the parents are that their children are at home in supervised care. It limits the stress of travelling to another location to drop off and pick up their children. <u>Disadvantages</u> might be in whether the child care provider has any training, and limited access that the children might have to social activities with their peers.

Many parents choose to send their school-age children to a <u>family home care setting</u> in their neighbourhood. The advantage of this option is that the children may be able to walk to and from school and are able to play with other school friends. Disadvantages may arise with regards to the training of the child care provider, the quality of activities the children are doing on a daily basis, and the quality of time that the child care provider can give to the school-age children if there are younger children in the home as well.

Children who attend a <u>school-age program</u> before school, at lunchtime, after school, and/or on school holidays have some advantages. They can participate in supervised activities and have new experiences, make friends within a wider circle than is available in their neighbourhood, and learn to get along with adults other than their parents. School-age children who attend a school-age program that is housed in their elementary school have an added advantage in that they can easily move between the school environment and the program setting before school, at lunchtime, and/or after school. A disadvantage of this option is that being in the same physical environment after school and during their school day may not give the children enough of a change.

Some parents with older <u>children who stay by themselves</u> during out-of-school times may also feel their children have advantages. Children do get to a stage where they are ready to be in self-care, usually around the age of 10. They relish the freedom to come home and do what they want. They grow in independence and self-esteem as they master emergency situations or do household chores. According to Manitoba's Child Welfare laws, however, no child under the age of 12 is to be left alone without suitable supervision. The challenge for parents is to know when their children are ready for self-care and how prepared they are to deal with safety situations. Regulations vary from one province/territory to another but are similar in terms of the age-12 cutoff.

In spite of the care options for their school-age children, many working parents feel tremendous stress. Their most frequently voiced complaint is that they never have enough time to spend with their children, do work around their home, or for their spouse. Fatigue and stress may cause family friction or result in adults taking out their frustrations on the children. Children may feel isolated because the adults have little energy left for being parents. Children may also feel abandoned or that their parents care more about work than about them. If the children do not attend a school-age program but stay home alone when they are not in school, they may feel lonely and sometimes frightened.

<u>When parents divorce</u>, another kind of stress is added to children's lives. Statistics Canada reports that there were 70,828 divorces in 2003. Between 2002 and 2003, divorce rates increased by only 0.7 percent. Most provinces and territories recorded a drop in their divorce rates, except more significantly in Ontario and Quebec (Canadian Council on Social Development, 2004).

Now, in many families both parents work outside the home, requiring them to search out different out-of-school care options for their children. Divorce can have a profound and lasting impact on children's behaviour. They may exhibit "acting-out" behaviours such as aggression or conflicts with authorities. The acting out may also be seen as withdrawal from contacts with others, depression, or anxiety. In addition to changes in behaviour, children of divorce often perform less well academically. Their grades go down, and they are less motivated to achieve. A few studies show that boys have more difficulty adjusting to divorce than girls, but multiple-gender studies find that boys do less well than girls only in their social adjustment (Amato & Rezac, 1994). There are also some age-related differences in children's development. Preschoolers are more concerned about maintaining relationships with both parents. In middle childhood children tend to assume responsibility for the divorce and have unrealistic expectations of their own ability to affect their parents' behaviour. They may believe they can reunite their parents. High school children tend to relate the divorce to their

Figure 3-2 ■ "Radio, Dad, me, stepbrother, brother, StepMom." Kevin, age 5

own identity and their ability to maintain relationships and make wise life choices (Kurkek, 1989).

However, if contact is maintained with both parents and if income and living conditions remain stable, these children do as well as those in an intact family. The reality, however, is that in many situations, the mother becomes the custodial parent, and family income is often far lower than during the marriage.

Children of mothers who have never been married can be well adjusted, but the odds are against fatherless children. These children are deprived of the special kind of child-rearing fathers can provide. Kyle Pruet (1988), a professor of psychiatry at Yale University and author of *The Nurturing Father*, says that whether roughhousing with a five-year-old or disciplining a delinquent teen, fathers have a different parenting style. Boys and girls both benefit from a male role model. Girls need a suitable male role model with whom they can identify with regards to appropriate male–female relationships.

Probably the most serious difficulty for the lone-parent family, especially when headed by a mother, is low economic status. Women often earn lower salaries than men, causing some of these families to have greater financial difficulties. In 2009, male lone-parent families earned an average total income of $65,400, while female lone-parent families had an average total income of $47,700; an increase from 2007 (Statistics Canada, 2009). Lone parents often suffer from "role overload" as they try to nurture their children, offer sensible discipline, and provide adequate financial support. Stressors increase when there is more than one child or when illness strikes.

Frequently, when the words "lone parent" are used, we assume that they apply to mothers. However, a growing number of men are granted custody of children. When fathers are motivated to provide a loving, nurturing environment, both boys and girls in father-only families do as well as those living with their mother ("Single fathers," 1995). However, boys are placed more frequently with their fathers than girls, and they seem to do even better in a father-only family than if they lived with their mother. Part of the reason may be that fathers seek custody because they want to care for their children; mothers are often given custody whether they want it or not. Also, the income level of a male-led family is more likely to be higher than that of a family led by a female, so the children benefit from a higher standard of living.

An increasing number of households include grandparents or are headed by a grandmother and/or grandfather. These adults provide valuable assistance when families have experienced divorce. They can provide emotional support for the children during difficult times, perhaps add some income, and assist with out-of-school-time care. Although there are advantages to this arrangement, there are also additional stresses on the adults and the children. Parents may find that they are caught between the needs of their children and those of their parents. Illnesses and physical limitations of older adults may require additional time and effort from members of the family to provide the necessary care. The extended family of grandparents, aunts, uncles, and cousins is more typical in traditional societies such as China, India and in our Canadian aboriginal populations.

When divorced adults find new spouses, the remarriage and resulting blended family are usually seen as an opportunity to start over and to resolve the difficulties of a previous union or of being a lone parent. For the children, the experience can be positive, negative, or mixed. If the children have been living with their mother, the economic situation often improves. Boys are sometimes helped by the presence of a stepfather, especially if he takes a personal interest in them. When the father remarries, there may be a more equal sharing of household chores and routines. Children in blended families often find they have more role models and choices. In addition, they may have the opportunity to live in new places and have new experiences. All of these are positives.

Many adjustments are difficult, however, and vary with the ages of the children. Younger children suffer more from loss of a close relationship with both parents. Some children continue to have problems of identity and self-worth in blended families. School-age children may go through a period of lower academic achievement.

Children from families who are immigrants or refugees have many challenges to face in their new country. Kenise Murphy Kilbride (1997) comments on interviews done with a mixture of immigrants and refugee parents from various cultural backgrounds about what they expect from the staff in the child care program. The parents responded that they wanted to be sure that their children were liked and valued for who they were; that child care professionals took the time to understand them and that their needs were met, as with all the children. These parents want to be involved in their children's program and to know how their children are doing. They too want to be understood, to share and talk about different child-rearing practices and cultural practices. They, along with their children, want to feel at home in the program and the community in which they live. These children often face discrimination from their peers. They need caring, sensitive, and watchful child care professionals who will step in, prevent and stop discriminatory behaviour, and plan a nonbiased curriculum that supports and celebrates the differences between people (pp. 31–32).

Aboriginal families also have special ways of interacting with people and have specific beliefs about nature and the environment that need to be recognized and

Figure 3-3 ■ "Barkley, Mommy and Me." Natalie, age 8

Chapter 3   Families: Where Children Are Nurtured

Figure 3-4 ■ "My family." Elizabeth, age 10

incorporated in a school-age program. Children from aboriginal families are taught to value the integration of nature and people into a more "harmonious whole." They believe that one is greatly dependent on the other; much respect must be given to our forests, lakes, rivers, and animals; and that we must work to preserve the natural elements of our country. Aboriginal cultures practise a more cooperative way of working together and making decisions. They place great value on the Elders of their communities and believe that they are very important in passing on cultural traditions. School-age child care professionals need to plan opportunities to incorporate these practices in their program by inviting Elders in the community to come and spend time telling stories and sharing skills with the children. School-age child care professionals will find that those from aboriginal communities communicate differently. Time should be taken to listen, to slow down, and not jump in too quickly to add information (Murphy Kilbride, 1997, pp. 34–36).

Same-sex-parent families may be the target of discrimination as many people still look upon these relationships with hostility. Children may feel something is wrong with them when they are the targets of negative attitudes. They may also consider themselves different from schoolmates who have a "mom and a dad." Despite this, a number of studies show that children in same-sex-parent families can and do adjust when given adequate support by adults. Studies by Laird (as cited in Ambert, 2003) and Patterson (2000) showed that children in same-sex-parent families were not disadvantaged emotionally and that they often possessed certain strengths of character, such as tolerance, empathy, and contentment. When children have an opportunity to seek out additional role models, they have an easier time developing their own identity.

A study comparing lesbian and heterosexual mothers, some single, some in couples, found no difference in children's adaptation and development around the age of seven. The children studied had all been reproduced by donor insemination, which would also be an additional complication for the child in terms of how he or she would define oneself (Chan, Raboy, & Patterson, 1998). "Lesbian mothers are similar to heterosexual mothers; it is not their sexual orientation that emerges as an important variable but their identity as mothers" (Lewin, 1993).

Although family composition does have an effect on children's development, the essential ingredients for emotionally healthy children can be found in any group. Successful families have the following common characteristics:

- They are affectionate. Members express their love and caring for one another.
- They have a sense of place. They either have a stable environment or they have a commitment to their place of origin.
- They pass on their cultural heritage.
- They connect with posterity. They honour their elders.
- They promote and perpetuate family rituals. Parents pass on traditions from their own past and encourage a sense of family continuity.

- They communicate with one another.
- They respect differences among their members.

As you can see, the ingredients for an effective family can exist no matter who makes up the group. Remember that as you work with children and families in your program.

Poverty

Statistics Canada releases figures on the numbers of people living below its low-income cutoffs (LICOs); from these figures we can describe trends in child poverty. These LICOs are broadly understood as Canada's poverty lines (Canadian Council on Social Development, 1998). As a result of recommendations from Campaign 2000 and government investments in child benefits, the rate of child poverty is slowly declining, from 11.9 percent in 1989 to 9.5 percent in 2009. However, there are still nearly 639,000 children (1 in 10 children), who remain in poverty in Canada (Campaign 2000 Report Card, 2011).

A more comprehensive measure of poverty lines is Canada was released in May 2003 and is called the Market Basket Measure (MBM). The MBM creates a detailed list of basic items that a family of four would need for food, clothing, and shelter. (National Council of Welfare, 2004).

Low-income, two-parent families remain far below the poverty line. Sixty-three percent of children under 18 are in low-income two-parent families. Families headed by women and immigrant families are more likely to be poor than other families. The highest risk for poverty is found in female-headed, lone-parent families, at 31 percent. Children of immigrants, of Aboriginal identity in racialized families, and those with a disability are also at a higher risk for poverty (Campaign 2000 Report Card, 2011).

Even though there has been a slight decrease of the numbers of children in poverty, government policies continue to establish a more comprehensive, multipronged social investment strategy, which would work toward achieving sustained reduction and a virtual end to child poverty in Canada. This strategy includes income security, more jobs, affordable housing, and a well-designed system of early childhood education and care (Campaign 2000 Report Card, 2011). Various provinces and territories have adopted their own poverty-reducing initiatives through social planning networks.

Poverty is a critical issue in First Nations communities and also for Aboriginal people living in urban areas (54 percent, more than half the Aboriginal population). Crucial factors for those in poverty include low income, low levels of education, and poor housing. Youth suicide is three to seven times greater in First Nations communities. The Canada–First Nations Joint Action Plan has been developed to set goals for improving the lives of First Nations citizens (Campaign 2000 Report Card, 2011).

Helping Children and Their Parents

Probably your most important function when working with children is to support the bond between parents and their children. Working parents agonize over how they can provide the best kind of upbringing for their children and still earn a living. They may be sad that they cannot spend more time with their family. Many find it hard to get back to being a parent at the end of the day after the pressures of their job. You can help them bridge the gap between their daytime activities and their role as parents.

The key word is to <u>communicate</u>! If you see the parents frequently, talk with them. If you seldom see some parents, you will have to find other means to communicate. Parent handbooks or newsletters provide an opportunity to present aspects of the program, make suggestions for parent/child activities, or announce upcoming events. A bulletin board in an entry area where all parents will see it can be used to give information and also to display children's artwork or show photos of children. Some programs set up their own website and e-mail addresses. Parents can log on to the website to get information about the program, upcoming events, or special services. School-age child care professionals can receive inquiries from parents by e-mail and answer in the same way. You can also use telephone calls to keep in contact with parents. It is important to take the time to ask parents how they see their child's experience in the program or to check on a child who has been absent. Be sure to check with parents to determine the best time to call them.

Figure 3-5 ■ **It is important for staff to support the bond between parents and their children.**

Figure 3-6 ■ **Bulletin boards can provide important information for parents.**

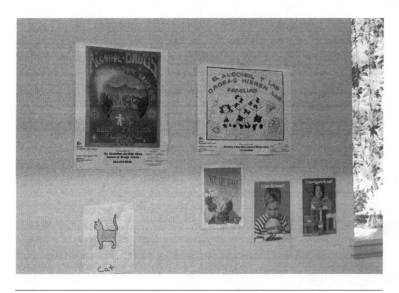

Some programs have found a <u>parent survey</u> to be an effective way to reach parents to determine their concerns or needs. Ask parents what they need to know about the program or their children's development. Additional questions might determine whether there are other ways that the centre could support parents. Once the information has been gathered, staff can decide on ways to respond. Parents appreciate knowing about any changes in their children since they left them in the morning. They want to know if the children are troubled or ill or are showing changes in behaviour. You can then work together to determine causes and bring about needed change. And communication is not one-way. Ask parents to let you know when there are variations in the home situation or when they see changes in their children.

Another means for keeping in contact with parents is through a <u>family journal</u>. Every child is provided with a notebook in which both school-age child care professionals and parents can write notes to one another. Staff can direct inquiries such as "What has Max been reading at home lately? He tells me he loves to read at home" or "Tell me the things Maya likes to do on weekends." The notebook can become a valuable tool for maintaining contact as well as providing a record of a child's progress.

Schedule <u>social events</u> that allow parents to get to know school-age child care professionals and other parents in a relaxed, fun situation. Many parents welcome a potluck dinner. They can meet their school-age children, along with younger children in the family, at the program and have dinner. As an added bonus, make it a multicultural dinner, with families bringing a dish specific to their culture or a family tradition. As recipes are shared and traditions discussed, everyone should gain an appreciation for how many families are alike even though their backgrounds are radically different.

Help parents see their children's behaviour realistically. Working parents often feel guilty about leaving their children in the care of others. When problems arise, they immediately think, "If I didn't have to work, these things wouldn't happen." That may or may not be so. Help parents to understand that some behaviours are developmentally predictable. Children will go through those stages whether the parent works or not. Often, time alone will resolve the situation. Sometimes simple changes within the family will work miracles.

Encourage parents to use their own knowledge of their children to bring about changes. Do not be too quick to offer advice based on your own experiences. Your family and your own child may be quite different. Instead, help parents think through the problem and come up with their own solutions. Discuss your observations of the behaviours, then ask them what happens at home. Encourage them to consider the causes. Let them suggest ways the problem might be alleviated. Obviously, if they have no suggestions, you can voice your own.

Recognize that parents sometimes express anger toward you as an outlet for their own fatigue. Try not to take it personally. The anger may be a way of expressing guilt about not having more time or energy to spend with their child. In addition, the cost of child care may consume a large portion of the family's income. Parents may feel, "I am paying a lot of money for this care. The least you can do is to see that he gets his homework done." If you understand the reasons for the parents' frustrations, you can deal with them more easily. Recognition of the fatigue helps. Most parents will respond to "It sounds like you have had a really hard day" or "Yes, it is hard to get him to do his homework. Do you have any suggestions as to how I can be any more successful?" It is important to clarify with the parent what role the program has in assisting children with doing their homework. Many programs provide a quiet space for children to do their homework and provide reminders for them when they come after school. Recognize that other parents prefer to help their children with homework at home. Accept differences in family organizations. Examine your own prejudices about what makes a family. If you grew up in a happy, intact family, you may see that as the only alternative. Instead, be open to recognizing the strengths of each family you work with. It will help if you increase your knowledge about the changes that have taken place in the last decade by reading further in the books listed at the end of this chapter.

Encourage families to share their cultural traditions with your program. This will be especially important to children in immigrant families. Visit the children's community and talk to the residents. Learn about the cultures through books, pictures, music, and observation. Actively involve the parents by asking them to share stories, songs, drawings, and experiences that portray important aspects of their culture. One of the best times to involve parents is during holidays. Some parents may be able to spend time in the classroom showing children the way they celebrate. However, avoid the "tourist approach," which teaches children about diversity *only* through holiday celebrations.

Some parents may be willing to bring you books, toys, or artifacts that are typical of their background. Still others may welcome an opportunity to get together at a workshop to make presents or decorations for the holiday. The addition of these kinds of resources would make the addition of diversity to the curriculum very meaningful for the children.

Help all children to increase their own self-esteem. As you read earlier parts of this chapter, you learned that this is more vital for children in some families than in others. But we know that children who feel good about themselves have a better chance of getting along and of becoming happy, functioning adults. So be aware of the ways you can let children know they are liked and successful. A later chapter provides specific strategies and activities.

As a school-age child care professional, you share the responsibility for children's welfare and education not only with parents but also with elementary school teachers. In a model situation, each of you would have close contact with the other. However, this does not always happen. Although you may see parents daily when they deliver or pick up the child, you may seldom have contact with elementary school personnel. If your program facility is connected to an elementary school, it is easier to bring about a close working relationship. If your facility is outside a school, it is harder to establish a liaison with teachers. In recognition of the Freedom of Information and Protection of Privacy Act, child care professionals are required to get signed permission from parents in order to share information about their child with professionals outside the program. This can be done by including a permission statement with the general intake forms that parents receive when they enrol their child in the program. See Appendix F for a permission form for the exchange of information.

When it is impossible for you to work directly with teachers, you can monitor the child's progress in other ways. Ask parents how their children are doing in school. Provide quiet places for the children to do their homework. Be aware of when report cards come out and inquire how children did.

Know when to refer parents for outside help. Find out what is available in your community so that you can suggest sources. Make referrals when the service needed is not something your program can provide. Medical or social services are examples. Make referrals when the problem with the child or within the family is acute or long standing.

Establishing a close relationship with parents can bring about immense rewards for you and the families you work with. Parents will find they are not alone in trying to provide the best for their children. You will find that getting to know parents will add to your ability to help their children.

Summary

As society has changed, the definition of a family has evolved. Several types of families are now recognized. The nuclear family consists of mother, father, and child(ren). This is often represented by married-couple families. However, there are a growing number of parents in common-law relationships with children or in lone-parent families where either the mother or father cares for the child(ren) ex-clusively or for a large portion of the time. Stepfamilies and blended families are another growing phenomenon; divorced parents remarry and combine their families, some-times conceiving additional children. Although all families are unique, immigrant families and aboriginal families have particular needs and face specific challenges that must be recognized by school-age child care professionals. Same-sex couples often bring children to or conceive children within their partnerships. The family is a system that affects children's development at every age level.

In many families, both parents work outside the home, requiring them to search out different out-of-school care options for their children.

Divorce can have a profound effect on children's lives. These children may exhibit acting-out behaviours such as aggression, conflicts with authorities, withdrawal from contacts with others, and depression or anxiety. They may also perform less well academically. Boys of divorced parents seem to have more difficulty than girls do in their social adjustment. Age also determines the kinds of problems children will exhibit. In middle childhood, children tend to assume responsibility for the divorce, while high school children relate the divorce to their own identity and ability to maintain relationships. Although adults see remarriage as an opportunity to start over, children in stepparent and blended families may experience some difficulties.

Immigrant children and children from same-sex-parent families may be the target of discrimination. Close contact between parent, school, and school-age child care professionals is vital. All parents suffer stresses and pressures, and staff can help by being understanding and establishing regular avenues of communication.

Visit the children's community and talk to community residents. Learn about cultures through books, pictures, music, and observation. Actively involve the parents by asking them to share stories, songs, drawings, and experiences that portray important aspects of their culture.

Key Terms

married-couple family	lone-parent family	blended family
common-law family	stepfamily	same-sex-parent family

Student Activities

1. Prepare a collage depicting your own family. You can do this on a large piece of poster board, using cutout pictures, words, and phrases from magazines. Display this collage to your class. Ask class members to discuss the family portrayed in the collage. Verify or refute your classmates' impressions.
2. Visit a school-age program at the time parents are coming to pick up their children. Write a short paper on your impressions of parent/staff/child relationships.
3. Bring to class an object that is meaningful to your family and representative of some aspect of your culture. It can be a picture, poem, or story, an article of clothing, or a handcrafted object. Show it to classmates and discuss its significance to you. Following the completion of all the presentations, discuss what you have learned. Have you learned something new about your own culture or another?
4. Interview a lone parent and parents in a two-parent family. Ask all the parents to describe the situations that create the most stress for them and their children. Are there similarities between the two families? What are the differences?

Review Questions

1. How has the definition of the word "family" changed?
2. List and describe five family forms.
3. What is likely the most serious difficulty for the lone-parent family headed by a woman?

4. What are the advantages to children when a parent remarries?
5. What are the problems faced by children in immigrant and Aboriginal families?
6. List three characteristics of an effective family.
7. What is your most important function as a school-age child care professional?
8. What are the advantages for children who live in a father-only household?
9. What government policies are needed to reduce or eliminate poverty in Canada?
10. List some ways that school-age child care professionals can share the responsibility for children's welfare with parents and elementary school teachers.

Case Study

For Mrs. Jolie and her family, the day begins long before it gets light. She and her children are on early, tight schedules to get to their various daytime commitments. Mrs. Jolie must travel 40 miles to her job as an elementary school teacher and must leave the house at 6:45. Often her oldest daughter, Anna, leaves even earlier, at 6:30, for before-school activities at her high school. Victor, age 10, is supposed to be picked up at 6:55 by the transporter service his mother has hired. This morning, when it doesn't arrive, he tries to reach his mother, but she is still en route to her school and doesn't have a cell phone. At 7:20 he calls the supervisor at his school-age extended day program. Chris, the supervisor, tells him not to panic and to keep cool, and they will work to contact his mother. He assures Victor his mom will have a solution. Chris leaves a message for Mrs. Jolie at her school's office. She returns his call immediately upon arriving at her school and quickly arranges other transportation for Victor.

Mrs. Jolie was really upset that this happened and said she felt guilty she had to leave her children to go to work. She has been divorced for only six months and knows that it has been hard on the children.

1. How would you assess the situation regarding the children's ability to cope with their early morning schedule?
2. What can you say to support Mrs. Jolie and recognize her feelings and frustrations?
3. Are there any additional suggestions that you can offer Mrs. Jolie to help in making the early-morning schedule run more smoothly?

References

Amato, P. R. & Rezac, S. J. (1994). Contact with non-resident parents, interparental conflict, and children's behaviour. *Journal of Family Issues, 15,* 191–207.

Ambert, A. M. (2003). Same-sex couples and same-sex-parent families: Relationships, parenting, and issues of marriage. The Vanier Institute of the Family. Retrieved April 5, 2005, from http://www.vifamily.ca/library/cft/samesex.html

Berger, K. S. (2001). *The developing person through childhood and adolescence* (5th ed.). New York: Worth Publishers.

Campaign 2000. (2004). One million too many: Implementing solutions to child poverty in Canada. *2004 Report Card on Child Poverty in Canada,* pp. 1–3. http://campaign2000.ca/rc/rc04/04National ReportCard.pdf

Campaign 2000 Report Card on Child and Family Poverty in Canada. (2011). Retrieved May 29, 2012, from http://www.campaign2000.ca/reportCards/national/2011EnglishRreportCard.pdf

Canadian Council on Social Development. (1998). *Child poverty in Canada: Recasting the issue.* Retrieved April 19, 2005, from http://www.ccsd.ca/pubs/recastin.htm

Canadian Council on Social Development. (2004). Families: A Canadian profile. Retrieved December 30, 2011, from http://www.ccsd.ca/factsheets/family

Chan, R. W., Raboy, B., & Patterson, C. J. (1998). Psychosocial adjustment among children conceived via donor insemination by lesbian and heterosexual mothers. *Child Development, 69,* 443–457.

Eichler, Margrit. (1988). *Families in Canada today: Recent changes and their policy implications* (2nd ed.). Toronto: Gage.

Human Resources and Skills Development Canada. (2011). Canadians in context—Households and families/indicators of well-being in Canada. Retrieved December 30, 2011, from http://www4.hrsdc.gc.ca/.3ndic.1t.4r@-eng.jsp?iid=37

Howard, J. (1978). *Families.* New York: Simon and Schuster.

Kurkek, L. (1989). Relationship quality for newly married husbands and wives: Marital history, stepchildren and individual predictors. *Journal of Marriage and the Family, 52,* 1053–1064.

Lewin, E. (1993). Lesbian mothers. Accounts of gender in American culture. Ithaca, NY: Cornell University Press. Retrieved April 19, 2005, from http://www.vifamily.ca/library/cft/samesex.html. Original work published in 1993.

Mandell, N. & Duffy, A. (1995). *Canadian families: Diversity, conflict and change.* Toronto: Harcourt Brace.

Marcil-Gratton, N. (1999.) Growing up with mom and dad? Lone parents and their children. *Transition Magazine, 29,* 1. Retrieved April 19, 2005, from http://www.vifamily.ca/library/transition/291/291.html

Murphy Kilbride, K. (1997). *Include me too! Human diversity in early childhood.* Toronto: Harcourt Brace.

National Council of Welfare. (2004). Full time workers still in poverty. Retrieved April 5, 2005, from http://www.ncwcnbes.net/htmdocument/reportIFL/PressReleaseIFL_e.htm

Patterson, C. J. (2000). Family of lesbians and gay men. *Journal of Marriage and the Family, 62,* 1052–1069.

Pruett, K. D. (1988). *The nurturing father.* New York: Warner Books.

Review panel on common law relationships. (2001). Vol. 1, p. 1. Retrieved April 5, 2005, from http://www.gov.mb.ca/justice/reviewpanel/vol1/summary.html

Single fathers: Doing it all. (1995). *Ebony, 50,* 60.

South Cochrane Child and Youth Services, Children's Mental Health Centre. (2004). *Children in step-families.* Timmons, ON: South Cochrane Child and Youth Services. Retrieved April 19, 2005, from http://cfi.vianet.on.ca

Statistics Canada. (2001). 2001 census: Families in private households by family structure and presence of children. In L. Wilson (Ed.), *Families and communities in early childhood development.* Toronto: Thomson Nelson.

Statistics Canada. (2004, April 7). Low income in census metropolitan areas. *The Daily,* 1–7. Retrieved April 5, 2005, from http://www.statscan.ca/Daily/English/040407/d040407a.htm

Statistics Canada. (2007). 2006 Census (Cat. No. 97-554-XCB2006007). Retrieved December 30, 2011, from http://www4.hrsdc.gc.ca/.3ndic.1t.4r@-eng.jsp?iid=37

Statistics Canada. (2009). Family portrait: Continuity and change in Canadian families and households in 2006: National portrait: Census families. Retrieved June 15, 2012, from http://www12.statcan.ca/census-recensement/2006/as-sa/97-553/p4-eng.cfm

Statistics Canada. (2009). Income of Canadians. http://www.statcan.gc.ca/daily-quotidien/110615/dq110615b-eng.htm

Vanier Institute of the Family. (2004). Contemporary family trends—Same-sex couples and same-sex-parent families. Retrieved April 5, 2005, from http://www.vifamily.ca/library/cft/samesex.html

Vanier Institute of the Family. (2010). Children growing up in step families. Retrieved December 30, 2011, from http://www.vifamily.ca/media/node/513/attachments/stepfamilies.pdf

Selected Further Reading

Ambert, A. (1992). *Effect of children on parents* (2nd ed.). Binghamton, NY: Haworth Press.

Ambert, A. (1997). *The web of poverty: Psychosocial perspectives.* Binghamton, NY: Haworth Press.

Brand, S. (1996). Making parent involvement a reality: Helping teachers develop partnerships. *Young Children, 51*(2), 76–81.

Hendrick, J. & Chandler, K. (1996). *The Whole Child* (6th Canadian ed.). Don Mills, ON: Pearson Education Canada.

Miller, P. A., Ryan, P., & Morrison, W. (1999). Practical strategies for helping children of divorce in today's classroom. *Childhood Education, 75*(5), 285–289.

Saracho, O. N. & Spodek, B. (1983). *Understanding the multicultural experience in early childhood education.* Washington, DC: National Association for the Education of Young Children.

Wallersein, J. (1993). Children after divorce. *Human development.* Guilford, CT: The Duskin Publishing Group.

Websites

For Parents

BC Council for Families
http://www.bccf.bc.ca

Foundation for Equal Families
http://archive.egale.ca/index.asp?item=62

ProudParenting.com
http://www.proudparenting.com

WomansDivorce.com
http://www.womansdivorce.com/divorce-and-children.html

Stepfamilies
http://www.vanierinstitute.ca/include/get.php?nodeid+756

Articles by Dr. Anne-Marie Ambert
http://www.yorku.ca/ambert/publications/index.html

General Family Information

Resources on 2001: Families in Motion Research & Information Group
http://www.uvic.ca/psyc/fmric

Articles by Dr. Anne-Marie Ambert
http://www.arts.yorku.ca/soci/ambert/writings/index.html

How Children Grow and Develop

Chapter 4

Development in Middle Childhood: Physical

Objectives

After completing this chapter, the student should be able to:

- Discuss the importance of understanding child development
- Distinguish between the progress of development and the process of learning
- Relate major changes and variations in growth patterns and motor skills among children
- Discuss determinants of good health and the impact of obesity and other health conditions on children's physical well-being
- Describe ways in which school-age child care professionals can enhance children's physical development and healthy well-being

Profile

A Discovery Asthma Camp called the ACT-Wilf Churchman Camp is a summer program for children, aged 7 to 13, who live with moderate to severe asthma. The camp is situated in a beautiful outdoor environment on the shores of Lake Diefenbaker, northwest of Regina, Saskatchewan. The program is able to accommodate 54 children, and eligibility to attend is based on the recommendation of the child's physician. The children are involved in a number of physical activities, including swimming, canoeing, hiking, softball, volleyball, crafts, dancing, and other special events, which are led by qualified staff. Developing friendships and "hanging out" with others who have a similar health condition provide a network of social and emotional support and an opportunity to talk about shared issues and concerns.

The promotion of an active lifestyle is important for everyone, especially for those who have asthma. There are many athletes, such as hockey player Gary Roberts and Olympic medallist Mark Spitz, who have well-controlled asthma, enabling them to participate in sports. *Pediatrics* reported that children with asthma were more likely to be active if they were enjoying physical activity, if parents believed that they could do as much activity as their peers, and if parents believed that exercise actually made their child's asthma better (Lang et al, 2004). Improved fitness levels are associated with decreased severity of asthmatic symptoms, and children with controlled asthma can do most of the things their friends do.

This camp has a fully trained multidisciplinary medical team of registered nurses and physical therapists, a respiratory therapist, a dietician, a pharmacist, and a physician who are available around the clock to provide care and support for the children. Educational sessions on the nature of asthma, the proper use of medication, and how to manage and control asthma are conducted by medical staff. This gives the children the knowledge and confidence they need to feel comfortable with taking part in physical activity (Lung Association Saskatchewan: http://www.asthmacamp.org).

The Importance of Understanding Child Development

The years between 5 and 12 bring about changes in children that make them more independent of adult assistance in the conduct of their daily activities. Children master new physical skills fairly easily when they have opportunities to practise those skills. Illnesses and death occur less frequently than during infancy and preschool years or later in adolescence. Gender differences in physical development and ability are minimal. Most children feel competent to manage their school and home lives and still want to perform in ways that earn recognition from adults.

A knowledge of the universal predictable stages of growth as well as an understanding of individual patterns of timing are absolutely essential for anyone involved in planning and operating a school-age program. The quality of a program may depend upon a variety of factors, but a major determinant is the extent to which activities and procedures are appropriate for the developmental level of the participating children. The learning environment and program activities should be based on an assessment of children's cognitive, social, emotional, and physical abilities at each stage of their development and also provide challenges to promote further development. A knowledge of child development will enable adults to choose effective techniques for guiding an individual child's behaviour and planning strategies for group interactions. Further, a knowledge of child development will enable school-age child care professionals to communicate more effectively with parents about a child's progress.

Development and Learning

The study of human development examines how individuals grow and change over the period of a lifetime, how they remain the same, and how some individuals may vary from typical patterns. Several characteristics of individuals are programmed by

Figure 4-1 ■ **School-age child care professionals who understand child development can provide an environment that allows children to enhance their skills.**

genetic makeup at the time of conception, whereas others are the result of environmental conditions and experiences. The relative importance of one over the other, known as *nature vs. nurture,* is a topic for debate among developmental researchers.

Nature refers to a variety of characteristics, such as eye colour and body type, which are inherited from parents. Physical limitations and certain diseases such as diabetes are also inherited, as well as some personality characteristics, such as activity level or verbal ability. **Nurture** refers to all the experiences and influences one is exposed to from the moment of conception on throughout a lifetime. These would include environmental factors, such as the level of maternal bonding experienced in infancy; cultural expectations; quality of home-life experiences; and influence of peer interactions, school, and other program experiences.

The dichotomy of influences on human development is also portrayed as *maturation vs. learning.* **Maturation** indicates the progression of changes that takes place as one ages. An example of this would be that a poorly nourished child may have some delays in development. **Learning** refers to the processes by which environmental influences and experiences bring about permanent changes in thinking, feeling, and behaviour. Children will thrive and learn when they are part of an enriched and interesting environment where they can freely explore developmentally appropriate activities at their own pace, with a supportive and motivating adult.

The basic question is the same no matter what labels are used: How much of development and human behaviour is the result of genetic inheritance, and how much is the result of all of life's experiences? Most developmentalists believe that both are important and that in fact the interaction between them is the determining factor in one's pattern of growth.

Physical Development

Middle childhood is a time when children grow more slowly than they did in the preschool years, and they will not experience another growth spurt until they approach adolescence.

Physical Growth and Change

Typically, children gain about 2.5 kilograms (5 pounds) and 5–7.5 centimetres (2–3 inches) per year. By the time they are 10 years old, most will weigh 32 kilograms (70 pounds) and be 138 centimetres (54 inches) tall (Berk & Levin, 2003). Up to the age of nine, boys and girls are about the same size, but then girls start to pull ahead in both height and weight. Around age 9 or 10, girls begin a growth spurt that precedes adolescence. By the end of the elementary years, girls are generally taller and heavier than boys. School-age children seem slimmer than they did during the preschool years because their body proportions change. Their arms and legs get longer, their torsos elongate, and their faces are thinner.

Yet there are wide variations in their appearance. Genetics also plays a large part in determining size as well as rate of maturity. While adults may understand that variations in size and timing of maturity are normal, it is often difficult for children to accept these differences. Physical development can affect peer relationships because children often choose friends who have a pleasing appearance and are physically, academically, or socially capable (Hartup, 1983). Children who are shorter, taller, or heavier than their peers, as well as those who are less capable, are often rejected.

nature

a variety of characteristics that are inherited from parents

nurture

all the experiences and influences one is exposed to from the moment of conception on throughout a lifetime

maturation

progression of changes that takes place as one ages

learning

processes by which environmental influences and experiences bring about permanent changes in thinking, feeling, and behaviour

Box 4-1 ■ Determinants of Good Health and Health Conditions

The World Health Organization defines health as:

> ...the extent to which an individual or group is able, on the one hand, to realize aspirations and satisfy needs; and, on the other hand, to change or cope with the environment. Health is therefore seen as a resource for everyday life, not the objective for living; it is a positive concept emphasizing social and personal resources, as well as physical capacity. (Pimento & Kernested (2004))

Sometime between the ages of 9 and 14, usually earlier for girls, children experience changes in their reproductive systems. With the onset of puberty in girls, their breasts start to develop and the onset of menstruation occurs. Boys experience an enlargement of their testes and a change in the colour and texture of their scrotum. Hair growth in pubic and underarm areas begins to occur. There is a great variation from individual to individual as to when these changes will take place. Children need supportive adults in their lives to talk to about the physical changes that they are experiencing during puberty (Berk & Levin, 2003).

Extensive research on the relationship between the physical development of the brain and children's overall development has indicated the importance of providing caring and nurturing relationships between adults and children beginning in early and continuing into middle childhood. Children need to be in settings where caring school-age child care professionals nurture development and thus allow for the maximum functioning and use of all areas of the brain. By age eight, the brain has achieved 90 percent of its adult size. During middle childhood, brain development involves more efficient functioning of various structures of the brain, such as the frontal lobes of the cortex, that are responsible for thought and consciousness. This part of the brain increases slightly due to the continuing process of myelination (Craig, Kermis, & Digdon, 2001).

In order to be healthy, children need access to nutritious food, clothing, housing, and a clean environment free of pollutants. Pimento and Kernested (2004) identify the following determinants of health: income/social status; healthy development; freedom from discrimination; communication and life skills (p. 5).

Poverty contributes to the poor health status of many children. Because of their living conditions they are subject to poor nutrition. With little money to buy food, they often have to resort to buying the cheapest food, which is often low in nutrients. Additives and high fat content is common in low-priced food. If consumed in large quantities, this can lead to further chronic and life-threatening diseases (Mandell & Duffy, 1995, 259). The National Forum on Health acknowledges that an individual's health improves with increased income and social status. This allows people to have more control over making decisions in their lives, which is also a large contributor to one's well-being (Pimento & Kernested, 2004, p. 5).

Immigrant families and children in aboriginal communities are often at greater risk of living in poverty and of not being able to provide for the development of healthy children in their communities. They are more inclined to be subject to discrimination and prejudice. Children and families who have access to quality public health care, community services, and community facilities demonstrate healthier social, emotional, and physical well-being. Children of aboriginal families who have more access to community-based programs of child care, recreation, culturally based activities, and aboriginal language instruction were reported by their parents to be in good to excellent health and to have better school performance (Statistics Canada, 2004).

Children also need access to clean air and water, and an environment that is free of contaminants in order to develop to their full potential (Pimento & Kernested, 2004, p. 9). There has been a general increase of respiratory illnesses, such as allergies and asthma, among children since the 1980s, with more than 20,000 hospitalizations for childhood asthma each year (Asthma Society of Canada, 2004). This is often attributed to air pollutants, lead poisoning, chemical toxins, and environmental tobacco smoke. Children are also at risk for later development of skin cancer due to higher exposure to ultraviolet radiation (Canadian Council on Social Development, 1996, p. 4). In 2007/2008, the Children's Task Group of the Federal/Provincial/Territorial Committee on Health and the Environment developed a national strategic framework on children's environmental health with the overall intent to protect children living in Canada from exposure to environmental hazards (Health Canada, 2011)

An illness that is becoming more common and is causing a great deal of concern is type 2 diabetes. With the rise in obesity in North America, the risk of children getting this disease is increasing. The Canadian Paediatric Society (2010) continues to monitor the increased prevalence of non-insulin-dependent diabetes mellitus in aboriginal people (Paediatric Child Health, 2010).

In 1997, along with the World Health Organization, the Canadian Committee on Antibiotic Resistance issued a mandate to decrease the use of antibiotics for respiratory tract infections by 25 percent. Using antibiotics when they are not needed (for example, to treat viral infections such as colds and flu) can lead to antibiotic resistance. Antibiotic resistance limits the effectiveness of antibiotics in treating bacterial infections, many of which are serious or life-threatening conditions like pneumonia. Hand-washing procedures, using regular soap, must be practised by all children and adults in school-age programs. This has been identified as the single most important key to reducing the use of antibiotics, thus ensuring that antibiotics can be effective in saving lives in the future (Blondel-Hill & Fryters, 2001, pp. 25–31).

💡 Implications for School-Age Child Care Professionals

School-age child care professionals can do a great deal to help children learn to maintain a healthy lifestyle as well as help parents be responsible for ensuring that children's health needs are met.

- Support children's questions about physical changes in their bodies.
- Help children evaluate the messages they receive from their environment concerning health. Provide activities that encourage them to question environmental risks related to health.
- Include program activities that stress good health and nutrition.
- Offer only nutritious meals and snacks. Offer supplementary nutrition to children who may be undernourished.
- Provide space within the physical facility for activities that encourage health and fitness.
- Become informed about community health services and resources. Refer parents to appropriate facilities.
- Support immigrant and aboriginal families to access language and cultural programs in their communities.
- Ensure that health procedures for disease prevention are practised, such as regular hand washing.

Obesity

The percentage of Canadian children who are overweight or obese continues to climb. In 2004, 26 percent of children and adolescents aged 2–17 were overweight or obese compared to 15 percent in a 1978/79 survey. This was based on the **body mass index (BMI)**, an international standard for the measurement of obesity. A BMI is found by dividing weight in kilograms by height in metres squared (BMI = kg/m^2). See Figure 4-3 for overweight and obesity rates by age in 1978/79 and 2004 (Statistics Canada, 2006).

A 2004 Canadian Community Health Survey found that 59 percent of children and adolescents ate fruits and vegetables fewer than five times a day. Those children were more likely to be overweight/obese than those who ate fruit and vegetables more often (Statistics Canada, 2006).

Overweight children are subject to several health risks, particularly higher blood pressure and blood cholesterol levels. These children may also have orthopedic or respiratory problems. The greatest risk is that they will become overweight adults, prone to developing heart disease at a young age or hypertension, diabetes, arthritis, and some forms of cancer (Canadian Paediatric Society, 2002, p. 3).

In addition, serious psychological distress can occur, since these children may be the object of teasing and rejection by their classmates. In the Western world, there is a strong cultural prejudice against obesity and an obsession with thinness, which can lead to stigmatization and discrimination. Obese children may be teased and harassed by their peers. Children acquire these negative cultural concepts about obesity, possibly as young as age 7 (Feldman & Beagan, 1994, p. 3). This results in lowered self-esteem, depression, and various kinds of behaviour problems. Obese children's unhappiness leads them to further curtail participation with their peers and to overeat to compensate for their unhappiness. Thus patterns are established that carry over into adulthood; overweight children are frequently overweight adults (Serdula, Ivory, Coates, Freedman, Williamson & Byers, 1993). It is estimated that 60 to 80 percent of obese children will become overweight adults (Lucas, 1991).

Figure 4-2 ■ School-age children master many physical skills.

body mass index (BMI)
a measure of the ratio of weight to height

Figure 4-3 ■ Overweight and Obesity Rate, by Age Group, 1978/1979 and 2004

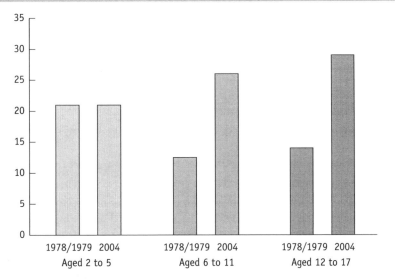

Note: Excludes the territories.

Source: Statistics Canada, Catalogue no. 82-620-ME2005001.

Another possible consequence of this poor self-image may be the development of other eating disorders such as anorexia nervosa in adolescence (Feldman & Beagan, 1994, p. 3).

Causes of Obesity

There is no one cause of obesity; rather, it is an interaction between several possible conditions. Patterns are often established in infancy and continue into adulthood.

- *Heredity.* Several factors that contribute to obesity are inherited: body type, height and bone structure, the amount and distribution of fat, metabolic rate, and activity level.

- *Activity level.* Children who are more active are less likely to be overweight since they burn more calories. Although activity level is influenced by heredity, an individual's willingness to engage in active play will also affect weight. For some children, the unavailability of safe places to play will also be a factor. In the National Longitudinal Study of Children and Youth, in 1998/99, fewer obese children (38 percent) were found to be active compared with nonobese children (47 percent) (Statistics Canada, 2002).

- *Media use.* Children are inactive when they watch television or play electronic games where they are sitting for long periods of time. During this viewing, children are also bombarded with commercials about foods that are high in fat and sugar. These are usually the foods children choose to snack on while they watch television.

- *High-calorie foods.* Overweight children are not necessarily overeaters. However, much of the food they consume is high in calories. Many children take in large quantities of high-calorie soft drinks and chips, as well as high-fat hamburgers and french fries. Often, too, parents give in to demands from their children for the high-calorie snack foods they see on television ads.

- *Attitudes toward food.* In some families, children are encouraged to consume large portions of food as a measure of the family's prosperity or their love for their children. Often, too, food becomes a symbol for love and comfort, causing people to overeat when under stress or unhappy. Parents who offer special foods as a reward or comfort set up a lifelong habit that can lead to obesity.

- *Specific event.* A traumatic event in a child's life can be a precipitating factor in the onset of increased weight gain. Hospitalization, parental divorce, the death of someone close to the child, or even a move to a new neighbourhood can all cause distress and a need for a substitute gratification in the form of food.

- *Physiological problems.* A small number of cases of obesity in children can be traced to abnormalities in the growth process or metabolism (Lowrey, 1986). The obesity is only one part of the problem that usually includes disturbances in normal physical and mental growth. Only about 1 percent of childhood obesity can be attributed to this cause, however.

- *Poverty or low income.* As family income increases, the proportion of overweight and obese children decreases (Statistics Canada, 2002). When families have little income they often resort to poor choices of foods, usually because healthy foods can be more expensive. As a result, children can have difficulties maintaining healthy body weight measures.

Implications for School-Age Child Care Professionals

Within any group of school-age children, particularly if there is a wide age span, there will be children of many sizes and shapes. Children compare their own appearance with their peers' and as a result often think they are too tall, too little, too heavy, or too thin. In addition, children who vary noticeably from their peers tend to get teased and labelled with unflattering names. Differing from the norm can cause a great deal of anguish and loss of self-esteem.

- An important task for adults who have responsibility for children's welfare is to assure them they are accepted no matter how they look and to help their peers be accepting. Further, all children need to know that they will change as they grow and develop.

- Obese children need special attention to help them change their eating patterns and activity level. They can learn about good nutrition and how to prepare good-tasting, low-calorie foods. See Chapter 14 for ideas that can be used in a school-age program. Although increased activity is the best way to lose weight, obese children may have a difficult time participating in active sports or games. They are often rejected as team members and are teased if they try to join in games. It is important to encourage them to start somewhere: walking to school, bicycling, or participating in the exercises suggested in Chapter 14. Pay special attention to the suggestions for choosing teammates also suggested in Chapter 14 and be sure to discuss any problems that arise due to teasing.

- The children's families need help to change the environment that created the obesity, whether it lies in the foods they eat, in the parental interactions, or in the kinds of activities children are encouraged to engage in. Remember that talking about food and weight is a sensitive issue for many parents. Therefore, in a nonjudgmental way, provide parents with information about nutrition. Help them find ways to discipline or reward their children other than with food. Provide suggestions for active things the family can do together.

Figure 4-4 ■ A game of tag can help to develop gross-motor skills.

- School-age child care professionals are responsible for planning and preparing nutritious snacks that are not high in fat, salt, or sugar using the *Canada's Food Guide to Healthy Living* as a basis for choosing nutritious foods.

Motor Skills

During the elementary school period children develop a wide variety of motor skills, particularly when they have ample opportunities to practise and are encouraged to try new things. Five-year-olds endlessly practise running, jumping, and throwing. Gradually their timing and coordination increase, enabling them to become noticeably more proficient. They soon learn to judge the time it takes to swing a bat in order to hit a ball or estimate the distance a ball will travel when thrown in order to catch it. Along with developing physical skills, children are also acquiring new ways to get along with their peers and are beginning to understand the importance of rules. The inter-action of these developing abilities accounts for the popularity of sports during middle childhood.

Gross-Motor Skills

Several skills that children acquire in middle childhood occur in play activities typical of this period. Developmentally appropriate practices for school-age children should include opportunities to develop both gross- and fine-motor skills (Albrecht & Plantz, 1993).

- *Running.* By age five or six most children have mastered the form and power required to run. They have learned to start, stop, and turn and can integrate these into their play activities.

- *Jumping.* Jumping requires a complex set of skills including balance, maintenance of equilibrium, and form. Jumping is usually not attempted by children until they have become fairly proficient in basic locomotion, but by age five most children have a good mastery of jumping skills.

- *Throwing.* At age five or six, there is a perceptible change in children's ability to throw. They learn to transfer their weight from one foot to the other during throwing. This weight shift, coupled with a horizontal movement of the arms and body, allows children to efficiently propel a ball forward. Most six-year-olds are able to perform an overhand throw.

Further practice and refinement of gross-motor skills allow children to participate in the popular activities of childhood: swimming, biking, soccer, ice skating, skipping, baseball, basketball, and gymnastics.

Figure 4-5 ■ "I like to play baseball." Lark, age 8

Fine-Motor Skills

During middle childhood, most children master a variety of tasks requiring the use of small muscles. They learn to cut easily with scissors, draw, write, or print accurately and sew or knit. By this time, most children will have established handedness. They are better able to paint or colour within lines. As their eye–hand coordination increases further, they can learn to play musical instruments, engage in hobbies such as model-making, or play games such as jacks. Their visual coordination is developing, which is necessary when they are learning to read.

Differences in Motor Skills

Boys and girls are fairly equal in their physical abilities during the middle childhood years except that boys generally have greater forearm strength and girls have greater flexibility. Boys are often better at baseball, while girls excel in gymnastics. However, when girls take part in sports like baseball or water polo, they can catch and throw a ball accurately and with sufficient strength. Likewise, with training, boys can do well in activities that require flexibility, such as gymnastics and dance.

Certain motor skills do not depend upon the amount of practice a youngster engages in. Some depend upon body size, brain maturation, or inherent talents. A good example of a skill dependent upon brain maturation is reaction time. A child's brain continues to mature into adolescence; therefore, older children usually do better where this skill is necessary.

Inherent traits are also important in determining how well a particular child performs a motor skill. Body size, particularly height, gives some children an advantage when playing basketball. Children also vary in their ability to coordinate body movements. Some children find it easy to kick a soccer ball with accuracy while others find it almost impossible. Heredity accounts for children's basic skill at these activities, but practice and experience can increase their proficiency.

Figure 4-6 ■ With practice, children can participate in difficult sports activities.

Implications for School-Age Child Care Professionals

Middle childhood is a time when children want to feel competent at whatever they do. In school they must use small muscles to be successful, while out of school they need well-developed gross-motor skills to participate in the sports, vigorous games, and strenuous individual activities that are so much a part of the school-age years. Since practice and experience help children enhance their inherited abilities and acquire new skills, it is extremely important that school-age programs offer as many opportunities as possible. School-age child care professionals can:

- provide a wide variety of activities that require skills at varying levels
- include opportunities to develop muscle strength with throwing balls, doing yoga, practising gymnastics, and playing on playground equipment
- encourage children to practise gross motor skills and experiment with balance and coordination through skipping, playing hopscotch, and participating in games and sports
- plan opportunities for children to practise fine motor skills by using smaller tools for writing, drawing, painting, and sewing, and by manipulating a computer keyboard
- allow children ample time to practise and refine new skills
- encourage both genders to participate in all activities
- offer children encouragement for their efforts rather than praise their achievements
- encourage children to teach their skills to others

Figure 4-7 ■ Girls generally have greater flexibility than boys.

Summary

A knowledge of the universal predictable stages of growth, as well as an understanding of individual patterns of timing, are essential for anyone involved in planning and operating a school-age program. The quality of the program may depend to a large degree on the extent to which all activities, procedures, and interactions are developmentally appropriate for the children who participate.

Human growth is affected both by maturation and learning. Maturation is the progression of changes that takes place as one ages and is influenced by nature, which refers to a variety of abilities, characteristics, and limits that are inherited from parents. Learning refers to processes by which environmental influences and experiences bring about permanent changes in thinking, feeling, and behaviour. Children grow more slowly during middle childhood than they did in the preschool years. They may gain 2.5 kilograms (5 pounds) and 5–7.5 centimetres (2–3 inches). Boys and girls are about the same size until age nine, when girls begin a preadolescent growth spurt. Variations in size are due to nutrition or heredity.

School-age children may suffer from a variety of health conditions due to issues of poverty, poor caring and nurturing environments (regarding adult-child relationships and settings that do not promote the overall development of the child), exposure to pollutants, and lack of awareness of or access to public health and community services. Adults working with children can help children and their parents become responsible for meeting their health needs; school-age child care professionals should become aware of environmental policies and find out about local community programs and share this knowledge.

Obesity is a growing problem among children and can affect a child emotionally as well as physically. Overweight children are often unhappy because they are rejected or teased by their peers.

Causes of obesity are heredity, activity level, types of food consumed, and attitudes toward food. In addition, specific events and psychological problems trigger various eating disorders.

School-age child care professionals can help children accept both the way they look and that as they grow, they will change. Obese children need special attention to encourage them to change eating habits and to be more active.

During middle childhood, children rapidly acquire a variety of new motor skills. Gross-motor skills include running, jumping, and throwing. Fine-motor skills include the ability to cut easily with scissors; draw, write or print accurately; and sew or knit. Boys and girls are fairly equal in their physical abilities during middle childhood except that boys generally have greater forearm strength and girls have greater flexibility. With training and opportunities to practise, the differences may be lessened.

School-age child care professionals can provide many opportunities for children to participate in a wide variety of activities requiring the use of large or small muscles. Staff should also allow plenty of time for children to practise, encourage both genders to participate in all activities, praise efforts rather than achievements, and inspire children to teach their skills to others.

Key Terms

nature	maturation	body mass index (BMI)
nurture	learning	

Student Activities

1. Ask the children in your school-age group to draw a picture of themselves and one best friend. Do they show themselves as taller or shorter than the friend? Is there any noticeable difference between the attractiveness of their own image and that of the friend?

2. Write a paragraph describing your appearance when you were six. Include the kinds of activities you engaged in during your out-of-school time. Next, describe yourself when you were 11. In what ways did your development follow the description in this chapter? In what ways did it differ?

3. Watch two hours of Saturday-morning children's-television programs. Count and list the commercials for food that are shown. How many are for high-fat,

high-sugar, or high-salt foods? Do they show children having fun while consuming these foods? Discuss the impact these commercials might have on children.

4. Do a survey of the neighbourhood near your home or the school-age program. Are there places where children can play outdoors? How do you think the environment affects the children who live there? What could be done to increase opportunities for physical activities? Share your information with your classmates.

Review Questions

1. Why is it important for school-age child care professionals to have a knowledge of predictable stages of growth and an understanding of individual patterns of timing?
2. Differentiate between maturation and learning.
3. What is another way to describe the dichotomy of influences on human development?
4. How much will an average well-nourished child gain in weight and height per year? The typical 10-year-old will weigh _____ kilograms and be _____ centimetres tall.
5. Boys and girls are about the same size for part of the middle childhood years. At what age do girls begin to increase in size faster than boys?
6. List the causes of obesity in children.
7. In what ways can school-age child care professionals help children who are different from the norm in body size or who are obese?
8. List eight motor skills developed by children during middle childhood. In what ways do children use these skills in their daily lives at school or at home?
9. In what ways do the motor skills of boys and girls differ?
10. What can school-age child care professionals do to help children enhance their inherited abilities and acquire new skills?

Case Study

Nine-year-old Ian is often called names by some of the other children. They refer to him as "Tubby," "Fatso," or "Lardo." He gets very angry and starts hitting, although sometimes he ends up crying in frustration. The school-age child care professional has noticed that he seems to have an ample supply of snacks in his backpack. There are often chips and candy bars, and he wants to have those for snack time rather than the food the program provides. When his request is refused, he stomps away from the table and refuses to eat anything. Occasionally he is seen sneaking food from his locker.

1. How would you respond when Ian stomps away from the table?
2. What can you say to his parents?
3. What can you do to help Ian change his eating pattern at the school-age program?

References

Albrecht, K. & Plantz, M. (1993). *Developmentally appropriate practice in school-age child care programs.* Dubuque, IA: Kendall/Hunt Publishing Company.

Asthma Society of Canada. (2004). Asthma at school. Retrieved April 5, 2005, from http://www.asthma.ca/adults/community/aas_parents.php

Berk, L.E. & Levin, E. (2003). *Child development, Canadian edition.* Toronto: Pearson Education Canada.

Blondel-Hill, E. & Fryters, S. (2001, Spring). Do bugs need drugs? Antibiotic use in respiratory tract infections. *Family Health,* 25–31. Retrieved April 5, 2005, from http://www.dobugsneeddrugs.org

Canadian Council on Social Development. (1996, November 13). *The progress of Canada's children 1996,* 1–9. Retrieved April 5, 2005, from http://www.ccsd.ca/pubs/archive/pcc96/hl.htm

Craig, G., Kermis, M. D., & Digdon, N. L. (2001). *Children today,* (2nd Canadian ed.). Toronto: Pearson Education Canada.

Feldman, W. & Beagan, B. L. (1994). Screening for childhood obesity. In *Canadian Task Force on the Periodic Health Examination.* Ottawa: Health Canada, 334–344. Retrieved April 5, 2005, from http://www.ctfphc.org/Full_Text/Ch30full.htm

Hartup, W. (1983). Peer relations. In P. H. Mussen (Ed.), *Handbook of child psychology: Vol. 4. Socialization, personality and social development.* New York: John Wiley & Sons.

Health Canada. (2006). Obesity. Retrieved June 5, 2012, from http://www.hc-sc.gc.ca/hl-vs/alt_formats/pacrb-dgapcr/pdf/iyh-vsv/life-vie/obes-eng.pdf

Health Canada. (2011). National strategic framework on children's environmental health. Retrieved May 30, 2012, from http://www.hc-sc.gc.ca/ewh-semt/pubs/contaminants/Framework_children-cadre_enfants/index-eng.php

Lang, D. M. et. al. (2004, April). Physical activity in urban school-aged children with asthma. *Pediatrics,* 112(4), 341–346.

Lowrey, G. (1986). *Growth and development of children* (8th ed.). Chicago: Year Book Medical Publishers.

Lucas, A. (1991). Eating disorders. In M. Lewis (Ed.), *Child and adolescent psychiatry: A comprehensive textbook.* Baltimore: Williams and Wilkins.

Mandell, N. & Duffy, A. (1995). *Canadian families: diversity, donflict and change.* Toronto: Harcourt Brace.

Paediatric Child Health. (2010). Risk reduction for type 2 diabetes in Aboriginal children in Canada. Child Health 2005; 10 (1), 49–52. Retrieved May 30, 2012, from http://www.cps.ca/english/statements/II/FNIH05-01.htm

Pimento, B. & Kernested D. (2004). *Healthy foundations in early childhood settings* (3rd. ed.). Toronto: Thomson Nelson.

Serdula, M., Ivory, D., Coates, R., Freedman, D., Williamson, D., & Byers, T. (1993). Do obese children become obese adults? A review of the literature. *Preventive Medicine, 22,* 167–177.

Statistics Canada. (2004, July 9). Aboriginal Peoples survey: Children who live in non-reserve areas. *The Daily,* 7–9.

Statistics Canada. (2006). Childhood obesity: A troubling situation. Retrieved May 30, 2012, from http://www41.statcan.ca/2006/2966/ceb2966_004-eng.htm

Selected Reading

Gold, M. (2003). *The complete kid's allergy and asthma guide.* Toronto: Robert Rose.

Statistics Canada. (2002, October 18). National longitudinal survey of children and youth: Childhood obesity, *The Daily,* 6–7.

Websites

Learning about growing up with asthma: Games, information for children and parents
http://www.asthma-kids.ca

Canadian Lung Association
http://www.lung.ca/children

Canadian Diabetes Association
http://www.diabetes.ca

Children's Environmental Health Project
http://www.cape.ca/children/resources.html

Chapter 5

Development in Middle Childhood: Cognitive

Objectives

After completing this chapter, the student should be able to:

- Discuss the major principles of cognitive theories
- List the contributions and concerns expressed by critics of each theory
- Describe the guidelines used for each theory to enhance children's development
- Discuss the ways in which children develop and use language and how school-age child care professionals can promote language growth

 Profile

A school-age care program provides care, supervision, and activities for elementary school-age children before school, at lunchtime, after school, and during professional-development days and school holidays. In Quebec, school-age care programs are offered by school boards, private schools, or community centres. There are no requirements for obtaining a license to operate a school-age care program. Programs that are situated in public schools fall under the jurisdiction of the Ministry of Education and follow minimal "Regulations Respecting Childcare Services Provided in Schools" ("Règlements pour les services do garde en milieu scolaires"). In recognized centres, parents pay a minimum fee ($7.00 per day) and the government subsidizes the remaining costs.

Because Quebec's regulations for providing school-age care are minimal, a team of child care experts compiled an additional list of quality standards for parents to follow when they choose appropriate care for their children. This was done in conjunction with the National School-Age Child Care Project in 1999. Here is a list of quality issues:

- staff–child ratios (1 staff for every 20 children)
- staff training in child development and first aid
- health and emergency procedures; policies for arrival and dismissal
- dedicated space for exclusive use with access to other facilities in the school
- a balance of activities, projects, and quiet and active play, including science, language, music, dance, games, arts and crafts, drama, and sports, to enhance all areas of development
- flexibility in scheduling activities; children's involvement in planning; time to do homework
- positive interactions among the staff with school staff, parents, and children
- staff assist children with solving problems by asking questions and encouraging independence
- older children assume responsibilities and make their own decisions by setting up book, sewing, dance, and sports clubs
- respect all individuals regardless of their gender, language, abilities, appearance, race, religion, cultural background, and/or other types of diversity
- positive behaviour management approaches; teaching conflict resolution skills
- making community connections; parent involvement
- integration of special-needs children

Quality Assurance and School Age Care 1997–1999, Social Development Canada. Reproduced with the permission of the Minister of Public Works and Government Services, 2012.

Cognitive Theories

Cognitive theories are used to explain all the mental processes that enable children to think or acquire knowledge and the way these processes affect how they perceive and understand their experiences. How individual children function is dependent partly upon hereditary factors and partly upon their experiences. As children's brains grow and mature, they are able to use different cognitive skills to gather and process information. Early brain development sets a foundation for overall well-being, behaviour, and learning, but later development plays a significant role in building on the base.

> Child and adolescent development can be compared to building a house walls and roof. We need to invest time and good materials into the walls and windows, and finally to the roof. (Bertrand, 2001, p. 17)

Child and adolescent development can be compared to building a house. The early development phase is zero to about age six and compares to the foundation. Middle childhood (from 6 to 12 years) is the walls and adolescence is the roof. A good foundation is important to the structure of the whole house, but it still needs the walls and roof.

The thinking processes of school-age children are markedly different from those of preschoolers. By middle childhood, children can selectively focus on tasks—that is, they are able to screen out distractions and concentrate on the relevant parts of the information at hand. This capacity helps them to remember and also to reason in logical steps in order to solve a problem. School-age children also learn strategies for increasing memory.

These are called **storage strategies.** School-age children rehearse the information, organize it into memorable units, or use mnemonic devices such as rhymes or mental images to aid in remembering. Language develops rapidly and is used to communicate ideas, interact with others, and develop competencies that are required by the society in which they live. All of these abilities enable children to perform tasks beyond the reach of younger children.

storage strategies
methods used to increase memory

Piagetian Theory

Swiss psychologist Jean Piaget was an important contributor to our understanding of how children think and learn. He began his work with children by helping to develop the first intelligence test. Piaget's task was to interview children and find the age at which most children could answer the test questions correctly. Instead, Piaget became curious about children's incorrect responses to items on the test and observed that children who were the same age gave similar answers. This began a lifelong search to understand children's thought processes and how they change with age. Piaget (1952) concluded that cognitive development follows predictable patterns through four major stages. Each stage has certain characteristics that form the basis for how children approach and process intellectual tasks. Everyone proceeds through these stages at their own rate, some slower, some faster, but everyone goes through them. Each stage is built on the skills of the previous stage. Piaget called the period from birth to two years the **sensorimotor period.** During this time infants use all their senses to explore and learn about the world around them. They put objects in their mouths, become attentive to sounds, poke or pat objects, react to tastes, and follow out-of-reach objects with their eyes. The information they gather is experience based; they can understand only what they experience directly. Limited memory of an object or experience is retained when the object is removed or the experience ended.

sensorimotor period
Piaget's first period, in which infants use all their senses to explore and learn about the world around them

Figure 5-1 ■ Children's thinking changes, and they are able to use logic to solve problems.

preoperational period
ability to begin to think symbolically and to remember experiences and objects independently of the immediate encounter

By contrast, preschool children, two to seven years old, are in the **preoperational period,** in which they can begin to think symbolically. They can remember experiences and objects independently of the immediate encounter. This is evident in their rapidly developing ability to use language. Words help them to remember past events or to talk about an object. They also begin to engage in pretend play, not always needing the real props to support the play. Preschool children can play out elaborate scenarios in which they relive familiar interactions with parents or with siblings.

Piaget observed that during the preoperational period children often come to the wrong conclusions. He believed that this was because they could not perform "operations." By operations Piaget meant the ability to internalize an action—that is, that it can be carried out in the mind and that it can go in one direction or reverse into the opposite direction. The preoperational child cannot perform these operations.

Piaget observed the difficulty children had with one of his conservation experiments. He placed two identical cylinders with equal amounts of liquid before four-year-olds. He then added two cylinders, one tall and slim, the other short. He poured the liquid from one glass into the tall cylinder and from the other into the short one. When asked which glass had more, most children would indicate the taller one. They could not mentally reverse the event to realize that when poured back into the original containers, the amounts were equal. In addition to an inability to imagine reversibility, children can focus on only one dimension of a form at a time. In the case of the liquids, they focused on the height of the fluid in the glasses. Piaget called this **centring.**

centring
Piaget's observation that young children focus on only one dimension of a form at a time

Another characteristic of preoperational children is that they believe everyone thinks and acts the same way they do. They are egocentric—incapable of understanding how others think or feel.

concrete operations
ability to think symbolically and to reverse processes when information is presented concretely

Between the ages of 7 and 11, children are in the **concrete operations** stage. They begin to think symbolically and can imagine reversing processes. The word "concrete" means that children can carry out this process only when the information is presented concretely. If a child is asked how many pieces of fruit there are if she has two apples and a friend gives her one, she will be able to figure out the answer. She can imagine two apples and then one additional one. She has experienced apples, can imagine them, and execute the solution. It would be difficult for her to figure out the answer to the question "What is two plus three?" in such an abstract manner. During this period children become less egocentric and much more social. Increased language skills enable them to interact more effectively with their peers and to begin to understand the views of others. The need to be a part of a group or to have friends requires discussion and negotiations over play activities. In the process children learn that others do not always think or feel the same way they do.

formal operations
ability to consider hypothetical problems without concrete examples

Piaget's last stage, **formal operations,** occurs between the ages of 11 and 15. During this period adolescents are able to consider hypothetical problems without concrete examples. They are also not limited by having to consider the here and now but can imagine situations they have not yet experienced or that are abstract. Thus adolescents begin to ponder questions about the effects of global warming or the importance of preserving wilderness areas for future generations to enjoy.

Several general principles underlie the concepts of Piaget's theory and are important to fully understand his perception of how children think and learn.

1. Children are active participants in the development of their own intelligence. Piaget believed that children actually *construct* their knowledge of the world through their activities. Experiences are the raw ingredients from which they organize and structure their knowledge, implying that the process takes place within the child rather than being transmitted from the outside. Through

Figure 5-2 ■ Children learn by doing.

experimenting with the objects and experiences in their environment, children actually create their own intelligence.

2. The development of intelligence is the result of a progression through stages. Each stage builds a foundation for the next stage. There is no finite division of the stages since each stage may carry vestiges of the previous period.

3. Due to differences in maturation rate, individuals will progress through the stages at different rates. However, each individual goes through the same stages in the same order.

Evaluation of Piagetian Theory

Piaget's ideas changed the way children's intellectual development is perceived, focusing more on how children come to know rather than on what they know (Berger, 2000). Yet there are criticisms from those who point to the formal nature of his experiments. These critics state that when children are closely watched in everyday situations, different interpretations of their abilities are possible. Some skills that Piaget relegates to later stages are clearly present in earlier ones. Therefore, critics contend that Piaget must have been wrong about just how early some cognitive skills develop.

Another concern of those who have looked closely at Piagetian theory is that children's abilities are not homogeneous within a given stage. In fact, each stage is entered gradually, with vestiges of the previous stage remaining for a period of time. Additional factors affect children's ability to think consistently at an expected level for their stage of development. Hereditary differences in abilities and aptitudes, as well as timing of maturation, play an important part. Environmental factors, such as the kinds of experiences children are exposed to and the kind of education they receive, also influence the rate of intellectual development.

The criticisms of Piaget's theory do not negate the importance of his ideas, however. We do know that children proceed developmentally from one stage to the next, changing their thinking processes as their maturity and experiences dictate. They continue to learn, taking in new information, organizing it, and deciding how it fits in with previous information.

Implications for School-Age Child Care Professionals

Piaget never claimed to be an educator, yet his theory is widely used to formulate educational programs for children. His theory provides a framework from which appropriate learning experiences can be designed. It enables educators to

- provide many different objects and experiences for children to explore so that they can incorporate them into their symbolic thinking process at a later time. There needs to be a balance between unstructured materials and guided ones. Art materials, sand and water, and building materials are examples of unstructured activities. Experiences such as cooking, in which children must follow a recipe, and classifying or seriating a group of objects, are guided activities.

- plan activities that are age-appropriate for the level of ability of most members of the group. In addition, teachers can add activities that meet the needs of individual children.

- allow plenty of time for children to explore freely and engage in play activities. Through play children have an opportunity to test out their own ideas and find out what is true and what is not.

Figure 5-3 ■ "Me doing my reading book." Sarah, age 6

- provide experiences that allow children to solve their own problems and make decisions
- set up situations in which children can exchange ideas, thus learning that others may think differently from themselves.

Behaviourist Learning Theory

Watson (1967) saw the need for a more exact study of psychology. He believed that in order to be a true science, hypotheses should be tested and measured. The only way that could be done was to measure those things that could be observed: behaviours and words rather than feelings or thoughts. His concepts were popular because they were different from the psychoanalytic theory prevalent at the time.

Watson studied Pavlov's (1960) **classical conditioning** experiments with animals and then used those ideas to formulate his own theory of human conditioning. In classical conditioning, a stimulus (anything that elicits a response, either a reflex or a voluntary action) is repeatedly followed by a specific response (behaviour). Dogs salivate when they see their food. Pavlov added a ringing bell along with the presentation of the food. After several repetitions the dogs would salivate when they heard the bell. The result is a connection that allows the response to occur without the need for the stimulus. An example is our response to a favourite food. When we are presented with that food, the sight and the smell cause us to salivate in preparation for tasting. When we see pictures of that food in a magazine or on television, we often have the same reaction—we salivate.

Watson was also influenced by the writings of Locke (1959), who saw human infants as a *tabula rasa,* a blank tablet upon which life experiences write a script. According to Watson, human behaviour could be shaped by controlling events children were exposed to and by offering rewards for proper responses. Give children appropriate rewards and the desired behaviour will follow. A parent who says "You are being so patient waiting while I pay for our groceries" is giving an appropriate reward to her child.

Skinner (1953) used both Watson's and Locke's (1959) ideas to formulate his theory. He proposed that infants are "empty organisms" that can be filled with carefully controlled experiences. He agreed that behaviour can be changed by conditioning but saw another type of conditioning that plays a larger role. He called it **operant conditioning.** Children play an active part by operating or acting on their environment and are reinforced for their behaviours. When a behaviour is followed by a pleasant response (reward), it is likely to be repeated. If the consequence of a behaviour is unpleasant, it is not likely to be repeated. Therefore, a system of positive or negative reinforcers can be used to shape an individual's behaviour. School-age child care professionals who tell children they have done a good job putting away their materials are using a positive reinforcer. At the next cleanup time, the children are more likely to go about the task willingly.

Bandura (1977) contributed another dimension to our understanding of how learning takes place. He felt that some behaviours cannot be explained as a simple conditioned response to a direct stimulus but occur through less direct learning. He believed children observe others behaving in given ways and then pattern their own behaviour accordingly. This type of social learning is more likely to occur when one is uncertain or unsure in a situation and when the object of observation is admired or seen as powerful. Called **modelling**, it is a technique that parents and child care professionals use to increase the likelihood of acceptable behaviour in children. In

classical conditioning
conditioning brought about by proximity of stimulus and response

operant conditioning
the process by which children act upon their environment and are reinforced for their behaviours

modelling
exhibit the behaviours that are expected of children

other words, model the behaviour you expect of children. It may also explain why four-year-olds pretend to be Superman or why teenagers want to dress like their favourite rock star. They are imitating the behaviour of people they admire.

Social learning changes as individuals mature. One has to be attentive to the behaviours of others, store the information for future retrieval, possibly mentally rehearse the behaviour, and then use the information when needed. The consequences of behaviours are also noted. One can then test out alternative behaviours and choose the one with the best outcome. A school-age child observes that when she gets mad and leaves a game, her friends do not ask her to play next time. She will try to curb her anger in order to be included.

Evaluation of Behaviourism

Learning theories have contributed a great deal to the study of how behaviours are shaped (Berger, 2000). The emphasis on the connection between stimulus and the resulting observable response allows a different interpretation of some kinds of behaviours. Previous notions that behaviour is the result of deep-seated emotional problems could be revised by observing the environmental causes of some behaviour. Behaviour can then be changed by changing the environment's response.

Learning theory has also contributed to a more scientific study of human development. Researchers are pressured to refine their hypotheses, define their terms, devise replicable tests for their hypotheses, and avoid reliance on concepts that they cannot test. On the other hand, there are valid criticisms of learning theory. The emphasis on observable behaviour and external influences does not take into account the inner life of children. Some behaviours result from complex relationships between biological maturation, an individual's thought processes, and the struggle to make sense of new experiences. If only observable behaviours are taken into consideration, we would have an incomplete picture of the wide range of influences on human behaviour.

When behaviourist-learning theory was first proposed, there were claims that behaviour modification through a system of rewards and punishments was manipulative. Present-day critics still voice the same concerns and also object to the kinds of reinforcers that parents or child care professionals sometimes use.

Implications for School-Age Child Care Professionals

Behaviourist theory provides some specific guidelines for adults who work with children:

- Carefully arrange the learning environment. Because the importance of the environment is stressed in behaviourist learning theory, anyone who works with children can use this information to arrange the setting to bring about positive responses. This means that the placement of furniture, the ways in which activities are presented, and the ways in which adults interact with children all have to be carefully considered with expected results in mind.

- Use appropriate reinforcers to bring about desired results. Carefully consider the implications of reinforcers, and choose those that will enhance positive, rather than negative, behaviours.

- Model the behaviour that you expect of children.

- Provide opportunities for social learning to take place among peers. Children are powerful models and can have extensive influence on one another.

- Help children find alternative behaviours to those that generate negative responses from others.

Sociocultural Theory

Only recently have the writings of Vygotsky (1978, 1987), a pioneer in the study of sociocultural influences of learning, become available. Studying sociocultural aspects of development as a means for helping children in a multicultural society is helpful. Vygotsky's theory assumes that social interaction and children's direct participation in authentic cultural activities are necessary for their optimum development. Several main ideas follow this basic assumption.

Cross-Cultural Variation; Cultural Mosaic

Cultures differ in the kinds of opportunities they provide children to develop the competencies they need. Every culture has hopes and expectations for the children growing up within that society. These expectations are expressed in terms of competencies or things children need to know or be able to do. A child in rural Africa will be encouraged to learn vastly different skills from one living in a public housing development in Vancouver, British Columbia. Vygotsky believed that knowledge and skills are taught by the older and more mature members of a group. In daily interactions within families, in the school or child care centre, and in neighbourhood groups, children are constantly being shown models or are being told directly. Children in rural Africa work beside their parents, learning how to nurture the crops or perform the daily tasks necessary for their existence. Children in Vancouver are taught by their parents how to behave within the neighbourhood environment, but they also learn from their friends as they play.

Scaffolding

scaffold
system that supports children as they move from one intellectual level to the next

The child is seen as actively constructing himself, constantly adding to his knowledge and skills (Berk & Winsler, 1995). The social environment is the necessary **scaffold**, or support system, sustaining the child as he moves from one intellectual level to the next. Parents and child care professionals carefully structure a child's participation in a series of learning experiences in order to facilitate learning.

Language

Language plays a crucial role in the development of cognitive abilities because it is the basis for social interactions between adult and child or between children. Through communication children can be guided to acquire the practical skills needed in their society. Communication also allows individuals to make mental contacts with others and provides a means for interpreting, storing, and using social experiences.

Zone of Proximal Development

zone of proximal development
the hypothetical environment in which learning and development take place

The **zone of proximal development** is the hypothetical environment in which learning and development take place (Berk & Winsler, 1995). It can be further described as the region between what a child can learn by herself and what she can learn through the guidance and tutoring of a more competent member of her society. Through carefully chosen and planned activities, the child gradually moves from assisted performance to independent performance. Crucial to this process is sensitivity to the child's level of competence and a means to encourage the child to move to the next level. When school-age child care professionals or parents help a child to acquire a new skill, they may begin with a demonstration, then carefully guide the child through the steps and encourage the child as she performs on her own.

Figure 5-4 ■ **Children learn from each other.**

Evaluation of Sociocultural Theory

Sociocultural theory has added a new dimension to the study of children's development, particularly in understanding diversity (Berger, 2000). It has increased knowledge of the ways in which cognitive development varies depending on the values and makeup of different societies. It further emphasizes the importance of understanding each culture's values and beliefs and their effect upon children's competencies.

Although the importance of Vygotsky's theory is recognized, present-day researchers are cautious in trying to generalize research findings from one culture to another (Cole, 1992). On the other hand, there is recognition that children's competencies should be examined through procedures that are relevant within their culture.

One limitation of sociocultural theory is that it does not take into account developmental processes that are not social. Some processes are the result of biological maturation. Another limitation is that Vygotsky did not consider how much children affect their own learning environment. According to Rogoff (1990), children often choose their own activities or their mentors. They often reject or resist help and support from parents or teachers.

💡 Implications for School-Age Child Care Professionals

Most school-age programs serve children who come from more than one cultural group and who, as adults, will live in an increasingly diverse society. It is important, therefore, that they learn to function comfortably in a multicultural environment without losing their identity within their own group. School-age child care professionals can help them achieve that goal in the following ways:

- Learn more about different cultures and be sensitive to cultural values, ways of interacting, and linguistic differences.

- Include families, integrating their values and culture into teaching and learning experiences. Learn about their expectations for their children.

- Encourage children to learn about and appreciate cultures other than their own.

- Help children to acquire the competencies that are important in their culture as well as those that are necessary in broader society.

- Carefully choose and plan activities that gradually move children from assisted performance to independent performance.

- Cultivate each child's communication skills as an important tool of learning.

- Establish a meaningful relationship with every child since it is through the interaction between adult and child that much learning takes place.

- Encourage cooperative learning so children can learn from each other.

Constructivist Learning Theory

Constructivist theories have emerged out of the works of Piaget, Vygotsky, Bruner, and Bandura, and gained popularity in the 1980s in North America. Learners construct knowledge individually and socially through active experiences in their environment and at the same time construct meaning as they learn. These theories emerged from ancient philosophical beliefs such as those of Plato who believed that learning was not stagnant nor just a collection of simple facts or perfect ideas. Learning is a continuous reconstruction of reality, ever changing and evolving as people understand and reflect on their experiences in life both individually and collectively.

Piaget recognized that children create mental maps and cognitive structures as they move along the continuum of developmental stages. Children assimilate experiences, adding them to existing structures of knowledge, and accommodate new experiences that may change or reconstruct their view about something they already know (Focus on Constructivists, n.d.).

Vygotsky's theories contribute to constructivism from a social perspective. He believed that children construct knowledge based on their social interactions and are influenced by culture and interactions with family, peers, teachers, and their community.

Bandura's social learning theory integrates many perspectives on constructivist learning theories. His theory recognizes that behaviour is a result of continuous interactions between the mind, behaviour, and environment. A strong belief in the importance of modelling and observation in providing a viable learning environment is seen as crucial to children's learning (Focus on Constructivists, n.d.).

Language is seen as an important element in constructivist theories. Both Piaget and Vygotsky recognized that children learn through "self-talk," or talking to themselves in order to figure out something or to understand it. Children also learn from interactions with each other and with adults. Children think in their first language and need this to learn effectively as they learn from and refine their daily experiences.

Constructivism is a process of learning rather than a product of facts and knowledge. It supports the process of critical thinking, problem solving, inquiry, exploration, and investigation. Dewey believed that learning is an active process of manipulating materials in concrete versus abstract ways. Children learn "how to learn" and come to see the value of life-long learning. In this way, learning involves a process that takes time to construct meaning, understand something, and then acquire new structures of mind. Learning needs to take place within a context that is real and that makes sense for children and integrates all aspects of social interactions.

Evaluation of Constructivism

The belief that learning is a constructive process where the learner builds an internal understanding of knowledge and a personal and interpersonal interpretation of experience emerges as a credible and viable means of the best way for children to learn. It is based on research coming through the postmodern age when psychologists such as Piaget, Vygotsky, and others were examining how children acquire knowledge in meaningful ways.

Understanding and implementing these theories is a challenge for many teachers and those interested in the teaching/learning process as it requires a change in moving the control over learning from the teacher to the student (Hein, 1991). Educational institutions maintain a behaviourist approach for designing programs that are based on prespecified objectives or outcomes. Constructivists believe that this does not provide the student with an opportunity to delve into the process of learning, which is situational and interactive between children and teachers. Constructivism often challenges the "status quo," whereby teachers are the only experts. Contrary to the belief that constructivism undermines the role of the teacher, the role of the teacher is simply different from an instructionalist or traditional perspective. Teachers facilitate the learning through careful planning of the teaching/learning environment and through their ongoing interactions with the children; coach, provide provocations, promote inquiry-based learning, and encourage the love of learning. Some say constructivism only makes students "reinvent something new." However, along with looking at how something could be done in a different way, constructivist learning supports children's exploration about how things work, how they function, how to apply the children's existing knowledge, how to relate to real-life situations and how to work with the scientific processes of discovery (Concept to Classroom, 2004).

Implications for School-Age Child Care Professionals

In a constructivist approach, children are seen as competent, curious, and motivated learners. They bring valuable knowledge and experiences to the teaching/learning process. They are active learners within a context of family, culture, and society. They come with various learning styles and ways of understanding and constructing knowledge, and can learn from each other as well as from teachers (Jacobs, Vukelich, & Howe, n.d.).

Those working with school-age children should consider the following guidelines that support of constructivist learning:

- Take time to observe and document children's interests and learning processes.
- Provide "hands- on" materials that actively engage children to explore, investigate, and discover new ways of looking at things.
- Engage in ongoing dialogue with children; ask open-ended questions to promote inquiry.
- Support children's participation in the room arrangement, material choices, and overall ownership of their room (Jacobs, Vukelich, & Howe, n.d.).
- Support children's participation in setting up classroom rules for getting along with one another, and respecting themselves, others, and the program's toys and equipment.
- Provide opportunities to take part in "real-life" experiences within their culture and their community.
- Remember that children develop in stages along a continuum and that they learn and acquire knowledge in different ways.

Intelligence Theory

Attempts to understand and measure intelligence have existed for many years. Tests were developed to try to quantify intelligence in relation to chronological age. Items on tests such as the Stanford-Binet focus on general knowledge, reasoning ability, mathematical skill, memory, vocabulary, and spatial perception. More recently, theories of multiple intelligences have interested professionals who are concerned with the education of young children. Sternberg (1996) delineates three types of intelligence: academic (measured by achievement or IQ tests), creative (measured by imaginative undertakings), and practical (seen in everyday tasks and interactions). Gardner (1983) describes seven distinct intelligences: body-kinesthetic, spatial, linguistic, logical-mathematical, musical, interpersonal (social understanding), and intrapersonal (self-understanding). More recently, Gardner has added naturalist intelligence, the ability to recognize and classify features of the environment (Gardner, 1999). According to Gardner, everyone has a basic aptitude for each of the intelligences, but most of us are stronger in one than in others. One person may have exceptional musical ability but have limited spatial skill and therefore gets lost easily.

Evaluation of Intelligence Theory

In recent years there has been much concern about intelligence as being viewed from only one perspective: that which can only be measured by standard intelligence tests.

Sternberg's theory recognizes that there is a combination of mental skills needed in everyday life. Children use different abilities both in and out of school, and cultures vary widely in determining which behaviours they regard as intelligent. Some cultures value more noncognitive capacities like motivation, self-management, and social skills as being more important than cognitive traits of problem-solving and reasoning.

Experts such as Howard Gardner have brought to light a greater scope of intelligence that involves the means of thinking and reasoning through a series of mathematical, vocabulary, and spatial skills; the creative side of intelligence, which involves the creation of art, music, and drama; and the inner understanding of self and social understanding of others.

Implications for School-Age Child Care Professionals

Theories of multiple intelligence are important to anyone who works with children because they can help us understand why some children do so well in some areas but have difficulty in others. These theories also tell us that learning experiences should provide children the opportunity to use all their senses and to express their abilities in a variety of ways (Gardner, 1991). Many schools focus primarily on the tasks that standard tests of achievement measure, but this does not allow children to develop other facets of intelligence. School-age child care professionals can encourage children to develop more than one intelligence by implementing the following suggestions:

- Understand that each child is unique and may be gifted in one area but not in others.
- Let children choose their own methods of learning and work at their own pace (intrapersonal).
- Use cooperative learning that includes feedback from others (interpersonal).

- Provide a variety of experiences that allows children to use their senses in different ways (body-kinesthetic).

- Encourage children to use language in word games, crossword puzzles, or debates (linguistic).

- Foster the ability to visualize by providing the opportunity to do puzzles, draw maps, and solve mazes (spatial).

- Provide games that require strategy planning or resolving problems (logical-mathematical).

- Help children use music in a variety of activities: writing songs, playing instruments, and creating musical plays (musical).

- Use the outdoors as another classroom by introducing science projects, creating a nature area, or nurturing animals (naturalist).

Language Development

Middle childhood is a time when the ability to use language to enhance cognitive skills and to manipulate social situations increases rapidly. Children acquire as many as 20 words a day, achieving a vocabulary of 40,000 words by grade five (Anglin, 1993). The list of words they understand and use may include some they have not experienced directly but understand through reading, conversation, television, and computers. They deduce the meaning of a word through knowledge of the context in which it is used.

School-age children define words differently from the way they did as preschoolers. When asked to define a word, preschool children give examples that are based on perceptions. "An orange is something to eat that tastes good." A school-age child will likely be more logical by saying "It's a fruit." Preschoolers also define words by using action-based statements, whereas older children analyze the relationship to other words. A four-year-old will say, "Under something is where I hide my toys from my brother." A nine-year-old might say, "Under is the opposite of over" (Holzman, 1983).

Children practise their language skills by trying to refine grammatical construction. By age six most children understand and use grammar correctly, but during middle childhood further improvement takes place. Preschool children acquire new language constructions by adapting what they have previously learned. They discover that "ed" is added to make a verb past tense and therefore say, "He goed." Gradually, school-age children learn the variations of verb forms and use them correctly. Older children may not always use correct grammar even though they know it. In conversation with their peers, for instance, they may say, "Me and my mom had a fight." In school they are able to correctly say, "My mom and I had a fight."

School-age children become adept at pragmatic uses of language. They choose words, modify sentences, or change voice inflections to fit the listener in a particular situation. They may use simpler words and shorter sentences when talking to a younger sibling than they would with their friends. The best example of pragmatic use of language is seen in the jokes told by elementary school children. In order to be successful humorists, they need

Figure 5-5 ■ **Learning to write is an important part of cognitive development.**

to recognize what the listener will think is funny and to remember the exact words (Yasilove, 1978).

Further indication that school-age children use language pragmatically is the switch to different forms as the occasion dictates. When making a request of possibly reluctant adults, they are careful to use a polite form of request: "Could I please go to the movie with Rachel?" A more extensive switch in language is called **code switching** (Holzman, 1983; Yoon, 1992). This means a complete change of form when addressing adults and another when addressing cohorts. They may use **elaborated code** in the classroom and change to a **restricted code** when they are on the playground (Bernstein, 1971, 1973). Elaborated code has a more extensive vocabulary, is correct grammatically, and is longer. In contrast, restricted code is more limited and may rely on gestures and voice intonation to communicate meaning. While they are required to use standard English or French in the classroom, children also learn the idiosyncrasies of speech specific to their ethnic group or in common usage in their particular region of the country. Some forms differ in minor ways, such as regional accents or colloquialisms in common usage. Certain speech patterns or accents are so distinctive that they can identify the region where a person lives or grew up. A Newfoundland accent is easily distinguished from Ontario English. Another variation is Black English, or Ebonics, which uses double negatives: "Nobody couldn't come to the party." Children for whom English or French is not their primary language face even greater problems. These children are forced to use a language they may barely understand and then get behind in school. They may also be teased by other children for their accent or misuse of words.

Second-Language Development

The influx of immigrants into Canada has rapidly increased the number of children who are second-language learners. They speak a native language at home and are learning English or French in their out-of-home experiences. Research points out the cognitive, cultural, and economic advantages of bilingualism (Hakuta & Pease-Alvarez, 1992). Hence children who have the opportunity to speak two languages should be encouraged to maintain both. Cognitively, school-age children are able to understand that others may perceive them as different if their language is not that of the majority. They fear they will become the targets of teasing, and this affects their self-concept.

Some basic principles have been drawn from theory and research on second-language acquisition (McLaughlin, 1995). The first is that it is rare for both languages to be perfectly balanced. As a child is learning a second language, one language will be predominant. The more the second language is used, the less the native (home) language is used, and hence both languages may appear less proficient. This is a temporary imbalance, and most bilingual children will reach age-level proficiency in their dominant language given adequate opportunities for use.

The second principle is that of the normalcy of code switching. Young children tend to insert single items from one language into the other (McClure, 1977) primarily to resolve ambiguities and clarify statements. A French-speaking child might say, "My grandmère [grandmother] came to visit." *Grandmère* is the familiar word associated with the grandmother. By around age nine, however, children tend to switch phrases or sentences. They will switch languages to convey social meanings following the manner in which they hear it switched at home and in the community. A child may say "Hey, that's cool, man" when talking to peers but when addressing a teacher say "That's really nice."

code switching

a complete change of language form when addressing adults and when talking to other children

elaborated code

a communication that uses a more extensive vocabulary, is correct grammatically, and is longer

restricted code

communications that are more limited and may rely on gestures and voice intonation to convey meaning

Third, there are different cultural patterns in the use of language. The communication patterns of some cultures do not encourage children to participate verbally in activities. Their home culture interprets this as calling attention to oneself or showing one's knowledge, which is regarded as an arrogant form of behaviour (Philips, 1972).

Finally, children internalize a second language more readily if they are asked to engage in meaningful activities that require using the language, if they have good models for language use, and if they are given encouragement and opportunity to experiment with language as they learn correct phrases and intonation.

💡 Implications for School-Age Child Care Professionals

The importance of language in children's development cannot be underestimated. Good language skills are essential for success in school, and children who can communicate their needs and feelings clearly get along better with their peers and with adults. Perhaps even more important, good language skills are needed for many of the jobs these children will pursue in the future.

- Provide a wide variety of reading material: books, magazines, comic books, and newspapers.

- Read to children frequently and encourage them to read alone or with others.

- Plan a variety of activities and experiences that help children expand their vocabularies and their ability to communicate clearly with others. Remember that listening is a part of communicating.

- Model correct English or French when speaking to children and accept children's forms of speech. Remember that the goal is for the child to communicate, not adhere to rigid rules about language. Do not correct grammar or pronunciation when children are communicating. Respond to the content of communication.

- Use demonstrations, modelling, and role playing to communicate the meaning of language. The more visuals presented to limited English or French speakers, the more likely they will comprehend what is being presented to them.

- Invite parents of children with different cultural backgrounds to provide activities and information about their culture such as language, food, and special customs.

- Develop buddy and peer groups that will be supportive and provide feedback to the second-language learner.

- Provide opportunities for children to use their primary language in ways that enhance their self-esteem. Encourage them to teach useful words or phrases to others. Allow them to use their speech forms in creative ways when writing stories, plays, or poetry.

- Include written or oral language in culturally based activities.

Summary

The thinking processes of school-age children are markedly different from those of preschoolers. Swiss psychologist Jean Piaget was a major contributor to our understanding of how children think and learn. Piaget believed that intelligence is the result of progression through four stages: the sensorimotor period, from birth to 2 years of age; the preoperational period, from 2 to 7 years of age; the concrete operations period, from 7 to 11 years of age; and the formal operations period, from age 11 to 15. Another general principle of Piagetian theory is that children are active participants in the development of their own intelligence. A third principle is that differences in the rate at which individuals pass through the stages are due to variations in maturation rate.

Behaviourist theory grew out of a need for more precise studies of human development and was proposed early in the 20th century by Watson. Watson's ideas were based on the classical conditioning of Pavlov and pointed to the connection between a stimulus and response. When a stimulus is followed by a pleasant response, the behaviour is likely to be repeated; if the response is unpleasant, the behaviour may disappear. Skinner started with Watson's ideas but went a step further. He proposed another type of conditioning, operant conditioning. He observed that children operate on their environment and are reinforced. When the reinforcer is pleasant, the behaviour will be repeated, and when unpleasant it is likely not to be repeated. Bandura also agreed with behaviourist ideas but felt that some behaviour could not be explained by simple stimulus and response mechanisms. He saw that some behaviour occurs as a result of less direct teaching, through observation of a model and then subsequent imitation of that behaviour.

Sociocultural theory, proposed by Vygotsky, has only recently been widely disseminated. Vygotsky assumed that social interaction and children's direct participation in authentic cultural activities is necessary for their optimum development. He pointed to the need to understand cross-cultural variation, the kinds of tools and activities different societies use to help children develop the competencies they will need as adults. Vygotsky believed that children construct themselves, adding to their knowledge and skills. Later researchers labelled this scaffolding. Vygotsky also pointed to the importance of language, since it forms the basis of social interactions between adult and child. According to Vygotsky, the zone of proximal development is the hypothetical environment in which learning and development take place.

More recent attempts to understand intelligence have brought theories of multiple intelligences. Sternberg delineated three: academic, creative, and practical. Gardner listed eight: body-kinesthetic, spatial, linguistic, logical-mathematical, musical, interpersonal, intrapersonal, and naturalist.

Constructivist theories support many theorists, but in particular Vygotsky's view that children construct their own knowledge from a teaching and learning environment that encourages collaborative learning. The adult is the facilitator, coach, and keen observer. He or she provides resources and materials to expand children's interests, allows for freedom to explore materials, and creates an atmosphere that encourages a process of inquiry learning.

Middle childhood is a time when the ability to use language to enhance cognitive skills and manipulate social situations increases rapidly. Children acquire as many as 20 words a day, achieving a vocabulary of 40,000 words by grade five.

Children practise their language skills by trying to refine grammatical constructions. They are adept at pragmatic uses of language, choosing words, modifying sentences, or changing inflections to suit particular situations. Children also demonstrate their pragmatic use of language when they switch to different forms as an occasion dictates. Code switching is a complete change of form when addressing adults and another when addressing peers.

Many children speak a non-English (or -French) primary language in the home and therefore are at various levels of proficiency in using English or French. Their attempts at learning and using English as well as their primary language should be encouraged. School-age child care professionals should provide an enticing, language-rich environment that supports reading, writing, and speaking English or French as well as home languages.

Key Terms

storage strategies

sensorimotor period

preoperational period

centring

concrete operations

formal operations

classical conditioning

operant conditioning

modelling

scaffold

zone of proximal development

code switching

elaborated code

restricted code

Student Activities

1. Observe a group of school-age children. Can you recognize any models the children are using to pattern their own behaviour? Are the models real people (familiar adults or their peers) or characters from television, films, or computer games? Why do you think they have chosen these particular models? In small groups, share your observations with classmates. Discuss these questions.
2. Visit a school program serving children from 6 to 12 years of age. Record the number of times the adults use positive reinforcers. What types of reinforcers seem to be most effective with this age level? Did they encourage repetition of the behaviour? What negative reinforcers were also used? Did they discourage the behaviour? Share your findings with classmates, and compile a list of responses that seem effective when working with school-age children.
3. In small-group discussions, ask members to relate their own methods of working with children to one of the theories described in this chapter. Do they choose one theory over others? Or do they tend to use each of the theories in an eclectic approach?
4. Plan two activities for a group of nine-year-olds that will help them increase their vocabulary. Share your plans with classmates.
5. Present a demonstration of an activity using only visual gestures and materials to convey your meaning. In small groups, discuss the difficulties of learning concepts and instructions if there is no understanding of the language being spoken. (It would be ideal to have someone who speaks another language, unknown by the majority of the classmates, do this presentation in their native language followed by small-group discussion.)

Review Questions

1. Why did Piaget observe that during the preoperational period children often come to the wrong conclusions?
2. Between age 7 and 11 children progress to the stage of concrete operations. What new abilities have they acquired?
3. State three applications of Piagetian theory in a school-age program.

4. How does operant conditioning, proposed by Skinner, differ from the social learning theory of Bandura?
5. What are some criticisms of behaviourist theory?
6. How is the constructivist theory used when planning an appropriate environment for school-age children?
7. What is meant by "scaffolding"?
8. What is meant by the "zone of proximal development"?
9. How can school-age child care professionals use Vygotsky's ideas in a multicultural community?
10. State three ways school-age child care professionals can help children increase their language skills.
11. List the seven intelligences delineated by Gardner. What is the eighth one he added in 1999?
12. Describe the role of the school-age child care professional as it pertains to children who are learning English or French as a second language. Consider curriculum, peer interaction on behalf of the second-language learner, and your own interactions with the child.

Case Study

Angela and Jennine wanted to learn to knit so they could make scarves for their dads. Nancy, one of the staff, promised to show them how since she had been knitting since she was very young. She told them to bring some #6 needles and a ball of yarn in the colour they liked. She also had some available for those who didn't have knitting needles and yarn at home. They came to the after-school program the next day, eager to get started. Nancy cast on the stitches on each of their needles since she felt it would be hard enough for them to learn the stitch without starting with casting on. She demonstrated for each of them, then guided their hands through several stitches. Angela was quickly ready to proceed on her own, but Jennine was having trouble. She would forget which way to wrap the yarn around the needle or how to pull the stitch through. Nancy again guided Jennine's hands, but she still had problems, and Jennine became increasingly frustrated. Then Nancy remembered that she had a knitting instruction book in the cupboard that showed the step-by-step process. She got it out and propped the page in front of Jennine. Jennine studied it and then cautiously tried each step. Finally she understood and was exuberant that she was successful at last.

1. Why did do you think that Angela found the instructions Nancy gave her easy to follow? Why was it difficult for Jennine?
2. How would you describe the methods that Nancy used to teach the girls?
3. What theory or theories of cognitive development would you apply here?
4. What does this tell you about other learning experiences that you provide for the children in your group?

References

Anglin, J. M. (1993). Vocabulary development: A morphological analysis. *Monographs of the Society for Research in Child Development, 58* (10, Serial No. 238).

Bandura, Albert. (1977). *Social learning theory.* Englewood Cliffs, NJ: Prentice-Hall.

Berger, K. S. (2000). *The developing person through childhood and Adolescence* (5th ed.). New York: Worth Publishers.

Berk, L. E. & Winsler, A. (1995). *Scaffolding children's learning: Vygotsky and early childhood education.* Washington, DC: National Association for the Education of Young Children.

Bernstein, B. (1971, 1973). *Class, codes, and control.* Vols. 1, 2. London: Routledge and Kegan Paul.

Bertrand, J. (2001). *Summary of research findings on children's developmental health.* Ottawa, ON: Canadian Child Care Federation & Canadian Institute of Child Health.

Cole, M. (1992). Culture in development. In M. H. Holzman (1983), *The language of children: Development in home and in school.* Englewood Cliffs, NJ: Prentice-Hall.

Concept to Classroom, Workshop: Constructivism as a paradigm for teaching and learning. (2004). Retrieved May 30, 2012, from http://www.thirteen.org/edonline/concept2class/constructivism/index.html

Focus on constructivists, 1995–2010. (n.d.). Pearson Education, Retrieved from http://wps.ablongman.com/ab_leverduffy_teachtech_2/23/6126/1568334.cw/index.html

Gardner, H. (1983). *Frames of mind: The theory of multiple intelligences.* New York: Basic Books.

Gardner, H. (1991). *The unschooled mind: How children think and how schools should teach.* New York: Basic Books.

Gardner, H. (1999). *Intelligence reframed: Multiple intelligences for the 21st century.* New York: Basic Books.

Hakuta, K. & Pease-Alvarez, L. (1992). Enriching our view of bilingualism and bilingual education. *Educational Researcher, 21:* 4–6.

Hein, G. (1991). Constructivist learning theory. Retrieved May 30, 2012, from http://www.exploratorium.edu/IFI/resources/constructivistlearning.html

Holzman, M. (1983). *The language of children: Development in home and in school.* Englewood Cliffs, NJ: Prentice Hall.

Jacobs, E., Mill, D., & Jennings, M. (1997–1999) Quality Assurance and School Age Care. Child Care Visions, Human Resources Development Canada.

Jacobs, E., Vukelich, G., & Howe, N. (n.d.) Pathways to constructivism: A self-directed guide for educators. Human Resources Development Canada.

Locke, J. (1959). *Essay concerning human understanding.* Collated and annotated by A.C. Fraser. New York: Dover Publications. (Original work published 1698)

McClure, E. F. (1977). Aspects of code-switching in the discourse of bilingual Mexican-American children. *Tech. Rep. No. 44.* Cambridge, MA: Berancek and Newman.

McLaughlin, B. (1995). *Fostering second language development in young children: Principles and practices.* Washington, DC: National Center for Research on Cultural Diversity and Second Language Learning.

Pavlov, I. (1960). *Conditioned reflexes: An investigation of the physiological activity of the cereral cortex.* (G. V. Anrep, Ed. and Trans.) New York: Dover Publications. (Original work published 1927)

Philips, S. (1972). Participant structures and communicative competence: Warm Springs children in community and the classroom. In C. B. Cazden, V. P. John, & D. Hymes (Eds.), *Function of language in the classroom.* New York: Teachers College.

Piaget, J. (1952). *The origins of intelligence in children.* (M. Cook, Trans.). New York: International Universities Press. (Original work published 1936)

Rogoff, Barbara. (1990). *Apprenticeship in thinking: Cognitive development in social context.* New York: Oxford University Press.

Skinner, B. F. (1953). *Science and human behavior.* New York: Macmillan.

Sternberg, R. J. (1996). *Successful intelligence.* New York: Simon & Schuster.

Vygotsky, L. S. (1978). *Mind in society: The development of higher psychological processes.* Cambridge, MA: Harvard University Press. (Original work published 1934)

Vygotsky, L. S. (1987). *Thinking and speech.* (N. Minick, Trans.). New York: Plenum. (Original work published 1934)

Watson, J. B. (1967). *Behaviorism* (rev. ed.). Chicago: University of Chicago Press. (Original work published 1930)

Yasilove, D. (1978). The effect of riddle-structure on children's comprehension and appreciation of riddles. Doctoral dissertation. New York University. *Dissertation Abstracts International, 36, 6.*

Yoon, K. (1992). New perspective on intrasentential code-switching: A study of Korean-English switching. *Applied Psycholinguistics, 13, 433–449.*

Chapter 6

Development in Middle Childhood: Psychosocial

Objectives

After studying this chapter, the student should be able to:

- Discuss the major principles of several theories of psychosocial development

- List the concerns expressed by critics of each theory as well as the points of agreement

- Develop strategies that enhance children's psychosocial development

 ## Profile

L ise provides child care in her home for five children; two children are three years of age, one child is four years old, and two children are seven and eight years of age. One of the three-year-olds is her own child. When she gave birth to her little boy, she decided to leave her job as a school-age child care professional at a municipal child care centre where she had worked for five years. She registered her home with the regional child care office and became a licensed home child care provider. A home child care consultant comes out to her home occasionally to talk about programming and meeting the challenge of providing care for a variety of age groups of children.

Lise has her child and the other three-year-old for most of the day; the four-year-old comes from junior kindergarten for lunch and the afternoon, and the seven- and eight-year-olds come after school, on professional-development days and on school holidays.

It is quite a challenge to provide activities that will interest such a variety of ages. Lise is sometimes tired at the end of the day when she sets up activities for the children after school and also has to get supper ready for her own family. She believes that it is important to provide interesting activities for the two children after school, along with the other children, knowing that the out-of-school time is still valuable time for children to be learning through play. She provides lots of choices of board games, cards, arts and crafts, building/construction and science kits, and a trunk of dress-up clothes. She also has a collection of appropriate software that the children can use on her computer. She is always watching and listening to their conversations, and encouraging them to help plan the activities. Sometimes the older children like to cook or bake, and they enjoy helping the younger children with different tasks. They spend some time outdoors each day.

Lise also provides a quiet area for the children to go to if they have homework to do. She has a good relationship with the parents and ensures that they feel comfortable sharing information about their children.

Theories of Social-emotional Development

The world of children between the ages of 5 and 12 expands as they enter school and begin to experience the environment outside their homes. Increased physical and cognitive skills allow them more independence to explore their neighbour-hoods, visit friends' homes, and use community facilities such as playgrounds or clubs. In the process they have many adventures and encounter new people. Parents are often unaware of and have little control over the kinds of challenges their children face as they manoeuvre in this new territory. How children manage depends a great deal on how they feel about themselves and the kinds of moral values they have learned within their families. Several theories are used to explain how children develop their sense of identity and learn to be successful members of a society.

Psychoanalytic Theory

Sigmund Freud

Sigmund Freud (1938) was an Austrian doctor and the founder of the psychoanalytic theory of human behaviour. While working with individuals diagnosed as "hysterics," Freud evolved the theory that irrational behaviours have underlying causes that come from unconscious sexual and aggressive drives that he called *libido*. He saw the psyche as having three parts: the **id**, the source of pleasure-seeking drives; the **ego**, or the rational aspect of personality; and the **superego**, which controls behaviour through the development of a conscience. Freud also proposed that the id is present at birth, whereas the ego and superego develop as one progresses through stages of development. In the process the ego functions as a mediating force between the desire to seek pleasure and the need to yield to the demands of parents and society. Each stage brings with it conflicts that a child must resolve. How well a child is able to do this is determined by the skills and competencies acquired along the way. Freud delineated five stages of development: oral—birth to 1 year of age; anal—1 to 3 years of age; phallic: 3 to 6 years of age; latency: 6 to 11 years of age; and adolescence: 11 years of age to adulthood.

id
in psychoanalytic theory, the part of the personality that is the source of pleasure-seeking drives

ego
in psychoanalytic theory, the rational aspect of personality

superego
in psychoanalytic theory, the part of the personality that controls behaviour through the development of conscience

Evaluation of Psychoanalytic Theory

Many of Freud's ideas are so widely accepted that they are no longer attributed to psychoanalytic origins (Berger, 2000). There is general agreement that unconscious drives affect some behaviours, although the source of those drives may not be attributed to sexual urges, as Freud proposed. Modified aspects of psychoanalytic theory are evident in research and popular writings about the importance of attachment between mother and infant, gender identity, parental discipline, moral development, and adolescent development.

Some facets of psychosexual theory, however, are no longer considered valid. There is little support for Freud's belief that the way in which conflicts during the oral and anal phases are resolved result in specific personality traits. An even more important criticism of psychoanalytic theory is that it was based on Freud's experiences with white, middle- or upper-class patients. Present-day developmental theory emphasizes that personality and behaviour are affected more by a person's heredity, life events, and the culture in which one lives rather than on conflicts that occur in childhood. There is little support as well for Freud's belief in the struggle between the id and the superego. The strongest criticism of psychoanalytic theory is that it cannot be proven through controlled scientific research.

Psychosocial Theory

Erik Erikson

Erik Erikson (1963) studied psychoanalytic theory with Anna Freud, the daughter of Sigmund Freud. He later moved to Boston, where he started a psychoanalytic practice. Erikson's work included children from a wide variety of backgrounds. Some were from middle-class, professional families, others from poor families, and some were delinquent children. At first Erikson found it difficult to apply psychoanalytic principles to his work with children who were not typically middle class, but eventually he found that all children have some common characteristics. Erikson expanded Freud's stages of development to encompass the entire life span, with each stage characterized by a challenge or developmental crisis.

Erikson's first five stages are similar to those of Freud, but Erikson added three stages of adulthood. These five stages are (1) **trust vs. mistrust**; (2) **autonomy vs. shame and doubt**; (3) **initiative vs. guilt**; (4) **industry vs. inferiority**; and (5) **identity vs. role confusion**. The significant difference between Freud and Erikson, however, lies in Erikson's emphasis on one's relationship to the social environment rather than on the body. He called his ideas the psychosocial theory of development. At each stage of development, the resolution of a crisis depends upon the interaction between the individual's personality characteristics and the support and guidance provided by the social environment. How successful or unsuccessful one is in resolving these crises depends a great deal upon competencies and the support and guidance that parents and society provide.

1. *Trust vs. mistrust: Birth to one year of age.* During the first year babies either learn to trust that others will take care of their basic needs or that others cannot be depended upon. The important factors are the sensitivity to the infant's needs and the love and warmth that caregivers show.

2. *Autonomy vs. shame and doubt: One to three years of age.* The primary focus of this stage is to become independent by gaining control over bodily functions: toileting, feeding, walking, and talking. The crisis arises when the strong drive for autonomy must be balanced by the demands of parents. Too much control by adults results in feelings of inadequacy, followed by shame and doubt.

3. *Initiative vs. guilt: Three to six years of age.* During this period children want to attempt many tasks they observe their parents or other adults performing. They sometimes attempt activities that are beyond their capabilities or are outside the limits set by their parents. If given support and guidance by their caregivers, the result will be feelings of success and pride in their own initiative. If they are unsuccessful, they will be left with feelings of guilt.

4. *Industry vs. inferiority: Seven to eleven years of age.* During this middle-childhood period children expend their energies on mastering new skills at home, in school, on the playground, and in their neighbourhoods. When they are successful, they acquire the tools they will need for important societal tasks such as getting a job and getting along with others. When they are unsuccessful, feelings of inferiority set a pattern for possible failure throughout life.

5. *Identity vs. role confusion: Adolescence.* This period is highlighted by adolescents' search for identity as individuals in a society. They must balance a desire to establish their own uniqueness with a need to conform to the standards set by the society or culture in which they live. Rebelliousness may lead to role confusion, and strict conformity to a stifling of individuality.

Erikson delineated three additional stages that follow the school-age years and extend into adulthood: intimacy vs. isolation, generativity vs. stagnation, and integrity vs. despair.

Evaluation of Psychosocial Theory

Erikson's perception of human development is more widely accepted than psychoanalytic theory even though it is based on Freud's ideas (Berger, 2000). Erikson's writings are more contemporary, not based on the Victorian culture of Freud's time. Many ideas taken from Erikson are currently applied to issues regarding care of infants, parenting programs, care of children in groups, and training of early childhood educators.

Figure 6-1 ■ These girls are best friends.

Figure 6-2 ■ Writing is an important societal task to be mastered.

Table 6-1 ■ Comparison of Psychoanalytic Theories

Approximate Age	Freud	Erikson
3–6	Phallic stage	Initiative vs. guilt
	Oedipal situation	Attempt adult activities
	Identification with same-sex parent	Gaining independence
	Superego, conscience	Overstep parental limits, feel guilty
7–11	Latency	Industry vs. inferiority
	Quiet period, less sexual tension	Becoming competent is important
	Psychic energy goes into learning skills	Can feel inferior if unsuccessful
Adolescence	Genital	Identity vs. role confusion
	Seeking sexual stimulation and gratification	Considering own identity
		Establishing ethnic and career identities

Implications for School-Age Child Care Professionals

Two themes are present in both Freudian and Eriksonian ideas about how children develop: the significance of childhood stages in the formation of personality and the importance of the manner in which adults respond to children's behaviour during each of the stages. These lead to several specific implications for persons working with school-age children:

- Remember that adults are active participants in helping children resolve the conflicts inherent in each of the stages of development. Provide guidance and support so that the conflicts can be resolved in ways that enhance children's self-image.

- Include families in decisions concerning a child's problem behaviours. The behaviours have been formed within the context of family interactions and will be more easily changed with cooperation from family members.

- Support children's need for competence by providing opportunities for them to acquire new social skills and to practise already acquired skills.

- Support children's need to be independent by allowing them freedom to make choices and do things without adult intervention. As shown in the profile at the beginning of the chapter, let children plan and carry out many of their own activities. As well, let them make their own rules within limits that do not interfere with others' rights.

- Let children know that their competence and responsibility are valued. Children in the program discussed in the profile feel competent and responsible when they help out with the younger children.

Moral Development

The process of acquiring and using moral values and attitudes continues throughout life. At each step of development, children learn that certain behaviours are acceptable whereas others bring disapproval and rejection. The years of middle childhood are particularly fertile grounds for learning the lessons taught by the family, culture, and society for several reasons. First, peer relationships become extremely important, sometimes taking precedence over family. Children want to be part of a peer group, so they learn to negotiate, compromise, and play "by the rules" in order to be included. Second, they have already acquired cognitive skills that allow them to think logically and even abstractly. They understand concepts of right and wrong and can consider moral issues related to their own behaviours. Finally, their world has expanded beyond the family into the school and the neighbourhood. Toward the end of middle childhood, children begin to look at broad moral issues that affect others: human rights, destructiveness of war, ecological devastation, and global hunger.

Jean Piaget's Theory

Jean Piaget's (1932) primary concern was the cognitive development of children, but he was also interested in how children begin to understand justice and develop a respect for social order. He believed that children's understanding of rules goes through stages as their thinking processes change. Their views are often based on concrete observable evidence and are reflective of their egocentric thinking. Piaget used two stories; one that talks about a (well-intentioned) child who breaks 15 cups by accident and another (ill-intentioned) child who breaks one cup out of anger. Children generally under the age of 7 will assume that the child who broke the 15 cups by accident is naughtier than the child who broke one cup on purpose. In the earliest stage, the preschool and early school-age years, children believe that rules are created by an all-powerful authority figure and that they are not to be changed. Piaget called this stage **moral realism,** in which justice is whatever the authority decides at a particular time. By age seven or eight, children reach another level. During this period they interact with their peers differently, often with give-and-take reciprocity. They also change their ideas about authority, recognizing that punishments may be fair or unfair, depending upon the transgression committed. As children approach adolescence, around age 11 or 12, a new stage emerges. Piaget called this stage **moral relativism.** At this level, children are able to be more flexible, change rules, and discuss moral issues. At this stage, children who have heard the story about the breaking of cups will understand that the child who broke the one cup out of anger is naughtier than the one who broke 15 cups by accident. Their higher level of cognitive thinking allows them to see situations from a broader perspective.

moral realism

a stage of moral development in which children believe that rules are determined by an authority figure and they are not to be changed

moral relativism

a stage of moral development in which children view punishments as fair or unfair, are more flexible in their thinking, and can discuss moral issues

Evaluation of Piaget's Theory

Subsequent research has found that Piaget's theory accurately describes the changes that children go through in moral justice. As children get older, outer physical conditions or fear of punishment give way to more subtle considerations, such as the person's intentions, needs, and wishes. Evidence supports Piaget's conclusion that moral understanding is supported by cognitive maturity, less conformity to authority, and more social awareness. Critics have questioned some of Piaget's findings about the extent of moral understanding that young children have (Berk, 2003). However, we must remember that Piaget believed that children move through each stage of development at their own individual pace rather than at a specific age or stage.

Lawrence Kohlberg's Theory

The most complete theory of children's moral development was proposed by Kohlberg, who used Piaget's theories as a starting point for developing his own theory of moral development. Kohlberg (1963) believed that children's moral thinking developed in stages along with the development of cognitive skills. As cognitive processes changed, the ability to consider moral questions also changed. To test his theory, he presented children with a set of hypothetical stories about moral dilemmas that required decisions involving human life, property rights, or human needs. He examined children's responses to these situations and concluded that children proceed through the following three levels of moral reasoning:

Level I, Age 4 to 10. Preconventional: Emphasis on Punishment and Rewards

preconventional
Kohlberg's first stage of moral development, in which there is an emphasis on punishment and rewards

Stage 1. Might makes right. At this level, behaviour is labelled good or bad based entirely on the consequences of an action. Children obey authority in order to avoid punishment: "If you do that, you'll get in trouble."

Stage 2. Satisfy your own needs. People take care of their own needs first and occasionally the needs of others. Children believe that if they are nice to others, others will be nice to them: "I'll invite you to my birthday party if you let me play with you."

Level II, Age 10 to 13. Conventional: Emphasis on Social Rules of the Individual's Family, Group, or Nation

conventional
Kohlberg's second stage of moral development, in which there is an emphasis on social rules of the individual's family, group, or nation

Stage 3. Interpersonal concordance. Good behaviour is behaviour that others approve of and reward. Approval is more important than any other kind of compensation. Children value conformity to stereotyped images of what majority behaviour is. A significant change occurs during this stage: Children recognize intent that is attached to behaviour: "He didn't really mean to ruin your building. He was just trying to help."

Stage 4. Law and order. Emphasis is on authority and obedience to the laws set down by those in power in order to maintain social order. Right behaviour means doing one's duty, showing respect for authority, and recognizing the need to maintain social order: "It's not right to take things that don't belong to you. Besides, you might get arrested."

Level III, Age 13 and Older. Postconventional: Emphasis on Universal Moral Values and Principles

postconventional
Kohlberg's third stage of moral development, in which there is an emphasis on moral values and principles

Stage 5. Social contract. People understand that laws and rules exist to ensure individual rights. Right action is seen in terms of standards that society has examined and agreed upon. Aside from what has been democratically agreed upon, right is also a matter of personal values and opinions. Laws might be changed if a consensus can be reached: "I think we should change the rules of this game so the little kids can play."

Stage 6. Universal principles. People behave according to universal ethical principles. These principles are abstract, like the golden rule, and involve a basic right for everyone to be treated equally and with dignity: "I don't think anybody should be discriminated against. Everyone should be able to live where he wants or go to school where she wants."

Kohlberg found that individuals progress through the moral hierarchy very slowly. He found that most school-age children function at Stage 1 or 2. He believed that children must be at the cognitive level of adolescents to make moral decisions comparable to Stage 3. Only then will they begin to consider another person's intent before judging behaviour as right or wrong. Once they reach that level of thinking, they may be able to go on to question authority and laws in terms of faithfulness to maintaining basic human rights. Each stage must be experienced before progressing to the next level, and no level can be skipped. Some individuals may become fixed at a certain level and never move on to a higher one. (People who are fixated at Stage 1 or 2 may not be able to consider a number of viewpoints or reasons for a certain behaviour when faced with a moral dilemma and may resort to a single judgement or conclusion.)

Evaluation of Kohlberg's Theory

Although Kohlberg's stages of moral development were originally praised by developmentalists as a way of understanding moral education, several researchers took a closer look.

Gilligan (1982) pointed to the fact that Kohlberg's scheme was validated on a group of only males, ages 10, 13, and 16. When women were tested, they scored lower than males; women on average were at Stage 3, and men at Stage 4. Moral development at Stage 3 is an interpersonal level, with emphasis on gaining approval for good behaviour. Stage 4 is a more objective acceptance of rules. Gilligan argues that girls develop what she calls a **morality of caring**, whereas boys judge right and wrong in terms of a **morality of justice.** Because they are socialized to be caring and nurturing, girls are reluctant to judge right and wrong in absolutes. When faced with making choices, boys immediately determine what is right or wrong and follow with a clear solution, whereas girls try to find a variety of alternatives.

One researcher tested Gilligan's ideas and came to a different conclusion. Walker (1988) found that during middle childhood, both boys and girls tended to seek justice when faced with a moral dilemma. Older and more mature subjects were more caring.

Turiel (1983; Turiel, Smetana, and Killen, 1991) pointed out that Kohlberg used hypothetical situations, not the daily circumstances children typically confront. When Turiel used real test situations more closely resembling children's own experiences, he found that children can reason better about familiar settings. When playing games, for instance, they function at a higher level of moral thinking. Turiel also found that when children have a chance to discuss issues repeatedly, they make wiser decisions.

A further criticism of Kohlberg's theory is that his stages reflect Western values and cannot be applied to other cultures. Reid (1984, 1989), studying Samoan and European families in New Zealand, found that the needs of family members sometimes take precedence over observing moral principles that apply to everyone.

Implications for School-Age Child Care Professionals

Because middle childhood is a period when children are learning to find their way in the world outside their home, it is important to facilitate their ability to live within

Figure 6-3 ■ "Me." Nicole, age 7

morality of caring
Gilligan's theory that girls are socialized to be caring and nurturing and reluctant to judge right and wrong in absolutes

morality of justice
Gilligan's theory that boys will determine what is right or wrong and then follow it with a clear solution when faced with making choices

society's rules and to get along with others. School-age child care professionals can play an important part:

- Expose children to both male and female school-age child care professionals.
- Involve children in solving moral dilemmas that occur in their everyday experiences. Give them opportunities to discuss the possible solutions to and the consequences of each decision, allowing them to find new ways of approaching moral dilemmas.
- Provide children with opportunities to interact with children and adults of different age groups, exposing them to higher levels of moral functioning.
- Create an environment in which a variety of individual and family value systems are accepted. It is easy to accept value systems that are like one's own, but it takes more practice to accept those that are different. Bring awareness to similarities and differences between cultures. In some cultures, such as some aboriginal and East Indian communities, the practice of not cutting one's hair is essential to their religious beliefs.
- Model the kind of behaviour expected of children. Behave in ways that are fair and just rather than imposing arbitrary rules that have no relation to values.
- Allow children to assist in forming the language of the program rules.
- Set up scenarios, using puppets or role plays on topics that relate to various moral issues such as lying or stealing, and discuss appropriate responses and actions.

The Adventure of Risk Taking: Child Development

risk taking
being able to challenge oneself and make appropriate decisions, with adult support

Whether children are climbing trees, sliding down a slide, swinging on a swing, or spinning around on a merry-go-round, they need opportunities for risk taking in their play.

What are the risks for children's futures of not taking risks?

Children who are good risk takers are confident, careful thinkers who make good choices and decisions. These children will most likely be prepared for the unexpected in life. They will have practised risk taking and know what to do when they meet everyday problems in life. They will be able to face their problems, step out of their comfort zone, and take action to get resolution. They will know how to struggle with uncertainty, accept possible failures, and work toward achieving and mastering their goals. They will feel safe in themselves, trust their instincts, and be able to express their ideas, beliefs, and convictions.

From a child development perspective, these children have strong social and emotional capabilities to face day-to-day challenges. They are more resilient and have a strong sense of self-esteem. They excel cognitively because they are critical thinkers and work through situations with tenacity and diligence. They enjoy physical challenges and are not afraid to make mistakes and learn from them. They are more tolerant and can accept differences more readily.

Ways and Means of Practising Risk Taking

Good risk-taking behaviour prevails in a program's climate of safety, security, and mutual trust between children and adults. Children need to know that teachers will accept them for who they are and that they will guide them toward developing into the best that they can be.

Teachers need to build attachments with children. Adults working with school-age children need to acknowledge their individual personalities and temperament styles, and know about their families and communities and help children build a good base of security.

Here are some guidelines to follow:

- Help children set realistic goals for themselves and let them try out, explore, investigate, and play.
- Guide them with problem-solving strategies and encourage them to reflect on their own experiences, both positive and negative.
- Help them discover ways to do things and see things in different ways, to see beyond superficial stereotypes and cultural prejudices.
- Have them practise sharing their emotions in constructive ways, using various practical and meaningful ways of expression.
- Do some story writing; draw, paint, act out scenarios; build, construct, and play active games.
- Remember that children are competent and resourceful, and they have many life experiences.

Build on these and help them become the best that they can be (adapted from Davis & Eppler-Wolff, 2009).

Summary

Freud's psychoanalytic theory of development asserts that there are hidden causes of behaviour that originate in the unconscious. He also believed that libido, general sexual or sensual energy, is the driving force behind all human behaviour. He saw the psyche as having three parts: the id, the ego, and the superego. The struggle between the pleasure-seeking id and the conscience-driven superego is facilitated by the mediating force of the ego. Individuals go through five stages during this process.

Erikson based his theory on psychoanalytic principles but felt that the resolution of the conflicts between the id and the superego takes place in the context of the social environment. How successful one is in resolving the crises of each stage depends upon the support and guidance of parents and society. Erikson delineated eight stages from birth to the end of life.

Although many facets of Freud's theory are widely accepted, there are criticisms. Erikson's theory is more easily accepted since it is not based on the Victorian culture of Freud's time.

The process of developing moral values continues throughout life. Piaget related moral development to the development of cognitive abilities. He wrote of the stage of moral realism during the preschool and early school-age years. By age seven or eight, children reach another level, moral relativism. At this level children are able to be more flexible, change rules, and discuss moral values.

Kohlberg formulated the most complete theory of children's moral development. He used Piaget's ideas as a starting point and related moral development to the acquisition of cognitive skills. Kohlberg proposed three levels of moral reasoning, with two stages at each level. He found that individuals proceed through the stages slowly and that most school-age children function at the first level.

Criticism of Kolhberg's theory comes from several researchers who noted that his research focused only on preadolescent and adolescent boys. Gilligan argues that girls develop a morality of caring, whereas boys develop a morality of justice. Turiel contends that Kohlberg's test situations were hypothetical, not actual day-to-day dilemmas children actually face and could understand. Further criticism is that his stages reflect Western values and cannot be applied to all cultures.

School-age children need strong attachments with adults in order to feel safe and secure enough to take risks in their play and thus develop into confident and independent individuals who can make good decisions and choices in the future.

Key Terms

id	initiative vs. guilt	conventional
ego	industry vs. inferiority	postconventional
superego	identity vs. role confusion	morality of caring
trust vs. mistrust	moral realism	morality of justice
autonomy vs. shame and doubt	moral relativism	risk taking
	preconventional	

Student Activities

1. Ask several school-age children to discuss some moral dilemmas they are likely to face in their everyday life. The following are some possible scenarios, but you can make up your own.
   a. You and your friend go to the store to buy some candy. You notice that your friend puts a chocolate bar in his pocket but pays for a package of gum. What should you do?
   b. Your friend's little sister wants to play a game with the two of you, but you know that it will be too difficult for her. What will you do?

   Write down the children's responses and then try to put them into one of Kohlberg's stages. Share the results with your classmates during your next class.
2. Ask your parents how they handled the following situations when you were growing up:
   a. toilet training
   b. thumb sucking
   c. questions about gender differences

   Determine whether their methods were influenced by psychoanalytic thinking. If so, in what way?

Review Questions

1. Freud saw the psyche as having three parts. List and define each.
2. How is Erikson's theory related to Freud's ideas, and how is it different?
3. Briefly describe children's development according to Erikson during the following stages:
   a. initiative vs. guilt
   b. industry vs. inferiority
   c. identity vs. role confusion
4. State some criticisms of psychoanalytic theory.
5. What are some ways school-age child care professionals can apply Freudian and Eriksonian theory to their work with children and families?
6. Piaget cited two stages in children's development involving a sense of justice and respect for social order. What are they?
7. Kohlberg proposed three levels of moral reasoning. He called Level I, age 4 to 10, preconventional. State and describe Stages 1 and 2 at this level.
8. Why did Kohlberg believe that school-age children would find it difficult to make moral decisions having to do with a person's intent behind a behaviour?
9. What was the basis for Gilligan's criticism of Kohlberg's theory?
10. Why is it important for children to take risks? Identify six ways that adults working with school-age children can support them.

Case Study

Jamahl is one of the staff members for a group of seven- and eight-year-olds. He would like to change the way some children react when there are problems among the children. Danisha, the youngest boy in the group, never does anything wrong, but when someone else does, he loudly says, "You're going to get in trouble for that." Emily maintains control over her two friends by threatening, "I won't invite you to my birthday party if you don't do what I want."

1. Why are the children reacting in this way?
2. Jamahl wants to reinforce the importance of rules but also wants to help the children move on to a higher level of morality. What could he say to the children?
3. When you are faced with helping children make decisions about appropriate/inappropriate behaviour, what do you want them to learn?

References

Berger, K. S. (2000). *The developing person through childhood and Adolescence* (5th ed.). New York: Worth Publishers.

Berk, L. (2003). *Child development* (Canadian ed.). Toronto: Pearson Education Canada.

Davis, S. & Eppler-Wolff, N. (2009). Raising children who soar. Teachers College Press, Retrieved May 31, 2012, from http://www.parentbooksummaries.com/raising-children-who-soar

Erikson, E. H. (1963). *Childhood and society* (2nd ed.). New York: Norton. (Original work published 1950) Freud, S. (1938). *The basic writings of Sigmund Freud.* (A. A. Brill, Ed. and Trans.). New York: Modern Library.

Gilligan, C. (1982). *In a different voice: Psychological theory and women's development.* Cambridge, MA: Harvard University Press.

Kohlberg, L. (1963). Development of children's orientation towards a moral order (Part 1). Sequence in the development of moral thought. *Vita Humana, 6,* 11–36.

Piaget, J. (1932). *The moral judgment of the child.* (M. Gabin, Trans.). New York: The Free Press.

Reid, B. V. (1984). An anthropological reinterpretation of Kohlberg's stages of moral development. *Human Development, 27,* 56–74.

Reid, B. V. (1989). Socialization for moral reasoning: Maternal strategies of Samoans and Europeans in New Zealand. In J. Valsiner (Ed.), *Child development in cultural context.* Toronto: Hogrefe and Huber.

Turiel, E. (1983) *The development of social knowledge: Morality and convention.* Cambridge, UK: Cambridge University Press.

Turiel, E., Smetana, J., & Killen, M. (1991). Social context in social cognitive development. In W. M. Kurtines & J. L. Gewirtz (Eds.), *Handbook of moral behavior and development: Vol. 2, Research.* Hillsdale, NJ: Erlbaum.

Walker, L. J. (1988). The development of moral reasoning. *Annals of Child Development, 55,* 677–691.

Chapter 7

Helping Children Develop Social Competence

Objectives

After studying this chapter, the student should be able to:

- Define social competence and self-regulation
- Describe the four RPCs of behaviour guidance
- State the steps used to help children resolve conflicts
- Describe behaviours that create challenges for individuals and the group
- Discuss strategies for helping children change their behaviour

Profile

For several years the Downtown Alternative School in Toronto has been using a Peacemaking model to assist children and empower them with strategies to find peaceful solutions to conflicts. From junior kindergarten on, children are taught the language of feelings. When children have to deal with small conflicts like someone taking something away from them without asking, they learn to use "I" messages. "I feel upset when you take that away from me when I am using it, and I need you to give it back."

When an issue or conflict is bigger, like someone calling another person names or excluding someone from a group, children are encouraged to follow a formal process of peacemaking. The children choose a peacemaker who helps facilitate empathetic listening and solution seeking. Any child could be a peacemaker. With practice and modelling from staff, children have internalized the process of identifying problems, engaging in dialogue to discuss problems, and exploring possible solutions.

"Peacemakers intervene actively; they do not take power away from participants (by bossing them), but rather exercise a new kind of power with them by collaboratively working through the conflict within the agreed-upon framework."

The DAS Code of Behaviour

We treat other people the way we would like to be treated.
We respect each other's bodies and feelings.
We speak to each other without teasing, name calling, swearing, or threatening.
We listen to each other.
We try to see each other's point of view.
We cooperate with each other to solve problems.
We take responsibility for our behaviour.

DAS Code of Behaviour. Reprinted by permission of the Downtown Alternative School.

Social Competence and Self-Regulation

Making and keeping friends is of major importance to children during middle childhood. Those who lack social skills do not have friends, tend to exhibit aggressive or passive behaviour, have difficulties in school, and have emotional problems. On the other hand, children who have good social skills have lots of friends, get better grades, and will probably function more effectively as adults (Hartup, 1991). Middle childhood is an optimum time for helping children develop the skills they need to get along with others. At this age they have begun to develop empathy and can consider how others think and feel. At times they are willing to give up gratification of their own needs in order to do what a friend wants. They are learning self-control and take responsibility for behaving in ways that do not conflict with others' rights.

Social competence or prosocial behaviour refers to the ability to get along with others, listen to other viewpoints, understand the importance of establishing and following rules, and use empathy.

Self-regulation is the ability to manage one's own energy states, emotions, behaviours, and attention in ways that are socially acceptable and help achieve positive goals, such as maintaining good relationships, learning, and maintaining well-being (Shanker, 2012).

This involves emotional and cognitive self-regulation, both of which have the same neural roots. As children get older and their brains develop, they are better able to take control of their thinking and feelings, thus inhibiting certain impulses (Bodrova & Leong, 2008). It is particularly important to help children nourish these abilities at an early age.

Antisocial behaviour refers to disruptive behaviour, bothering others, fighting, and other forms of physical and verbal aggression (such as name calling and excluding others from a group).

social competence
getting along with others, listening to other viewpoints, understanding the importance of establishing and following rules, and using empathy

self-regulation
ability to recognize how one's own emotional and cognitive abilities can facilitate positive relationships

antisocial behaviour
disruptive behaviour, bothering others, fighting and other forms of physical and verbal aggression (name calling and excluding others from a group)

In the socialization process, at a young age children become part of the values, attitudes, and behavioural standards established by the social setting they are part of. At the same time, children progress into a stage of "values clarification." They need to be part of a social setting that creates an atmosphere in which children can discuss their thoughts and feelings openly. School-age child care professionals need to establish an atmosphere of trust, one where judgements of behaviour are reserved until all the facts of the situation are discussed.

The school-age program is an ideal place to help children learn how to make and keep friends. The atmosphere is less structured and more relaxed than that in the school classroom. There is time for group discussions or individual conversations. Effective school-age child care professionals are intentional about focusing on developing an environment that nurtures a sense of community, where people get along with one another, explore differences and various viewpoints, and at the same time experience principles of democracy, fairness, and justice. Children experience why it is important to have rules in their school-age program community, which later transfer into learning about the importance of laws for the general welfare and protection of individuals in their greater community.

While establishing a positive atmosphere of behaviour guidance that supports the continued development of self-regulation skills, professionals working with school-age children should include an additional curriculum to the 3 Rs of reading, writing, and arithmetic. The following framework of the four RPCs provides a foundation for establishing a socially and emotionally healthy program that is responsive to the children's developmental needs. These guidelines can assist school-age child care professionals in developing written policies regarding behaviour guidance practices and discipline procedures for dealing with challenging behaviours. These policies should be part of a parent handbook as well. Various provincial regulations require programs to establish behaviour-guidance policies.

A number of learning experiences related to understanding and exploring these concepts can be organized into games and other fun things to do.

Four Rs

Responsibility

School-age child care professionals have the ultimate responsibility to improve the quality of the social environment. They also have the responsibility to involve the children and parents in the process of establishing behavioural guidelines and practices. Although school-age child care professionals encourage the development of positive experiences with friendships, school-age children also need to develop a sense of **responsibility** in terms of how to regulate their own behaviour, recognize the impact of their behaviour on others, and develop strategies of self-control. At this stage children like to have certain responsibilities in their program, such as assisting staff with various tasks, like serving snack or setting up and cleaning up activity areas. Being a keen and careful observer is key to identifying possible causes of conflict. See the checklist for possible causes of conflict in Appendix E.

Rights

All individuals in the program need to know that they have the **right** to be themselves, to be listened to, to express their feelings in appropriate ways, to be treated with compassion, and to enjoy a general sense of happiness in their day-to-day experiences with

responsibility
professional duty of school-age child care professionals to promote and improve the quality of the social environment; also the children's ability to regulate their own behaviour, to recognize the impact of their behaviour on others, to practise strategies of self-control, and to take care of their physical environment

rights
to be oneself, to be listened to, to express one's feelings in appropriate ways, to be treated with compassion, and to enjoy a general sense of happiness

their friends. The school-age program should establish a fair and democratic setting where the rights of individuals to stand up for themselves in appropriate ways when they are involved in situations that feel uncomfortable to them are recognized.

Respect

It is essential to develop an atmosphere in a school-age program where everyone is treated with kindness and understanding regardless of their size, age, gender, or ethnic or cultural background. This extends into setting up practices whereby children learn to take care of their environment, including equipment and materials. Practising **respect** also assists school-age child care professionals in building a caring and supportive sense of community for the children and their families. Children learn to understand what it means to be a friend. Children need to be acknowledged in terms of their own strengths, talents, and the uniqueness that they each may offer to the program.

Rules

In keeping with establishing a cooperative and democratic climate in the school-age child care program, it is important to discuss a simple set of **rules** with the children. Get their input about what rules would be important to them. Rules should be established when the program is set up and should be reviewed regularly to ensure that children's needs are being met. Children should be part of this process at each stage so that they feel more commitment to the rules, understand the reasons for rules, and subsequently are able to follow those rules more easily.

Children find great comfort in rules, knowing that things will be fair and that they will feel safe in their social setting. It is a good idea to display rules in writing in a place where staff and children can refer to them. Even though rules are discussed at the beginning of the year, children need gentle positive reminders. Sometimes children "test the limits," and they may demonstrate negative behaviours in order to force adults to show them the boundaries. Staff need to be cautious about setting up too many rules and focus on only those rules that are necessary. Too many rules are hard for children to remember, and they will rebel. Also, consider the natural order of things in the environment or "built-in rules." For example, when you want to limit the number of children at an activity, set out the number of chairs at the table that would accommodate that activity comfortably. Set up the environment with clearly labelled shelves and buckets so that it is easy for children to put equipment and materials away.

Table 7-1 outlines some further guidelines for establishing and reinforcing appropriate behaviour in a school-age program.

respect
treating individuals with kindness and understanding regardless of size, age, gender, or ethnic or cultural background, plus taking care of toys, equipment, and the physical environment

rules
a simple set of guidelines that are developed with input from the children in order for everyone to feel safe and secure in their social setting

Table 7-1 ■ Guidelines for Establishing and Reinforcing Appropriate Behaviour

- *Realistic rules.* Establish rules that are easy to follow. Rather than "No talking in line," a more reasonable expectation would be "Talk softly in line." Limit waiting periods and transitions. No one likes to wait in a lineup for extended periods of time.

- *State rules positively.* The purpose of rules is to help children to know what to do, not what they did wrong. Instead of saying "Don't leave the games on the table," say "Put the games on the shelf when you are done with them."

- *Be sure rules are understandable.* Discuss what certain words might mean. Children might not understand what you mean when you say "Respect property." It is important to talk about what respect means, and also what property means. "Respect property" means "take care of our toys and equipment."

- *Understand the reasons for rules.* When adults explain the importance of rules and involve children in the process of making rules, children develop a sense of self-control. Talking about how laws and rules are made in a "grown-up" world helps children understand their importance.

- *Give gentle reminders.* Give children plenty of time to play at activities. Let them know in plenty of time when they need to make a transition to move to another room or activity. Clarify rules and expectations with them before entering into a particular setting or activity. This will need to be done a few times until the expected behaviour comes more naturally and routinely.

- *Reinforce rules and expectations consistently.* Children gain comfort in predictability. They need to trust that when a rule or expectation of behaviour is established you will follow through. Otherwise, they will feel vulnerable, mistrustful, and will often take matters into their own hands—causing more misbehaviour.

Guidelines for Establishing and Reinforcing Appropriate Behaviour. Adapted from Todd, C. M. (1992). Establishing rules. In Todd, C. M. (Ed.), *School-age connections*, 1(6), pp. 3–5. Urbana-Champaign, IL: University of Illinois Cooperative Extension Service. Used by permission of Christine M. Todd, University of Georgia.

Strategies

- Coach children to find more effective ways of behaving toward friends. Ask what behaviour causes friends to dislike or reject them. Discuss alternative behaviours and urge children to try them.

- Praise children for times they are successful while interacting with others.

- Model good social skills as you interact with colleagues and parents. The children will observe you and want to use you as a model for their own behaviour.

- Discuss with children the characteristics that foster friendships. Encourage them to discuss a time they had fun with a friend and what made it enjoyable. How did they and their friend act toward one another?

- Talk about what "respect" means.

- Discuss the laws and rules of the community and why it is important to follow them. Talk about what it means to have democratic rights.

Activities

■ Make a Friend

Purposes: *practise respectful interaction skills*
                demonstrate respectful approaches to other children

Facilitate mini-dramas of role playing, in which each child plans what he or she would do to make a friend. Play out the scene. At the end of the scene, discuss what happened and how the participants might have felt. Possible scenarios are the following:

You are playing a game of basketball with your friends, and a child you do not know stands at the side watching. Your friends think he is too little to play.

A new girl comes into your classroom. She has just moved into the neighbourhood from another part of the city. Your best friend whispers that she is "kinda ugly 'cause she's too fat."

A new family moves into the house next door to you. You see that they have twins who look about your age. You are a little shy but would like to have somebody next door to play with.

■ Getting to Know You

Purposes: *develop friendship skills*
increase respect and awareness of similarities and differences between people

Encourage children to get to know others in the program. Make a roster with children's names and pictures. Or make a book with a page for each child. Information on the page can include a picture, the names of family members, the child's birthday, the child's likes and dislikes, or whatever she chooses to say about herself. Leave the book in a place where children and parents can look through it.

For a more extensive project, have the children make an individual book all about themselves. The purpose of this book is to provide helpful information for the adults who work with these children. (See Appendix A for reproducible pages that can be used for this purpose.)

■ Best Friends Are _____

Purposes: *identify characteristics of friendships*
practise communicating appreciation for friends

At group time, tell the children that the topic for discussion is "What makes a friend?" You might relate that when you were their age, you had a best friend, and one of the things you liked about that person was _____.

Encourage the children to tell one thing they like about one of their friends. Write down the characteristics they describe on chartpaper. Encourage each child to add to the discussion while the rest of the group listens. Read the list and ask the children to think about how many of the characteristics they have themselves. Conclude the discussion with ways they can become more like the best friend they want for themselves.

■ Group Caring Project

Purposes: *increase responsibility*
foster feelings of empathy for others

Involve the entire group in planning and implementing a caring project. It can be raising money for a worthy cause, getting involved in a community cleanup drive, or visiting a retirement home. Allow the children to research community needs, then choose a project. Have them plan ways to implement their ideas. Encourage them to assign tasks and coordinate ways to follow through. When the project is completed, evaluate what they learned and what they might have done differently.

These are some of the ways you can encourage children to feel better about themselves and learn to function effectively in a group. However, in spite of all your efforts, you may find that some children are still troublesome to themselves and their peers. These children may need extra thought and care.

Four Ps

Power

School-age children need to feel a sense of "appropriate power" that they typically do not feel in an "adult world." They will often use negative ways to assert their **power** by playing super-hero roles, playing with toy guns, and exerting aggressive actions that are imitated from violent movie or television images they have seen. Children need positive ways to "feel powerful." They need opportunities to have a say in the contents of their program, to make choices of activities, to have a say in the rules of the program, and to solve their own problems with adult assistance. They need to be in a climate that makes them feel "in control," not "being controlled."

power
appropriate ways for children to feel that they have some say about activities and practices in their program

A primary goal in guiding children's behaviour is for them to have a chance to develop independence and control over their own behaviour.

One way to facilitate this feeling of "appropriate power" is by planning group meetings. Children can work with school-age child care professionals to discuss problems, share ideas and feelings, and propose and choose solutions. These meetings can be scheduled on a regular basis, perhaps at the beginning of each day of the program, or they can happen quite spontaneously, as the need arises (Adams & Sasse Wittmer, 2001, pp. 11–12). These meetings provide an opportunity to have discussions with the children about what it means to be powerful—to have "power with" versus "power over" others (see Table 7-2).

Children need to feel that they are in "positions of power." This can be done by assigning them to different tasks or responsibilities, such as serving snack or setting up and putting away equipment and materials. Some children, especially the older ones, may be interested in helping staff in other parts of the child care centre, such as the toddler or preschool programs. It is important to be aware of school-age children's developmental needs (Table 7-3) in nurturing their feeling of "power."

Table 7-2 ■ You Are Powerful When You

- Help each other.
- Make a new friend.
- Say you're sorry.
- Try to get along with each other.
- Share toys, games, and equipment.
- Ask for help.
- Talk through problems and conflict.
- Say how you feel.
- Invite others to play with you.
- Ask if you can join the group.
- Help someone who is hurt or sad.

Adapted from *Teaching young children in violent times, building a peaceable classroom*, 2nd ed. (p. 142), by D. Levin, 2003, Washington DC: NAEYC.

Table 7-3 ■ School-Age Children's Needs

- to have a recognized identity
- to feel a sense of autonomy
- to make choices and make decisions
- to be independent and have a degree of freedom
- to feel competent
- to interact with peers and develop friendships

Positive Self-Image

Figure 7-1 ■ Children who have a good self-image behave in acceptable ways.

Self-image has two components: our perceptions of ourselves and the perceptions conveyed to us by others. Throughout a lifetime, self-image changes as physical abilities evolve, cognitive functions change, and interactions with others are refined. During middle childhood, self-image is tied closely to feelings of competence. Children compare themselves to their contemporaries in terms of physical abilities, academic success, and popularity with their peers. Evaluations of themselves are sometimes realistic and at other times radically unrealistic. In addition, adult attitudes and behaviours play a significant role in how children feel about themselves. Adults need to recognize how different personalities and temperaments "fit" with their own expectations of behaviour. Some children are easygoing, others are more impulsive, and some are slow to warm up. When adults react positively to them, children feel they are valued and therefore have self-worth and a **positive self-image.** At times, adults will approach children only if they approach them first. Especially for children who are "slow to warm up," adults may need to take the first step to make the child feel welcome.

How children feel about themselves has a direct effect upon their behaviour. If they like themselves and see that others react positively to them, they behave in ways that gain further approval. If children have negative perceptions of themselves, they may use unpopular tactics to gain attention or satisfy their needs. This solidifies each child's perception of himself as someone who is unlikable or who cannot succeed. Therefore, it is essential that anyone who works with children convey attitudes that help, rather than hinder, children in the development of their identity and self-esteem.

positive self-image

good image of oneself as well as good feelings based on perceptions conveyed by others

Peacemaking

There are a number of approaches found in communities today that outline how to promote a healthy emotional, social, and nonviolent climate in the classroom. This may take the form of training some children to be "mediators," "peacemakers," or "conflict managers" who assist other children with conflicts. Sometimes a "peace table" is used as a location for discussing problems, exploring feelings, and deciding on solutions. The Fussbusters program uses this approach. The day after the program was introduced in Head Start programs, and the children had tried it out, they sat together to develop a list of rules and procedures that were then posted at the peace table. The children listed some of these **peacemaking** guidelines in their own words as follows:

peacemaking

a program approach that is used to promote a healthy emotional, social, and nonviolent climate

1. Keep your hands and feet to yourself.
2. No name calling.
3. No put-downs.

4. Talk things over.
5. One person talks at a time.
6. Ask for help.
7. Work the problems out.
8. Talk about how you feel. (Wilson, Gillespie & Chick, Childhood Education, 2001, pp. 192–197)

Problem Solving

"The classroom climate improves as incidences of aggression and victimization decrease and positive social skills are promoted" (Adams & Sasse Wittmer, 2001, p. 10). The social **problem-solving** model is one that children begin to use in their preschool years. As children progress in terms of their cognitive capabilities, they become better at focusing on more than one aspect of a situation at a time and can then consider more than one point of view.

problem solving
the ability to focus on more than one aspect of a situation at a time, to consider more than one point of view, to generate and agree on solutions and implement them

They understand that more than one attribute defines a category. For example, a child will begin to understand that "If I tell my friend John that I didn't like it when he took my hockey cards without my permission, he will still be my friend."

School-age children begin to think more abstractly and can make logical causal connections between events. In this way, they are better able to follow the basic steps of solving problems: defining the problem; listening to different viewpoints; sharing feelings; generating possible solutions; agreeing on a solution; and following through with the evaluation of the chosen solution.

School-age children are also better able to distinguish between reality and fantasy. They can separate what they see on television and movies from real-life situations. They then have more realistic fears and may feel more vulnerable in the face of possible disasters like tornados, hurricanes, and terrorism. Adults need to have discussions to increase understanding about disasters and periodically practise drills with children in order for them to know what to do if they face these kinds of situations. In this way children can feel some sense of control, feel safe, and carry on with their day-to-day activities.

Strategies

- Develop a genuine interest in every child. Find opportunities to spend time with children individually. Get to know them, listen to them, and try to understand their concerns. Offer help when needed, but also support their ability to find their own solutions to problems.

- Be open to individual styles, personalities, and temperaments of children.

- Recognize every child's unique qualities and respect their differences. Eliminate prejudice or bias in your own thinking or in the behaviours of the children. Ensure that all activities are nonracist and nonbiased.

- Support self-esteem by involving children in intrinsically meaningful activities. Plan challenging projects in which children and adults work together and in which children develop skills and gain knowledge. As they acquire skills and feel more competent, children's belief in their own self-worth increases.

- Conduct group meetings that allow all children to ask questions, express concerns, discuss problems, or make plans. During group meetings there should be a peaceful exchange of ideas that encourage a problem-solving process. Each contribution should be shown respect and consideration, and children should learn to consider all sides of an issue.

- Provide many ways for children to feel a sense of "power." Offer a variety of activities appropriate for children at different developmental levels. In that way, all children will be able to choose, according to their needs, some activities that are easy for them and others that offer a challenge. Writing and illustrating a simple story is a fairly easy task for nine- or ten-year-olds. Older children might tackle the more difficult task of writing a play complete with dialogue.

Activities

■ Puppet Talk—Role Play

Purposes: *practise problem-solving skills*
                    increase organizational skills and a sense of power
                    provide an outlet for the expression of ideas and feelings
                    explore fairy tales and stories from other cultures

Set up a puppet stage. Provide books of fairy tales, fables, or stories from other cultures. Assist children in writing scripts using the stories from the books or a story of their own devising as the framework. Make available materials and instructions for making puppets. Chapter 11 has some suggestions for making puppets.

■ Getting to Know Me

Purposes: *increase self-esteem*
                    understand how people are alike and different
                    communicate each person's uniqueness to others
                    develop appreciation for others' individual traits

Figure 7-2 ■ Children want to get along with each other.

Ask children to bring things from home that are special to them and that represent who they are. These may be things they like to collect, photos of special people, or mementos of special occasions in their life. The objects must be small enough to fit into a shoe box.

Provide each child with a box, and distribute materials they can use to decorate their box. Wallpaper pieces, wrapping paper, construction paper, collage materials, paint, marking pens, and pictures from magazines are examples.

Allow time at group meetings to have each child show the items from her box and explain why they have special meaning to her.

■ Picture Problems

Purposes: *increase ability to understand (decode) non-verbal communications in pictures recognize and accept others' points of view practise with problem solving and group decision making*

Glue pictures of people in a problem situation onto the front of a large manila envelope. You can find pictures in magazines, colouring books, discarded newspapers, and posters. Have children work in groups of three. Give each group a picture and some paper. Ask them to reach an agreement about the problem portrayed in the picture, then write a description of it. Tell them to put their paper into the envelope and then pass it on to the next group until all groups have looked at all the pictures. Allow three minutes for each picture.

Collect the envelopes. Read each of the descriptions. Discuss how different groups saw the problem differently.

■ *Come on Up*

Purposes: *increase awareness of others' feelings*
        foster group cohesiveness
        practise problem solving

This game is the opposite of "King of the Hill." One child stands at the top of a hill, then one by one asks others to join. The object is to get everyone onto the hill without anyone falling off. (If no hill is available, use a mat.)

Discuss what they had to do to keep everyone together at the top of the hill. How did it make them feel to be included? How did it make them feel if they fell off and could not be included? See Chapter 10 for other cooperative games.

Four Cs

Cooperation/Compassion

Cooperation with others does not come easily to children. As infants, toddlers, and young preschoolers, they are intensely egocentric. During those years their main concern is satisfying their own needs and achieving their own goals with little focus on the needs of others. Gradually, during middle childhood, cognitive development enables children to see others more clearly, and they begin to understand that others have needs, too. When others' needs conflict with their own, they learn to compromise and cooperate in order to have friends. Key factors in helping children to learn cooperative behaviours are supportive parents and well-qualified staff in the school-age program. Provide opportunities for children to work together to achieve a common goal. This gives children a chance to discuss and share ideas; to take on leadership and follower roles, and to listen to various viewpoints.

As children work together, they develop some sense of **compassion**. They learn to respect each others' differences and unique personalities, and begin to understand the feelings of others. They learn to treat others as they would like to be treated. They learn that name-calling, harmful teasing, and laughing at others for their ideas is not productive and doesn't provide for a pleasant and cooperative atmosphere.

Consequences

Child development professionals agree that children learn best from **natural consequences.** An example of this in a school-age program would be when a child cheats

cooperation
ability to work together to achieve a common goal

compassion
respect of differences and unique personalities, and understanding the feelings of others

natural consequences
results of one's behaviour that have an implicit effect on another's reaction; allows children to learn from their actions

at a game of cards and later the children don't want that child to play such games with them anymore. This would be an important time for the school-age child care professionals to discuss the problem with the child and help him understand how his behaviour of cheating affects others.

logical consequences

a tool for changing behaviour in which the result of a child's misbehaviour is related to the behaviour

Logical consequences can be identified where natural consequences don't connect easily. An example would be telling a child who is careless with putting sports equipment away that if she does not put the sports equipment back after using it, she will not be able to use it and will have to find another activity to do. Consequences should not be presented as a punishment, but more in terms of assisting children with understanding what happens if we don't follow expectations or the rules that are set in place for the program. Often children at this age do not understand their actions much beyond their own needs at any one time. For example, in the situation discussed above, staff could pose a question to the child who doesn't want to put the equipment away after she has used it. "What would happen if we didn't put the sports equipment back in the storage room after we are finished with it at the end of the day?" The child may respond, "It may get stolen, and we will not have it to play with the next day." Logical consequences encourage children to think through their actions, make predictions, "think outside the box," and find alternative actions to their problem. This is a nonpunitive approach, one that teaches children about what is appropriate behaviour in various situations rather than focusing on the negative behaviour. After discussing the logical consequences of a negative situation, it is hoped that next time the child encounters a similar situation she will understand why she needs to act in an appropriate way.

Communication

The ways in which adults respond verbally to children's behaviour can either increase the likelihood of repetitions or bring about changes in behaviour. It is normal to become exasperated with children's behaviour, particularly at the end of a difficult day. The tendency is then to respond with anger, generalizations, or labelling. At one time or another most adults have made comments such as, "Dominic, why are you always getting into fights?" or "Marila, you're such a loudmouth." These kinds of verbal responses may momentarily relieve the adult's angry feelings, but they do nothing to help the child change. In fact, they may bring about the opposite, a tendency for the child to repeat the behaviour. The child knows how to irritate the adult and takes pleasure in doing it again or may feel the negative label gives him status with his peers. School-age child care professionals can learn to respond in ways that are appropriate to the situation and that will help children gradually change their behaviour.

Acknowledge the Range of Children's Feelings

Often adults respond to children's expressions of their feelings, such as sadness and anger, by denying their existence or trying to change the feelings. Constant denial of feelings or a rush to change them makes children distrust their own inner senses.

Example Callan has been lying on the book-area pillows since getting off the bus from school. One of the staff members wants her to get involved and asks why she does not find something to do. Callan answers by saying: "Can't you see I'm tired?"

Here is an inappropriate response:

Adult: "How can you be tired when you haven't done anything yet?"

An appropriate response might be:

Adult: "Yes, I know some days at school are tiring. You decide when you're rested and ready to do something."

Describe the Situation

Children are sometimes unaware of all aspects of a situation. They are concentrating on achieving their own goals and are oblivious to anything else.

Example It is cleanup time before a field trip, and there are still materials that have not been put away.

Here is an inappropriate response:

Adult: "You guys haven't finished cleaning up, so maybe you won't be ready to go on the trip. Why are you always such slobs?"

An appropriate response might be:

Adult: "I can still see some puzzles on the table and some paints that need to go into the sink. The bus will be here in five minutes, so let's all be ready."

Figure 7-3 ■ **It helps to acknowledge a child's feelings rather than deny them.**

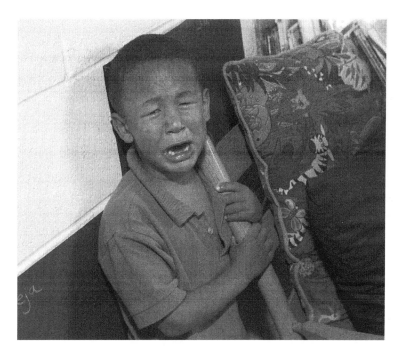

▦ *Angry Body Drawing*

Purpose: *To recognize areas in the body where one might feel anger.*

Talk about signals in our bodies when we get angry. Children can draw their own bodies and mark where they experience these angry feelings, such as a red face, shaking, heart beating faster, clenched fists, tight muscles, etc. Share situations where children were really angry.

▦ *The Raging Volcano*

Purpose: *To understand how anger builds up and how to calm down and think through the process.*

As a group, make a volcano out of clay or papier-mache. Mix baking soda, vinegar, and red food colouring in your volcano. Talk about situations that make the children angry. Talk about ways to handle anger and strategies of calming down so the children don't lose control.

Help Children Recognize How Their Behaviour Affects Others

Until children reach a stage of maturity at which they are less egocentric, they often fail to understand that what they do affects others.

Example Two girls are beginning to dress up with some costumes that are kept in a large trunk. Shari pulls out a white dress and says that she wants to be a princess and wear it. Khaya looks at her and tells her she can't be a princess because she is too fat.

Here is an inappropriate response:
Adult: "Hey, you girls. No name calling."
An appropriate response might be:
Adult: "Shari, how did it make you feel when Khaya said you couldn't be a princess?"
Another appropriate response might be:
Adult: "Khaya, when you tell Shari she cannot be a princess because of the shape of her body, it really hurts her feelings. Did you notice how she quickly put away the dress and looked like she was about to cry? Everyone's body is different, including princesses'."

Encourage children to recognize wrongdoings and find ways to recognize others' feelings and apologize for hurting others' feelings. Apologies should be genuine and meaningful and not be just a routine of "I did something wrong so I have to say I'm sorry." At this stage, children have a better understanding about what it means to say "I'm sorry." This may involve a letter of apology sent to the one who has been hurt, or it might involve doing a special deed for the person. School-age child care professionals should help the children to understand the connection between the wrongdoing and the apology.

Give praise for positive behaviour, but be careful not to overdo it. Be sure to keep your messages genuine and fitting within the language and experiences of the school-age children. For example, giving a "high-five," by clapping the palm of your hand with the palm of a child's hand is a good way to show your appreciation for a job well done. Remember that the positive atmosphere that you create by greeting the children at the beginning of the program and asking them how their school day was goes a long way in modelling good **communication** skills. Being part of their ongoing conversations and talking with them on a one-to-one basis makes them feel important, rather than just talking to them when "trouble" breaks out.

communication

ways that individuals respond verbally and nonverbally to each other

Conflict Resolution

Children are growing up in a world where they may witness violence almost every day. They learn ways of dealing with conflict by watching the adults they see at home, in their neighbourhoods, on TV, and at school. Often adults behave in ways they really do not want children to imitate. Yet, children often "try on" behaviours they observe in others and only gradually learn to resolve conflicts in more effective ways. Preschool children will call upon adults to intervene in resolving disputes. School-age children gradually learn to negotiate a compromise, bargain, or use humour to lessen angry feelings. However, at times those strategies do not work, and children resort to fighting.

Violence is a confrontational and harmful way of settling disputes for children and adults. The act can be physical, verbal, or emotional. These methods of settling disputes are counterproductive. Violence often escalates until serious injury or death results. However, violence is only one of the styles people use to resolve conflicts. Avoidance is also frequently used. When confronted with a difficult situation, the person turns away, withdraws completely, or is silent. This method does not resolve the conflict but only internalizes the angry feelings. After repeated incidents, the anger may intensify until it erupts either in violent behaviour or displays of anger out of proportion to the particular situation. The most effective way of dealing with conflicts is problem solving, yet many adults and children find it difficult to do.

In many ways, conflicts are a normal part of life. A conflict is defined as a dispute or disagreement between two or more people (see Box 7-1).

It may be somewhat unrealistic to believe that one could completely eliminate conflict in a school-age program. In reality, we face conflicts every day. Therefore it would be important for children to learn strategies of how to deal with conflicts. Children will feel more empowered and develop more self-control if they know what to do when they face a conflict situation.

Conflict resolution is a process of mediating between children who are not getting along in a way that helps them to think situations through for themselves, make decisions, and solve problems (Haas-Foletta & Cogley, 1990, p. 27).

The process of conflict resolution involves mediation. **Mediation** is a process in which a person who is not involved in the conflict (the mediator) helps those who are in a conflict. The mediator does not act like a judge and doesn't decide how to resolve the conflict. The mediator helps the people in the conflict come up with their own solutions (Edwards, 1989, p. 43).

The process is a "win-win" vs. a "win-lose" approach. It is collaborative, not competitive, and requires children to work together. It focuses on the needs and interests of both parties and promotes open communication. The children leave the conflict feeling that there are two winners as opposed to a winner and a loser (Edwards, 1989, p. 18).

Negotiating is a strategy that is also involved in the process of trying to resolve differences. Ongoing discussions about thoughts, ideas, and feelings bring about a cooperative problem-solving process, whereby children attempt to come to some agreements.

School-age child care professionals can help children go through the steps necessary to resolve their conflicts so that each feels validated and empowered. Initially, adults in a program may be the mediator. Through the process of modelling, teaching, and learning, children will eventually become mediators for each other. All parties should be satisfied that they have been heard, that their feelings have been considered, and that the solution is mutually agreeable. When all parties are gathered, the adult can facilitate a discussion that takes the children through the following steps:

1. *Decide to resolve the conflict.* All the children involved in the dispute must agree to solve the problem. "I am willing to try to settle this argument." Set some ground rules:
   a. Each is committed to solving the problem.
   b. One person talks at a time; be truthful.
   c. Name calling and put-downs are not permitted.
   d. Confidentiality is agreed upon; keep what's discussed in the group

conflict resolution
process of mediating between arguing children in a way that helps them to think situations through for themselves, make decisions, and solve problems

mediation
process in which a person who is not involved in the conflict (the mediator) helps those who are in a conflict to come up with their own solutions

negotiating
strategy that involves ongoing discussions about thoughts, ideas, and feelings and emphasizes cooperative problem solving to assist in resolving differences

---

Box 7-1

Definition of Conflict:

... a struggle between opposing principles or aims

... a clash of feelings and interest

Webster's Encyclopedic Dictionary of the English Language, Canadian Edition. (1988). New York: Lexicon Publications, Inc.

Chapter 7   Helping Children Develop Social Competence

Figure 7-4 ■ Children working together to solve a problem.

2. Each child tells what happened; identify the problem
   a. Use "I" messages. "I get mad when you …" "I am unhappy when …" "I feel sad when …"
   b. Describe exactly what happened.
   c. Relate how each felt about the incident.
   d. Listen to what the other person has to say.

   Example: "I was waiting for my turn at the CD player, but she grabbed it. I got mad because she does that all the time." "I had been waiting a long time, and I didn't know she was, too. I was surprised she got so mad at me."

3. Each child states what he or she needs to resolve the conflict.
   a. Be specific; use "I" messages.
   b. Listen to the other person's needs.

   Example: "I just want to have a turn so that I can play the music I like." "I don't always want to hear what she likes."

4. Explore possible ways of solving the conflict.
   a. Brainstorm options.
   b. Evaluate the suggestions.
   c. Decide which will be satisfactory to both parties.

   Example: "Let's think of ways to solve this problem." "Will that solution satisfy both of you?"

5. After an interval of time, get the children together to determine whether the solution is working or whether a new approach should be considered.

   Example: "How has it been working to have a sign-up sheet and a timer for using the CD player?" The adults can be powerful motivators to help children change their behaviour so they can become part of a group, feel good about themselves, and achieve their personal goals. The process may be difficult along the way, but it helps to remember that change takes time and effort.

Strategies

- Model cooperative behaviour, or what parents call "setting a good example." When children see adults helping others, being kind or compassionate, and assisting others to achieve their goals, they see how it can be done. They have a model to follow when confronted with situations in their own daily activities. Conversely, children will also imitate selfishness, cruelty, and noncooperative behaviours they observe in adults.

- Emphasize cooperation rather than competition. During middle childhood, children are striving to succeed at whatever they attempt and constantly compare themselves to others. They want to be the "best, the first, or the fastest." Some competitiveness is inevitable because many of the sports that are popular among youngsters are based on someone winning and someone losing. Competitiveness cannot be avoided, but it can be minimized by staff. Each child can be recognized for his or her participation during the game, rather than praising only the winner. In addition, there should also be games that do not involve someone emerging as the winner. Several of the games described in Chapter 10 require cooperation and do not have a real victor.

- Design space to accommodate groups of varying sizes. When children play in proximity to others, they are forced to compromise or to engage in negotiations concerning the use of space or materials. Space should not be so limited, however, that children feel crowded, for that causes tension and squabbling. Within the workspace, materials should be close at hand, adequate in number for all to share, and stored in an uncluttered manner. In this way children can work comfortably and with fewer conflicts.

- Develop more cooperative behaviour by leading discussions about sharing, fairness, taking turns, and negotiating when working together. They can use examples from daily occurrences or hypothetical situations. As an example, fairness is an important issue for school-age children, and conflicts occur frequently. A sensitive school-age child care professional will use these situations to discuss what happened, why a situation may have seemed unfair, or what the children can do differently next time. It is also important to help children become aware of the fact that sometimes one child or another has needs that may seem to take precedence over her own. Equity does not always mean fairness but implies that each child's needs will be met to the greatest extent possible. Equity should be part of the philosophical approach in a school-age program.

- Include activities that require children to work cooperatively toward a common goal. A good example is the production of a play. An entire group could work on this kind of project with some children writing the script, and others making costumes, taking roles, designing stage sets, or directing the final presentation. Another example is producing a newsletter. Children have to work together to gather news, write articles, decide upon format, and print and distribute the paper. Both of these projects require a great deal of discussion, negotiation, and compromise and can be effective techniques for helping children to develop those skills.

- Increase children's ability to read nonverbal cues from others. Sometimes a look or gesture is misinterpreted, and an argument ensues. When an altercation takes place, encourage the participants to discuss what they saw and what they thought it meant. If there has been a misunderstanding, help them to clarify their meaning. Does ignoring an invitation to play just mean "I didn't hear you," or does it mean "I don't want to play right now. Go away"? Does an angry look mean, "He's mad at me about something" or "He had a bad day at school"?

- Let children know that sometimes we do get angry at one another. It can be scary at times when someone is angry. Encourage them to use "I" messages to explain their feelings, recognize the degree of anger within themselves and others, and put their actions into a positive context by being direct and honest.

- Help children to see that others may have a different view. Use discussions to let all children express their own perspectives or state their own needs. One way to accomplish this is to involve children in planning parts of the program. They may all have good ideas based on their own interests or what is most important to them. Each contribution should be accepted and valued even though it may not be put into action.

- Provide many opportunities for children to learn by trial and error. They have to practise conflict negotiation and ways to cooperate with one another.

- Write notes to children who have a history with difficult behaviour to recognize them as being important people who are valued and cared for.

Activities

▉ Silent Stories

Purposes: practice in reading nonverbal cues
             increase understanding that others have different points of view

Have children work in pairs. Tell them to use nonverbal ways to tell their partner something about themselves. For instance, they can use gestures to tell their age or things they are interested in. Facial expressions can be used to indicate something that makes them mad or sad. Set a time limit of 5 or 10 minutes. At the end of that time, each child tries to relate to the other what has been learned. Have them clarify any misinformation and discuss another way they might have conveyed the information.

▉ Shopping Trip

Purposes: practice in working together as a group
             develop decision-making skills
             resolve conflicts effectively

Divide the children into groups of three. Give each group a catalogue. Tell them they have $100 to spend buying presents for a boy and girl who are both nine years old. Explain that they all must agree on what to buy. Set a time limit. When they make their decision, they can cut out the pictures and paste them on a sheet of paper.

Have each group share their choices. Ask children about the problems they encountered and how they resolved them. Why did they make the choices they did?

▉ Brainstorming

Purposes: foster divergent thinking skills
             strengthen ability to negotiate conflicts
             amplify group cohesiveness

Tell children that many great inventions are the result of a group of people getting together to create something new. You might remind them that it takes numerous scientists and engineers to design and build space vehicles. Divide the children into groups of four. Tell them they are going to invent a new bicycle. Give each group a piece of paper, and tell them to assign one member to write down ideas. When they have several designs, ask them to choose one that should be built. Set a time limit of 10 minutes.

Let each group relate their ideas to the entire group. Discuss the value or difficulties of creating as a group. How did they decide on the design that should be built?

▧ Sculpture

Purposes: *provide opportunity for sharing ideas*
           increase ability to work under time pressure
           strengthen conflict-resolution skills

Divide the children into groups of three. Give each group a pile of toothpicks, some glue, a piece of styrofoam, and some small corks. Tell each group that they are to make a single sculpture. Each member gets to help decide what to make and to participate in the construction. Set a time limit. (You can also use other objects: clay, blocks, beads, etc., as suggested in Chapter 11.) Have each group share their sculpture.

Discuss how they decided what to make. What kinds of conflicts were encountered? How did they resolve the conflict?

Changing Children's Behaviour

Helping children reverse recurring cycles of behaviour that interfere with reaching the goals they set for themselves is one of the most important tasks for staff in school-age programs. The challenge is to stop harmful or destructive behaviours; encourage children to act in ways that others approve of, thus enhancing their self-esteem; assist children with developing self-control; allow children to express themselves clearly; and help them learn skills of problem solving and conflict resolution. This is a process that can take a long time. It is easy for staff to get discouraged when changes in behaviour do not occur readily. It is important to help children set realistic goals for making changes in their behaviour, to talk about a step-by-step process of achieving these goals, to celebrate successes, and to involve other people in the children's lives, such as their parents and teachers in the school, in the process.

Stopping destructive behaviour begins with a clear understanding of the children and trying to find the reasons behind the behaviour. This requires staff to practise skills of keen observation along with diplomatic discussions with parents and teachers. Here are some guidelines for questions to ask when exploring the reasons behind disruptive behaviours:

Figure 7-5 ▧ Hitting or hurting another person is never an acceptable response to anger.

- What kinds of stressors are happening for the child at home? Are there some changes in the child's regular family routines, such as moving, a new sibling, parent separation, or divorce?

- What methods is the child familiar with regarding regulation of his behaviour? Is the child familiar with practices of problem solving and conflict resolution or is he more used to external controls and rewards of behaviour?

- What is the child's overall temperament? Does she approach situations impulsively or does she take time to think before she acts?

- What is the overall physical and emotional well-being of the child? Does he experience any health conditions such as allergies, sleep problems, or eating disorders?

- What is happening between the child and her peers? Is the child accepted or rejected by her peers? Does she have a significant friend?

- What is happening in the child's school life? Is he feeling some success in his academic work or is his experiencing some difficulties?

Mistaken Goals

Behaviour is often a result of mistaken goals on the part of the children. Certain behaviours, such as stealing, telling lies, being defiant, hitting others, swearing, and fighting, cause adults to feel and react in certain ways: annoyed, angry, hurt, helpless, or defeated. It is important for staff to put their feelings into words along with helping children to do the same. When school-age child care professionals identify their feelings clearly to the children, the children will learn to do this as well. For example, in a power-struggle situation, the adult should overcome the impulse to respond angrily or give in and instead try to gain the child's cooperation by giving the child power in situations where she can use it productively. (See the National Network for Child Care, http://www.nncc.org/Guidance/sac33_behav.mgmt.stress.html, for examples of mistaken goals by the child, how adults feel in reaction to the behaviour, and what adults should do.)

Individual Contracts

Sometimes there are particular behaviour situations where, within the process of communication and problem solving, the school-age child care professional should meet privately with the child. During this conference-style meeting, the child and school-age child care professional discuss the problem, relate feelings, and identify possible solutions and desired changes in behaviour. At this time it may be fitting to compile a contract. The contract would clearly identify the desired change in behaviour, steps to achieve the behaviour, and a short timetable of desired outcomes. School-age children often enjoy printing and signing a contract. It makes them feel important and gives them power and control in changing their own behaviour (Borman Fink, 1995, p. 37). See Appendix G for an example of an individual contract.

Alternatives to Time-Out

Time-out is a frequent response to children who exhibit unacceptable behaviour, such as aggression, toward another child. The child who misbehaved is removed from an activity area and expected to sit by himself for a specified period of time. He is told to cool off and to think about what he did. This process of adults imposing a time-out on children is directive, controlling, and a punitive approach to guiding behaviour. Opponents of time-out argue that it damages children's self-esteem by punishing, embarrassing, and humiliating the child in front of his peers. Some critics say that time-out may worsen the problem by increasing the child's anger and anxiety. Time-out brings focus to the negative behaviour and may inadvertently reinforce such negative attention–seeking behaviour (Kaiser & Rasminsky, 1999, p. 31). It is an approach that doesn't fit within the overall goals of assisting children to develop self-control, problem-solving skills, and identify and relate their feelings. Staff resort to time-out as a quick fix. It stops the behaviour at the time but does little to assist the child with understanding his behaviour and implementing strategies to effect change.

A better approach for staff to take in difficult behaviour situations where someone is getting hurt is to

1. Stop the behaviour, separate the individuals involved.
2. Stay calm and take a deep breath.
3. Assess whether the children need a cooling-off time for a few minutes.
4. Get the children back together.
5. Avoid prejudging the situation; get the facts.
6. Consider the options.
7. Accept strong feelings of anger, which are natural reactions.
8. Listen, then help children put their feelings into words.
9. Mediate and problem solve.

Other Strategies

- Allow children to express their feelings in ways that are not hurtful to others. Because some children may not be able to put their feelings into words, a discussion with a caring adult sometimes helps them to find acceptable ways to relieve the feelings. Some children may need active ways to relieve feelings, particularly anger. Provide them with pillows to pound or a place to run.

- Help children devise additional ways to act on their feelings of empathy by discussing possible ways to behave. Their own limited experiences may not be enough for them to know what to do, and fear of failing may prevent them from acting. "Let's think of some ways to help a friend who is having a difficult day."

- Create a non-aggressive environment. Physically, provide plenty of spaces to play and enough age-appropriate materials so that children can engage in activities with minimal conflict. Socially, adults and children should focus on supporting and respecting others, offering encouragement when needed. Wherever possible, make it clear that aggressive behaviour gets negative results.

- Encourage children to appreciate random acts of kindness.

- Help children through transitions, letting them know ahead of time what the expected behaviours need to be.

- Be consistent. School-age child care professionals need to communicate with each other on how behaviours are to be handled.

- Help children find appropriate outlets for their feelings, such as painting, playing a musical instrument, jogging, or writing poetry.

Build Positive, Supportive Relationships

Parents and families are your best allies. Show interest in the children's families. Ask them about the activities their children are interested in. Ask parents to share any issues or changes that are occurring in the child's home life. Be open and receptive to the parents' daily challenges of juggling the demands of work, home, and child care. Establish written policies of guiding behaviour that can be included in a parent handbook, which may also be used. It is also important to communicate with the teachers and the principal of the school. Obtain a permission form from the parents to allow you to hold discussions about their child with professionals in the school setting. This is best done at enrolment time. Most parents view this exchange of information between the school and the school-age program to be appropriate and to be in the best interests of the child. The Freedom of Information and Protection of Privacy Act, 1989, requires that parents give written permission when personal information regarding their children is shared between school-age child care professionals and the school. See Appendix F for a permission form for exchange of information.

Building positive, supportive relationships with parents, siblings, grandparents, and school staff is an important part of an overall philosophy of cooperation, democracy, and respect for one another in a school-age program. Children notice responsive, caring adults and as a result will emulate these behaviours and continue to seek positive as opposed to negative attention (Fox, Dunlop, et al., 2003, p. 49).

Behaviours That Create Challenges for the Individual or the Group

Even with knowledge of child development and good intentions, school-age child care professionals often find they are baffled by the behaviour of one or more children in their group. These are the children who exhibit similar behaviours to other children, but their behaviour has increased in intensity and is therefore potentially harmful. There may be a child who is aggressive in an obvious conflict situation, but there are others who bully children for no apparent reason. Another child may spend a good portion of her time alone and resist any attempts to be included in group activities. Still another may be in a perpetual whirl of motion, hardly stopping long enough to be contacted by either adults or children. Each of these children desperately needs, and probably wants, help to become a part of the group and to be accepted by others.

The Overly Aggressive Child/Bullying

Nearly every group has at least one child who seems to be angry all the time and who dislikes both children and adults. Although he often complains that others are picking on him, in reality he is usually teasing other children. At times he may resort to outbursts of physical aggression or verbal attacks. This may be a child who has experienced many failures. He may be feeling powerless and feels good only when he is bullying others. He may also come from a family background that is harsh and punitive and that provides very little nurturing.

bullying
violent behaviour imposed by individuals who wish to intimidate, harass, alienate, and isolate others they perceive as weaker, vulnerable, and easy targets

"**Bullying** is violent behaviour imposed by individuals who wish to intimidate, harass, alienate and isolate others they perceive as weaker, vulnerable and easy targets" (Chodzinski, 2004, p. 11). A survey of Canadians revealed that 6 percent of children admitted bullying others "more than once or twice" over a six-week period and 15 percent of children reported that they had been victims of bullying at the same rate (Pepler et al., 1997). Research done by Craig and Pepler (1997) found that bullying occurs once every 7 minutes on playgrounds and once every 25 minutes in classrooms in Canada.

Research suggests that up to 60 percent of identified bullies incur at least one criminal offence by age 24, and 40 percent have three or more convictions (Chodzinski, 2004, p. 23).

The Canadian Centre for Addiction and Mental Health's report on Youth Violence (2002) indicates that in coordination with social support services, after-school programs help to reduce the incidence of juvenile crime.

Children who are bullied often lose self-esteem, feel alone, withdraw, and may turn to violence to protect themselves. There is no doubt that bullying can be a very serious behavioural problem in a school-age program. Behaviour-guidance practices discussed earlier, such as establishing the four RPCs, help to prevent situations from degenerating into bullying; other practices such as conflict-resolution skills assist in sorting out actions and feelings for those who are being bullied or who bully others.

Parents and school-age child care professionals should be aware of warning signs that a child is a target of bullying or is bullying others (see Table 7-4).

School-age child care professionals must be very careful to distinguish between developmentally appropriate behaviour of school-age children, bullying behaviour, and abusive behaviour. Specific policies and practices need to be put into place to let parents and school-age child care professionals know how to deal with the latter two situations.

Table 7-5 outlines guidelines about how to respond to children who are being bullied or who bully others.

The key to dealing with bullies and being bullied is to use keen supervision skills and anticipate problems before they occur. Always be available to children and establish a trusting atmosphere so that children can come to you if they are being bullied or if they see someone being bullied. It is important that children know that you will step in promptly, be assertive, and follow through on expected behaviour and consequences. Children need to feel safe and to know that violence is not an acceptable way of dealing with problems. Take part in anti-bullying campaigns such as "pink shirt day" to help "empower young people to reject bullying, celebrate diversity and promote positive relationships" (www.pinkshirt.ca). School-age child care professionals can become the significant adults in children's lives, helping them to change their behaviour:

- Win trust by showing you care; listen carefully.
- Make sure the rules and standards for behaviour are understood.
- Follow through with logical consequences.
- Help children see the difference between teasing, tattling, and bullying.
- Teach problem-solving and conflict-resolution skills.
- Try to anticipate situations that are likely to cause outbursts. Suggest safe alternative actions or activities.
- Praise and reinforce acceptable behaviour whenever possible. Do not overdo, but when praise is warranted, give it. Include a description of the behaviour to be repeated: "I'm happy to see that you were able to wait your turn without pushing."
- Encourage intrinsic motivation for appropriate behaviour. "You should feel proud of yourself for solving your problem with Mano by listening to what he had to say and working out a solution."

Table 7-4 ■ **Identifying Signs That a Child Is Being Bullied or Is Bullying Other Children**

A child who is being bullied may show the following signs:

- physical injuries
- torn or missing clothing
- missing money or a favourite personal belonging
- personality changes
- overly shy, little communication
- sadness and tears
- not wanting to play with friends, lonely
- low self-esteem
- feels stressful and anxious
- headaches, lack of appetite, and sleep deprivation
- disruptive
- overly assertive, calling attention to themselves
- sudden change in academic performance

A child who is bullying other children may show the following signs:

- physical aggression
- gossiping
- excluding others
- expresses little empathy
- ridicules others
- constant teasing
- uses physical size and strength to intimidate others
- disruptive, impulsive temperament
- challenges authority inappropriately
- disrespectful; uses inappropriate jokes
- encourages peers to exclude others
- takes over situations—constantly "bossy"

Sources: *Bullying: A crisis in our schools and our communities*, by R. Chodzinski, 2004, Welland, ON: Soleil Publishing; and *Bullying: A crisis in our schools and our communities*, by National Strategy on Community Safety and Crime Prevention (n.d.), retrieved April 25, 2005, from http://www.prevention.gc.ca/en/library/publications/fact_sheets/bullying.

The Withdrawn Child

The withdrawn child is often overlooked in a group because she is hardly noticed. She does not create problems and does what she is told, but stays by herself. Sometimes she may appear to be depressed or anxious. Behind this behaviour the child may just be shy or may feel she is not competent to do the things others do. She

Table 7-5 ▨ Responding to Children Who Are Being Bullied or Who Bully Others

For the child who is being bullied:

- Take the situation seriously: bullying can have an emotional impact on the child (fear, humiliation, anger, sadness).

- Listen carefully, discuss concerns, avoid blame.

- Assist children in understanding that they don't have to deal with it on their own; adults are responsible for keeping children safe.

- Explain the difference between telling (to get help from someone) and tattling (to get someone in trouble).

- Teach problem-solving skills: set up role-plays or scenarios about common situations; identify strategies.

- Focus on building the child's self-esteem and feelings of pride and success.

- Encourage and promote friendships in the group.

- Discourage "fighting back"; encourage assertive and nonviolent responses.

- Communicate with the parents and focus on a team support for the child.

For the child who bullies others:

- Stay calm: discuss concerns privately with the child and work toward a positive solution.

- Let the child know that bullying is unacceptable: discuss negative impact for the other child and for the bullying child.

- Assist the child to find ways to express anger that do not involve verbally or physically hurting others.

- Ensure that there is adequate supervision and reasonable rules to follow.

- Decide on logical consequences.

- Model appropriate behaviour in dealing with conflicts.

- Promote positive friendships (good role models).

- Provide positive outlets and activities for surplus energy.

Sources: *Bullying: A crisis in our schools and our communities*, by R. Chodzinski, 2004, Welland, ON: Soleil Publishing; and *Bullying: A crisis in our schools and our communities*, by National Strategy on Community Safety and Crime Prevention (n.d.), retrieved April 25, 2005, from http://www.prevention.gc.ca/en/library/publications/fact_sheets/bullying.

may also be afraid of rejection by other children. School-age child care professionals can help:

- Capitalize on her interests, initially allowing her to pursue them in seclusion. Gradually encourage her to talk about her interests with one other child, then with two children. From there, it may be possible to move her into related activities in a small group of children.

- Involve the child in puppetry either alone or with a small group. She may be able to participate behind the stage or by acting through the puppet.

- Practise pretend telephone conversations. Start by engaging her in a conversation with you. Choose a topic that is likely to interest her. "I know you have a dog at home named George. I certainly like that name. Tell me about him." Encourage further conversation by additional prompting. "What are some of your favourite things to do with George?" Encourage her to practise with another child. Suggest topics for the conversation, such as telling one another about favourite things they do on weekends or their favourite movie.

- Plan activities that will allow her to be successful. Acknowledge her achievements by describing the behaviour that allowed her to succeed. "You were really creative when you figured out how to make a curtain for the puppet theatre. That was good thinking!"

- Make specific suggestions about things to say to other children or things she can do to enter group activities. Praise her efforts when she is successful, pointing out what she did that worked.

The Overly Active Child

The overly active child creates a lot of problems for teachers and school-age child care professionals. During group times, he fidgets, talks loudly, or pokes whomever sits next to him. He never settles down to an activity but moves randomly from one to another. His path through the room may be marked by a trail of destruction. When asked to wait his turn for a snack or during games, he gets very angry. He has a hard time making or keeping friends because he is often argumentative or manipulative. This may be acting-out behaviour due to stress factors in his life such as a disrupted family life or not enough attention from his parents.

Some of these children may be classified as suffering from attention deficit hyperactivity disorder (ADHD). When attempts to moderate the behaviour are unsuccessful, it is important to encourage the parents to get a professional evaluation. Before referring an overly active child, however, some behaviour changes can help him control his own behaviour. School-age child care professionals can help:

- Be consistent about rules. Make sure the child understands the rules, then enforce them after every misbehaviour.

- Anticipate unstructured times that are likely to create problems. Examples of these times are when the group moves from indoors to outdoors or in the transition between an activity-oriented period to snacks. Give plenty of warning that one period is ending and another will begin. Assign him a specific task during the time; have him help prepare the snack, then pass it out, or let him hold the door while the other children go outside.

- Give this child plenty of support. Seat him nearby at group times, accompany him to an activity, and help him get started.

- Help him acquire social skills. Suggest ways he might enter into others' play. Remind him of expected behaviour while with other children.

- Praise him for times he is able to exercise impulse control. "I saw that you were able to stop yourself that time. You must be proud of yourself for that."

- Avoid using negative statements whenever possible. Say "You can build your buildings over here," rather than "Don't knock down Axl's block building."

- Encourage physical exercise to use up excess energy. Physical activity also helps to stimulate beneficial hormones that bring about greater calmness.

- Simplify your environment. Consider whether there are ways you can eliminate clutter and disorder in the classroom. Are materials easily accessible without having to pull out other materials? Do materials get put back in their place so they are available the next time they are needed?

ADHD

Children with true attention-deficit disorders display many of the same behaviours as children who are classified as merely overactive. The difference may lie in the intensity or frequency of the behaviours. A diagnosis can be made only by a physician, pediatrician, or psychologist who specializes in childhood disorders. Brain scans measure the number of dopamine transporters in the brain. Dopamine transporters send signals from one brain cell to another by releasing dopamine. A group of researchers at Harvard Medical School have found that ADHD sufferers have 70 percent more dopamine transporters than their non-ADHD counterparts (Fischman et al., 1999). It is uncertain, however, whether the increased number of dopamine transporters is a cause or an effect of the disorder.

In addition to brain scans, observation and evaluation of a child's behaviour are necessary to make an accurate diagnosis. The behaviours most frequently seen in children with ADHD are distractibility, impatience, impulsivity, and a short attention span. Children with ADHD may also perform acts without awareness of the consequences or risks. ADHD is diagnosed six times more often in boys than in girls (Arcia & Connors, 1998; Safer & Krager, 1994).

The most frequent treatment is the use of several drugs, most often Ritalin or Dexedrine. These medications increase the production of the neurotransmitters dopamine and norepinephrine, which results in increased attention and less restlessness. Decreasing food additives in children's diets may be effective. Some diagnosticians also recommend the addition of vitamin B1 and magnesium. The suggestions made for managing the behaviour of overly active children given in the previous section apply as well to the child with ADHD and will not be repeated here. School-age child care professionals can help in the following ways:

- Refer the family to reliable sources for testing and diagnosis.
- If medication is prescribed as a treatment, ensure that the child takes it as recommended.
- Maintain close and supportive contact with the family to continue to evaluate the child's progress and condition.
- Give positive reinforcement for the child's attempts to control behaviour.
- Consider adaptations to the environment: limit the amount of open space, monitor the noise level, and help the child to adjust to the choices of activities.
- Assist the child with transitions; give a few minutes warning before changing activities.
- Try different approaches to the child; listen attentively and show empathy.

Assistance from Other Behaviour-Intervention Programs

School-age child care professionals may need to reach out for assistance from other professional organizations in the community to assist with strategies and other intervention programs that focus on working with children who have challenging behaviours.

Childhood community resource centres, children's mental health centres, and child and youth organizations may be good places in the community to go to for help.

There are a number of behaviour-guidance intervention programs, such as the **Second Step Violence Prevention Program,** that can be incorporated in various areas of the curriculum. This program focuses on developing prosocial behaviour and reducing impulsive and aggressive behaviour. Empathy training, impulse control, and anger management are key components of the program.

Grossman, D., et al. (1997) report an increase in positive social interactions and less physical aggression of grade two and three children who were involved in the Second Step Program.

Reaching In … Reaching Out (RIRO) is a unique evidence-based program in Canada that teaches resiliency thinking and coping skills to young children. This program helps children develop strength and resilience, reducing their sense of helplessness in the face of conflict, violence, and risk of depression. The program incorporates a motto for a "Road of Life" Travel List that recognizes the importance of outside supports such as caring relationships, positive role models, and community involvement. It also strives to help children build inner strengths or self-control, thinking skills, confidence, a positive outlook, responsibility, and participation (www.reachinginreachingout.com).

Roots of Empathy is an evidence-based program that has shown significant benefits in reducing levels of aggression in school-age children. As children are involved with observing the relationship between babies and their parents who are invited to the classroom, they begin to understand feelings and emotions, raising their own social/emotional competence and increasing empathy. Children who participated in this program demonstrated more prosocial behaviours such as kindness, sharing, and understanding with their peers (http://www.rootsofempathy.org).

Zero tolerance is a common buzzword used in many school-discipline policies to curb violence in elementary and secondary schools across Canada and the United States. The Ontario Safe Schools Task Force introduced this approach in schools in the early 1990s in response to reports of increasing violence in schools. The intent of the message of zero tolerance for violent behaviour and the use of weapons was sound; however, its implementation has come under great criticism. The approach has become a "quick fix" to get rid of the problem, usually by suspending or expelling the child from school for a few days or permanently.

Little is done to address the behaviour itself or to help the child develop strategies to control her behaviour. The Canadian Association of Principals is currently aware of the problems associated with this "lockstep disciplinary approach" and wants to explore alternative behaviour-management methods. They acknowledge that this may require the need for additional resources for greater staff supervision

Second Step Violence Prevention Program
behaviour-intervention program that focuses on developing prosocial behaviours and reducing impulsive and aggressive behaviours of children

zero tolerance
policy used for discipline procedures in elementary and secondary schools to curb violence

Figure 7-6 ■ **Sometimes parents need to be referred to special programs or services to get help for their children.**

on playgrounds and during transition times as well as more time for staff to develop and implement other behaviour-intervention programs (Canadian Association of Principals, (n.d.); Hoffman, 2001).

It is important for school-age child care professionals to be aware of elementary school discipline policies and practices of zero tolerance. School-age child care professionals can assist children with understanding the differences between behaviour-guidance policies in the school-age program and the school.

The aim of providing a healthy, safe, respectful and nonviolent environment in which to play and learn in is the same for both organizations: tolerance of violence is unacceptable in any school-age program. Policies and procedures for dealing with behavioural challenges need to be developed by the staff and communicated to the children and their parents.

Summary

During middle childhood, children want to have friends. Those who lack social skills have a difficult time and may be either aggressive or passive, perform poorly academically, and have emotional problems. Those who have good social skills will have lots of friends, get better grades, and probably function effectively as adults.

As children develop better cognitive abilities, they learn to delay personal gratification and attain important attitudes and values about getting along with others, as well as those that help establish a cooperative sense of community. School-age child care professionals can assist children in developing social competence by creating a positive climate or atmosphere in which their developmental needs are recognized. School-age child care professionals can facilitate the Four RPCs as a means of assisting children with developing sound self-regulation skills and establishing policies about socially appropriate behaviours.

All members of the school-age program community have a responsibility to "make it work": to work and play together in a positive social climate. School-age child care professionals have the responsibility of setting clear expectations of behaviour and involving the children in the process; the children have the responsibility of learning to follow those expectations.

Children and staff in the program need to acknowledge individual rights; that everyone is a unique individual and that each person should be treated with compassion, listened to, and allowed to express feelings in appropriate ways. In order to build a healthy emotional and social climate, children have the right to a general sense of happiness each day in their work and play.

In the same way, children and school-age child care professionals establish an understanding of respect. Together they discuss actions and behaviours that demonstrate kindness and empathy for one another. Being respectful of others regardless of their size, age, gender, ethnic or cultural background, as well as taking care of the program environment, are key aspects of a cooperative social atmosphere.

A few simple rules are an important part of a democratic and peaceful program. Children should take part in talking about what kinds of rules would assist everyone in getting along. Rules need to be realistic, understandable, and reinforced with positive, gentle reminders.

School-age children need positive ways to feel powerful. They can do this by making choices to participate in certain activities, taking part in setting up rules for the program, and working through their problems. By knowing the children's needs, school-age child care professionals work toward creating a climate where the children can be "in control" versus "being controlled." Class meetings can be planned where children and school-age child care professionals can discuss what works for their program.

Self-image has two parts: our perceptions of ourselves and the perceptions conveyed to us by others. Throughout a lifetime, self-image changes as physical abilities evolve, cognitive functions change, and interactions with others are refined. How children feel about themselves has a direct effect upon behaviour. When adults react positively to children, the children will develop a positive self-image.

The process of peacemaking gives children the opportunity to take some responsibility in discussing problems and conflicts that they are experiencing. Sometimes this process involves individuals, called "peacemakers" or "conflict managers," who assist children with conflicts.

In this process of "peacemaking," children follow the steps of problem solving. Initially, they define the problem, listen to different viewpoints, clarify ideas and feelings, generate solutions, agree on a solution, and follow through. These are skills that children will use all through their lives as they face day-to-day challenges.

Cooperation with others does not come easily to children. Gradually, during middle childhood, they learn that others have needs and that they must compromise and cooperate in order to have friends.

Children learn from natural consequences, where they learn that certain behaviours such as cheating, lying, and fighting among their peers are not welcome. At other times, staff need to implement logical consequences, where children can take responsibility for their actions and learn what behaviour is expected.

A positive means of communication is important when working with children in a cooperative and respectful climate in a school-age program. Using "I" messages and identifying children's feelings shows that you respect how they feel and that their feelings are real and not denied. Staff can assist children with recognizing how their behaviour affects others and what they can do the next time they are in a similar situation.

Children learn to resolve conflicts by observing adults at home, in their neighbourhoods, in movies, on TV, and at school. They witness others' violent ways and imitate their actions until they acquire more effective methods. Some types of conflicts are a normal part of life. Children can learn effective ways of dealing with conflicts through mediation, negotiation, and problem solving. School-age child care professionals can help children resolve conflicts in ways that allow each party to feel validated.

Children's behaviour can be changed when adults take time to build some understanding about the motivations behind them. School-age child care professionals should find out what is happening in the child's home life, school work, and peer group. Children's physical health will also have some effect on their behaviour. Sometimes children will behave in negative ways to gain a sense of inappropriate power, receive negative attention, or for revenge. Staff are often angry and frustrated and need to learn how to deal with these behaviours positively. Building positive relationships with parents and school personnel from the beginning is essential to the process of helping children change their behaviour. Some children exhibit behaviours that are similar to those of other children but are more intense or potentially harmful to the individual or the group. Both the overly aggressive child and the quiet or withdrawn child can be helped. Bullying is a concern in many programs. School-age child care professionals and parents must be aware of warning signs in children who are being bullied or who are bullies. Children need to know that they can trust adults in their program so that they may feel comfortable about reporting incidents of bullying. School-age child care professionals should know the difference between bullying and a behaviour that is part of the normal course of child development and then how to respond effectively.

Some children are overly active and may be suffering from ADHD and should be evaluated. There are a number of intervention programs such as Second Step Violence Prevention Programs, RIRO, and Roots of Empathy, which have demonstrated some success in helping children deal with stress, develop resiliency, understand empathy, and reduce aggressive behaviours.

Key Terms

social competence	positive self-image	conflict resolution
self-regulation	peacemaking	mediation
antisocial behaviour	problem solving	negotiating
responsibility	cooperation	bullying
rights	compassion	Second Step Violence Prevention Program
respect	natural consequences	
rules	logical consequences	zero tolerance
power	communication	

Student Activities

1. In class, practise problem solving using the steps of conflict resolution listed in this chapter. Work in pairs, with each member of the pair assuming one side of a controversy. Choose one of the following situations or describe one from your own experience.
   a. Two school-age child care professionals share a room. One never cleans up thoroughly when an activity is finished, so at the end of the day, the room is in chaos.
   b. On the playground one school-age child care professional spends a lot of time with individual children rather than supervising the group. The other adult is left to intervene when altercations occur, stimulate additional activities, and generally manage a large group of children.
   Share the results with classmates. Was the process easy or difficult? Were you able to use "I" messages when telling what happened? Did each of the partners feel satisfied with the resolution?
2. Work with one of your classmates to determine whether your perception of yourself is the same as or different from how others see you. First, write down five words that describe your partner. Next write five words that describe you. Compare your partner's list with your own. Did each of you agree when describing the other? How close was your self-evaluation to the way your partner described you? How does this activity contribute to your understanding of the complexity of self-image in children?

Chapter 7 Helping Children Develop Social Competence

3. Interview a school-age child care professional. What methods does she use to promote children's ability to develop self-control and cooperate with one another?

Review Questions

1. State the four RPCs of guiding behaviour and why school-age child care professionals use these to support the development of self-regulation and social competence.
2. Outline five guidelines for introducing rules in a school-age program.
3. List and explain the steps in problem solving.
4. Why is it important to help children increase their ability to read nonverbal cues?
5. List five things an adult can do to establish a nonviolent, peaceful classroom.
6. State three strategies for helping children learn to resolve conflicts effectively.
7. Describe three activities that you could use to foster social competence, one from each of the RPCs of guiding behaviour.
8. Describe why time out is not effective and identify an alternative approach for staff to take when they are dealing with challenging behaviour.
9. Define bullying. List 10 possible signs of a child being bullied and outline five ways to respond to a child who is being bullied.
10. Describe the behaviour of an overly active child. What might be the cause of this behaviour?

Case Study

The room where Rowan's school-age group meets has only one computer, which is much sought after by all the children. This afternoon Mei wants to e-mail her friend in China and is eager to get started. Three other children are clamouring to get online as well. They each have urgent things they want to do. Natalia has a homework assignment; Gregory wants to finish a game he started the day before; and Xavier just wants to explore some information about stars, his newest interest. They all begin squabbling, each declaring he or she should be first. Rowan is so tired of the fighting over the one computer that he would like to just get rid of it but knows the children benefit by using it. One of the volunteers in the program thinks that the children should all be told that no one can use the computer until they learn to share.

1. Do you agree with the volunteer's advice that none of them should be allowed to use the computer until they learn to share? If you disagree, why?
2. If you were Rowan, what would be the first thing you would do to assist them with resolving the conflict?
3. Can you think of a plan that would prevent problems like this in the future?

References

Adams, S. & Sasse Wittmer, D. (2001, Fall). "I had it first": Teaching young children to solve problems peacefully. *Childhood Education*, 10–16.

Arcia, E. & Conners, C. K. (1998). Gender differences in ADHD? *Journal of Developmental and Behavioral Pediatrics, 19*(2).

Bodrova, E. & Leong, D. (2008). Developing self-regulation in kindergarten: Can we keep all the crickets in the basket? *Young Children*, March: 56–58.

Borman Fink, D. (1995). *Discipline in school-age care, control the climate, not the children.* Nashville, TN: School-Age Notes.

Canadian Association of Principals. (n.d.). Zero Tolerance Policies in Context: A Preliminary Investigation to Identify Actions to Improve School Discipline and School Safety. Retrieved April, 20, 2005, from http://www.schoolfile.com/safehealthyschools/whatsnew/capzerotolerance.htm#Executive%20Summary

Canadian Centre for Addiction and Mental Health. (2002). *Youth and violence: What's the story?* Retrieved March 21, 2005, from http://www.camh.net/pdf/scoop_sheet_youth_violence.pdf

Chodzinski, R. (2004). *Bullying, a crisis in our school and our communities.* Welland, ON: Soleil.

Craig, W. & Pepler, D. (1997). *Naturalistic observations of bullying and victimization on the playground.* Public Safety and Emergency Preparedness Canada, Bullying in Canada. Retrieved March 21, 2005, from http://www.prevention.gc.ca/en/library/publications/fact_sheets/bullying/#1

DAS. (n.d.). *Peacebuilding.* Retrieved March 21, 2005, from http://schools.tdsb.on.ca/downtownalt/peacebuilding.html

Edwards, C. (1989). *Conflict resolution for kids: Learning a lifeskill.* Toronto: Author.

Fischman, A. J., Daugherty, D. D., Bonab, A. A., Spencer, T. J., Rauch, S. L., & Madras, B. K. (1999). Dopamine transporter density in patients with attention deficit hyperactivity disorder. *Lancet, 34* (9196).

Fox, L., Dunlop, G., Hemmeter, M., Joseph, G., & Strain, P. (2003, July). The teaching pyramid, a model for supporting social competence and preventing challenging behavior in young children. *Young Children*, 48–52.

Grossman, D., et al. (1997). The effectiveness of a violence prevention curriculum among children in elementary school. *Journal of the American Medical Association, 277,* 1605–1611.

Haas-Foletta, K & Cogley, M. (1990). *School-age ideas and activities for after school programs.* Nashville: TN: School-Age Notes.

Hartup, W. W. (1992). Having friends, making friends, and keeping friends: Relationships as educational contexts. *ERIC Digest.*

Hoffman, J. (2001). Violence at school. *Today's Parent.* Retrieved April 21, 2005, from http://www.todaysparent.com/preteen/education/article.jsp?content=3525 *Making a difference: Responding to bullying and peer abuse.*

Kaiser, B. & Sklar Rasminsky, J. (1999). *Meeting the challenge, effective strategies for challenging behaviors in early childhood environments.* Ottawa: Canadian Child Care Federation.

Levin, D. (2003). *Teaching young children in violent times, building a peaceable classroom* (2nd ed.). Washington DC: NAEYC.

National Network for Child Care. (n.d.). *Behaviour management: The big stressor.* Retrieved March 21, 2005, from http://www.nncc.org/Guidance/sac33_behav.mgmt.stress.html

National Network for Child Care. (n.d.). *Establishing rules.* Retrieved March 21, 2005, from http:/www.nncc.org/Guidance/sac16_estab.rules.html

National Strategy on Community Safety and Crime Prevention (n.d.). *Bullying in Canada.* Retrieved April 25, 2005, from http://www.prevention.gc.ca/en/library/publications/fact_sheets/bullying

Pepler, D. J., Craig, W., O'Connell, R., Connolly, J., Atlas, R., Sedigdeilami, F., Smith, C., & Kent, D. (1997). Prevalence of bullying and victimization among Canadian elementary and middle school children. In *National strategy on community safety and crime prevention, bullying in Canada.* Retrieved March 21, 2005, from http://www.prevention.gc.ca/en/library/publications/fact_sheets/bullying/#1

Safer, D. J. & Krager, J. M. (1994). The increased rate of stimulant treatment for hyperactive/inattentive students in secondary schools. *Pediatrics, 94,* 462–464.

Shanker, S. (2012). Self-regulation. Presentation—Conestoga College, April.

Webster's Encyclopedic Dictionary of the English Language, Canadian Edition. (1988). New York: Lexicon Publications.

Wilson, C., Gillespie, C., & Chick, A. (2001). Fussbusters: Using peers to mediate conflict resolution in a head start classroom. *Childhood Education*, Summer, 192–195.

Selected Further Reading

Akin, T., Cowan, D., Dunne, G., Palomares, S., Schilling, D., & Schuster, S. (1990). *The best self-esteem activities for the elementary grades.* Torrance, CA: Innerchoice Publishing.

Bullying—About kids' health. Hospital for Sick Children. Retrieved June 5, 2012, from http://www.aboutkidshealth.ca/En/HealthAZ/FamilyandPeerRelations/PeerRelations/Pages/Bullying.aspx?gclid=CMjR8qLNkbACFSWFQAodGHeIqw

Bully B'ware Productions. Take action against bullying; Bullying hurts and keeps on hurting. Retrieved April 5, 2005, from http://www.bullybeware.com

Coloroso, B. (1995). *Giving your child the gift of inner discipline.* Toronto: Somerville House Publishing.

Coloroso, B. (2003). *The bully, the bullied and the bystander.* Toronto: Harper Collins.

Drew, N. (2010). *No kidding about bullying—125 ready to use activities to help kids manage anger, resolve conflicts, build empathy and get along.* Minneapolis, MN: Free Spirit Publishing.

Goldberg, S. (1991). *Times of war and peace, dealing with kid's concerns.* Toronto: Annick Press.

Holden, G. (2001). *The C-A-R-E project, Conflict And Responsibility Education.* Carthage, IL: Teaching & Learning Co.

Honig, A. S. & Wittmer, D. S. (1996). Helping children become more prosocial: Ideas for classrooms, families, and communities. *Young Children, 51*(2), 62–70.

Lamm, S., Groulx, J., Hansen, C., Martin Patton, M., & Jimenes Slaton, A. (2006). Creating environments for peaceful problem solving. *Young Children,* Nov., 22–28.

Reaching In … Reaching Out Program. http://www.reachinginreachingout.com/about-program.htm

Roots of Empathy. http://www.rootsof empathy.org

Vance, E. & Jimenez Weaver, P. (2002). *Class meetings: Young children solving problems together.* Washington, DC: NAEYC.

Visual Media

Take a stand against bullying. Sunburst Media. http://www.learn360bullying.com/index.html

Out on a limb: A guide to getting along. http://urbanext.illinois.edu/conflict/intro3.html

Children's Books

Family and Children's Services. (2007). *What happens next? Information for kids about separation and divorce.* Canada, Dept. of Justice.

Ludwig, T. (2005). *My secret bully.* New York: Crown Publishing.

Romain, T. (1997). *Bullies are a pain in the brain.* Minneapolis, MN: Free Spirit Publishing.

Soronson, B. & Dismondy, M. (2010). *The juice box bully: Empowering kids to stand up for others.* Northville, MI: Ferne Press.

Thomas, P. (2000). *Stop picking on me.* Hauppauge, NY: Barron's Educational Series.

Whitehouse, E. & Pudney, W. (1998). *A volcano in my tummy: Helping children to handle anger.* Gabriola Island, BC: New Society Publishers.

Background

Chapter 8

Program Planning

Objectives

After studying this chapter, the student should be able to:

- Reinforce the various theories that support curriculum development
- Describe the different approaches for curriculum
- List the components of an effective developmentally responsive program
- Plan a program that supports real-life learning experiences

 Profile

Connaught School Age Program in Ottawa offers an emergent project-based curriculum, one which comes from the children themselves. After observing a staff member sewing items for the centre, the school-age children became interested in trying it themselves. A project of learning to sew on machines and decorating handiwork emerged over several months. Some of the floor cushions were sewn by the children. Younger children also wanted to learn to sew and did some simple pieces by hand. Their work was documented with photographs and works of art. Web drawings were also used to record emerging projects and projects in progress.

The children also take part in regular physical exercise, spending as much time as possible outdoors. Developing life skills like cooking and caring for their environment by cleaning up after themselves and watering plants in the centre is a key element of the program. A sense of community is also an essential part of the program. The school-age program and the school share resources and the principal and teachers in the school are invited to their annual potluck supper. They have developed a positive relationship with the second-hand

Developmentally Responsive Practice

Theories of child development have provided the basis for curriculum development in child care and education since the late 1800s (Goffin & Wilson, 2001, p. 196). New understandings about the interplay of heredity and environment have influenced a changing perspective away from a heavy reliance only on developmental theory as a basis for curriculum design (Goffin & Wilson, 2001, p. 199). Development is seen as a process that continues through life, based on the contributions of heredity and environmental conditions. Critical periods are identified as unique times in a child's growth when specific environmental or biological events must occur for development to proceed normally. Social competence and emotional development are key components in this process. The adults' role in children's learning and development—by providing a supportive and nurturing environment that is **developmentally responsive**—is crucial (Goffin & Wilson, 2001, p. 200).

When planning a program for school-age children, consideration should be given to Howard Gardner's belief that different areas of the brain work together to engage a particular action. As explained in Chapter 5, Gardner's Theory of **Multiple Intelligences** outlines eight areas of intelligence. This theory supports various developmental theories but takes a different dimension by looking at how children learn and develop in different ways as opposed to a predictable developmental stage-by-stage process. Gardner believed that the two most important foundations of growth and development are the nurturing of interpersonal and intrapersonal skills. When children develop a good sense of self, they can then develop a sound understanding and acceptance of others. Other areas of intelligence include linguistic, logical-mathematical, spatial, bodily-kinesthetic, musical, and naturalist (Powell, 2001, p. 9).

It is important for school-age child care professionals to observe the differences in how children learn and to plan a curriculum that provides children with the experiences to practise these intelligences in a variety of ways. For example, many children learn best through bodily-kinesthetic ways or through somatic sensations. They love to dance, run, jump, build, touch things, and use many gestures. They need opportunities to role-play, build things, play sports and physical games, and take part in tactile experiences and hands-on learning. Children can practise their understanding of the formation of letters by playing a game of "letter makeup," where groups of four to five children work together to use their bodies to copy a letter from a card.

Developmental research leads us to the conclusion that the most successful programs for school-age children are based on the premise that an active child in an active environment constitutes the optimum conditions for bringing about developmental changes. Studies by both Jean Piaget (1952) and Len Vygotsky (1978) pointed to the importance of children's interactions with their environment and the impact of the social environment on development. Piaget identified stages of qualitative changes in a child's thinking that allow him to construct knowledge through interactions with his

developmentally responsive planning
programs are responsive to individual growth and changes that occur on a continuum of development

multiple intelligences
eight different ways that children learn: interpersonal, intrapersonal, linguistic, logical-mathematical, spatial, bodily-kinesthetic, musical, and naturalistic

environment. Vygotsky believed that thinking changes as a result of instruction or support (scaffolding) from the environment and as language skills increase. According to Albrecht and Plantz (1993), developmentally appropriate school-age child care programs should be tailored to the developmental characteristics and needs of the children they serve. Quality programs must address the fact that children change tremendously in middle childhood and that there are great variations in the rate and types of change in all developmental areas. Even within an individual child there is great variation from one stage to another or within a stage of development.

More recent awareness has arisen from the theories of Loris Malaguzzi (1994) who emphasized the importance of seeing children as active participants in the construction of learning; that families and teachers are equal partners in promoting learning; that attention should be paid to the visual arts in providing an aesthetically pleasing environment; that documentation and dialogue of children's efforts should form the basis of curriculum planning; and that children should participate in the creation of projects.

Theories of **constructivism** discussed in Chapter 5 also bring forth some important guidelines with regards to program planning. These include the following: children are curious and competent learners. They bring valuable knowledge, ideas, and experiences about the world around them. They are active, social learners—learning through exploration and investigation. They are influenced by family, gender, culture, and previous experiences. They use a variety of learning styles and ways of understanding and constructing knowledge (Jacobs, Vukelich, & Howe, n.d.). For example, from an observation that one of the staff did, Tommy has been trying out some new artistic drawing techniques in his drawings. The school-age child care professional decided to bring out some different kinds of brushes, drawing pencils, and charcoal to see what he would do with them. Tommy was fascinated by the new art tools and he began to sketch new drawings. He talked about seeing drawings done in charcoal in a book called *Make Way for Ducklings* by Robert McCloskey. Tommy used various words such as "shadow," "bold," and "light" to describe his work. Other children became interested in trying out the new drawing tools. They shared other experiences about different kinds of art that they had seen in picture books and in their homes. One girl talked about a print by Picasso, and that her father told her Picasso used an art form called "cubism" in his art. The children thought they might like to explore this type of art too. In this example, the children were encouraged to explore and investigate their interest to construct some understanding and knowledge about something that was meaningful to them. At the same time, they were communicating and sharing their learning experiences together and making sense of the world around them.

constructivism

based on a belief that children are curious, capable, and interested in learning; allowing for opportunities to build on their interests and ideas that extend on their current knowledge

Table 8-1 ■ IPA Declaration on the Child's Right to Play

PLAY, along with the basic needs of nutrition, health, shelter and education, is vital to develop the potential of all children.

PLAY is communication and expression, combining thought and action; it gives satisfaction and a feeling of achievement.

PLAY is instinctive, voluntary and spontaneous.

PLAY helps children develop physically, mentally, emotionally and socially.

PLAY is a means of learning to live, not a mere passing of time.

IPA Declaration on the Child's Right to Play. International Play Association, http://www.ipaworld.org/ipa_declaration.html

Play also becomes an important consideration when designing curriculum for school-age children. Piaget outlines the various stages of play and the different types of play in which children engage. School-age children become more involved with symbolic or make-believe play and are ready for playing games with rules. They spend more time in the stage of cooperative play, where they work together with other children on pre-planned goals of what they want to achieve. Theorists such as Spencer, Lazarus, Groos, and Hall refer to play as a means of relaxation and recreation, where children can expend energy, restore energy after their school day, and practise various physical skills. Vygotsky views play from a sociocultural perspective, where children engage in various tasks (symbolic play experiences) that are familiar to them from their own lives in order to bring some understanding to what they see and hear in the real world. Freud and Erikson believed that play allows children to master their physical and social skills in order to build self-esteem.

play

self-motivated, pleasurable, and process-oriented aspect of children's daily life that is vital to their social, emotional, cognitive, and physical development

With play comes the opportunity for children to be creative. Being creative means viewing the world in ways where there are no right or wrong answers, only possibilities. Adults need to plan curriculum that will allow children to "push the boundaries" and explore possibilities. Children need to manipulate and transform ideas and materials, and take things apart and put them back together in different ways. Opportunities to solve problems, to try and figure things out, ask questions, and challenge accepted ways of thinking should be encouraged (Crowther, 2003, p. 182).

The International Association for the Child's Right to Play (IPA) supports the United Nations statements on the Rights of the Child. The declaration in Table 8-1, which the Association has developed, is based on the UN's Rights of the Child, which states that "all children have the right to rest and leisure, to engage in play and recreational activities appropriate to the age of the child and to participate freely in cultural life and the arts" (International Play Association, n.d.)

UNICEF states that besides developing physical skills and capabilities; sport, recreation, and play provide children with an opportunity to "practice for life." Children learn self-discipline, trust, respect for others, leadership, and problem-solving skills. They learn to value rules, develop self-confidence, and experience self-expression. Play is something that children have done throughout history and in all cultures. UNICEF is a great proponent of inclusive programs with children who have special needs. The organization supports leisure activities that are planned to include interactions between people of all cultural backgrounds and ages (UNICEF, n.d.).

The guidelines in Table 8-2 address all areas of an <u>effective program for school-age children</u> beginning with the role of school-age child care professionals. Qualifications of school-age child care professionals have been discussed in Chapter 1, but we should emphasize here that they should play a supportive role to children. As young people strive for independence from their parents, they look to other adults to guide them through the process of adjusting to the outside world. Albrecht and Plantz (1993) discuss the importance of adjusting interactions with children according to their age and stage of development. There is a difference between the needs of children who are five to seven years of age and those who are approaching adolescence. The youngest children may need more direction and motivators; the oldest children want more autonomy and adult-like responsibilities. The guidelines also indicate the importance of peer relationships as children move toward independence.

Both friendships with one or two others and a sense of belonging to a group are essential to children's self-esteem. Adults can facilitate <u>peer</u> relationships by supporting children's developing social skills. School-age child care professionals can also initiate activities that encourage children to discuss the causes of conflicts and ways to resolve them. Additionally, developmentally appropriate school-age child

In addition to "developmentally appropriate practices" as outlined in Table 8-2, "developmentally responsive practices" in school-age child care support the recognition that children are capable and competent; that they come with current knowledge, and that school-age child care professionals are responsive to their interests and needs by providing experiences that encourage a learning process of exploration, investigation, and inquiry.

RESOURCE SHEET

Canadian Child Care Federation

Developmentally Appropriate Practices in School-Age Child Care*

Developmentally appropriate practices are based on the developmental needs of the children they serve. There are two aspects: age-appropriateness and individual appropriateness. Developmentally appropriate practices should be designed for the age group being served, taking into consideration the specific needs and differences of each child, including culture and language. Experiences for children should be interesting and mentally challenging as well as active and enjoyable.

To encourage developmentally appropriate practices, the children's environment should be well organized, clearly defined and easily accessible. Furniture should be arranged to promote both small group interaction and group discussion. Children learn best when they can construct their own knowledge and figure things out for themselves. As children grow, they develop and acquire new skills and experiences that facilitate learning. Developmentally appropriate practices are based on seven principles that acknowledge children as active learners.

Figure 8-1 ▪ Children work together to plan their activities.

PRINCIPLES OF DEVELOPMENTALLY APPROPRIATE PRACTICE	ENVIRONMENT
To provide resourceful, caring staff	Be responsive to children's questions; give children enough time to play and interact with materials
To recognize the importance of peers	Provide opportunities to interact with peers; encourage friendships
To provide opportunities for same-age and mixed-age groupings	Encourage physical activities such as games, sports, field trips, kids' clubs, drama, music, dance and art
To promote self-selected activities and experiences	Offer open-ended activities; provide choice; allow children to organize activities themselves
To exercise positive guidance and discipline techniques	Involve children in rule making; help them understand limits; encourage problem recognition and solving
To provide a wide variety of activities individually as well as in small and large groups	Allow children to use modelling clay, to cook or to paint; offer opportunities for individual and team sports; let children choose books based on their age and interests
To provide for the whole child	Provide opportunities to modify and personalize the environment; allow for independence

Canadian Child Care Federation. (2001). Resource sheet #23: Developmentally appropriate practices in school-age child care. Ottawa, ON: CCCF.

care programs use both mixed-age and same-age grouping to help children develop relationships with their peers according to their own developmental needs. School-age child care professionals should use positive guidance strategies to help children achieve inner control and self-discipline. This means that adults encourage children to resolve their own differences and that they listen to children and encourage them to verbalize their feelings. Positive guidance also means that school-age child care professionals help children behave productively by describing problem situations and encouraging group problem solving.

Developmentally appropriate programs include space for a wide variety of activities for individual children and small and large groups. The program should include more self-selected activities than staff–selected activities in order to provide a balance to the child's after-school time, which follows the more structured content of her school day.

Plan activities and experiences that meet children's desire to be competent in all aspects of their development: psychosocial, cognitive, and physical. A developmentally appropriate program will provide activities and experiences that help children develop their self-concept and need for independence. Children want to feel successful and gain control over their own actions. This can be achieved by allowing children to direct their own activities and having supportive school-age child care professionals who allow independence but offer guidance as needed. Children also need to be challenged to increase their cognitive abilities. There should be varied and interesting activities that are neither too easy nor too difficult for their developmental level. The importance of physical competence and well-being should not be overlooked by those planning developmentally appropriate programs. Children should have a wide variety of activities in which they can practise skills requiring both large- and small-muscle coordination. A developmentally appropriate program will encourage children to develop sound attitudes and practices to ensure their own health and safety. There should be opportunities to learn what constitutes fitness, how to maintain health, and what to include in a healthy diet.

The Importance of Planning: Observations, Child–Staff Interactions, and Documentation

If you think of yourself as a spontaneous and flexible person, you may wonder whether you really need to plan. Nevertheless, when you work with children, looking ahead is essential. Without it, a day can lead to chaos, unhappy children, and irritable adults.

Planning ensures there will be a variety of play opportunities that will attract and stimulate children. There should be a balance between old and new activities. Some should be familiar things children like to do over and over again. Others can be new things or provocations to spark their interest.

Planning ahead allows you to provide the materials that children might be interested in based on your observations from the previous days.

Have an abundance of open-ended materials such as fabrics, glue, water paint kits, boxes, tubes, blankets, string, etc. available for children at all times and store them in a place where they can find them easily.

Involving the children in planning reduces the number of conflicts between children. A group of children can engage in free play for periods of time, but eventually differences will arise.

During the hours that children are in the school-age program, taking part in free play as well as planned activities will keep children interested and involved. Petty arguments and irritability will decrease and children will have opportunities to practise their skills of self-regulation.

Plans allow staff to divide responsibilities. Everyone should know specifically what they will be required to do during a period of time. Some may have responsibility for playground supervision and others for setting up materials in the classrooms.

Every step of the day, including transitions, activities, snack, and free play, should have some plan that is familiar to the children. At the same time, be flexible and recognize the ongoing needs of the children.

The most important function of program planning is to ensure that both the children and the staff are partners in the process and that experiences emerge out of observations and conversations with the children about their interests, needs, and abilities.

Planning also helps school-age child care professionals apply the guidelines for developmentally responsive practices. As each day's experiences emerge, they can be measured according to the guidelines. Will they allow children to develop their physical skills? Are there opportunities for creative expression? Is there a balance between staff-initiated activities and time for child-initiated ones? Are there activities at different levels of difficulty so that children at diverse developmental levels can participate and feel successful? School-age child care professionals need to pay keen attention to the children's interests and needs, the age group combination, the space that is used for the school-age program, the talents and abilities of the staff, and the role of the parents and community. This process of program planning requires continuous observation, reflection, and adaptation.

observation

means of gathering information about children's interests, needs, and developmental abilities through recorded methods to further relevant learning opportunities

Observations should be recorded and be visible so that parents and professionals such as other teachers and the principal can be kept informed about the children's interests and experiences. These can be anecdotal in nature and be recorded on sticky notes and put in notebooks, binders, or folders.

documentation

means of recording children's learning processes through written, verbal, or visual methods such as a web drawing, thus providing validation of their play and work

Documentation of the children's experiences should be displayed on bulletin boards in prominent places in their room and other areas of the building. It can be a grouping of photographs with children's comments underneath, a collection of stories and drawings, or a class book. It can be an art gallery format, showing the children's creative artwork or a video taping of a dramatic play production. If the school-age program is situated in a school setting, it is important that the school staff and administration can also see what the children are involved with in their school-age program. A web drawing can be used to record and document ideas, interests, and responses from the children. It often provides a visual way of identifying the processes used in integrating curriculum ideas and making connections between learning experiences. This process is used in emergent curriculum approaches and in Reggio Emilia programs. It is particularly meaningful for the children to take part in the process of developing a curriculum web if the school-age child care professional provides sufficient time and an opportunity to do so. Web drawings are also used to document children's projects as they progress or to outline their completion. Sometimes a web might provide a drawing of their exploration of a particular concept, such as lightning, velocity, or friendship. Others may come from children's particular interests, such as castles, giants, or underwater sea life. See Figure 8-3.

This process provides a launching pad for extending children's ideas. The relationships and connections made between each of the experiences and activities enable children to make better sense of their world, build concepts, and think of things in new ways. This strategy helps school-age child care professionals and children work together, learn together, make connections to previous experiences, make their learning visible, and construct notions of similarities and differences (Workman & Anziano, 1993, 8).

What Should Be Included?

- *Start with the routine things you and the children do every day.* Plan for one of the staff to welcome the children, and consider what the children will do when they first arrive at the program. Decide who will take attendance, when you will have the snack, who will supervise the playground, and what materials will be ready. All this may seem trivial, but it is not. Children enjoy a predictable environment. Careful planning of your schedule makes the day run more smoothly for both adults and children.

- *Plan time for meaningful observations.* Watch the children in their play and listen to their conversations; keep notes and refer to them often while considering what ideas will be explored and what materials and equipment you might need.

- *Capitalize on children's interests.* Some children may want to continue themes they are working on at school, whereas others may have some current interests unrelated to school. Holidays, too, create excitement that can generate ideas. Videos and DVDs may also pique interests you can use. Sometimes one child has a special interest that can be shared with others. Use this child to generate enthusiasm in other children as they work together on projects. Ask parents about their children's particular interests.

- *Build on the staff's interests, abilities, and hobbies.* The school-age child care professionals may have similar interests in music, play, and sports activities as the children. Share these with the children. This will help to secure a bond between the children and the adults, making more of a home-like or cooperative atmosphere.

- *Involve children in the planning process.* Plan class meetings and ask the children for input on what they would like to do in the next week or month in the program. Stimulate ideas based on observations of their play that you have made previously. Be aware of activities the children have been involved in outside the program that could be extended. Brainstorm ideas, use of space, and daily schedule, and record the plan on paper.

- *Increase children's awareness of and respect for diversity.* Plan activities that promote an antibias approach that is inclusive of people of different abilities, races, cultures, family compositions, classes, genders, religions, and sexual orientation. Promote an atmosphere of respect and acceptance of differences, and help children to look at similarities between people and their backgrounds. Make this an integral part of your program, not just something you do on special occasions. Parents and the children are good resources for getting information about customs that are representative

Figure 8-2 ■ Encourage children to try all kinds of activities.

Figure 8-3 ■ Web Design: Documentation of Children's Interest in Octopi

of their culture. Help children develop positive attitudes about male and female roles in society. Beware of falling into the trap of unconsciously planning different activities for boys and for girls. Encourage all children to try all activities. Include opportunities for children who have English or French as a second language to share their language with others.

- *Foster children's desire to become competent.* Let them help with daily routine tasks that allow them to use real tools. Demonstrate how to cut up fruit for snack time. Let them answer the telephone and take messages. Include them in the maintenance of your environment. Plan projects that use tools. Show them how to use a saw, hammer, and drill for woodworking projects. Let them use blenders, food processors, and other tools for baking and cooking. Be sure to carefully supervise children using these tools. Ensure that children are aware of safety concerns and proper procedures.

- *Encourage children's natural play and recreational interests.* Keep a store of props that inspire music, drama, and dancing. Help children also to be more competent with fads that sweep through groups of children. Yo-yos and hackie-sacks are not just "time wasters" but allow children to develop their skills. Play sports such as road hockey and flag football, and other games outdoors. Use these interests to foster their physical development and greater self-esteem. Be aware of safety concerns.

- *Promote creativity.* Encourage children to take pride in the process of what they are doing with their activities. Ask questions that encourage divergent thinking where they can explore many different paths. Pose problems and initiate the creative process of looking for alternative solutions, brainstorming, making predictions, and evaluating ideas.

- *Plan a balance of activities.* Plan for activities in a variety of curriculum areas: visual art, drama, music, science, technology, games, and active play. Include both group and individual activities. Have quiet times interspersed with more active play. Allow times for activities the children themselves initiate and conduct as well as those you choose and direct. Encourage adult/child and child/child interactions. Sometimes set up activities so you can be involved with children. At other times, encourage children to work together. Plan and develop projects together.

- *Have enough choices so all children can find something to do.* Variety will allow for different interests and levels of capability. Be sure to rotate materials, such as games, puzzles, and books, in order to prevent boredom and possible behaviour issues and support chances for the children to engage in self-regulation.

- *Include some activities that will recreate everyday experiences.* Bring in real items such as keyboards, guitars, and machines for children to explore. Make connections between play experiences and the "real world." Do some research and discuss where and how things happen in the world around them.

- *Allow time to meet the special needs of school-age children.* Let them be alone or give them time to do what they want. Provide opportunities for them to make new friends or spend time with existing friends. Some children may need time to rest or just do nothing.

- *Plan how transitions will be accomplished.* Will the children go from one activity to another in a whole group or individually? Will one adult stay on the playground to receive children as they leave the classroom? Provide snack as a free-flow option and allow the children to eat as they are hungry.

- *Document the process.* Have the children create a drawing, such as a web, of the learning experiences. Involve the children by recording their comments about the activities. Ask them their opinions about the time and efforts that they put into the activity or what they learned when doing the activity. Take pictures recording the process of their work and display them along with projects that they have created for families to see.

- *Be flexible.* If your plans are not working, change them. Or allow children to decide they want to do something different from what you had planned. Vary the settings for activities. Try painting outdoors or put on a play under a tree. Be spontaneous. Jump in and suggest a new game when the children look like they need a change. Have ideas at hand and know where you could access materials and equipment easily.

Organizing the Program: Curriculum Approaches

The curriculum that is developed defines the direction that the program has for the children, centre, school-age child care professionals, and parents. A curriculum is a multileveled process that encompasses what happens in a program each day, reflecting the philosophy, goals, and objectives of the centre (Jackman, 2005). Establishing what approach to take with the curriculum should be based on what one believes in terms of child development, learning styles, and general philosophies about play, leisure, and recreation. The philosophy is usually established by the staff in the centre or program and expresses their basic principles, attitudes, and beliefs about working with children and families (Jackman, 2005).

Various curriculum approaches are being practised and adapted in the fields of child care and education today. The desire to adopt a particular curriculum approach in place of existing practices has largely been fuelled by the need to improve the quality of child care programs. Child care professionals often feel the need to continue to justify their existence and value in the face of government policies and funding for child care. Much of the need to enhance the quality of child care programs has had its influence then on children's academic performance in school.

In light of the importance of improving the quality of school-age child care in our provinces and territories, a number of regions have instituted Quality Assurance Programming Practices and are using the School-Age Care Environment Rating Scale (SACERS) as a basis for training and the evaluation of program quality. This is discussed in Chapter 16.

Goffin and Wilson (2001, p. 226) talk about the premise or reasons that child care professionals choose one or more curriculum approaches. Choosing any one particular curriculum approach needs to be considered in light of the program's philosophy, values, and beliefs. It should be a process of consideration that relates to your program's goals and intentions regarding quality, implementation, and a process of continuous reflection, taking into consideration the vitality and growth being experienced by children and staff.

In each of the following curriculum approaches, learning through play is the central component. Children are viewed as being partners in the teaching–learning process with staff. Remember that children need opportunities to explore, investigate, ask questions, and talk about their experiences. Also keep in mind that children need to relate their learning to real-life situations and have opportunities to connect to their families and community.

Emergent Curriculum

An **emergent curriculum** evolves through continuous dialogue and documentation, frames learning as children devise and engage in projects (Essa, Young & Lehne, 1998, p. 80).

In this approach the experiences and activities emerge from the children's interests. Staff spend much time observing, talking to children, and taking notes while children take an active role in planning what they would like to do in their program. School-age child care professionals assist by connecting the children's ideas with their curriculum goals. In this approach, staff take on the role of facilitator: asking questions, posing problems, and extending play experiences by adding information and other materials. This allows for a certain amount of spontaneity, which is crucial in implementing a program for children. Here is an example of an emergent approach to curriculum planning:

The staff observed a group of children playing "dress up" with a box of clothing, hats, and shoes that was brought in by one of the parents in the program. With the available large blocks and mats, the children made a "runway" to walk along to show the clothing they were wearing. When the children sat down to have their snack, they talked with staff about a recent community fundraiser fashion show that they had been involved in. The staff extended the discussion to talk about fashion shows for weddings, sports wear, and seasonal clothing. They talked about people who design clothing and about people who work in factories where clothing is made. From this point, the children and staff planned different projects that various children could work on. One group did some drawings of clothing designs to display. Another group of children took some old clothing and, by cutting and sewing or gluing on other materials, they made new designs. Another group made a stage and backdrop that they could use for a fashion show. A couple of children worked on choosing some music for the show. The project evolved into a full production of a fashion show featuring the children's fashion designs that the parents and younger children in the centre attended.

Project-Based

Project-based approach is often used in combination with emergent curriculum. A project is defined as an in-depth investigation of a real world topic worthy of children's attention and effort (Chard, 2001). In most cases ideas emerge from the children's interests, but the staff can initiate them as well. The topics that are developed often come from personal experiences or events. These projects develop over time and can last for several weeks. Children can work on their own or in groups. Older children can help younger children in small groups. The school-age child care professional assists the children by offering suggestions, asking questions, encouraging children to have conversations, and asking questions or collecting information and materials together. Silvia Chard of the University of Alberta has developed a process for a project approach that involves three phases: beginning the project, developing it, and concluding the process. The process involves discussion of ideas and experiences with the children, field work that involves connections with parents and expertise in the community, representation through various means of play experiences, investigation by means of questioning and problem-solving, and display of the children's shared experiences. Development of different topic ideas can be found at her website, http://www.projectapproach.org.

Here is an example of how one idea that the children had about dinosaurs developed into a project:

Box 8-1 ■ Dinosaur Project

One day a group of children decided to create their own "life-size" dinosaur after two of the children, who are siblings, visited the Museum of Paleontology in Drumheller, Alberta. First they sat down with one of the staff to talk about how they would begin—what materials they would need, where and how they would collect what they needed, and where they could find some pictures of dinosaurs. The group had to decide where they would keep their project, since they would have to work on it for several weeks. The school-age child care professional helped them decide what kind of dinosaur to make and collected information about different kinds of dinosaurs. As the children worked on their project, the staff took videos and pictures of the stage-by-stage process of the work. After their "life-size" dinosaur was complete, the children had a chance to review the process with the staff and record comments.

To add to the development of various projects, staff can put together containers of items based on a particular topic of interest to the children. These containers should be easy to transport if the program is sharing space in a classroom in a school or in a gymnasium. Containers could be anything—a cardboard box, knapsack, bag, or old suitcase. Topics that might interest school-age children include the following:

- survivor kit
- washtub band kit
- magic kit
- Olympic sports kit

Many programs, such as Reggio Emilia (see below), use a project approach to planning curriculum.

Reggio Emilia Programs

Interest in the philosophy of **Reggio Emilia programs** for children in preschool programs has also resulted in Reggio Emilia programs for school-age children. School-age programs are often in the same facility as the preschool children and will follow the same philosophy that the child care centre has adopted. A Reggio program incorporates constructivist theories and adopts elements of emergent curriculum. Curriculum focuses on the integration of graphic arts as tools for cognitive, linguistic, and social development. School-age child care professionals learn alongside the children. They facilitate learning, do research on topics that the children are interested in, and work closely with families and the community. They act as provocateurs by listening, observing, comparing, and encouraging children to hypothesize, problem solve, and engage in conversation about various topics. School-age child care professionals are resources of knowledge and expertise to be shared with the children. There is a great deal of documentation of the children's work through drawings, pictures, and transcriptions of children's discussions and comments (Katz & Chard, 1996, p. 2).

Reggio Emilia programs
programs that incorporate elements of emergent curriculum and project-based approaches, focusing on an integration of graphic arts as tools for cognitive, linguistic, and social development

Figure 8-4 ■ Documentation of the process of children's projects.

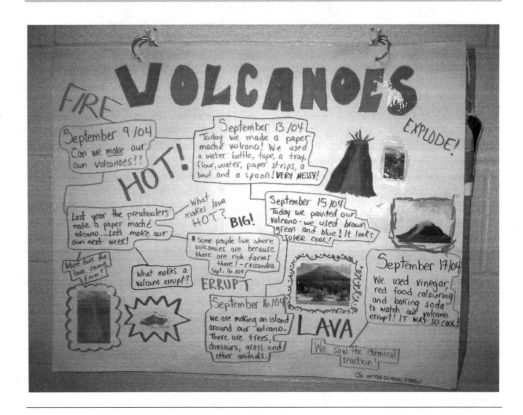

The environment is a key component of the program, with specific attention given to the design of the room, gardens, and furniture; there is an emphasis on colour, shape, texture, size, uniqueness, and beauty (Morris, 1995, pp. 2–3). There is a consistent collaboration between home, school, and community in the support of the children's learning and development.

The "100 Languages of Children of Reggio Emilia" includes drawings, dramatic play, sculptures, and paintings that represent children's processes and theories. Children are encouraged to think through various problems and represent their understanding in various ways. Teachers and children together continuously revisit, modify, and represent their expressed intentions.

High/Scope Programs

High/Scope programs
child-centred approach that involves the children in planning and reviewing their day along with active "doing," which involves workshop time

Before- and after-school programs that adopt a **High/Scope** approach have similar components and philosophy as their preschool and elementary classrooms: daily routine, learning environment, observations (strengths, needs, and interests) and adult–child interaction with a few unique adaptations that accommodate the needs of children during their extended day.

In terms of the daily routine, the plan-do-review sequence is still a key component for developmentally responsive practices in a school-age program. When the children arrive after school, they take part in a large group. This is a non-competitive time where they play games and take part in music and movement experiences. School-age child care professionals take the children's lead in determining what they want to do at this time. They might make up a new game, based on traditional rules, or change the words to familiar songs.

After this time, the children split into two groups with a caregiver and talk about their plans for the afternoon. The way the children share their plans may vary. They might draw them, write about them in a journal, act them out, play a guessing game, or simply talk about them.

Unlike the traditional High/Scope program, the school-age program does not have a structured small group time. Because these children are in structured classrooms throughout the day, High/Scope programs for the extended day allow for more flexibility and freedom, meeting the children's unique needs. These programs have borrowed from the elementary High/Scope model for the "do" or work time portion with a workshop time. During this time, children can make choices to go to any area of the classroom or join in a particular workshop at any time. Caregivers plan the workshops, but they are based on the children's interests and needs, which are identified through careful ongoing observations. High/Scope's five elements of active learning—materials, manipulation, choice, language, and adult support—are inherent in these experiences. A quiet area is always available during this work time for children who choose to do homework. Snack is offered as a free-flow choice in a designated area of the room. Children are encouraged to learn to self-regulate their food choices and the amount of food they eat. Interaction strategies of High/Scope are practised including problem solving, conflict resolution, and encouragement. Playing and engaging as a partner with children, and actively responding with questions and conversation, is essential. Learning environments are flexible, adapting to the interests of the children. For example, a block play area might turn into a stage for a play. Observations have been adapted to reflect the needs of this program by combining the preschool and elementary tools to include six areas of development: Language and Literacy, Logic-Math/Science, Fine Arts, Physical Movement, Music, and Social-Emotional Development. At the end of the day before the children leave, they review their day and share their experiences with a teacher and parent individually or in a traditional group time. Again, this may be done in different ways through conversations, drawings, writings, stories, and games (Kruse, 2003).

Waldorf Programs

Schools with **Waldorf programs** also may offer before- and after-school programs, and care on PD days and holidays to meet the needs of working parents whose children attend these schools. The Waldorf educational philosophy carries through these programs. Their focus is on preparing children to be dynamic, resilient lifelong learners. The following attributes are nurtured: creative thinking, imagination, flexibility, and focus; emotional intelligence, empathy, and self-esteem; physical vitality, stamina, perseverance, and spiritual awareness; along with appreciation and responsibility for nature, work, and fellow human beings (http://www.waldorf.ca)

Waldorf programs
child focused; develop attributes of a well-rounded person to think creatively, be socially responsive, and have a strong sense of emotional and physical well-being

Montessori Programs

The key concept of a **Montessori program** is the prepared environment, offering a wide variety of exciting learning opportunities at the end of the day. Students can make choices of the activities available that relate to their interests and expand on their knowledge and skills. Some of the choices offered at the Glebe Montessori School in Ottawa include paint, palettes, and brushes; language labs—rench, Spanish, Italian, Mandarin; drama; comic illustration; creative cooking; 3-D

Montessori programs
a prepared environment that supports each child's independence and ability to plan his or her own activities after school

engineering; lacrosse; chess and knitting, crocheting and stitching, to name a few. As is characteristic of Montessori philosophy, children are encouraged to be independent and to take charge of their own learning (http://www.glebemontessor.com).

Full-Day Early Learning–Kindergarten Programs

full-day early–learning kindergarten programs
child-centred, developmentally appropriate, integrated, core day and extended-day programs of play-based learning for 4- and 5-year-old children

Full-day early learning–kindergarten programs are child-centred, developmentally appropriate, integrated core day and extended-day programs of learning for 4- and 5-year-old children. The purpose of the program is to establish a strong foundation for learning in the early years in a caring, safe, play-based environment that promotes the development of children in all areas: physical, social, emotional and cognitive growth, as well as a healthy well-being. The program also will help to provide a smoother transition to grade 1, establish a foundation for lifelong learning and improve children's future overall success in school and beyond. Partnerships with families and communities and respect for diversity, equity, and inclusion are key elements of the program. Play is seen as the core of learning that capitalizes on children's natural curiosity and desire to learn. Each child is viewed as being unique, and needs opportunities to learn in ways that best suit his or her needs and individual development. A planned curriculum provides opportunities for children to engage in experiences that fall within their zone of proximal development and supports differing strategies that teachers might use to assist them.

Kindergarten programs see self-regulation as essential to a child's capacity to learn. This is based on Charles Pascal's report in "Every Child, Every Opportunity: Curriculum and Pedagogy for the Early Learning Program" that stated "self-regulation is the cornerstone of development and a central building block to early learning" (p. 4).

Social, emotional, and cognitive self-regulation and the ability to communicate with others gives children the tools they need to establish their own internal motivation for adapting and understanding themselves and others. In so doing, children are able to attend to tasks, follow instructions, cooperate, be aware of their own feelings and those of others around them, and know how to respond in appropriate ways.

A kindergarten teacher and an early childhood educator form a team approach in a full-day early learning–kindergarten program. As reflective learners themselves, they work together to provide a program that provides a balance of educator-initiated and child-initiated activities. Some activities include whole-class instruction, small group time, and independent learning at various learning centres. Learning experiences promote integrated learning, with opportunities to explore, inquire, investigate, and experiment with materials that bring connections to real life. See "The Inquiry Process in Early Learning–Kindergarten Classrooms" in Appendix B. Understanding and incorporating children's social and cultural contexts is also seen as essential for optimal learning.

The full-day early learning–kindergarten program comprises six learning areas: personal and social development; language; mathematics; science and technology; health and physical activity; and the arts (Elementary Teacher's Federation of Ontario, 2010). Children demonstrate their learning by saying, doing, and representing their ideas, and the teaching team supports their learning through intentional interactions by responding, challenging, and extending their learning through various means of observing, documenting, and authentic assessments. The extended-day (fee-based) component is complementary to the core day program and provides a seamless and consistent experience for 4- and 5-year-olds. It is a play-based learning program that is offered before the core day begins and continues at the end of the day, and is delivered by a team of registered early childhood educators. (Ontario Ministry of Education, 2006).

Anti-bias Curriculum

Anti-bias philosophy promotes attitudes of respect and acceptance within an atmosphere of inclusion and diversity. This fills the need for inter-group harmony and equity (Saderman Hall & Rhomberg, 1997, pp. 2, 17).

Figure 8-5 ■ Web Drawing: Children's Ideas About Castles

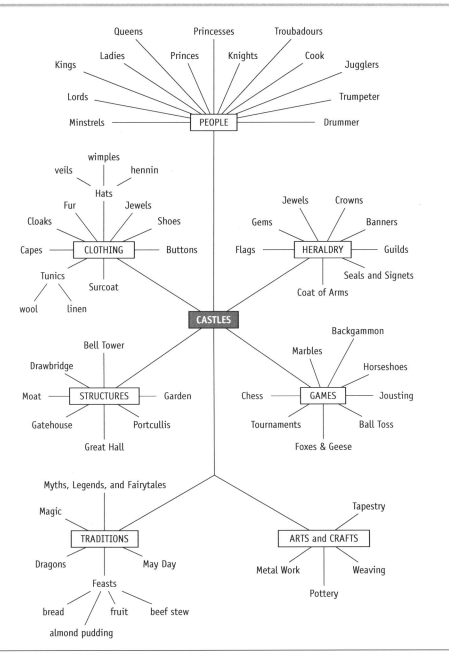

At an early age children become aware of differences among people. Four-year-olds notice and begin to ask about the differences between boys and girls, why one child has dark skin, why another speaks with an accent, or why another cannot walk and is in a wheelchair. By the time children reach middle childhood, they may stop asking the questions because adults are embarrassed or do not know how to answer them. The result can be the development of prejudices or stereotypes. In a bias-free environment, Derman-Sparks (1989) says, "children should be free to ask questions about any subject, to use their own ideas in problem-solving, to engage in real dialogue with adults, to make choices, and to have some say in their daily school life." School-age child care professionals can assist children by being open to their questions, challenging stereotypes, and pointing out similarities and differences as being a natural part of our world.

School-age child care professionals set program goals and guidelines that address the needs of all children and families. An **anti-bias curriculum** focuses on policies and practices that acknowledge the development of children's positive self-worth, self-identity, and well-being. Program goals should positively address the 10 areas of potential bias: ability, age, appearance, beliefs, class, culture, family composition, gender, race, and sexuality. A **bias** is a point of view, belief, or attitude that can be demonstrated verbally, nonverbally, or physically. It is unrealistic to expect that every person would be completely unbiased. We are all products of our time and environment; therefore, we all have preferences. However, to act on them would exclude others and then constitute a bias (Saderman Hall & Rhomberg, 1997, pp. 2–3).

Wolpert (1999, p. 13) identifies four goals for implementing an anti-bias currriculum:

1. Nurture the construction of a knowledgeable, confident identity as an individual and as a member of multicultural groups (such as gender, race, ethnicity, or class).
2. Promote comfortable, empathetic interaction with all people from diverse backgrounds (majority and minority groups).
3. Foster each child's ability to recognize bias and injustice (to identify unfair stereotypes, comments, and discriminatory behaviours).
4. Cultivate each child's ability to stand up, individually and with others, against bias and injustice.

Wolpert, E. (1999). *Start seeing diversity—The basic guide to an anti-bias classroom.* St. Paul, MN: Redleaf Press. Page 13.

In order to help children develop positive self-esteem and a confident identity, school-age child care professionals must incorporate the children's world into the program. "When children see their lives reflected around them, whether in music, art, cooking, books or other media, they feel that sense of belonging that is such a fundamental condition of positive self-esteem" (Murphy Kilbride, 1997, p. 97). It is important to include activities and materials that reflect the diverse lives of the children in your program. It is also crucial to provide interesting materials and experiences with the children that would introduce them to the diversity of the world. A good example of this is in the book *Crow Boy* by Taro Yashima (1955). In this story Crow Boy's skill of imitating the sounds of animals in the forests around his home are ridiculed and unappreciated by the children in his school. His teacher notices this and comes to his rescue. The teacher talks to the children about how unique and valuable this talent is to Crow Boy's culture and then he is asked to demonstrate the ability to imitate crow's voices in a talent show (Murphy Kilbride, 1997, p. 95).

anti-bias curriculum

policies and practices that acknowledge the development of children's positive self-worth, identity, and well-being; addressing the impact of stereotyping, bias, and discriminatory behaviour

bias

point of view, belief, or attitude that can be demonstrated verbally, nonverbally, or physically; areas of potential bias include ability, age, appearance, beliefs, class, culture, family composition, gender, race, and sexuality

Feelings of belonging in children can be nurtured through an atmosphere of **inclusion.** Inclusion means "not leaving anyone out" or "helping everyone to feel a part of an activity or situation." School-age child care professionals play a large role in modelling these aspects of inclusion:

1. Seek out "teachable moments" to stimulate questions and discussion in situations involving bias. Challenge stereotypes and correct misinformation.
2. Initiate activities that get children to think about antibias ideas. Perform puppet plays with Persona Dolls (dolls that represent unique qualities of people, such as race or ability) to present a problem situation; ask the children to come up with some possible solutions.
3. Organize group discussions about diverse abilities, different types of families, and gender roles.
4. Encourage acceptance of different points of view, acknowledging that young school-age children are still somewhat egocentric developmentally.
5. Focus on similarities before exploring the differences. For example, "Everyone has a birthday, but it may be recognized in different ways in different homes."
6. Avoid the "tourist approach" that teaches children about diversity *only* through holiday celebrations, ethnic art activities, and cooking ethnic foods. In contrast, an antibias approach takes into account children's developmental levels, their interests, and their concerns.
7. On the other hand, be inclusive in the celebration of various holidays. Don't leave any one holiday out, even if it is the one that is practised most by the children in the program.
8. Encourage respect for the variety of celebrations, traditions, and religions in the world.
9. Provide accurate information about holidays in a developmentally appropriate manner.

inclusion
sense of belonging with a blending of differences; not leaving anyone out and helping everyone to feel part of an activity or situation

Blisson, J. (1997). *Celebrate! An anti-bias guide to enjoying holidays.* St. Paul, MN: Redleaf Press. Page 27.

You can create an antibias approach by including the following in the program environment:

- photos of children and families that reflect the racial/ethnic background and family composition of the group and the surrounding community if the group is particularly homogenous
- images of both men and women doing a variety of jobs, not just those that are typically associated with a gender
- images of differently abled people doing jobs or interacting with others in recreational settings
- various colours, patterns, and textures of materials and items that represent different cultures
- opportunities for children to see or hear different languages through signs, labels, story tapes, or songs, including braille and sign language

Figure 8-6 ■ Learning to knit.

Chapter 8   Program Planning   **143**

- music, dance, activities, and games from different cultures
- diverse places and people to visit and invite to the program as guests

Toys and materials in an antibias classroom should include

- books that reflect diversity of gender roles and ethnic differences as well as people with different abilities and in different kinds of jobs
- books that include different languages, either through stories or alphabets
- dramatic play materials that encourage children to engage in common, everyday tasks without concern for gender roles
- implements and tools used by different ethnic groups, such as cooking equipment, holiday decorations, clothes, or personal objects
- art materials that can be used to depict people of different skin tones or are representative of different cultures and that can be used by children with different abilities, such as left-handed scissors
- small toys and manipulatives, such as puzzles, puppets, and dolls that depict various aspects of diversity (family composition, ethnicity, ages, physical abilities, and appearances)

Planning for Cultural and Linguistic Diversity (Bicultural and Bilingual Children)

In Canada the Canadian Charter of Human Rights and Freedoms promotes the rights and freedoms of people to equality, cultural heritage, and official language usage (see Table 8-3).

Table 8-3 ■ Canadian Charter of Human Rights and Freedoms

The Charter of Human Rights and Freedoms (1982) provides protection of the following:

- Fundamental freedoms
- Democratic rights
- Equality rights to all individuals
- Official languages of Canada
- Minority language education rights
- Canada's multicultural heritage
- Aboriginal people's rights
- Rights to employment

Section 15: Equality Rights, that states that every individual is equal under the law, without discrimination based on race, national or ethnic origin, colour, religion, sex, age, or mental or physical disability.

Section 27: Multicultural Heritage, that preserves and enhances the diversity of ethnic cultures in our communities.

Section 28: Equality of the Sexes, refers to guaranteed equality to male and female persons.

From *Include me too! Human diversity in early childhood*, by K. Murphy Kilbride, 1997, Toronto: Harcourt Brace & Co., Canada, p. 216.

In addition to recognizing that each child is unique and has an individual pattern of growth, remember also that children come from varied backgrounds and cultures. Children's sense of self-worth stems partly from their experiences within the family and their community and their ability to master the skills expected of them in those settings. They will learn best if the expectations and values of their school or school-age program are congruent with those of the family and community. As an example, children who can communicate well with their family or neighbourhood friends in a language other than English or French may find it difficult to be understood or to learn in other environments. They are learning to adapt to a new language and culture, and at the same time they are trying to preserve the culture and language of their country of origin. In this situation, children become bilingual and sometimes multilingual; when retaining an original culture while adopting a new culture, they become bicultural. To this end, the National Association for the Education of Young Children (NAEYC) (1996) states that developmentally appropriate programs should

> recognize that all children are cognitively, linguistically, and emotionally connected to the language and culture of their home.

Bredekamp and Copple (1997), broadened statements about diversity to recommend that programs develop a positive climate for learning within a democratic community.

Accomplishing this means knowing each child well, taking into account individual differences, and being aware of each child's developmental level. It also means bringing a child's culture and language into the program so children can feel they belong. Children learn through reading books or hearing books read to them about other cultures and current events, and by discussing cultural values. Staff can also group children flexibly in small cooperative groups to work on projects so they can learn through discussions in which they share information or expertise. A democratic community also means that children with disabilities are included as members of the group.

Another aspect of cultural and linguistic diversity is embodied in NAEYC (1996):

> Acknowledge that children can demonstrate their knowledge and capabilities in many ways.

This statement recognizes that children have acquired many cognitive skills and knowledge before entering school or child care. They should be able to demonstrate those skills using their own language and then begin to build upon that base while learning a second language.

> Understand that without comprehensive input, second-language learning can be difficult.

Children may be able to learn a second language, but learning more complex cognitive skills requires an integrated approach. They need a learning environment in which to build on the skills they acquired in their first language while gaining new skills in the second.

Research in the past 15 to 20 years has shown that bilingual or multilingual children perform better on school tests and other school work, are better thinkers, and improve their cognitive abilities as they learn more than one language. Being able to speak more than one language gives children more opportunities for employment in the future (Murphy Kilbride, 1997, p. 168).

Other recommendations focus on families. NAEYC (1996) suggests that parents be actively involved in the program, that staff help parents become knowledgeable about the cognitive value of knowing more than one language, and that programs support the family's cultural values.

Recommendations for programs and practice in these guidelines recognize the importance of respecting and supporting children's home language.

> Recognize that children can and will acquire English even when their home language is used and respected.

Children should be able to build upon cognitive skills they have already acquired using their home language. When children have lots of opportunities to read and be read to in their home or in a group setting, they will develop literacy in a second language more easily (Krashen, 1992).

The recommendations also suggest supporting and preserving children's home language. Ideally, this can be done by an adult speaking the language and by providing many examples of the language within the environment. Books, bulletin boards, tape recordings, labels on materials, and signs are all ways to incorporate the home language into the environment. If the school-age child care professionals do not speak the child's language, they should learn words and phrases from that language. This will help to establish a rapport with the children and their families. If several languages are spoken by children in a group, the task may seem overwhelming. In this case, children who speak the same language can be grouped together at times to work on specific projects. However, it is important to ensure that these children do not become isolated and are incorporated into other groups as well.

Planning Field Trips and Involvement in the Community

Field trips can be a simple walk around the block or an all-day trip to the beach. Both should be planned carefully, although obviously a walk takes less planning than an all-day excursion. Start by deciding the purpose of the trip. A walk can reinforce a project to map your neighbourhood or collect material for a nature collage. A trip to the beach can include collecting rocks or studying wave patterns. As with all other activities, fit this into the overall pattern of activities.

Figure 8-7 ■ On a field trip to the airport.

Plan each detail so that both you and the children know what to expect (see Appendix C). Inform parents about the trip well in advance and obtain permission (see Appendix D). Arrange for lunch for day-long trips, and transportation. Make sure there are enough adults to properly supervise the children. Discuss the arrangements with your administrator and other school-age child care professionals. Tell the children where they are going, what they will do, and what the rules will be. (Make sure you visit the site ahead of time so you will know what to expect and can plan appropriately.) Be prepared with alternate plans in the case of inclement weather. You could also help the children to do some fundraising for the trip if necessary. Fundraising activities can be as simple as the children making and selling popcorn on a movie day or asking families to sell plants or other typical fundraising products.

Plan further with the children so they will get maximum benefit from the trip. For instance, if they are going to the beach to gather rocks for a collection, prepare ahead. Read books, look at pictures, and talk about different kinds of rocks they might find. If you have a video or digital camera, take it along to record interesting finds and to document where the rocks were found or what the children saw.

Do a follow-up when you return to the program or on the following day. Ask children to share what they collected and tell about what they saw. They should also be encouraged to relate what they learned from the trip, what they liked best, and perhaps even how they would change the trip if they went again. You can then create a book documenting the field trip by having each child draw a picture and briefly write about the trip.

See Chapter 15 for suggestions of places to visit. Develop partnerships with individuals and groups in the community and use them as resources to provide children with a wider range of activities. Invite guests who have interesting hobbies that the children might enjoy. Plan ways that children can get involved in their community and develop a sense of citizenship by visiting senior citizens in a retirement home, collecting toys for less fortunate children during holidays, and getting involved in environmental awareness programs. See Chapters 13 and 15 for other ideas.

Making a Schedule

A good program is more than just a series of activities. The structure of those activities within the context of the day allows children to enjoy their time in program. Greet the children when they arrive, ask them about their day, and provide time to look at any of their projects from their school day. Be available to talk with the parents when they come to pick up their children and pass on any messages. You may also need to coordinate with the school about how different age groups of children will move from the centre to the school and back again if the centre is attached to the school. Younger children will need more assistance, while older children may be allowed to make these transitions with less supervision. For example, one staff member may be designated to bring the children down to the kindergarten classroom and pick them up each day. This could also be an important job for a volunteer in the program.

From reading the previous pages you know what goes into a typical day with children. Start by writing down the specifics for your program. Include everything you do each day, then add things that have to be done less frequently. Next, estimate how much time to allow for each activity. As you put your schedule into effect, you will probably revise it a few times.

Here are a few guidelines to follow in putting together a schedule:

- Make transitions as smooth as possible—be available and keep the routine consistent.
- Some familiarity with consistent routines provides comfort for children on a day-to-day basis.
- Allow time for kindergarten children to rest if needed.
- Limit waiting periods. No one likes to stand in line for a long time. With careful planning of the schedule, this will avoid any problems with negative behaviour.
- Ensure that children have enough time to finish what they are doing. Give them lots of warning ahead of time.
- Access individual and group needs—allow for choices where possible.

Figure 8-8 ■ **Staff greeting the children as they arrive at the school-age program by bus.**

Chapter 8   Program Planning   **147**

- Give responsibility where appropriate—self-serve snack, work with younger children in the centre, cleaning up.
- Plan for group meeting times for discussion, reflection on learning, and problem solving.
- Plan for clubs such as drama, art, cooking, or whatever the children are interested in.
- Be flexible and adjust to the needs of the children. Incorporate the children's ideas.
- Plan according to the space the program is using. Incorporate the children's ideas.
- Plan for inclement weather days; have an alternate schedule (with the use of additional space, such as a gymnasium) posted so children can predict what may happen on such days.
- Plan special events and trips based on their interests on days when the children will be there for a full or half day.
- Outside time is very important after a long day of school.
- Provide time for individual children to do homework in a quiet place.
- Allow for older children to attend lessons and team sports with permission from the parents.

A <u>typical schedule</u> for a before- and after-school program may look like the following:

6:00 a.m. *Children arrive individually. Breakfast is available for children who are hungry. Some children may want to finish homework, others may finish a project from a previous day. Still others may want to work quietly at an art centre or read. A few may want to expend some energy outdoors.*

8:15 a.m. *Children complete whatever they are doing and prepare to go to school.*

8:30 a.m. *Children board the bus for their elementary schools.*

When children return to the centre at the end of the day, they may follow this schedule:

3:00 p.m. *Children arrive in a group on the bus. Some may be hungry and need a snack. Others may want to rest a bit before joining activities. Still others may need to spend time with their school-age child care professional to talk about what happened at school.*

3:15 p.m. *Most children want to be outdoors after a day of sitting in school. Schedule outdoor free play, exercises, games, or sports.*

4:00 p.m. *Group time, planning, observations, discussions, reflection, problem solving.*

4:15 p.m. *Indoors for a variety of activities: homework, clubs, individual projects, music, reading, cooking, or talking with friends.*

5:30 p.m. *Finish activities, straighten environment, and collect belongings. Children may read alone or in a group until parents arrive.*

Your job as a school-age child care professional should be enjoyable, exciting, and engaging. Planning with the children's interests and needs in mind will help to avoid many of the frustrations that may occur.

Summary

Theories of child development form the basis for planning a program and its curriculum. Development is seen as a process that continues through life and is based on environmental and hereditary influences. Research has identified critical periods of development in middle childhood that are strongly influenced by adults' ability to provide a supportive and nurturing environment for children. Gardner's Multiple-Intelligences Theory identifies eight areas of intelligence that work together in a holistic manner in the brain, in order for children to learn. The developmental research of Piaget and Vygotsky points out the importance of viewing development from a predictable stage-by-stage process in the context of a social–cultural context of learning. Programs should address the needs of school-age children in all areas of development: psychosocial, cognitive, and physical.

Play is an essential component in designing a program for school-age children. Play is the process through which children can explore their environment, learn, be creative, and bring some relaxation and recreation to the end of their day.

Guidelines for developmentally responsive practices address all areas of an effective program for school-age children. They include the role of school-age child care professionals, provision for the development of peer relationships, the use of positive guidance, an environment that accommodates small and large groups, and activities that are geared to the interests and developmental needs and abilities of the children.

Planning is essential to a good school-age program; it ensures that a variety of activities will emerge from observations and that lots of open-ended materials will be always be ready. Conflicts between children will be less frequent. Staff can share responsibilities for planning with parents and children, implementing both short- and long-term goals. Parents should be involved in the program, and children should have lots of opportunities to explore their community and make connections to real life.

When planning activities for your school-age group, capitalize on children's interests. Increase their awareness of cultural differences. Foster children's desire to be competent by showing them how to do real jobs using real tools. Encourage their play interests and provide enough choices of things for them to do. Try to balance activities between group and individual, quiet and active, child initiated and adult initiated. Incorporate intentional teaching-learning practices of observation and documentation. Include everyday experiences such as a trip to the grocery store or a walk around the block.

In the pursuit of quality, professionals in the field of school-age child care continue to explore the numerous curriculum-planning approaches. Emergent curriculum, project-based, High/Scope, Waldorf, and Montessori approaches are each related to a particular philosophy of how children play and learn. Many of these approaches are integrated within one another and emphasize the importance of planning, at the same time allowing opportunities for the children to be involved in various ways. The Reggio Emilia Program incorporates an emergent curriculum- and a project-based approach to planning curriculum. Full-Day Early Learning–Kindergarten and Extended-Day programs provide opportunities for 4- and 5-year-olds to get a strong start in school, to be involved in play-based integrated learning experiences, and be given the opportunity to develop as healthy, confident and lifelong learners.

An antibias approach promotes respect, acceptance, and understanding. It is designed to be inclusive of all people. In middle childhood, children will develop prejudices or biases. In fact, we all have certain biases or preferences. Areas of bias include ability, age, appearance, beliefs, class, culture, family composition, gender, race, and sexuality. School-age child care professionals need to recognize their own biases and those demonstrated by the children. They need to be open to talk to children about similarities and differences in people and challenge stereotypes and discriminatory behaviour by providing accurate information. Materials and activities need to be carefully planned to reflect the diversity of children and families in the program, as well as to give children a diverse perspective of the world around them.

The NAEYC has made recommendations for working with children whose home language is other than English or French. Adults should recognize the importance of children's home language and acknowledge that children can demonstrate their knowledge and capabilities in many ways. Learning a second language can be a challenge, and children need to be able to build upon their cognitive skills using their home language. They will then be able to move on and gain new skills in the second language that can give them long-term benefits.

NAEYC recommends that programs support children's home language by providing examples of the language in the environment. Books, bulletin boards, audiotapes and CDs, labels on materials, and signs are all ways to incorporate the home language into the school-age program environment. Adults should also learn some words and phrases from the children's home language. When several languages are spoken by children in a group, it helps if children who speak the same language can work together at times.

Plan field trips and involvement in the community, developing partnerships and connections with people in various organizations.

Draw up a schedule by first listing everything you do each day. Allow adequate time for each activity but not so much that children get bored. Allow time to meet each child's needs. Do not forget to plan for transition times. Involve the children in making decisions about their day.

Key Terms

developmentally responsive planning

multiple intelligences

play

constructivism

observation

documentation

emergent curriculum

Project-based

Reggio Emilia programs

High/Scope programs

Waldorf programs

Montessori programs

full-day early-learning kindergarten

antibias approach

bias

inclusion

Student Activities

1. Talk to a group of school-age children. Find out what they are interested in by asking what they do after school, what they read, or what they watch on television. Is there a difference between boys' interests and girls' interests? Are there age-level differences?
2. Write a short paragraph about what you liked to do when you were between 6 and 10 years old. How did you develop these interests? Did your parents encourage them? Did your friends?
3. Survey school-age programs in your community to determine the curriculum approach used. Ask what reasons they have for choosing their approach to developing the curriculum.

4. Set up a schedule for an all-day program for a holiday when the school is closed and the centre is open, such as on a professional development day. Include as many of the suggestions from this chapter as possible.

Review Questions

1. List and describe three theories of child development that have an influence on program planning.
2. Describe five principles of developmentally responsive practice.
3. State five reasons for careful planning when you work with school-age children.
4. Identify the best approaches to curriculum development that would give children the opportunity to be involved in the planning.
5. What are the benefits of constructivism in developing an approach to curriculum?
6. In what ways can parents help you to plan a good program?
7. Suggest three activities you can include in the program that would promote an antibias and inclusive approach.
8. Why is it important to encourage parents to continue to use their first language with their children?
9. In what ways can field trips be used to enhance a school-age program?
10. How can children who attend a school-age program be more involved in their community?

Case Study

François and Marissa have both been assigned to a group of 9- to 11-year-olds in a YMCA after-school program. Marissa had been a preschool teacher in a Reggio Emilia centre and has a degree in early childhood education. François worked for many years as an assistant teacher in a grade-four classroom. They have widely differing opinions about how their program should be planned. Marissa believes they should rely to a great extent on what the children want to learn or do and develop the curriculum from there. She is familiar with observing the children's play, documenting their ideas, and developing a curriculum plan from there. François is more familiar with thematic-based and curriculum areas-based approaches, and he has several project theme boxes that he has collected over the years that he uses quite easily to set up a weekly or monthly curriculum plan. He feels that it is important to have a plan of activities ready each day when the children arrive to the program and to display it on the bulletin board for the parents to see.

1. How would you describe the program's different approaches to curriculum planning?
2. How can they resolve their differences so they can work together and the children gain the maximum benefit?
3. Can you think of a way to combine their two viewpoints of looking at curriculum to ensure that they maintain a child-centred approach?

References

Albrecht, K. M. & Plantz, M. C. (1993). *Developmentally appropriate practice in school-age child care programs* (2nd ed.). Dubuque, IA: Kendall/Hunt Publishing Company.

Arce, E. (2000). *Curriculum for young children—An introduction.* Albany, NY: Delmar Thomson Learning.

Blisson, J. (1997). *Celebrate! An Anti-Bias Guide to Enjoying Holidays.* St. Paul, MN: Redleaf Press.

Bredekamp, S. & Copple, C. (eds.) (1997). *Developmentally appropriate practice in early childhood programs* (Rev. ed.). Washington, DC: National Association for the Education of Young Children.

Canadian Child Care Federation (2001). Resource sheet #23: Developmentally appropriate practices in school-age child care. Ottawa: Canadian Child Care Federation.

Chard, S. (2001). *Project approach: Five structural features of the project approach.* Retrieved April 5, 2005, from http://www.project-approach.com/foundation/learning.htm

Crowther, I. (2003). *Creating effective learning environments.* Scarborough, ON: Thomson, Nelson.

Derman-Sparks, L. (1989). *Anti-bias curriculum: Tool for empowering young children.* Washington D.C.: NAEYC.

Elementary Teacher's Federation of Ontario. (2010). *Thinking it through: Teaching and learning in the kindergarten classroom.* 480 University Ave. Toronto, ON M5G 1V2, 1-888-838-3836.

Essa, E., Young, R., & Lehne, L. (1998). *Introduction to early childhood education* (2nd Canadian ed.). Scarborough, ON: ITP Nelson.

Glebe Montessori Schoo.l After School Programs. Ottawa. Retrieved June 2012, from http://www.glebemontessori.com/programs/after-school-programs

Goffin, S. & Wilson, C. (2001). *Curriculum models and early childhood education—Appraising the relationship* (2nd ed.). Upper Saddle River, NJ: Merrill Prentice Hall.

International Play Association. (n.d.). *The child's right to play.* Retrieved April 5, 2005, from http://www.ipaworld.org/ipa_declaration.html

Jackman, H. L. (2005). *Early childhood curriculum: A child's connection to the world* (3rd ed.). Toronto: Thomson Delmar Learning.

Jacobs, E., Vukelich, G., & Howe, N. (n.d.). *Pathways of constructivism: A self-directed guide for educators.* Human Development Resources Canada: Social Development Partnerships program.

Katz, L. & Chard, S. (1996). *The contribution of documentation to the quality of early childhood education.* Retrieved April 5, 2005, from http://www.cariboo.bc.ca/ae/literacies/reggio/reggioarticle1.htm

Krashen, S. (1992). *Fundamentals of language education.* Torrence, CA: Laredo Publishing.

Kruse, T. (2003). Using the High/Scope approach in before-and after-school programs. High/Scope Press, A Magazine for Educators. Spring, 9–14, 19–29.

Lowe, E. (2000, Winter). A school-age program with a difference. *Interaction,* CCCF, 30–34.

Malaguzzi, L. (1994). Your image of the child: Where teaching begins. *Child Care Information Exchange,* 61.

Morris, J. (1995, Fall). A glimpse of child care in Italy. *Child & Family Canada,* CCCF.

Murphy Kilbride, K. (1997). *Include me too! Human diversity in early childhood.* Toronto: Harcourt Brace & Co., Canada.

NAEYC. (1996). NAEYC position statement: Responding to linguistic and cultural diversity— Recommendations for effective early childhood education. *Young Children, 51*(2), 4–12.

Ontario Ministry of Education. (2010–11). *The full-day early learning–kindergarten program—draft version.* Retrieved June 2012, from http://www.edu.gov.on.ca

Ontario Ministry of Education.. (2010–11). *The full-day early learning–kindergarten program—the extended day draft version.* Retrieved June 2012, from http://www.edu.gov.on.ca

Piaget, J. (1952). *The origin of intelligence in children.* (M. Cook, Trans.). New York: International Universities Press. (Original work published 1936)

Powell, J. (2001). *Multiple intelligences activating young minds.* Grand Rapids, MI: McGraw-Hill Children's Publishing.

Saderman Hall, N. & Rhomberg, V. (1995). *The affective curriculum—Teaching the anti-bias approach to young children.* Toronto: Nelson, Canada.

UNICEF. (n.d.) *Sports, recreation, and play.* Retrieved April 21, 2005, from http:www.unicef.org/publications/files/5571_SPORT_EN.pdf

United Nations (1989, November 20). Article 31. Retrieved April 5, 2005, from the International Play Association website at http://www.ipaworld.org/ipa_article31.html

Vygotsky, L. (1978). *Mind in society: The development of higher psychological processes.* Cambridge, MA: Harvard University Press. (Original work published 1934)

Waldorf Education. Retrieved June 2012 from http://www.waldorf.ca/index.cfm?pagepath=Waldorf_Education&id=19491

Wolpert, E. (1999). *Start seeing diversity—The basic guide to an anti-bias classroom*. St. Paul, MN: Redleaf Press.

Wood, C. (1997). *Yardsticks, children in the classroom, ages 4-14: A resource for parents and teachers*. Greenfield, MA: Northeast Foundation for Children.

Workman S. & Anziano, M. (1993). Curriculum webs: Weaving connections from children to teachers. *Young Children*, 48 (2), 4–9.

Yashima, T. (1955). *Crow Boy*. New York: Viking.

Selected Further Reading

Bergstrom, J. M. (1990). *School's out*. Berkeley: Ten Speed Press.

Boutte, G., Van Scoy, I., & Hendley, S. (1996). Multicultural and nonsexist prop boxes. *Young Children, 52*(1), 34–39.

Cech, M. (1991). *Globalchild—Multicultural resources for young children*. New York: Addison-Wesley.

Graeme, J. & Fahlman, R. (1990). *Hand in hand, multicultural experiences for young children*. Toronto: Pearson Education Canada.

Haas-Foletta, K. & Cogley, M. (1990). *School-age ideas and activities for after school programs*. Nashville, TN: School Age Notes.

Hendrick, J. (Ed.). (1997). *First steps toward teaching the Reggio way*. Upper Saddle River, NJ: Merrill Prentice Hall.

Katz, L. & Chard, S. (1991). *Engaging children's minds: The project approach*. Norwood, NJ: Ablex Publishing Corporation.

Koralek, D., Newman, R., & Colker, L. (1995). *Caring for children in school-age programs. Vol. 1 & 2*. Washington, DC: Teaching Strategies.

Parry, C. (1987) *Let's celebrate! Canada's special days*. Toronto: Kids Can Press.

Sisson, L. (1990). *Kids club, a school–age program guide for directors*. Nashville, TN: School-Age Notes.

Whitney, T. (1999). *Kids like us; Using persona dolls in the classroom*. St. Paul, MN: Redleaf Press.

Websites

A Framework for Ontario Early Childhood Settings: Developmental Continuum Charts: 2.5–6; 5–8 years
http://www.edu.gov.on.ca/childcare/oelf/continuum/continuum.pdf

Early Learning Framework Ontario
http://www.edu.gov.on.ca/childcare/oelf

Kindergarten GAINS: Series of professional videos and resources
http://www.edugains.ca/newsite/fulldaykinder/index.html

Kindergarten Matters: Intentional Play-Based Learning: Thinking, Inquiry, Self-regulation, Documentation
http://resources.curriculum.org/secretariat/kindergarten

Multimedia Resources for Professional Learning—Kindergarten
http://resources.curriculum.org/secretariat/kindergarten/files/ KindergartenGuide.pdf

Ontario Ministry of Education—Full Day Kindergarten and Child Care
http://www.edu.gov.on.ca/kindergarten

Project Approach in Early Childhood & Elementary Education
http://www.projectapproach.org

Reggio Emilia—The Hundred Languages of Children
http://www.reggiokids.com/about/hundred_languages.php

Chapter 9

Creating an Environment: Designing the Space

Objectives

After studying this chapter, the student should be able to:

- Describe ways in which the physical environment is responsive to learning and development
- State general guidelines for planning indoor and outdoor space
- Draw a plan for a room for a school-age program
- Discuss ways to adapt the environment when space must be shared

Profile

Samara and Tom are school-age child care professionals who operate a school-age program for 8- to 10-year-olds in a gymnasium in an elementary school. Tom is trained in Early Childhood Education and has a post-diploma certificate in school-age programming, and Samara has a diploma in Recreation Leadership. They are aware of the importance of providing a "home-like" environment for the children after school, with a variety of choices of activities. At first they wondered how they would provide a balance of active and quiet activities and how they would set up and store a variety of materials in the space they had. They also had to consider how they would set up snack and activities in the simplest way possible to allow for their time constraints. They decided they were up to the challenge and were willing to experiment. They also wanted to include the children in planning the space.

Samara approached the principal of the school and was able to obtain permission to store equipment and materials under the stage in the gym. The school-age program was able to use the stage, so some additional activities could be stored there as well, including a number of prop boxes for dramatic play, such as one about "Dragon Boats" and one about "Magic Hats." Children use the items to create their own plays. The children may also take out a basket of books stored on the stage and some pillows to a corner of the stage for a quiet activity.

A wheel-in cupboard that can be separated into two parts is stored under the stage. One side of the cart is stacked with a variety of board games that are rotated from supplies kept in the child care centre down the hall from the gym. On the other side of the cart, children can choose from paper, markers, pencils, watercolour paint trays, and scissors for art work, as well as small science kits. One fold-out table can be set up with folding chairs, and carpet pieces can be set up, with the children's help, on the floor for board games. A CD player provides the children with an opportunity to play songs that are approved by Tom and Samara. These activities are set up on one half of the gym; the other half can be used for active play. Balls, hoops, floor hockey sticks, and other sports equipment are stored under the stage. Snack is picked up by one of the children from the child care centre that is down the hall from the gym. It is brought in on a wheel-in cart, and set up near benches for the children to sit on. The children use the washrooms that are near the gym, and they also have access to the outdoor play yard on a daily basis. Once in a while, the children enjoy a really messy art activity outside, using lots of paint and mural paper. They ensure that there is a pail of water, soap, paper towels, and a garbage can for cleanup.

How the Environment Responds to Learning and Development

The physical environment is the basic component of a school-age program, the foundation for everything that happens there. The very best program activities, materials, or equipment will be less effective if the physical setting does not meet the needs of the children for whom it is designed. This means that the physical setting should be developmentally appropriate, supporting and enhancing all areas of children's development: physical, cognitive, emotional, and social. The environment should encourage children to participate in activities that will respond effectively to their ongoing development.

Earlier chapters indicated that children's physical development is proceeding rapidly during middle childhood, although fine-motor control lags slightly behind gross-motor control. Indoor areas can be planned to provide children opportunities to increase both these skills. To develop fine-motor control, they need space where they can work puzzles, do art projects, build with small blocks, or construct models. There should also be space for dancing or active games that will increase gross-motor control and eye–hand coordination. Outdoor areas provide many opportunities for gross-motor activities, such as running, jumping, and throwing, but care should be taken to see that there are a variety of activities that progressively enhance physical development. As children become more adept at using their large muscles, they should have a place where they can play hopscotch, baseball, or soccer, and where they can swim, bike, or in-line skate. Space can also be provided for some activities that increase small-muscle control. Planting seeds in a garden bed, doing nature collages, and modelling with clay are some examples.

A developmentally responsive school-age environment will provide many places where children can enhance their cognitive abilities. In Chapter 5, you read that Piaget and Vygotsky believed that children need to be active participants in the development of their own intelligence. In order to do that, the environment must invite participation and offer a wide variety of choices. Children must be free to explore and discover, to hypothesize and experiment in order to increase their knowledge about the world around them. Each area must include space for children to work comfortably and to have their materials close at hand. There should also be storage space to keep ongoing projects safe or to display their work.

Social skills and language are also components of cognitive development. Work areas should be conducive to verbal interactions among the children. Round tables for some activities and enclosed spaces for others encourage children to talk to one another. Comfortable places for reading also encourage children to increase language skills.

During middle childhood, peer relationships and a sense of belonging to a group become extremely important. Children will usually find places where they can get together, but an effective school-age environment will structure places that foster both a group rapport and friendships between children. This means that the setting needs to have a space where all of the children can gather at one time for activities or discussions. There should also be places where two friends can just "hang out" and talk. Spaces for clubs also allow children to form relationships and share interests within a small group.

Brain research reported in *Scientific American Mind* (2009) as cited in Exchange Every Day (2009), reported that the spaces we are in affect our thoughts, feelings, and behaviour. How high the ceilings are, the degree of natural lighting in the room, and how much exposure we have to nature can affect our ability to pay attention and to learn (Exchange Every Day, 2009). This means then that we should consider the aesthetics in the school-age program environment. Reggio environments in particular strive to design a setting that provides lots of natural materials, such as wood and fabrics. Making it home-like is essential with a vase of flowers, pots of plants, real photos and prints, or real artwork on the walls. In the dramatic play area you might find real tablecloths, dishes, and pots and pans. Colours, shadows, and light are used to create a pleasing, but not overwhelming appearance. This might be done with colourful bottles on windowsills or prisms displayed in the windows.

There might be dried flowers or twigs hanging from the ceiling and coloured sheer materials draped over dowels to divide different play areas. This is a sharp contrast to traditional classrooms with teacher-made bulletin boards of traditional images on commercial posters and letters of the alphabet displayed, or a setting with plastic furniture and pretend dishes and food. (Tarr, 2011).

Developing the Plan

The originators of child care centres seldom have the luxury of choosing or building a facility that fits the program they envision. Most often, school-age extended-day programs are housed in classrooms, multipurpose rooms, cafeterias, or gyms. However, within any physical space it is possible to create an environment that welcomes children, makes them feel safe and secure, and enhances their development. It just takes more thought and ingenuity in some situations than in others.

If you are not sure where to start, get a feel for how children play. Watch them playing in your neighbourhood, at a park, or on a school playground. Note how the children group themselves. Do they all play in one large group, or do two or three children do something together? You probably will see that the groups are small and that children tend to stake out their own territory. They meet in specific places each day and then continue play activities together. Watch, as well, how they change their space whenever they can. Many use boxes for forts, some build tree houses from scrap lumber, and others pitch tents so they can be alone. Some children add materials to already existing structures to suit their own needs. They place a wide board on the jungle gym to make a platform for their space ship or enclose a climbing structure with large packing boxes for a clubhouse.

Consider the characteristics of your particular group of children. Their diversity should be reflected in your environment. Look at their age level. Are they all about the same age, or is there a wide variation? What skills and abilities do they have in common? What are their interests? Is there a predominant ethnic group? Do some children have special needs? Through the process of careful observations, each of these should be considered when planning your environment.

Think next of the goals of your program. Your space should allow children to do the things stated in your program philosophy and goals. If you want children to be able to work independently, you have to provide a place where they can do that. If you want to encourage a group feeling, there have to be places where the whole group can gather or do something together. If your goal is for children to develop their physical skills, you must provide space and equipment where that can happen.

When you have followed the preceding suggestions, you should have a fairly good idea of your constituents—the children who will use your environment. In addition, your goals tell you what you want these children to be able to do. It is up to you to set the stage where children and activities can mesh. There are some general considerations that may guide you in planning both indoor and outdoor space.

Figure 9-1 ■ **This reading area is partially enclosed by book racks.**

Overall Design of Indoor Space

Make the indoor space attractive and homelike. Add colour. Place plants on a shelf or table and hang paintings by artists and artwork done by the children on the walls. Paint some of the furniture an interesting colour or, in many cases a natural wood colour is preferred. Put a colourful rug in a corner to set off that space with a touch of brightness. Try changing the lighting. A harsh light is somewhat jarring and distracting; a softer light might create a more relaxed atmosphere.

Provide a consistent environment. Organize supplies and materials, so that children can find and return things. This promotes respect of the environment and offers kids a sense of order, security and belonging (School-Age Notes, 1989, p. 2)

Figure 9-2 ■ Well-planned indoor space allows for both individual and group activities.

Figure 9-3 ■ Children need a place to put their belongings.

Consider opportunities that children might enjoy to engage in quiet or loud play. A corner of the room invites privacy. Make it more secluded with a free-standing rack for books. A table and shelves can define space where individual projects are to take place. A rug tells children that this is a place for floor activities. A large space that is left open can accommodate group meetings.

Keep in mind that areas could be used for several purposes. The block area is usually used for block building, but children may want to build a stage and bring dramatic props to add to their play. The space used should be flexible, meeting the ongoing needs and interests of the children. If a space is not working as planned, discuss it with the children, then be open to their suggestions as to how the area can be rearranged. In general, for safety purposes, leave pathways for easy access to all activities and to entrances and exits. Look at the most likely traffic patterns children might use to move around the room or from indoors to outdoors. Arrange work areas so they are undisturbed by children walking through them. Make areas readily identifiable by children, staff members, and parents. The kinds of materials you place there, the furniture, or the arrangement should inform everyone of the purpose. Children may want to make signs for their play areas. Consider many different ways to integrate curriculum across all traditional areas of the room. Children may build a museum and want to include art work displays or books in the dramatic play area.

Minimize crowding in activity areas by allowing enough space for large group functions, and be aware of the number of children who can work comfortably at other areas. An open area where the entire group can meet should be spacious enough so that children are not pushing right up against one another. Be flexible; move tables and chairs to accommodate more children if they are interested in a particular activity.

What Should Be Included?

There Should Be Enough Space so Children Can Move About Safely

Check the licensing regulations in your province/territory to determine the number of square metres per child you will need. Add enough school-age child-size tables, chairs, shelves, and cabinets to accommodate your program. Leave enough room so children do not bump into furniture or trip on equipment.

Include Places Where Children Can Work on Individual or Group Projects

Children will probably need a table, some chairs, and a place to keep their work until it is completed. This area may also include a place where children can display their completed work. If children need to take their completed work home as soon as it is completed, pictures can be taken of their projects and then posted on a bulletin board or in a photo album.

Have a Place Where Children Can Keep Their Belongings

Children will be coming to you from school carrying backpacks, lunch pails, and jackets. Everyone should have a cubby, shelf, or box in which to deposit these articles until they are ready to go home.

Make Room for Messy Activities Near a Water Supply

Many art projects such as clay, painting, or *papier-mâché* will require a ready supply of water. Cooking projects, too, tend to be messy. These two areas can be right next to each other and share a sink for water. If a sink is not available, pails of water can be carried in from the washroom, along with soap, paper towels, and a garbage can.

Set Aside an Area for Quiet Reading, Alone Time, Resting, or Just Talking with Friends

An enclosed corner will serve this purpose. Furnish it with a low sofa, beanbag chairs, large pillows, and a soft rug. Add books and magazines, and rotate them frequently. These can be displayed on a book rack or set out in a large basket.

Leave an Open Area Where Your Whole Group Can Be Together at Times

Many programs leave the centre of a room for this purpose. This space can also be used for large-muscle activities indoors when you cannot go outside. You can dance or do exercises or gymnastics when the space is unobstructed. Set up an area for children to listen to music on a CD and tape player, along with a simple storage box for CDs and tapes.

Set Up an Area for Snack

Children will like to serve themselves. Provide a table and chairs for snack time. This is a good social time for the children to gather and talk about their day's activities. Make the setting interesting by adding colourful placemats and centrepieces made by the children. These can be theme or seasonally related.

Remember to Arrange a Place Where Children Can Complete Their Homework

Have computers and printers available for homework. Provide access to the Internet. A table and chairs in a quiet area of the room are needed. Make sure the lighting is adequate so children can see well. Some children will be able to work together at one table, whereas others may need their own work place. You may have to set up a small individual table for any child who needs to work alone.

If You Can, Provide High Spaces and Low Spaces

Many centres with limited floor space resort to a double-decker approach. Imagine a climbing structure that could serve as a dramatic play area in the upper level with a quiet hideaway underneath. The upper level might even become a stage for dramatic productions. Provide dramatic prop boxes on various topics that children can use to create their own plays. This would also be an ideal quiet area for children to read, play board games or do their homework.

Designate places to hang artwork, display photographs, or feature news items. This can be a bulletin board near the entrance so parents can also enjoy it. If you do not have a bulletin board, use appropriate adhesive tape or reusable adhesive to attach items to the wall.

Provide Adequate Storage

Storage should include both closed cupboards and some that are accessible to the children. Use closed cupboards for the items used infrequently, such as special art or project supplies, games, table activities, or books. Some materials should be on open shelves or cupboards so children can use them as they wish. Always keep a basic assortment of art materials readily available and in good condition. Rotate these periodically with those you have stored away.

If Your Curriculum Includes Club Activities, Arrange a Place for Children to Meet

Let the children decorate the space and add a sign with the club name. Furnish the club area with whatever is needed for their particular activity. A collector's club will need a table and chairs. A drama club could use a stage and a place to store props.

Consider the Need for Extra Space If Larger Numbers of School-Age Children Are in the Centre When the Preschool Children Are There as Well

This need for extra space may occur on bad weather days, professional development days, or school holidays. Additional suitable space may need to be accessed in the school or in other areas of the centre. Sometimes the older preschool children may enjoy a change from the child care centre and could go to another area. Inform children ahead of time where they will be going when regular routines change, so they will feel more secure.

If Your Group Includes Some Older Children (Children Between the Ages of 9 and 12), Design a Special Place for Them

A separate room would be best, but if you cannot provide that, set up a corner for them. Make it their special place, in which younger children are not allowed. The equipment might include a CD player/tape recorder/radio, model kits and games, beanbag chairs, or large pillows. If the room size permits, add a ping-pong table or an air hockey or pool table.

Do Not Forget the Adults When You Design Your Indoor Space

Designate a place where you can prepare materials and keep any records required by the program administrators. In addition, assign a lockable cupboard or drawer where you can keep your personal belongings.

Parents, too, Must Be Considered

There should be a place for sign-in/sign-out sheets and mailboxes for notes to individual families. In addition, you might install a bulletin board where you can post schedules, pictures of the children, reminders of upcoming events, or any other items of interest to all the parents. Designate a space for lost and found articles.

Now that you know what must be included, you can conceptualize the placement of activity areas. Try using a scale drawing of your room. Mark the doors and windows, then designate areas. Check that you have included an area for each activity in your program plan. Try to imagine yourself and the children living in the space. When you place furniture and storage cabinets in the environment, walk through it again, thinking about how it will function. If you are satisfied, try it with your group of children. Later, evaluate your arrangement and get input from the children. Do not be afraid to change it, however. As long as everything is movable and not built in, you can reorganize. Be flexible.

Figure 9-4 ■ Mats or large pillows invite children to relax, read together, or just talk.

When You Have to Share Indoor Space

You may not have the luxury of a space that can be set up and left intact at the end of each day. It can be overwhelming to have to arrange your environment at the beginning of each day, but with a bit of preplanning and some imagination, it can be done. It is important to try to keep the plan not only simple, but also one that will provide an interesting and challenging program for the children. If the materials are not plentiful enough or activities are not based on the interests of the children, difficulties with behaviour may arise. Space needed for children in a school-age program should not be considered only as a room but as a space where children live. A room such as a classroom in a school where children cannot touch materials after school that they use during the day may be an inadequate space for a school-age program.

> It's cruel and unfair to keep children in a room where they can't touch things, especially if the things they are not allowed to touch after 3:30, they are allowed to touch during school hours. The children will be much more respectful of the space and the needs of others if their needs are also respected. (Landy, 1991, p. 7)

If you use adaptable materials and have movable cabinets, your task can be managed easily and quickly, and the children will enjoy assisting with the setup. If possible, ask for storage space in the room—for example, a movable cabinet or a locked storage cupboard. The following are some suggestions that have worked for other programs, but each space may require different strategies.

- Set up activities based on children's interests each day. Have a collection of open-ended materials always available such as blankets, different kinds of materials, scarves, ties, etc. for dramatic play. This will be easier if you plan ahead by having all the materials you will need in a basket, a large box, ice-cream cartons, or shoe boxes. Children can help carry them to the table or area where they will use them.

- Provide other open-ended materials for construction such as door knobs, switches, clamps, pipes, nuts and bolts, hinges, and pulleys. Include a box of tools. Keep them in a covered box or bin that can be stored on a movable shelf or in a storage cupboard that children can access each day.

- Provide art materials that are easy to use such as watercolour pallets and brushes, pastels, different kinds of crayons, markers, sketching pencils, charcoal, drawing paper, and inexpensive paint canvases.

- Install large casters or wheels on cupboards, bulletin boards, or dividers used to designate areas. Sometimes it helps to label these to specify their use. Put locks on the cupboards.

- Design furniture that can be taken apart when it must be put away at the end of the day. Buy or construct modular furniture made from sturdy, lightweight building material. Add large vinyl pillows and vinyl beanbag chairs to be used in reading or listening areas. Bring a small CD and tape player for sharing music.

- A large pegboard on wheels is adaptable for many uses and can provide visual appeal. It can be a convenient place to display documentation of children's work such as photographs, children's stories, or art creations. These can be used to divide one work area from another. (You can divide spaces with folding screens, sheets, or blankets, as well.) Have some shelves that are also equipped with casters. Use these for art materials, games, block accessories, and science materials. Include plastic coverings such as inexpensive shower curtains to protect floor coverings.

- Carefully observe if and how children are using materials that are stored on wheel-in shelves to see if they need to be changed and rotated from time to time. Add new games, puzzles, books, art supplies, etc. based on children's interests.

- Use plastic stackable containers for the children's belongings, with each child having her own if there are no individual cubbies available. This demonstrates a respect for children's things, which becomes a model for children in terms of being respectful of other people and their possessions.

- Carpet squares, mats, or blankets can be used to sit on to do an activity on the floor such as a game or a puzzle.

- For more active play, ask for permission to use an unoccupied hallway, foyer, or gym in the school. Also ask for permission to share some equipment such as floor hockey sticks or basketballs between other school or community programs. Storage space for and easy access to this equipment would need to be considered as well.

- Allow children to rearrange the indoor environment. They may be able to see possibilities that adults have not considered. Before starting, however, discuss with them the kinds of activities that must be provided for, then have them offer suggestions. Compile their suggestions, then let them vote on the ones to be implemented. Draw up a plan and execute the changes. Evaluate with the children how the plan is working after a trial period.

- Work with other occupants of your space so that everyone has an understanding of what can be done and what cannot. Meet with the principal or building administrator on a regular basis to reinforce mutual commitments to serving children and their families, to discuss issues that arise regarding sharing equipment, and to resolve any problems. Maintain contact with teachers to determine ways in which the goals of the program can complement those of the school. Set up an agreement about use of office equipment and the telephone. Have an explicit understanding with the janitors about who is responsible for cleaning and taking out the garbage and who will clean up when others use the space.

Overall Design of Outdoor Space

School-age children who have been inside all day, except during designated recess and lunch periods outdoors, need more outside play time at the end of the day. The social, emotional, physical, and cognitive benefits of spending time outdoors has been researched over the years.

As cited in Head Start (2012), research by Fjortoft (2004) and Burdett and Whitaker (2005) found that children who play outdoors regularly maintain a healthier weight and fitness level. They develop stronger immune systems, have more active imaginations and lower stress levels, play creatively, and have a greater respect for themselves and others (Head Start, 2012).

It is rare that staff members are able to design a new playground; most have to adapt an existing facility to suit the needs of their program and the children they serve. Whether starting from scratch or adapting an existing playground, it helps to visit other school-age programs, parks, or schools to see how others have planned play spaces for children. Note how the children use both the open spaces and any permanent equipment. Are some areas not used at all? What kinds of equipment attract the greatest number of children or hold their interest the longest? What kinds of play occur? What do children do in the open spaces? This valuable information will be useful when planning outdoor areas.

The next step is to take an inventory of everything in the outdoor space that will be available to the centre. Map out areas that cannot be changed, and indicate the places that are open. Brainstorm ideas for the space with other staff members. If

Figure 9-5 ■ **Children like to test their skills on outdoor climbing equipment.**

Figure 9-6 ■ A natural play setting.

children are already enrolled in the program, get their input. They may have wonderful suggestions. Make a priority list of what will be needed, and calculate the cost of each item. If financial resources are limited, plan to purchase first items that are likely to be used the most or that have the greatest capability for multiple uses. Are there things that staff members or parents can build or install, thus decreasing the cost?

Clarify program goals that will be supported by the outdoor environment. What is it that you want children to be able to do as a result of using the space? Remember that outdoor space not only helps children develop physical skills but also can help them grow cognitively and socially. Outdoor play can involve problem solving, investigating, observing, listening, matching/naming objects, and predicting, to name just a few cognitive skills. Socially, outdoor play can help children learn to cooperate, share, develop friendships, engage in group fantasy play, and foster a group cohesiveness.

A playground should be based on a knowledge of child development. Review the chapters on development at the beginning of this text to remind you of school-age children's development. School-age children are extremely active and like to have lots of space to run, jump, and throw. They want to be competent at any activities that require physical agility and need places where they can practise their skills. They want to have places where they can be with their peers, either one on one or within a group.

Design your space with children's special needs in mind. When the group includes children with physical limitations, include spaces to which they will have access. Some possibilities are to include paved pathways that are wide enough for a wheelchair, a raised sandbox or a sand table, wheelchair-accessible areas for throwing balls, and climbing equipment with a transfer station, allowing a child to go from chair to climber. Many playground equipment companies will offer advice on how to adapt their pieces to fit the needs of children with disabilities.

Include natural play spaces that provide opportunities for climbing, rolling down hills, playing with sand and water, planting and watching a garden grow, and moving about on pathways that wind around between trees and shrubs where the children might see birds, squirrels, and various kinds of insects.

Safety

Canadian Standards Association (CSA)

sets standards for safe planning of equipment and design of outdoor play space for children in public playgrounds and child care centres

Children's safety should be a top priority for all programs for children and is therefore treated here as a separate subject to consider when planning or renovating outdoor play areas. In May 1998, the **Canadian Standards Association (CSA)** approved and released "A Guideline for Children's Playspaces and Equipment" (CSA Z614-98), outlining standards of safe planning for equipment and design of outdoor play space for children in public play areas, including child care centres. This is a standard similar to those set for playground safety in Europe and the United States. Operators of child care centres work diligently to achieve these standards in order to achieve optimal safety and also to provide space and equipment that meet the developmental needs of the children by challenging them physically. Educators must refer to the CSA's publication whenever a new playground is built or when additions, changes, and renovations are made. Daily **safety checklists** of indoor and outdoor play spaces are required. Some municipalities require that a complete written safety checklist is prepared on a daily basis. Weekly, monthly, and yearly safety checklists are required to identify any hazardous items, broken or faulty equipment, and general maintenance requirements. Information can be obtained from the following sources:

Canadian Institute of Child Health
384 Bank Street, Suite 300
Ottawa, ON K2P 1Y4
(613) 230-8838
Fax (613) 230-6654
http://www.cich.ca

Canadian Standards Association (CSA)
178 Rexdale Blvd.
Toronto, ON. M9W 1R3
(416) 747-4000 or toll-free 1-800-463-6727
http://www.csa.ca

Safe Kids Canada
555 University Ave.
Toronto, ON M5G 1X8
(416) 813-7288
http://www.safekidscanada.ca

Canadian Paediatric Society. (1996). *Well beings* (2nd. ed.). Ottawa: Canadian Paediatric Society, pp. 971–997. (Weekly, Monthly, and Yearly safety checklists).

safety checklist
survey of all playground structures in comparison to standards, guidelines, and laws set by municipal, provincial/ territorial, and federal agencies

At the same time, children need opportunities to challenge themselves and it is the responsibility of adults who design and supervise playgrounds to ensure that risks and safety are equally weighted. As children engage in outdoor play, they can learn about managing risk, and what is a safe risk and what is a dangerous one and why. Adults need to be actively present and engaged with children during outdoor play, helping them understand and notice unsafe situations, and empowering them to assess these situations on their own. Exposure to natural risks is important for children to learn about and manage future situations that they may face on their own (Gleave, 2008).

What Should Be Included?

Include Both Single-Purpose and Multipurpose Equipment

Most children love the old standbys: swings, climbing structures, slides, and a sandbox. Swings are **single purpose**: they can be used only for swinging. A climbing structure can be **multipurpose**, having many different kinds of play possibilities. A sandbox seems to be single purpose at first glance, but children can find almost endless ways to incorporate other kinds of play into this area. They will build dams, cook elaborate foods, and search for dinosaur bones, to name just a few. Thoroughly washed brick sand, or an equivalent, such as seaside sand, should be used. Check

single-purpose equipment
play equipment that can be used for only one kind of play

multipurpose equipment
equipment that has many possibilities for play activities

Table 9-1 ■ Guidelines for Planning a Safe Outdoor Environment for Children

1. Ensure the equipment is appropriate for the age of the children who will be using it. Your knowledge of developmental stages and abilities should help to determine whether equipment is too easy or too difficult.

2. Do a daily environmental inspection, looking for bottles, cans, other garbage, animal waste, standing water, or anything else that may create a hazard. Include a survey of equipment, looking for rust, splintering wood, or exposed bolts.

3. Follow the legal requirements regarding cushioned surfaces beneath equipment as a fall zone. Do not use asphalt, grass, packed dirt, and concrete. Choose satisfactory shock-absorbing surface material such as pea gravel, sand, or hardwood fibre/mulch. The height of the equipment will determine the depth of the material used. Usually 30 cm (12 in.) of loose fill will be adequate for equipment up to 2.4 cm (8 ft) in height. If synthetic material is used, the manufacturer will recommend the depth. Double-check that the manufacturer's recommendation meets local standards.

4. There should be a cushioned fall zone 1.8 m (6 ft) in front and 1.8 m (6 ft) behind the pivot height of the swing. The cushioned zone should also extend 1.8 cm (6 ft) to each side of the support structure.

5. Ensure that all climbing equipment meets the required safety standards. Steps on ladders should be in good condition, and handrails should have appropriate grip sizes. Ensure that protective barriers are at the right height for the age group.

6. Slides should be securely anchored. The steps should have firm handrails and provide good traction. Drainage holes in the steps will prevent moisture that makes them slippery. Make sure there is no space between the slide platform and the bed where strings from clothing can catch. If the slides are metal, they should be in a shaded area.

7. Provide access to open areas for games such as tag, ball hockey, soccer, or hopscotch.

8. Ensure that all areas with potential hazards are easily supervised and can be seen from various vantage points. There should be no trees or other structures that block your view. Ensure that any plants or shrubs are non-poisonous.

9. Always provide adequate supervision when children are using playground equipment by having an adult in the playground attending to what the children are doing.

10. Develop a selection of realistic rules that represent the developmental abilities of the age group. Involve the children in this process. Be sure the rules are not overly restrictive, thus limiting creative play. State rules in a positive manner, giving consistent and gentle reminders. Re-evaluate rules on a regular basis with the children.

with the CSA Standards with regards to the dimensions of the sandbox needed for each group size and the required depth of the sand needed. Be sure to have a suitable cover for the sandbox so that animals do not get in.

Add Some Materials so Children Can Construct Their Own Equipment

Large blocks, boards, boxes, cable spools, and crates present interesting possibilities. Consider using sheets of fabric, wood, or cardboard to make a roof. All materials should possess the characteristics of a safe toy (suitable dimensions with smooth, rounded surfaces) for children. Children can be marvellously inventive in what they devise.

As Needed, Bring Out Equipment to Stimulate New Play Ideas

Balls, racquets, hoops, hockey sticks, jump ropes, tumbling mats, bats, and nets are just a few choices. (Do not forget a pump for rejuvenating deflated balls.) You may also want to add chalk for sidewalk games, yo-yos, and marbles depending upon the interests of the children. A play parachute is a nice addition for cooperative games. When it is hot, bring out a hose, buckets, sprinklers, a small pool, and boats. For winter months when there is snow, provide shovels, sleds, and toboggans.

Include Areas Where Children Can Have Some Privacy

A playhouse, park bench, treehouse, or even a secluded corner under a tree can be a place where children can gather to chat with a friend or just be alone.

Allow Spaces for Special Activities, Some Protected from Inclement Weather

Some games need a hard surface, others dirt. Set aside a safe place away from pathways where children can practise skateboarding or in-line skating. Use a covered area for art or table activities that can be enjoyed when the sun is hot or even when it rains.

Have a Variety of Surfaces on Your Playground

Include grass, dirt, shock-absorbent surfaces, sand, or wood chip areas for added interest. In addition to these surfaces, it is nice to leave some planted areas in the yard. Trees, flowers, shrubs, or a garden area add interest to any yard.

Provide an Opportunity for Children to Learn About and Gain Respect for Their Natural Environment

Growing urban areas have almost obliterated any wild and natural places for children to play. As a result, many children today have little contact with the outdoors, and many even express fears of insects, snakes, and plants. The playground can allow children to explore the outdoors within a relatively safe setting. Create an area that contains unmanicured grass, bushes, plants, some rocks, a small hill, some trees, and a birdbath and feeder. Add a garden, including wild grasses or native plants, where children can grow vegetables or flowers, which may attract butterflies or hummingbirds. In addition, allow children to construct their own play spaces or private hideaways with tree limbs, boards, boxes, and large tires. Children will strengthen their appreciation of the outdoors if they share responsibility for maintaining the area. Check to be sure that all plants are safe.

Remember to Have a Water Outlet in the Yard, with Both a Drinking Fountain and Hose Faucet

Active children get thirsty, and water is needed for many art projects. If hoses are added, children will be able to build dams in the sandbox, learn how water sculpts any area where it runs freely, maintain a garden, or observe how sunlight shining through sprinkler spray makes a rainbow. Be aware of potential problems concerning flooding and be sure to secure faucets and remove hoses when not in use.

Provide Proper Protection from the Sun and Insects

Be aware of places where children can sit in the shade in order to get some relief from the sun. Take note of times of the day, between 11:00 a.m. and 2:00 p.m., when the sun is most intense. Ensure that the children are protected with the appropriate sunscreen and insect repellents and that proper permission forms are filled in, if required. Check with Health Canada for guidelines for protecting children.

The outdoor area of the program may be the only opportunity some of today's children have to engage in free, active play. Many may live in apartments or areas where they cannot play outside their houses because it is not safe. In addition, many will get home after dark. Therefore, you should put as much thought into the kinds of activities you provide for children outdoors as you do for inside time. Play outdoors is not only a chance to run around and let off steam but also an opportunity for additional learning and the acquisition of skills.

When You Have to Share Outdoor Space

If you have to share outdoor space with other programs or with neighbourhood children, you have an additional challenge. You probably will not be able to change the environment, but you can add your own movable play equipment. Bring out easels and painting materials, a box of balls or other sports equipment, digging tools in a crate, or games to play on the grass. You will have to look at the possibilities of the space available and add whatever you can.

Daily walks to a local playground may be an alternative; however, daily safety checks of that playground would need to be done by the staff before children arrive. Check with provincial regulations and insurance policies to determine whether a statement of permission is required from parents in order for children to go to a community park or playground.

Allow your children to mingle with others using the space. It would be awkward if your children felt different from neighbourhood youngsters in a park just because they were in a school-age program. Establish clear rules about where they can go and what they can do, but allow as much freedom of movement as you safely can.

Environment affects us all in subtle ways. A good atmosphere will encourage children to be relaxed and engage in productive play. Poor conditions may result in upset children who cannot settle down to sustained activities. Design your space with thought, and be willing to change it as needed.

Figure 9-7 ■ "Me on the bars." Mariah, age 10

Summary

The physical environment is the basic component of a school-age program, the foundation for everything that happens there. A developmentally responsive environment will support and enhance all areas of children's development: physical, cognitive, and social. Few child care professionals have the luxury of designing a facility that exactly fits the program they envision. Most have to adapt space in unused or dual-use spaces within another facility. With thought and ingenuity, it can be done, however.

There are some overall guidelines to help you plan indoor space. Provide open-ended materials that encourage creativity, inquiry learning, investigation, and problem solving. Traditional areas in the room can be adjusted to meet the interests of the children by enlarging a space or adding other equipment, toys, and materials to enhance the richness of their play. Consider ways to make the play space aesthetically pleasing, using natural and real-life materials. Leave pathways to doorways and exits, as well as to all classroom areas, accessible.

Children's safety should be a top priority. Planners should obtain guidelines, regulations, and laws that govern playgrounds. Ensure the equipment is age appropriate and has cushioned surfaces beneath potential fall areas. Climbing equipment should meet consumer-safety standards and legal requirements, steps and ladders should be in good condition, and all equipment, such as slides, should be securely anchored in the ground.

Include in your indoor environment the following:

- enough space to meet licensing requirements
- a place for individual or group projects
- a cubby for each child to keep his belongings
- a water supply for messy activities
- an area for reading, resting, or talking
- an open area for large gatherings or active games
- a place for children to do homework
- an area for snack
- high places and low places
- a bulletin board for art, notices, and parent information
- adequate storage
- an area for clubs
- a place to go on inclement-weather days
- a special place for older children
- a place for staff and parents

When you have to share indoor space, organize materials in easy-to-carry boxes or crates, install casters on all furniture, use shelves or pegboards to divide work areas, use carpet pieces to delineate a space, allow children to set up the environment, and work with other occupants to share equipment and storage space and avoid misunderstandings. Rotate materials to meet children's ongoing interests and needs.

Before you begin to draft a design for a playground, visit a variety of places where children play: other child care centres, school playgrounds, or parks. Your playground should reflect what you know about children. All outdoor areas should be safe but also offer some challenges to children. If you have children with special needs in your group, you will have to do additional research to know how to meet their needs.

Include in your playground the following:

- both single-purpose and multipurpose equipment
- some materials children can use to construct their own equipment
- balls, hockey sticks, jump ropes, etc.
- space for special activities
- a variety of surfaces
- a water outlet
- a natural, unstructured space
- protection from the sun and insects

When you have to share outdoor space with other programs, add movable equipment, allow children to mingle with others using the area, and establish clear rules with children about what is safe and not safe to do.

Key Terms

Canadian Standards Association (CSA)

safety checklist

single-purpose equipment

multipurpose equipment

Student Activities

1. Obtain several catalogues from companies that supply playground equipment. Select a climbing apparatus and three other articles for a school-age playground. In class, explain your choice in a group of two other students. Compile the list of choices from each group member, then negotiate and agree on buying only three items.
2. Visit three school-age programs that are under different auspices: recreation program, part of an elementary school, community organization, or privately owned. Record the kinds of furniture and equipment available in their indoor space. Share your findings with your classmates.
3. Draw a floor plan of an ideal indoor space for a group of 20 children from the ages of 6 to 12.
4. Use the list of things to include in an indoor environment discussed in this chapter. How might you adapt your plan to accommodate a child in a wheelchair?

Review Questions

1. List five general guidelines to remember when planning indoor space.
2. Indicate how the following activities would benefit from being integrated together; for example, block building and music, or visual art and science.
3. State five things to be included in indoor space.
4. List five possible storage containers for children's belongings. Can you suggest any others?
5. Describe how you would arrange an art area.
6. How would you set up an area where children could do their homework?
7. What is meant by single-purpose and multipurpose equipment? Give examples of each.
8. Why is it important to provide wild spaces for children in an outdoor play area?
9. List some equipment you might take outside to stimulate new play ideas.
10. In what ways can you adapt both indoor and outdoor equipment when you have to share space with other programs?

Case Study

Dion and Hazel have been hired to set up a school-age program for 18 children, 6 to 12 years of age, in a classroom in an elementary school. As they start to plan, they realize they have quite different ideas about what should be in the room. The teacher who uses the classroom during the day is willing to allow the children to use the equipment and some materials. However, he would like the school-age program to provide its own perishable supplies like paper, paint, and markers. The parents want their children to be successful in school, so they want their children to have time to do their homework.

1. If you were responsible for planning this environment, where would you start?
2. How can you take into consideration the differing ideas of the two school-age child care professionals, the concerns of the classroom teacher, and the demands of the parents?
3. Is there a way to make the environment flexible so that it can be changed if needed and also to recognize some of the unique needs of the older children?

References

Exchange Every Day. (2009). *Environments matter.* Exchange Magazine. Retrieved June 24, 2012, from http://childcareexchange.com/eed/issue.php?id=2244

Gleave, J. (2008). Risk and play. Play Day Give Us a Go. Retrieved May 2012, from http://www.springzaad.nl/litdocs/doc_73.pdf

Head Start. *Outdoor play benefits.* Retrieved May 2012, from http://www.aahperd.org/headstartbodys-tart/activityresources/upload/benefits-of-outdoor-play-2.pdf

Landy, L. (1991). Construction of a good school-age environment. *Exploring Environments*, 1, 1, 6–7.

School-Age Notes. (1989). *A space of their own, a space of our own.* September/October, 2–31.

Tarr, P. (October 2001). Aesthetic codes in early childhood classrooms, art education. Retrieved May 2012, from http://www.designshare.com/Research/Tarr/Aesthetic_Codes_2.htm

Selected Further Reading

Clemens, J. B. (1996). Gardening with children. *Young Children, 51*(4), 22–27.

Haas-Foletta, K. & Cogley, M. (1990). *School-age ideas and activities for after school programs.* Nashville, TN: School-Age Notes.

Herman, M. L., Passineau, J. F., Schimpf, A. L., & Treuer, P. (1991). *Teaching kids to love the earth.* Duluth: Pfeifer-Hamilton Publishers.

Louv, R. (2008). *Last child in the woods.* NY: Workman Publishing.

Morris, L. & Schultz, L. (1989). *Creative play activities for children with disabilities: A resource book for teachers and parents.* Champaign, IL: Human Kinetics Books.

Nabhan, G. P. & Trimble, S. (1994). *The geography of childhood: Why children need wild places.* Boston: Beacon Press.

Wardle, F. (1997a). Outdoor play: Designing, building, and remodeling playgrounds for young children. *Early Childhood News, 9*(2), 36–42.

Wardle, F. (1997b). Playgrounds: Questions to consider when selecting. *Dimensions, 25*(1), 9–15.

Wilson, R. A., Kilmer, S. J., & Knauerhase, V. (1996). Developing an environmental outdoor play space. *Young Children, 51*(6), 56–61.

Websites

Canadian Parks and Recreation Association (CPRA)
http://www.cpra.ca

Canada Safety Council
http://www.safety-council.org

Natural Play Spaces: The New-Style Playgrounds
http://www.healthyalberta.com/HealthyPlaces/532.htm

Learning Through Play

Chapter 10

Games Support Self-Regulation

Objectives

After studying this chapter, the student should be able to:

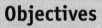

- Discuss why games should be part of a school-age program's curriculum
- Facilitate a variety of games for outdoor and indoor play
- List some guidelines for making games fun
- Identify the benefits of using computers
- Outline the guidelines for the use of electronic games, safe use of the Internet, and selecting appropriate software

Profile

Bonica works in a full-day kindergarten and extended after-school program for children who are 4 years of age to 8 years of age in an elementary school. She starts in the program at 9:30 a.m. and works alongside the kindergarten teacher with the children until 3:30. At that time she gets ready for the other school-age children who will arrive. Three days a week, the school-age children can use the gym after school.

Bonica has observed that the children enjoy playing a number of traditional games such as musical chairs. She has found a number of variations of this game that the children also enjoy. Instead of playing the traditional "Musical Chairs" where someone is eliminated, the children play a cooperative version. In this version, instead of being eliminated, when the music stops, the child who is left sits on the lap of another child, and another, and another. Each time a chair is removed, until there is one chair left and everyone is piled on one chair.

Another cooperative version of the game is called "Human Musical Chairs," where the children form a circle, facing each other's backs. When the music stops, the children sit on the lap of the child behind them. They have to work together, balancing themselves so that no one in the group topples over.

Bonica has also shown them how to play the game with carpet pieces, or "islands," that are spread out around the gym. Children move from one island to another and when the music stops, they have to find a mat. The one left out is eliminated from the game and another island is removed.

The children suggest variations of other activities. They have made up a version of baseball, called soccer baseball. The game is played like baseball, but instead of hitting the ball with a bat, they kick a soccer ball.

Bonica talks with the children and helps them understand the rules of the game before beginning. She encourages problem solving, cooperation, and healthy competition. She has a lot of energy and enjoys playing the games with the children. Bonica ends her day at 5:30. She gets a great deal of fulfillment from working with school-age children and providing them with an opportunity to participate in a range of activities after school each day.

How Games Can Enhance Development

Games are a big part of school-age children's play at any time of day. However, especially after school, games offer children a change of pace. Children's choice of activity in the after-school hours, though, will depend on their energy level and personality. Some have a lot of energy after sitting down all day and need to be active; others are tired and want to rest. Some children are gregarious and ready for playing in groups; others want to be alone and choose solitary activities. Fortunately, games offer a wide variety of options. They can be intensely vigorous or played quietly. Participants can be in large or small groups, or one child can play alone.

Games provide many opportunities for children to practise their physical skills. Although boys and girls have just about equal motor skills, boys generally have greater forearm strength and girls generally have greater overall flexibility. Their body size, coordination, and inherited talent will also affect their agility. As a result, children often select games at which they can excel; boys often prefer basketball or volleyball, and girls may choose gymnastics. Encourage them to try new activities by emphasizing the fun of participating, not the degree to which they are successful.

Children learn to take turns and work together; through this process, they develop self-regulation skills. By middle childhood, most understand that rules are for everyone and that they must abide by the rules to be a part of a group. Typically, they often spend more time discussing and negotiating the rules of a game than they do actually playing. In the process, however, they learn about fairness, how to take turns, and to accept that each person can be a leader or a follower. In addition, they experience the fun of a group effort.

Games reinforce and extend children's cognitive skills. They are using logic when they have to plan the next move in checkers or a series of strategies in chess. "If I do this . . . then next I do that . . . this will happen." Many games involve problem solving as well. A marvellous example is a game called Jenga®. The game begins with a completed tower, 18 levels with three blocks at each level. Each player removes one block

Figure 10-1 ■ **A computer and a selection of games can help children develop new skills.**

and places it on the top of the tower without toppling the structure. It takes a great deal of looking, thinking, and predicting before deciding which block can be safely removed. Trivial Pursuit® encourages children to remember facts. Dice games or Yahtzee® require math skills.

Children can gain an appreciation for their own or other cultures by playing the games of different countries. They learn that games are often played as part of celebrations, for holidays, or to bring groups of people together in a common activity. They will also find that in some cultures, games teach children skills they need for survival. See Figures 10-3 and 10-4 for two examples of cultural games. *The Multicultural Game Book* (Orlando, 1993), lists many more.

There will probably always be some children who will view games as an opportunity to win or to be the best in order to enhance their self-esteem. You may not be able to entirely eliminate this tendency toward competitiveness since it is so much a part of their environment at school, on television, and in the news. However, you can minimize this tendency by including games that are noncompetitive and encourage creativity. Also, reinforce children for their efforts and their skills, rather than being best or first. A poem by Zwerling, published in the January 1991 issue of *Young Children*, addresses the matter of competition. He wrote:

Child's Play

I watched the relay races today,
First grade recess
Filled with teachers' whistles and students' squeals,
with shouts and seeming delight.
The winning team screamed and jumped,
Gave high-fives and handslaps just like on T.V. One winner clenched his fists
    and put on a game face,
Almost grim, Will Clark in the Series
Giving high-fists and raising arms in triumph.
The other team slowly walked away;
And I thought this really is the beginning.
Surely, surely, there is a better way.
How can there be losers in children's play?

Games and Safety

Chapter 9 addressed planning a safe outdoor environment, but some specifics need to be considered when children are engaged in games or other outdoor activities. School-age children often overestimate their competence and attempt feats beyond their capabilities. School-age children also compare themselves with their peers and want to be the best at whatever they do. Watch a group of boys and girls on skateboards and observe the risks they take. The following guidelines will help prevent serious accidents to the children in your care:

1. Set clear rules for using all equipment, and make sure the children know the rules. Ensure that the rules are vigorously enforced.
2. Never allow children to use equipment in inappropriate or unsafe ways, or engage in an activity that is potentially injurious.
3. Before planning any vigorous activity, consider all the ways children might get hurt, and eliminate the most serious hazards. When the activity is introduced,

make the children aware of the possible hazards, ask them to suggest ways to prevent injury, and add additional cautionary measures if necessary.

4. Provide appropriate safety equipment for sports activities such as knee and elbow pads, helmets, protective eye wear, and catchers' mitts. Ensure that the safety equipment is worn every time and that it fits the child.

5. Have enough adults to supervise the activities and maintain the required ratio of adults to children. Train staff to position themselves where they can see the widest area under their supervision and to be vigilant at all times.

6. Apprise every staff member of the centre's policies and procedures for managing accidents. There should be a written statement easily accessible to every room that includes procedures for dealing with an accident, telephone numbers for nearby emergency services, and information regarding notification of parents.

7. All staff members should know first-aid procedures. They should be able to treat minor injuries such as scrapes or bruises as well as recognize when an injury requires medical attention.

8. Staff members should carry out a follow-up after an accident, reviewing the causes and making suggestions for preventing a similar mishap in the future.

9. Do a follow-up with the children. Children may be upset by the accident and need to be comforted. They may want to know what happened and why. Make sure the discussions with children are low key but factual and honest, focusing on ways to prevent the same kind of injury in the future. Never tell children the accident would not have happened "if Bryn had only listened to me when I told him to stop." Honestly describe what happened. "Bryn was going too fast around the skateboard area and wasn't able to make the turn."

Figure 10-2 ▪ Outdoor games—potato sack race.

Outdoor Games

Many outdoor games have been played by generations of children. If you look at pictures painted several centuries ago, you are likely to find children playing some of the same games they still play today. Pieter Bruegel's paintings done in the 16th century, for instance, include children playing blindman's buff, hide-and-seek, and drop the handkerchief. The street games played in cities and towns across the country have been passed down from parent to child, with each generation adding its own variations. Many popular games find their origins from other countries. For example, many tennis and racket ball games originated with the game of Palm Ball, which was played by played by Roman soldiers 2000 years ago (Orlando, 1993, p. 81).

Most of the following games are noncompetitive but are designed to test the player's skills; however, many games can be played in a competitive or cooperative way. This section will remind you of some old favourites as well as provide you with some new ideas.

Activities

▪ *Jump Rope*

Purposes: *develop physical coordination*
              promote cooperation to maintain rhythm
              enhance language development, especially for children learning a second language

Jumping rope is often done to a rhythmic song or chant. The beat sets the timing for jumps and counts the number of times the individual jumps before making an error.

Hopscotch

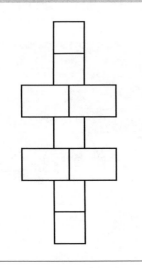

Hopscotch variation

5	6
4	3
1	2

In other chants, words direct the individual to perform different motions while continuing to jump.

> Cinderella, dressed in yellow,
> Went upstairs to kiss a fellow,
> By mistake, she kissed a snake,
> How many doctors did it take?
> 1, 2, 3, . . .

> Teddy bear, teddy bear, touch the ground,
> Teddy bear, teddy bear, turn around,
> Teddy bear, teddy bear, jump real high,
> Teddy bear, teddy bear, pat your thigh.

▪ *Hopscotch*

Purposes: *develop balance and large-muscle strength*
encourage play by traditional rules
increase eye–hand coordination necessary for aiming

Paintings by 16th-century artist Pieter Brueghel show children playing hopscotch, and a hopscotch board can be seen on the floor of the forum in Rome, indicating that generations of children have played the game. In Italy, the game is called "Heaven and Earth," earth being the starting point, and heaven the finish.

Draw the traditional pattern for hopscotch (see above). Vary the rules by hopping with the stone held on the back of the hand. Or hop without the stone, but with eyes closed.

Instead of the usual pattern for hopscotch, set up a set of six squares, three on each side (see beside). Number them from one to six. Have children jump through the squares in sequence with a stone held between their shoes, with both feet together like a kangaroo. If the stone is dropped, that player's turn is lost.

▪ *Sock Ball*

Purposes: *develop eye–hand coordination*
reinforce playing by rules

Push a tennis ball or sponge ball into the toe end of a tube sock. Tie a knot close to the ball. Children can toss this ball back and forth holding the open end. Vary the throws: twirl the sock before throwing, toss it underhand. To make catching more difficult, especially for older children, rule that they can catch the ball only by the tail.

▪ *Leapfrog Race*

Purposes: *foster trust in others and group cohesiveness*
develop large-muscle coordination

Have the children line up single file in two separate lines. When the starting signal is given, the first player in each line crouches down on hands and knees. The next player jumps over his back and then becomes a second back. The third player then must leap over two backs before becoming the third back. This continues until all players have had a turn. When the first player has jumped over all his teammates' backs and is at the head of the line again, he stands up. Each player at the end of the line follows the same procedure until all players are standing. The first team to have all players standing is the winner.

Hoist Your Sails

Place of Origin: Canada

Skills: Large motor, visual perception, and problem solving

Ages: 7 and older

Players: 10 or more

Materials: Coloured ribbon and materials to make flags

Playing the Game

1. Two teams are chosen by randomly assigning children two different sets of coloured ribbons. Each team can make up a name for themselves and make a flag for their team.
2. One team takes a treasure, which can be a collection of inexpensive items from a discount store, and goes off to hide it. The team can set up some natural obstacles along the way, such as jumping over a log. Each member of the team should mark each obstacle with the team's ribbon. Once the treasure is hidden, the team returns to the other team. One team member uses a stick to draw a map on the ground showing where the treasure is hidden. The team identifies all obstacles that will be encountered.
3. The other team goes off in search of the treasure. They may have to return to refer to the map several times. Along the way they collect the ribbons from each obstacle. Each person on the team should have one from each obstacle. When they have found the treasure, they come back and hoist their sail (a stick with their flag attached). They now go off to hide the treasure, set up some obstacles, and come back to draw a map that will show where to find the treasure.
4. Time limits can be set up and a limit of the number of obstacles can be determined before the game starts. Staff can talk about some possible obstacles, ensuring safety and the capabilities of the group. The time that each team takes to find the treasure can be taken.
5. At the end of the game, each of the children can take his or her "booty" from the treasure.

Figure 10-3 ■ Hoist Your Sails.

Based on "Hoist Your Sails," submitted by Miss Ella Des Brisay from Halifax in *Children's Games from Many Lands*, ed. N. Millen; Friendship Press, New York, 1943.

■ Catch the Dragon's Tail

Purposes: *promote group cooperation*
              practise being leaders and followers
              increase gross-motor skills

Eight or ten children line up, one behind the other. The last person in the line tucks a handkerchief in the back of her belt. At the start signal, the dragon begins chasing its own tail. The object is for the person at the head of the line to snatch the handkerchief. When the head finally gets the handkerchief, she becomes the tail. The second in line then becomes the new head. This is largely a cooperative game; however, it could be played with two teams competing by having the head of one team trying to catch the dragon's tail of the other team.

A version of this game is played in China, where the dragon is a symbol of good fortune. The game is often played at Chinese New Year celebrations.

In the Chinese version, the children line up, putting their hands on the shoulders of the person in front. The first person is the head and the last one the tail. The tail calls out: "1, 2, 3, dragon." The head leads, running and twisting trying to catch its tail. If the body of the dragon breaks, the dragon dies. The head then moves to the end of the line and becomes the tail. The game continues with a new head leading until everyone is too tired to play.

■ Pom-Pom Paddle Ball

Purposes: *develop eye–hand coordination*
              practise pair cooperation

Make paddles using five-inch lengths of broom handle or dowel. Drill a hole in one end of the handle. (Do this with the wood securely held in a vise.) Using wire cutters, cut the hook off a wire coat hanger just below the twisted part and discard the hook. Shape the remaining wire into a triangle. Pull a knee-high nylon stocking over the triangle. Secure the end with a bit of tape. Push the two ends of the wire into the handle and tape them there.

Make a pom-pom by looping yarn around a six-inch piece of cardboard. Use enough yarn to make a small ball. Slip the yarn off the cardboard, then secure the middle with a piece of yarn. Clip all the ends and shape into a ball.

Children can play in pairs, tossing the pom-pom back and forth. Vary the game by having children form into two lines facing each other. A group of six children works best. Have them toss the pom-pom back and forth between one team and the other.

■ Obstacle Course

Purposes: *develop large muscles*
              foster self-confidence by presenting increasingly difficult tasks

Set up an obstacle course using whatever equipment you have available. Place a sign showing the number at each station so children can proceed in sequence. Start with easy tasks and make them increasingly difficult. However, be sure that all activities are safe and that all the children can complete most of the tasks. Some suggestions are:

*   walk through a ladder that is lying flat on the ground without touching the ladder steps
*   crawl through a tunnel made of tables or large cardboard cartons
*   balance on a balance beam or walk on the edging of a sandbox
*   jump in and out of a staggered series of tires lying flat on the ground
*   jump from wooden packing boxes of several heights

- swing from a knotted rope
- climb a rope net
- shinny down the pole of a jungle gym

■ *Snake*

This game is played by children in Ghana, where there are many different kinds of snakes.

Purposes: *develop coordination*
              practise cooperating with others
              increase gross-motor skills

One person is chosen to be the snake. The snake goes to his home, an area that is large enough to fit several children. When given a signal (blow a whistle), the snake comes out of his home and tries to tag other players. Anyone who is caught holds hands with the snake and tries to catch others. The original snake is the head and determines who is to be tagged next. The end person, or "tail," can also tag players. If the snake's body breaks, the group must return to its home and start again. Free players can try to break the snake's body, forcing the snake to return home. The game ends when all the players have been caught or when everyone is out of breath.

■ *Rope Pull*

At one time, this game was a portrayal of the battle between the forces of good and evil. In Burma, the battle represents the natural occurrences of rain or drought. The custom is to allow rain to win. In Korea, villagers play the game to determine which village will have the best harvest. This version is played in Afghanistan.

Purposes: *develop gross-motor skills*
              increase coordination
              practise balancing
              increase the ability to plan strategies

Provide the players with a baseball bat or a wooden board about 1 m (3 ft.) long (sand all edges carefully so they are smooth). The players draw a line on the ground and stand on opposite sides. Each player clutches the board. The object of the game is to pull the first person on the other team across the line.

Picking Teams

No one likes to be the last person picked for a team. Box 10-1 describes some ways to help children pick individuals for a team and still maintain each child's dignity and integrity.

Box 10-1 ■ Creative Ways to Pick Teams

1. Number the children according to the number of teams you need (e.g., one, two, one, two).
2. Have every child put one shoe into the pile and then divide the shoes into teams.
3. Divide the children by the initial of their first name.
4. Divide the group by the colour of their hair or eyes.
5. Divide the group by the months of their birthdays.
6. Divide the group by the colour of the clothing they are wearing.

Chapter 10   Games Support Self-Regulation

Active Games That Can Be Played Indoors

You should know a few active indoor games children can play when the weather prohibits outdoor play. Even on warm days, children sometimes need to be moving around while inside. Children enjoy playing simple hand games and string games with partners as well as playing games that involve groups of children. Most of these games are **cooperative** types, where the children are always involved in the game; they might be moving places or taking on different roles in the game. There is no distinct winner or loser. The following are some games that can be played indoors, but you can set them up outdoors if you wish.

Activities

▥ People to People

Purposes: develop cooperation skills
listen and follow directions

Children move around in an area in the room. A caller, who could initially be a staff member, gives out different cues in a rhythmic pattern. The caller starts by chanting, "People to people, people to people …." Children move around and nod their heads and greet each other in the group. Then the caller may say, "Toes to toes," and the children move around the group connecting their toes with someone else's. The caller signals various other cues: elbow to elbow; head to knee, etc. You can vary the game and use colours asking the children to join with someone who is wearing the same colour clothing as they are. This is a good warm-up activity to help children become familiar with each other at the beginning of the year (Shadd, 2000).

▥ Upset the Fruit Basket

Purposes: practise taking turns
develop listening skills

Set up chairs or carpet pieces in a circle for the number of children in the group minus one person.

The children find a place to sit in the circle and each child is given the name of a fruit, such as papaya, orange, pineapple, etc. The children are asked to remember their fruit. One child goes into the middle. She calls out a certain fruit name or "Upset the fruit basket." If the child in the middle calls a certain fruit name, such as oranges, everyone who has that fruit name finds a new spot, but *not* beside them. During this time, the child in the middle has to find an empty seat in the circle. The child who has no spot in the circle goes into the middle to call out the next fruit name. If "Upset the fruit basket" is called, everyone finds a new seat, but *not* beside them. The person left without a seat goes into the middle to call the new fruit. Continue the game until everyone has had a turn.

▥ Human Pinball

Purposes: increase hand–eye coordination
encourage cooperation
increase strategic thinking skills

In a gym area or large indoor space, everyone stands in a circle facing into the circle. Players should stand with their feet planted firmly on the ground and touching the person's foot beside them. Players bend over with their arms dangling like flippers. They must stay in this position during the game and cannot hold the ball. The person who is the human pinball stands in the centre of the circle. A mid-sized ball like a soccer ball is set into the circle. The players in the circle try to hit the moving target in the middle by rolling the ball across the circle. Whoever hits the target becomes the next human pinball (Becker, n.d.).

▨ Beanbag Shuffleboard

Shuffleboard

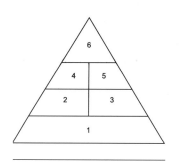

Purposes: *practise motor skills of throwing, pushing*

   improve math skills: writing numbers, adding

   taking turns, being scorekeeper and player

Use masking tape or chalk to mark off a court on an area of smooth floor. The court should be a large triangle, sectioned into six segments (see beside). Number each segment, giving the smallest segment the highest score. Children sit on the floor at the large end of the triangle and slide their beanbag along the floor. Each has two turns. Each can keep his own score, or a scorekeeper can be appointed. After a set number of turns, the scores are totalled.

In a variation of this game, a broomstick or long dowel can be used as a shuffleboard stick. Instead of sitting, children stand, then push the beanbag with the stick.

▨ Ping-Pong Jai Alai

Purposes: *refine hand–eye coordination*

   encourage cooperation when working in pairs

Provide a ping-pong ball and tall can for each child. Children drop or toss the ball with one hand, then try to catch it in the can. You can vary the game by suggesting they let the ball bounce twice or three times before catching.

Children might also work in pairs, with one child releasing the ball while the other catches. The catcher then puts the ball in play for her partner.

▨ Box Marble Shoot

Purposes: *develop small muscles of hand and fingers*

   increase math skills: number recognition and addition

For this game you need a shoe box, markers, scissors, and marbles. Draw five arches on one side of the box. Make one large, two medium, and two small. Mark number values above each arch, with the smallest arches having the highest value. Cut out the arches. Each player gets three marbles and several turns to complete the game. Players shoot their marbles, trying to get them through the slots. At the end of a set number of turns, each player totals his score.

▨ Kulit K'rang

Children in Indonesia play this game with small shells.

Purposes: *develop hand–eye coordination*

   increase reaction time

   predict where pieces will fall

The players sit in a circle around a bowl. Each player is given an equal (10–15) number of playing pieces (dried beans, peanuts, pebbles, or seashells). Leave about 20 pieces in the bowl. Each player places his pieces on the floor in front of him.

The first player puts a piece on the back of his hand, then tosses it in the air. He must grab another piece from his pile, then catch the falling piece. If he has successfully caught the falling piece, he takes one piece from the bowl. If unsuccessful, he must put one piece in the bowl. Play continues until the bowl is empty or all the players are out of pieces. The player who then has the most pieces wins the game.

Floor/Table Games

There are many commercial games you can use in a school-age program. Ask the children what they like to play at home, and recall the games you enjoyed when you were a child. Visit toy or game stores to find games that are appropriate for school-age children. In addition to the commercial board games, there are some that you and the children can make, such as a large floor version of Snakes and Ladders or Checkers. Also, encourage the children to think of their own ideas for games.

Introduce children to simple card games, which are inexpensive. Some are described here, but you can find others in the books suggested at the end of this chapter.

Activities

■ *Aboriginal Stick Dice*

Purposes: *develop mathematical skills of addition*
   use deduction; predict results when moves are made

Make an envelope from construction paper that will fit three craft sticks. Put the directions for the game on the outside of the envelope. Paint the three craft sticks red on one side and white on the other side.

To play the game: toss up all three sticks at once. The colours that come up each time will tell you how many points you score: 3 red = 10; 3 white = 5; 2 red + 1 white = 3 and 2 white + 1 red = 2. Use tally marks to keep score: 2 white + 1 red = // or 2 red + 1 white = ///.

This is a good game for the children to make themselves.

■ *Memory Game*

Purposes: *practise the ability to match like symbols*
   develop the ability to remember placement of objects in space

Find 20 pairs of pictures. You can use playing cards from two decks or secure your own matching pictures. They should all be the same size and with no identifiable marks, patterns, or colours on the back. Two to four children can play this game.

Mix the cards, then place them face down on a table. Players take turns selecting two cards at a time. The cards are shown to the other players. If the cards are a matching pair, the player keeps them. If not, they are placed back in their original spot. The next player then has a turn. The game ends when all the pictures have been picked up. The player with the most pairs is the winner.

■ *Twenty Pairs*

Purpose: *practise ability to match like pairs*
   develop thinking strategies

This game can be played by three or more and requires a pack of 52 cards. Remove one queen from the deck, then deal the remainder to the players. The goal of the game is to get rid of one's cards by getting matched pairs and laying them on the table. Each player picks up and examines his cards. He can discard any matching pairs by placing them face down on the table. If he has three cards of the same value, he can discard only two of them.

To begin the game, the player to the left of the dealer fans out her cards and offers them face down to the next player on her left. That player takes one card and incorporates it into his hand. If he now has a pair, he places it face down on the table. He, in turn, offers his cards to the next player. The procedure continues around the table until all the players have managed to pair and discard their cards. One person is left holding the odd queen.

■ Rotation Dice

Purposes: *practise taking turns*

enhance math skills: set recognition, adding

Two or more players can play the game, and all you need is a pair of dice. Each player takes turns trying to get a specified number on each throw. There are 11 rounds to the game.

In the first round each player tries for a two. In the second, each tries for a three. In the third round, each tries for a four. Succeeding rounds follow the sequence to the last round, when the sum of both dice must be 12.

If a player succeeds in throwing the number she is trying for, she gets that number of points. For instance, if she is trying for a five and succeeds, she can add five points to her score. If she does not succeed in throwing the number she needs, she ends that turn with no points. At the end of the eleventh round, the scores are totalled, and the player with the most points wins.

■ Tic-Tac-Toe Dice

Purpose: *strengthen math concepts: writing numbers, number recognition, adding*

Two or more players can play. You need two dice, a score card, and pencil for each child. (The score grid can be drawn on a piece of paper or an index card.) Have each player make a score grid with 12 squares.

Write the numbers from 1 to 12 in the grid (see beside). Each player throws the dice only once each turn. On each play players cross out a number or numbers on the score card. They can cross out the total or each of the two numbers. Players also can cross out any combination of numbers that equals the total on the dice. As an

Figure 10-4 ■ Nim Game

Nim

Skills:	Counting, creative thinking and planning skills
Ages:	8 and older
Players:	2
Materials:	16 toothpicks, beans, or other small markers

About the Game

This is the thousand-year-old Chinese game of *Nim*. It doesn't have any set patterns or rules. Here, however, is one way it might be played.

Playing the Game

1. Players will need 21 toothpicks or other small game pieces. Arrange the sticks in one row as shown in the picture.

2. Taking turns, the players pick up 1, 2, or 3 sticks at a time.

Winning the Game

The player to pick up the last stick, loses.

From *THE MULTICULTURAL GAME BOOK: MORE THAN 70 TRADITIONAL GAMES FROM 30 COUNTRIES.* Scholastic Inc./Teaching Resources. Copyright © 1993 by Louise Orlando. Reprinted by permission.

Tic-Tac-Toe

1	5	9
2	6	10
3	7	11
4	8	12

example, if a five and a two are thrown, the following combinations can be crossed out: six and one, or five and two, four and three, or one, two, and four. The first person to cross out all the numbers is the winner.

■ Solitaire

Card games that are played alone in North America are called "solitaire." In England these games are called "patience."

Purposes: *increase ability to concentrate*
                reinforce ability to count accurately
                practise recognition of symbols for suits

Shuffle a deck of cards. Deal out seven cards in a line, with the far-left card face up and the others face down. Deal out the cards on the line again, starting with the second column, and have that card face up and the others face down. Follow this pattern starting consecutively with the third, fourth, fifth, sixth, and seventh cards.

If an ace is showing, remove it and put it above the line of cards. Turn over the card exposed by your move, or, if it was the first card, replace it with one from the deck. The object of the game is to use all of the cards to fill each of the suits from the ace to the king in stacks above the game line.

Remove three cards at a time from the remainder of the deck, looking only at the top card. Play a black card on a red card, sequencing the numbers from largest to smallest. Cards can be removed from one pile to place on another, thus freeing another bottom card. The game ends when all four suits have been filled or no more plays can be made from the remaining deck cards.

■ Ajaqaq

During the dark winters Canadian Inuit children play a variety of games to pass the time. At one time they believed that playing this game would make the sun return earlier.

Purposes: *develop fine-motor skills*
                increase eye–hand coordination

Give each player a curtain ring or similar weight ring about 8 cm (3 in.) in diameter, a 30-cm (12-in.) stick, and 80 cm (30 in.) of string. Tie one end of the string to the ring and the other around the end of the stick. Hold the stick in one hand. Flip the ring in the air, then try to catch it on the end of the stick.

■ All Ears

Purposes: *develop listening skills*
                associate sound with familiar objects
                discriminate similar sounds from one another

This is a game for a group of children. Collect several objects that make a sound. Sit where you cannot be seen by the children (behind a shelf or a hanging bed sheet.) Make a sound with each of the objects. Players must guess what the object is or what action made the sound.

Some ideas for making a sound:
- shake a rattle
- bounce a ball

- pour water
- cut a piece of paper with scissors
- staple two pieces of paper together
- open a soft-drink can that has a pull tab
- snap your fingers
- crumple a piece of cellophane
- rub two pieces of sandpaper together
- saw a piece of wood
- pound a nail into a piece of wood
- bite an apple
- unwrap a candy bar
- rotate a hand eggbeater
- jingle some coins together

At the end of the game, ask the children to think of other objects that can make a sound. Add some of those to your next game.

Guidelines for Having Fun with Games

Before introducing any game to children, play it yourself. Know how the game is started and how the first player is determined. Although you want children to read the rules of a game, you should be familiar with them.

Introduce new games periodically. Although children like to play the same games over and over, they also need to keep extending themselves. Once they master a game, there may be little challenge. Therefore, look for new games. Talk to other caregivers to get ideas.

Encourage children to invent their own games. All games start with an idea of something that would be fun. Let children make their own board games, develop new ways to play outdoor games, and think of new ways to use available materials.

Help children feel competent when they gain new skills. Provide **authentic feedback** by describing their real accomplishments. Praise their efforts to improve their own performance, for being able to solve a problem, or for being a committed team player.

Encourage children to share their own favourite games with the group. Suggest that they bring games that are part of their cultural background.

Encourage youngsters to try increasingly difficult tasks. Once they have mastered one task, they are often more willing to try harder ones. Encourage them to do so, but do not pressure them. Praise them for their efforts.

Stress cooperation rather than competition. You cannot avoid having a winner and a loser when playing some games, and children

authentic feedback
a description of a child's real accomplishments

Figure 10-5 ■ Children enjoy the challenge of new games.

need to learn that they do not win all the time. Some of the challenge in playing certain games is to see who can be first or fastest. However, you do not want children to have winning as the primary focus of games. Therefore, do not set up contests or give prizes. Instead, offer genuine praise to all children for their participation, their teamwork, their sporting behaviour, and their efforts.

As children become older and gain more cognitive abilities, they will come to understand rules and competition more. The emphasis that is put on the process of playing the game by the school-age child care professionals will go a long way in teaching the children about themselves and others in the future when they are more involved in organized sports.

Assist them with problem solving, coming up with strategies as they meet various challenges.

Be flexible about rules. Be sure that children understand the rules before you begin the game. However, young children like to change rules or develop their own. Allow them to do so when all the players agree.

Enjoy physical activity yourself. Feel the joy children experience when they run, catch balls, or shoot baskets.

Remember the games you especially enjoyed in childhood. Teach the children how to play them. Your enthusiasm will be contagious. Be well prepared and encourage everyone to play the game or have some role in the play. Children can also retrieve balls, monitor line boundaries, or keep score. Make adaptations for children with physical disabilities. Play wheelchair basketball or make changes in an obstacle course to suit the abilities of the children involved.

Explore worldwide events such as the Deaflympics, Paralympics, Special Olympics, and Extremity Games for people with disabilities.

Enjoy the challenge of indoor games. Sit down and play solitaire, or try Trivial Pursuit® with some friends. Above all, have fun.

Electronic Games: Computers

With the proliferation of computers in today's society, professionals in the fields of child care and education have a responsibility to help the children in their programs keep up with technology. Many people need to have strong computer skills in order to be successful their jobs. However, questions arise for those working in school-age programs, such as how available should the computer be—whenever children want it, or on some kind of limited schedule? What about hand-held electronic and video games: do they have a place in a school-age program or not? Bigger questions include where to get the money to buy equipment and who will repair it when there are problems. Finally, who will monitor children's Internet explorations? All of these questions need to be addressed when setting up a computer in a school child care program. The answers should come from both staff members and parents.

One important reason for including computers in school-age programs is that some children may not have any other access to this technology. For children in economically deprived neighbourhoods, the school-age program may be the only source for learning how to use this tool that seems to be pervading our society. "Most children from Canada's low(er) income families do not have a computer at home, causing them to face yet another disadvantage in comparison to their more privileged peers" (Schoeber & Hiltner, 1995, p. 9).

Even though a school may have computers, the school-age program might be able to allow children more open-ended computer time than in the classroom. Girls may lag significantly behind boys in computer use, and free exploration time could allow them to feel more at ease. Computers have also been proven to be very beneficial for children with special needs; computers can assist children with developmental challenges by providing them with an avenue to express ideas, to participate in games with their peers, and to communicate their needs (Mulligan, 2003, p. 50).

Children use Internet search engines to research information on various topics. Many children also enjoy sending e-mail to friends or distant e-mail correspondents. Some electronic pen pals are found through chat rooms and newsgroup postings. Staff should monitor this process at all times and ensure that the sources for e-mail connections are safe.

Computers provide children with an opportunity to develop skills in a number of developmental areas:

- fine-motor control
- finger dexterity
- eye–hand coordination
- self-confidence/mastery
- self-regulation
- creativity/inventiveness/imagination
- reading comprehension and vocabulary
- language and communication skills
- listening skills
- mathematical skills
- decision-making skills
- problem solving
- cooperation and social skills

The phenomenon of <u>hand-held and video games</u> is also a highly significant component of contemporary children's culture today. As with computer games, children are very motivated by the nature of the games themselves (Kafai, 2001). One of the problems that occurs when children bring these games to the program is that the hand-held games are generally used by only one person at a time. This can create difficulties if the child who brings the game into the program is not willing to share it. Another problem relates to the nature of the games themselves. Violence is one of the most prominent features in commercial video games (Provenzo, 1991). Female game figures are not generally featured in main roles, and the themes of hunts embedded in most video games often hold little interest for girls (Kafai, 2001). Staff in the school-age program need to pay particular attention to their policies regarding when, where, and how toys and games from home can be used in the program, and share this information with parents. School-age child care professionals also should be sure that the games that come into the program are ones that match the overall philosophy of the program in terms of values and beliefs.

Box 10-2 ■ Rules of Internet Safety

The following are basic rules of Internet safety:

- Personal information such as a home address, phone number, e-mail address, or school location should not be given out without parent's permission.

- Download games or buy anything online only with permission from parents or staff in the school-age program.

- Sending insulting or rude messages is called "flaming" and can be a form of bullying.

- Tell the school-age staff or a parent right away if any message makes you uncomfortable.

- Check all sources of information with the school-age child care staff or parent to be sure it is a reliable resource

The question of <u>Internet safety</u> should be carefully considered. Children who are adept at "surfing the net" can get into websites that give them inappropriate or incorrect information, or put them in dangerous positions. Software programs can filter Internet access to sites you do not want children to explore. You should also solicit active participation from staff, parents, and children to decide the kinds of access that will be available to children, and find ways to prevent problems.

<u>Choose software programs</u> carefully, reviewing them before introducing them to the children. Computer software that is selected for the children should be focused on play, self-correcting, creative, explorable, multilevelled, and easily shared with a friend.

Because many computer games are violent or teach children questionable values, the National Association for the Education of Young Children (NAEYC) (1996) states that principles of developmentally appropriate practice should be applied. NAEYC believes that "in any given situation, a professional judgement by the staff is required to determine if a specific use of technology is age appropriate, individually appropriate, and culturally appropriate." It is also important to choose software that is non-biased in terms of gender preferences. Choose software that both boys and girls would enjoy, while staying away from the gender-biased choices. You can also find reviews of software and help in choosing appropriate programs on the Internet at the following websites:

Child & Family Canada: 10 Tips for Selecting Children's Software
http://www.cfc-efc.ca/docs/cccf/rs062_en.htm

University of Alberta, Faculty of Education: Evaluating software
http://www.quasar.ualberta.ca/techcur/whatis/software/reviews.htm

Teaching Teachers Technology: Choosing software appropriate for children
http://www.educ.uvic.ca/StuLab/ed359/software.html

The Canadian Toy Testing Council: 2000 Toy Report
http://www.toy-testing.org/contents/reports/toys-4+a.htm

4Teachers.org: Integrating technology into the curriculum and classroom
http://4teachers.org

Technological Tools: creating safe online environments for children
http://www.bewebaware.ca/english/TechnologicalTools.aspx

Cyberpatrol: Internet Safety Software
http://www.cyberpatrol.com

Superkids™ Educational Software Reviews
http://www.superkids.com

Junior Net.com: Provides easy e-mail access to children and advise parents on teaching tools
http://www.juniornet.com

Wide range of software from different sources as well as a special page for educators; includes product reviews and demonstration programs that can be downloaded
http://www.knowledgeadventure.com

Guidelines for Program Staff

Although this section on computers has been placed in the chapter titled "Games and Other Fun Things to Do," that should not be construed as meaning that computers are not an important tool for learning. Computers can be a vital element of learning if they are integrated into the total curriculum. Teachers and school-age child care professionals often use the term **"integrated learning"** to describe the use of interrelated disciplines such as language, math, or science to achieve a goal. This can be seen most often in a project approach where children work on self-initiated projects individually or in a group. The explorations to complete the project may entail the use of a word processor to write letters, stories, poems, or reports. Even children who are just learning to write can be adept at this since they can delete and rewrite easily, without the difficulties that come with laboriously handwriting words. The Internet can be used to research information to include in a report or to follow additional areas of interest. Technology is discussed in more detail in Chapter 12.

integrated learning
using interrelated disciplines such as language, math, or science to achieve a goal

In order for children to make the most effective use of computers, school-age child care professionals must play several roles depending upon the level of competence of the children:

Instructor. When computers are first brought into the program, children will need time to become familiar and comfortable with the hardware (the computer) and software (the programs). At this time school-age child care professionals must take the most active role, guiding the children through the various steps necessary to explore the new medium.

Coach. As children gain experience, staff can begin to withdraw active participation, allowing children to work independently or to rely upon peers to provide help as needed. The staff member becomes a facilitator, providing support when needed or ensuring appropriate behaviour.

Model. Children will more likely use computers as an important tool for learning if they see school-age child care professionals using them. The staff can demonstrate the ease with which a story can be recorded on the computer or classroom materials and charts can be produced.

Summary

Children need a change of pace after long hours at school. Some like to be active while others need to rest. Some are ready for socializing, but others want to be alone.

Games allow children to practise motor skills self-regulation, and skills of working together. They also help to reinforce and extend cognitive skills. Active games that can be played indoors allow children to work off energy. Many popular games have been played by generations of children. Games originate from many countries around the world, and help build children's appreciation for cultural diversity. Provide opportunities for children to appreciate different abilities in sports, such as in wheelchair basketball, rugby, and hockey.

Some children will view games as an opportunity to win, but school-age child care professionals can minimize this tendency by including noncompetitive games.

Always be aware of safety. Know the regulations and guidelines regarding the safe use of equipment and first aid practices in your program. Set clear rules and enforce them consistently. Have enough adult supervision.

Although there are many commercial games children like to play, there are others you can make.

Games should be fun. Guidelines for enjoying games with the children in your school-age program include the following:

- Introduce new games periodically.
- Help children feel good about themselves when they acquire new skills.
- Encourage children to try increasingly difficult tasks.
- Stress cooperation rather than competition.
- Be flexible about rules.
- Enjoy physical activity yourself.
- Remember the games you played as a child, and teach them to the children.
- Enjoy the challenge of indoor games.
- Have fun.

Computers can be an important addition to the school-age program; children can work at their own pace writing stories or poems and researching information for school projects. The school-age program may be the only place some children will have access to a computer.

Questions about the use of hand-held electronic games, safety of the Internet, and appropriateness of software programs must be considered. Adults must take several roles while helping children to become knowledgeable about computer use: an instructor who actively participates, a coach who provides support as children work independently, and a model who demonstrates how to use computers in a variety of ways.

Key Terms

cooperative games   authentic feedback   integrated learning

Student Activities

1. Visit a school-age program. Interview two children about their favourite games. Ask them the following questions:

   - What is your favourite game?
   - What do you like best about that game?
   - What do you dislike about it?

   Summarize your findings. Were there similar games mentioned by the two children? Why do you think those games were popular? Share your findings with the class.

2. Choose one of the indoor or outdoor games listed in this chapter. Teach the game to a group of school-age children. Was it successful? If not, why not?

3. Make one of the games described in this chapter. Try it out with a group of adults and children together. Did both adults and children enjoy the game? How do you think the participants benefited from playing the game?

4. Interview a senior citizen. Ask her to describe a favourite childhood game. Why was it a favourite?

Review Questions

1. What are the factors that affect children's choice of active games?
2. What should be done to ensure the safety of children when they engage in vigorous outdoor play?
3. Name three skills that are reinforced when children play floor/table games.
4. List four outdoor games.
5. Name three indoor games that allow children to move around.
6. Briefly describe how Twenty Pairs is played.
7. List eight guidelines for having fun with games.
8. What are some of the concerns about the use of computers, hand-held electronic games, and video games in a school-age program, and what can school-age child care staff do to limit any problems?

Case Study

Ryan, Joel, Trevor, Melissa, and Tavia were playing a game of Twister®. The children were taking their turns; as the colours came up on the board, they were moving their hands and feet to the appropriate places. Trevor fell over, but insisted that he was not out and still wanted to play. Joel, Melissa, and Tavia said that it wasn't fair, because the rule says that if you fall, you are out. Trevor says he didn't know that if he fell, he would be out of the game. The school-age child care professional, Anthony, came over and asked what the problem was. Trevor said he doesn't want to play anymore, because the game was stupid.

1. Is there a way this situation could have been prevented?
2. What would you say to Trevor?
3. How would you help the children get back into the game and to play fairly?

References

Becker, E. *Games*. Retrieved April 22, 2005, from http://troop851.ellenbecker.net/Games.htm

Child and Family Canada. (n.d.) *10 Tips for Selecting Children's Software*. Retrieved April 5, 2005, from http://www.cfc-efc.ca/docs/cccf/rs062_en.htm

Kafai, Y. B. (2001). *The educational potential of electronic games: From games-to-teach-to games-to-learn*. Chicago, IL: University of Chicago, Cultural Policy Center. http://culturalpolicy.uchicago.edu/conf2001/papers/kafai.html

Mulligan, S. (2003). Assistive technology—Supporting the participation of children with disabilities. *Young Children* 58(6), 50–51.

Orlando, L. (1993). *The multicultural game book*. Toronto: Scholastic Professional Books.

Provenzo, E. F. (1991). Video kids: Making sense of Nintendo. In Kafai, Y. B. (Ed.), *The educational potential of electronic games: From games-to-teach-to-games-to-learn*. Chicago, IL: University of Chicago, Cultural Policy Center.

Schoeber, T. & Hiltner, A. (1995, Winter). Children and computers in school-age care. *Interaction*, 9–10.

Shadd, D. (2000). *Cooperative games workshop*. Kitchener, ON: Conestoga Collage Institute of Technology and Advanced Learning.

Selected Further Reading

Davies, A. (1986). *Co-operative games for people who love to play*. Toronto: Public Focus.

Drake, J. & Love, A. (1998). *The kids' cottage games book: Official book of games to play*. Toronto: Kids Can Press.

Eagan, R. & Hoover, G. (1995). *Game for a game: Games, trivia, folklore & fun*. Carthage, IL: Teaching & Learning Co.

Gryski, C. (1985). *Cat's cradle, owl's eyes: A book of string games*. Toronto: Kids Can Press.

Haugland, S. W. (1999, November). What role should technology play in young children's learning? *Young Children*, 54(6), 26–34.

International Platform on Sport and Development: Sport and Disabilities. http://www.sportanddev.org

National Association for the Education of Young Children. (1996, November). NAEYC position statement: Technology and young children—Ages three through eight. *Young Children*, 51(6), 11–16.

Orlando, L. (1993). *The multicultural game book*. New York: Scholastic Professional Books.

Orlick, T. (1982). *The second cooperative sports & games book*. New York: Pantheon Books.

Petricic, D. & Gryski, C. (1995). *Games of childhood*. Toronto: Kids Can Press.

Stassevich, V., Stemmler, P., Shotwell, R., & Wirth, M. (1989). *Ready-to-use activities for before and after school programs*. West Nyack, NY: The Center for Applied Research in Education.

Wilmes, L. & Wilmes, D. (2000). *Parachute play*. Elgin, IL: Building Blocks.

Chapter 11

Inquiry Learning Through the Arts

Objectives

After studying this chapter, the student should be able to:

- Identify the process of inquiry learning through the arts
- Discuss the value of integrated play opportunities in the areas of art, music, and dramatics
- Plan for the incorporation of children's interests and needs through art, music, and dramatics

Profile

Jan runs a camp every summer outside Guelph, Ontario, for 15 children aged 6–12, called Spirit Connections. Jan is an Early Childhood Educator and also plans literacy-based programs for preschool children. She is an accomplished storyteller. Jan is one of the aboriginal leaders in the Guelph community and she takes care of the community medicine bundle. She shares knowledge of aboriginal traditions in art, storytelling, music, and drama with the children. An adult volunteer also helps in the program on a daily basis. Jan's program focuses on developing a keen sense of community, where every person learns to accept and respect each another as unique individuals and everyone works together to ensure that believe they are like valued and important members of the group. Lower ratios enable the adults to build trusting relationships with each of the children and to find ways to ensure that each child feels she or he is honoured within the group. The adults draw on each child's strengths to support a healthy sense of community based on cooperative, collaborative learning. The children's experiences enable them to recognize the connections they have with one another and to become more compassionate, respectful, and caring.

The program is situated in a beautiful, serene, rural setting where children can freely explore with minimal physical risk. A pond, small forest, and a large variety of flowers allow the children to take part in environmentally focused activities and learning experiences. As a result, they develop respect for all living things. A large, open green space houses a full-size tipi that the children help to construct. The tipi is used as the formal gathering place, where adults and children bring greetings to one another at the beginning and at the end of the day. Children have ample safe, open areas to play some traditional aboriginal games as well as time for quiet observation and reflection.

The arts are well integrated in the program. Jan believes that the arts encourage children to tap into their creative energies and to manifest their feelings, beliefs, and questions within a variety of tangible experiences. The visual arts offer opportunities for children to express themselves through the exploration of a variety of media without judgment and evaluation.

Music is symbolic of the rhythms and emotions of life that the children are encouraged to experience. Opportunities to dance enable the children to use their bodies creatively to "paint a picture" in response to the rhythms and emotions they feel. Drama gives children a chance to act out stories based on their own personal perspectives on life by creating props, masks, and costumes. Storytelling provides a chance to share cultural traditions, values, and beliefs, and helps children recognize the commonalities between their own stories and the stories of others.

Role of the Arts in Inquiry Learning

Watch a group of children as they paint at easels, dance with scarves, or listen to music and stories. Notice their expressions of concentration, joy, or relaxation. Creative activities satisfy children in a way few other experiences can. Children enjoy the arts because everyone can be successful. There is no right or wrong answer or just one way of doing things. Children also find it a way to communicate things they might not be able to put into words. For example, they can use bright colours when they are happy or subdued colours to show sadness. They often feel more relaxed after they pound, roll, or cut clay to release pent-up emotions. They learn what their bodies can do when they dance to music. They relive and remake their own experiences with puppets or in plays and bring to life their own stories.

Art can be shared with others or experienced privately. Painting alone lets a child express feelings or ideas that might not be easy to put into words. Group painting on a mural entails planning, compromise, sharing, and cooperation—all important social skills. Listening to music by oneself can be a way to release tension and achieve a sense of inner peace, experience emotions vicariously, or just enjoy the sounds and rhythms. Even dancing can be enjoyed by oneself and offers opportunities to increase physical abilities such as large-muscle control and coordination. Group dancing can be a social activity requiring sensitivity to one's partner or to the group. Patterned dances necessitate remembering sequences, an important cognitive skill.

Art, music, and drama can help children from diverse cultural backgrounds gain a greater appreciation for their own culture as well as share their heritage with others. Children can view art done by prominent artists from different countries, and they can use the same materials. Some cultures use sand for painting, others use brilliant colours, while still others use only black on white paper. Music can tell stories about a people, convey values or ideas, or use a rhythm that can be identified with a way of life. Children can dramatize a folk tale, write their own plays, or use puppets from different countries. Through each of these media, children learn how others live their lives. The result should be a greater tolerance for differences and a greater appreciation of similarities from one country to another.

Very young children use art experiences simply to try out materials. In preschool, children use all their senses to investigate the properties of art materials. They want to find out how colours mix together, how a paintbrush works, and how clay feels. They seldom know ahead of time what they are going to create. In kindergarten, children still enjoy just trying out materials for the pleasure of the experience, but they are beginning to realize they can express feelings and past occurrences as well. By the middle to the end of the elementary years, they set goals for themselves and want recognition for their accomplishments: "I want to learn how to paint with oil paints."

The arts can provide children with a lifelong interest in all creative media. When children view others' creations, they are introduced to new ways of expressing ideas and feelings. When they study paintings or sculpture, they appreciate how artists use colour and form to create something beautiful. While they listen to music, they hear how other people express emotions. When they watch a play, they share in others' experiences.

Children have a natural ability to explore and inquire about new discoveries. They watch, observe, ask questions, make comparisons, talk about their experiences, and communicate their feelings and desires. An important function of the arts is the opportunity to use both sides of the brain. There are two distinct hemispheres of the brain, and each performs different functions. This division or **lateralization** is most often associated with adults, but studies of children show that even though there is an early tendency to specialization, children's brains are still malleable (Brooks & Obrzut, 1981). The left side of the brain specializes in language and logic, uses deductive thinking, and is associated with science and mathematics. The right side of the brain uses an intuitive approach associated with creative processes. The arts can give children the opportunity to use their creativity while at the same time use language skills, explore scientific concepts, and practise mathematical skills. Opportunities for children to use both sides of the brain in a fully integrated approach to curriculum encourages a more well-rounded developmental approach. Staff should watch for situations in which they can introduce questions and comments that expand beyond the obvious nature of the activity. For example, when the children are "drop painting," (dripping paint from various heights onto paper that is set out on the floor), staff can talk about gravity and help the children make a chart showing predictions and measurements of the size of the drops they have made on the paper.

Most important, art is a perfect medium for helping children develop **divergent thinking** and **convergent thinking.** Divergent thinking is a process of thought or perception that involves considering alternatives and taking a line of thought that is different from the usual. In art there are no right or wrong answers and no single way to accomplish a creative task. So children can ask themselves "What if I used a different kind of paper for my picture?" or "I wonder if this would sound better in a different key or with another instrument?" Convergent thinking is just the opposite. It means to narrow down many ideas to a single, focused

Figure 11-1 ■ **Three-dimensional art experiences allow children to recreate a view of things in their world more realistically.**

lateralization
specialization in function of the two hemispheres of the brain

divergent thinking
a process of thought or perception that involves considering alternatives and taking a line of thought that is different from the usual

convergent thinking
a process of thought that narrows down many ideas into a single focused point

point. A child may want to express a feeling generated from a past experience. His thinking process will consider the many ways in which this could be done: through a painting, a sculpture, a piece of music, or a dance. Through a process of considering and eliminating, he will decide which will serve his purpose most effectively.

When you plan any creative activities, start first with children's interests. Capitalize on these to formulate your program. Encourage children to expand their interests or to find new ways to express them. Find out also what they are learning in history or social studies at school so you can plan activities that complement these school experiences. For some children, the creative activities they experience in the school-age program will be all they have. Cutbacks in school boards' money or personnel are often felt first in school art programs. For these children your program will become an even more important part of their lives. Let them enjoy one or more of the arts every day, integrating a variety of curriculum areas. Provide lots of different ways for children to re-create their work in two-dimensional drawings and three-dimensional constructions.

The most effective curriculum will meet the needs of both the youngest children and the older ones. Younger children want plenty of opportunities to freely explore what they can do with materials. They should have lots of materials available at all times and time to use them in any way they want. The result of their efforts should be less important than the experience. As children get a little older, approaching the end of the elementary years, their work becomes more goal directed, and they become more interested in a final product. Their drawings become more representational of what they see in their world around them, more organized spatially, and also use more geometric lines and shapes. Children become more critical of what they produce. As they gain better fine-motor control they learn how to use real tools such as palette knives, crochet hooks, or knitting needles to enhance their efforts. They appreciate the opportunity to learn techniques from real artists or people who have special skills, and they enjoy working together on long-range projects.

Experiences with the arts give opportunities to integrate other areas of curriculum. Children can practise their language and literacy skills by writing and sharing stories with one another. They can use their mathematical skills to measure, count, estimate, sort, or classify materials as they construct their two- and three-dimensional projects.

Ways to Promote Inquiry Learning Through the Arts

inquiry learning
a process of exploring, observing, gathering information, and engaging in a sense of wonder

To promote **inquiry learning**, ask questions that invite constructive input and validate prior knowledge. Ask open-ended questions such as "What would happen if …." Or "Tell me what you are thinking about …." Encourage children to ask questions of each other and share stories about their discoveries, such as how they solved a particular problem when putting something together in a construction so it wouldn't fall apart. Encourage them to think for themselves. Repeat or paraphrase what they say, allowing them to critique the process of their creations (Ogu & Reynard Schmidt, 2009).

The Ontario Full-Day Early Learning-Kindergarten Program identifies four elements of the child's inquiry process:

1. Initial engagement—noticing, wondering, playing
2. Exploration—exploring, observing, questioning
3. Investigation—planning, using, observations, reflecting

4. Communication—sharing findings, discussing ideas

(Ontario Ministry of Education, 2010–2011)

Visual Arts

Because there are so many art activities children enjoy, this chapter can give ideas for just a few. Read the books listed at the end of this chapter, investigate what is available at your local library, and talk to other teachers or school-age child care professionals. Attend workshops sponsored by local early childhood associations and other professional organizations. Look around you at all the possible materials children can use to construct, paint, or draw. Throw nothing away, for it might become part of your art program! Ask parents to collect potential art supplies, such as cardboard, tubing, fabrics, empty plastic bottles, and empty boxes. Some activities may be classified as crafts versus art in that they require children to follow specific directions and particular patterns. Some examples of these types of activities include learning to knit or crochet, using learn-to-draw books, and rug hooking. These activities will give children practice with using convergent thinking skills. Nevertheless, opportunities to use creative, divergent thinking skills should also be encouraged. For example, allow the children to make decisions about what colours they want to use for their knitting or assist them with solving a problem they may come across, without providing a solution yourself. Provide lots of opportunities for children to explore open-ended materials to develop their own projects: empty boxes, cartons, different kinds of fabric, yarn, string, tape, paint rollers, kitchen utensils, wood pieces, etc. can be used in many different ways.

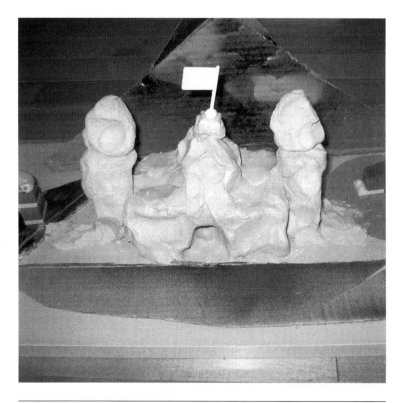

Figure 11-2 ■ **Joshua, Kevin, and Seth tell their story about King Arthur as they play with clay.**

Activities

Clay and Other Kinds of Modelling Media

Purposes: *develop fine-motor coordination*

enhance understanding of spatial relationships

transform an idea into a three-dimensional object—from symbolic to concrete

Grey or terra cotta clay. Provide lots of clay on a plastic-covered table. Add little dishes of water that children can dip their fingers in to rub on the clay. Provide plastic forks or knives, small combs, garlic presses, and small pieces of sponge for varying the texture of sculptures. Add real sculpting tools for further interest. Children may create and build interesting structures like towers and castles with the clay. If you ask them to tell you about what they are doing, they may share some very imaginative stories like the one in Box 11-1.

Story told by Joshua, Kevin, and Seth (ages five to six), while playing with clay with picture of their castle scene.

The King Arthur Story

This is a very old England castle. King Arthur lives there. There is a statue of a person who died in the war. There is no moat. There is a lake near the castle with water in it. The roof is just about to fall off. Their roof is nearly going to break. When the roof fell, it almost will break the castle. We don't take cars around there. We take boats and walk around. There is a cliff near the castle. It was made out of cement. The boat is parked between the cliff and the castle.

If you have a kiln, pieces that the children make can be fired and then displayed. Children can make bowls, plates, cups, or other kinds of pottery. Items may be painted with acrylic, water-based paints and then cover them with shellac or glaze. Display pictures of pottery created by local artists.

Plasticine. Plasticine is readily available but tends to be difficult to soften and work with. It comes in a variety of colours. It will not harden for a permanent sculpture. Store colours separately because when combined, they blend into grey.

Dough. Homemade dough provides opportunities for children to be creative by making whatever they like. Children enjoy making dough beads of different shapes such as cubes, cylinders, and spirals. Holes can be made with a straw, pencil, or toothpick. Children can also mix different coloured pieces of dough to make multi-coloured beads or paint their beads if you use a neutral colour of dough. Beads can be set out to dry in a warm dry place for a couple of days. See Box 11-2 for the recipe.

Box 11-2 ▪ Flour-and-Salt Dough Recipe

Ingredients

0.5 kg (4 cups) flour

250 mL (1 cup) salt

food colouring

water to moisten

Mix the dry ingredients together. Add food colouring to water. Add water to dry mixture to achieve the desired texture. This dough will dry hard in the air and then can be painted. If a reusable dough is desired, add two tablespoons of cooking oil.

Children can make Diwali lamps by flattening balls of dough and pinching up the edges to create small bowl shapes. Children can put a birthday candle (with the wick cut off) in the centre of their lamps. (Caution: the candles are not to be lit.) Diwali, or the Festival of Lights, is celebrated in late October or early November.

Papier-mâché. Use newspaper strips and liquid starch, white glue, or a flour-and-water mix to create *papier-mâché*. Use a balloon for a base. Dip the paper in the starch mixture, then lay it on the surface of the balloon. Overlap the pieces and make at least two layers. Let it dry thoroughly, then prick the balloon and pull it out. You should have a fairly solid round sphere. (This finished product can become the head or body of an animal, or a puppet head. Use paper towel tubes as the legs and neck.)

For added interest, bring a Mexican piñata to the program. Show the children that it has been made of a *papier-mâché* sphere similar to the ones they have made. Encourage them to make their own piñatas with balloons and *papier-mâché*. When the *papier-mâché* is dry, prick the balloon. Help the children cut a slit at the top of the sphere so that the piñata can be filled with candy or small toys if desired. Pull out the balloon. Provide tissue paper in a variety of colours, scissors, a small brush, and liquid glue. Show the children how to cut fringed strips from the tissue paper. Brush the sphere with the glue and lay the tissue-paper strips evenly on the sphere, each slightly overlapping the previous one and leaving the fringe free. Remember to leave the slit visible if the piñata is to be filled and then cover the slit with strips of tissue paper and glue.

Construction

Purposes: reinforce divergent thinking through exploring possibilities in found objects
enhance understanding of spatial relationships
develop fine-motor coordination

Toothpicks, natural or coloured. Combine with small corks, drinking straws cut in different lengths, or small wooden beads or mini marshmallows. Lengths of copper or coloured wire can be added. This sculpture can be freestanding or pushed into a base of styrofoam.

A variation of this type of construction would be to use chopsticks. Explain to the children that some people in Asia use chopsticks instead of forks. (This activity might follow preparation of a Chinese or Japanese meal.) Pieces of Plasticine can be used for a base.

Wood. Use a flat piece of wood or heavy cardboard as a base. Add lumber scraps cut into interesting shapes, wooden beads, wooden buttons, tongue depressors, wooden stir sticks, and wood lathe scraps. (Many interesting shapes can be obtained from a furniture manufacturer or a high-school woodworking class.) Use white glue to create structures. For a variation, add pieces of tree bark, small twigs, or seed pods. Make bark boats, adding sticks and leaves. Sail the boats in a big tub of water and have a boat race.

Recyclable cans. Create "can creatures" using clean soda or juice cans. Provide construction paper in assorted colours, fluorescent paper, felt, water-based acrylic paints, markers, scissors, white glue, and assorted objects (yarn, buttons, googly eyes, beads, pipe cleaners, feathers, etc.). Instead of using the can in its regular shape, the children could bend the side of the can inward by placing it on a flat, protected surface and smashing the can with their foot. They can paint the can with water-based acrylic paint. Encourage the children to imagine a "creature" with the can as the body. Cut out feet or arms from the paper or felt, make hair from fringed pieces of paper or yarn, and use buttons or beads for eyes or clothing decorations. Display the "creatures" when they are finished.

Towers and castles. Provide lots of building items, such as egg cartons, cereal boxes, shoe boxes, paper towel rolls, and plastic water bottles. Include white glue or a glue gun with low-temperature glue sticks. Encourage the children to work together to make their structure, which may take a number of days. Talk about famous towers like the CN Tower in Toronto, Ontario, and the Eiffel Tower in Paris, France, and bring in books about medieval castles, towers, and drawbridges.

Ice sculpture. Make a hand-shaped ice sculpture by filling a rubber glove with water. Secure the open end with a rubber band and prop it upright outside in the winter to freeze, or place it in a freezer. You can freeze water in containers like cake moulds, muffin tins, and loaf pans. Place pennies, bottle caps, or pebbles in ice cube trays and freeze them. When you look through the ice, shapes will be altered. To unmould sculptures, you may need to briefly run warm water over them for a moment. If temperatures are below freezing, keep the sculptures outside.

Collage

Purposes: *increase appreciation of the natural environment*
enhance sensitivity to differences in colour, texture, and appearance of different materials
develop fine-motor skills

Nature collage. Have children collect natural objects outdoors or on a walk; include leaves, twigs, bark, dried grass, seedpods, acorns, pine cones, feathers, and rocks. Give each child a base of heavy paper, tagboard, styrofoam, or wood, and provide strong white glue. Discuss and label each of the collected items. This is an especially fun project for the fall.

Shapes and origami. Provide children with a piece of drawing paper on which you have drawn one of the following shapes: square, triangle, rectangle, circle, oval, parallelogram, etc., from construction or other kinds of paper. Challenge the children to create a picture with the shape as the base. Provide marking pens, paints, an assortment of paper and fabric pieces, scissors, and white glue. Include some origami paper. A definition and history of origami can be found at http://www.creased.com/origami/origamidefinition.htm and a basic pattern is found at http://www.creased.com/origami/diagrams/cranediagram.htm.

Weaving Projects

Weaving projects can be done with various kinds of branches. Provide different colours of yarn, fabric, felt, ribbons, and string that children can use to wind in and out of the branches. During the summer, the children may enjoy weaving through the wires and slats of a playground fence. You may want to purchase or borrow a weaving loom that the children could use in the program. Children can also make dream catchers, which are common in North American First Nations Cultures, or Ojos de Dios (God's Eyes), which originate with the Huichole People of Mexico.

Paper Quilt

Collect small pieces of wallpaper, gift wrap, greeting cards, paper doilies, construction paper, aluminum foil, and cellophane, and give each child a base of cardboard, heavy textured paper, or thin box top (from stationery or shoe box). Provide white glue. These materials could be used to create treasure boxes or wrapping paper for special gifts.

Children can also work in groups to make paper quilts based on topics that interest the children, such as Harvest Time, Friendship, Winter Holidays, or Endangered Animal Preservation. Give children 22.5 cm × 22.5 cm (9 in. × 9 in.) squares of coloured construction paper and ask them to paint, draw, or glue items on each square of construction paper. These square patches will form the quilt when they are attached at the back with tape. Read books about making quilts like *Selina and the Bear Paw Quilt* by Barbara Smucker.

Fabric

Small pieces of felt, lace, ribbon, yarn, buttons, coloured beads, small silk flowers, and dried or paper flowers can be used for many crafts. Include various types of fabric that represent different cultures. For example, Kente cloth is used for shirts, ties, and hats in many African countries. Display pictures of Kente cloth or obtain samples. Point out that the cloth is made up of simple geometric patterns on square or rectangular shapes. Give each child a base of coloured bristolboard, construction paper, or a thin box top. Provide white glue, assorted construction paper, rulers, scissors, crayons, or marking pens. Display their fabric designs when they are finished.

Sewing projects. Give children opportunities to try some traditional crafts like sewing, knitting, crocheting, and rug hooking. Provide embroidery hoops, needles, thread, and simple patterns for older children. Younger children can do some sewing with larger darning needles, wool, or yarn, and squares of plastic canvas that can be purchased at craft stores. Children can also make a fabric quilt with the squares (see "Paper Quilt," above). Invite a guest to come to the program and teach the children some simple knitting and crochet stitches. The children will be more successful using larger knitting needles and crochet hooks. See http://www.knitting-crochet.com/knisti.html for knitting instructions and http://www.knitting-crochet.com/crochet/crosti.html for instructions on how to crochet.

Large Masks

Masks have been used for ceremonies to bring power and spiritual forces to the people who wear them. They often have intricate designs or carvings and are representative of mythological beings or spirits. Display pictures of ceremonial masks or visit a museum that displays them. Ensure that the children are aware of the sacred nature of the mask to some aboriginal peoples, and share stories and legends that are related to aboriginal cultures. Make some comparisons to celebrations today, like Mardi Gras and Halloween, where masks are worn.

Collect supplies for masks: large pieces of tree bark or basket-weaving pieces (large pieces of corrugated cardboard can also be used), scissors, white glue, construction paper, leather pieces, feathers, and various colours of paint. Remind the children they can build up parts of their masks with construction paper pieces or add objects to make the masks more authentic.

Another way to make creative masks is to cut out pictures of different eyes, noses, and mouths from magazines. Children can choose various combinations of eyes, nose, and mouth and glue them onto a paper plate. Punch holes in the sides of the paper plate and tie yarn or string in the holes so that the mask can be placed on the face.

Painting and Drawing

Purposes: *increase language by learning new words relating to artistic endeavours*

provide opportunity to move from one intellectual level to another in a nonthreatening environment (scaffolding)

increase awareness of cultural differences and similarities through appreciation for art from various cultures

Crayon rubbings. Use any thin paper over flat stones, leaves, sandpaper, corrugated paper, or cardboard shapes. Use the flat side of a crayon to cover the entire sheet of paper, picking up the design underneath.

Chalk painting. Cover a sheet of paper with a thin layer of liquid starch. Provide several colours of chalk, either sharpened to a point for a thin line or blunted for a thick line. Use a rag, paper towel, or fingers to mute or brush colours together.

Melted crayons. This is a good way to use old crayons. Remove paper coverings from pieces of wax crayons. Allow children to smash crayons in a heavy bag with a mallet, sprinkle crayon bits onto a piece of wax paper, and cover it with a second sheet. After covering the paper with an old tea towel, children should press the paper with a warm iron. When cool, cut the pictures into interesting shapes, punch a hole in the top, attach a string, and hang in a window.

Tempera or water-based acrylic paint. Provide a variety of colours and allow children to place their own selection on a small plastic paint palette, which can be bought inexpensively at a craft store. Give children a choice of brushes (thin, fat, stiff, or soft), and a variety of textures of paper (rice paper, grocery bags, parchment, newsprint, wallpaper, or plain white cloth sheeting). Use various shapes of paper (long, thin rectangle; large or small oval; large or small square; triangles; hexagon). Provide small containers of water for cleaning brushes between colours.

Figure 11-3 ■ Art activities might include painting with different tools or using different materials.

Rock painting. Go for a walk and collect rocks of different sizes. Wash and clean them with water. Provide various colours of paint and different sizes of paintbrushes to create designs on the rocks. Aboriginal people used rock paintings (pictographs) as a method of communicating ideas. Do some research and provide pictures and books about some of the symbols that have been found on rock paintings across Canada and around the world.

Splatter painting. Add some interest by setting up a painting activity where the children can drop thin liquid tempera paint with a brush from different heights onto paper that is placed on the floor. Always be sure to cover the floor surface with lots of newspaper or set up areas where children can paint outdoors.

As a variation, put thin paint in spray bottles and put large sheets of paper on a wall. Cover the area in front of the wall with lots of newspapers and have two or three children paint at a time. Talk about the importance of keeping the spray paint on the paper. This would be a good activity to do outside in good weather or on snow.

Textile paint or fabric crayons. Provide a variety of colours of textile paint or fabric crayons (obtain from a fabric store). Give children a choice of fabrics of different colours, textures, and sizes. Paint or draw designs on white T-shirts, socks, shoe laces, or small pieces of white cloth. Add other decorative items like sparkles or tin foil confetti. If children bring their own items from home, ensure that you get permission from the parents. For an outdoor summer activity, tie-dye with the children. Prepare vegetable and plant dyes, such as onion skins, tea, or food colouring. If you use commercial fabric dyes, it is essential to use disposable gloves and remind the children to dress in old clothes. Children use rubber bands to wrap different parts of the cloth into twisted shapes, then dip the cloth in the dye. Hang cloths to dry overnight.

Paint with different tools. Provide toothbrushes, feathers, roll-on deodorant bottles, small sponges, cotton balls, sponge-top bottles, Q-tips, foam swabs (used for cleaning audio and video equipment), flexible spreaders (used in cake decorating), and squeeze bottles.

Cut out round pieces of paper that will fit into the bottom of a salad spinner. Squeeze different colours of liquid tempera paint onto the paper. Spin the spinner, take out the paper, and admire the designs.

Murals. After discussing a topic of interest with children, collect a variety of art media such as paint, collage materials, construction materials, crayons, and markers. Provide white glue or glue guns and low-temperature glue sticks, scissors, tape, and large white mural paper or large white cloth sheeting. Encourage the children to work together to create a display of what they think is important about the topic they have chosen. Display books and pictures about the topic the children have chosen for their mural.

Figure 11-4 ■ "Under the Sea" mural.

Field trip. Visit an artist's studio. Ask the artist to demonstrate some techniques to the children and explain the safety precautions the artist uses. Visit a museum or art gallery and request a tour with a docent who can tell the children about the exhibits. Children will enjoy seeing how artists painted people, landscapes, or abstract designs.

Equipment to Have Available for Art Projects

- aprons or old shirts
- brushes—various sizes and shapes
- boards for clay—Masonite, plastic, or wood
- drying racks
- easels—floor and table
- paint palettes

- paper cutters—for single sheets and for large rolls of paper (caution: these are for staff use only)
- craft sticks, palette knives
- rags and towels for cleanup
- reproductions of fine art and traditional crafts
- rulers, measuring tape
- scissors—assorted sizes, left- and right-handed
- sculpting tools, garlic press
- sponges—large and small, natural and manufactured
- staplers
- sewing items—needles, thread, yarn, wool, knitting needles, crochet hooks, rug hooks
- the work and styles of artists: painters, dancers, musicians, storytellers, and actors
- visits to art museums, plays by local theatre groups, or concerts by musicians
- different types of tape, glue, glue guns with low-temperature glue sticks

Discussion

Enhance children's experience by helping them learn more about art. Discuss the following topics with them:

- how things look: light, texture, colour, position, patterns
- effect of using contrasting colours: light and dark, bright and dull
- two-dimensional surfaces: forms, variations in size and shape
- drawing techniques: line drawings, imaginative and decorative styles
- painting techniques: dry or wet brush, stippling, finger painting, colour mixing
- new words: ivory, crimson, burnt sienna, primary, embroidery
- professions: painter, sculptor, ceramist, illustrator, cartoonist, designer, museum director, weaver
- the work and styles of artists: painters, dancers, musicians, storytellers, and actors
- visits to art museums, plays by local theatre groups, or concerts by musicians
- cultural traditions and origins of various techniques

Music and Movement

When children enter kindergarten, most are able to sing simple songs, although they may not always be on pitch. Children seem especially attuned to music with a pronounced rhythm, and, given a few simple instruments, they will imitate rhythms they have heard or create their own. They develop self-expression when they move to music, using their whole bodies or just their hands or feet. By the end of elementary school, most children have developed a good sense of rhythm and beat. They can remember and sing a large selection of songs and may have added the new skill of being able to sing in harmony. Some are able to play instruments, and a few will be able to write simple musical patterns or songs.

Music education has been linked with success in other subject areas. Lamb and Gregory (1993) found that there was a strong relationship between musical sound discrimination and reading ability. The process of developing the ability to discriminate pitch enhances their phonemic abilities when they are learning to read, and music opportunities assist in developing spatial reasoning skills and social skills. Music also gives children an opportunity to express their feelings in appropriate ways.

Music should be a part of every day. It does not have to be a formal music time but can be integrated into the daily routine. Play CDs, tapes, and videotapes during activity times. Children often enjoy traditional camp songs, as well as different kinds of music that they hear on the radio. They may want to bring CDs from home to play at the school-age program. Staff should be careful to screen some music CDs for inappropriate messages relating to sex, violence, and discrimination. Music chosen should be reflective of the program's philosophy and goals.

Provide opportunities for children to play different musical instruments like drums, tambourines, shakers, rhythm sticks, and a small keyboard, if feasible. Children like to play "real" instruments and learn some of the musical notations associated with writing musical scores. Invite a guest who plays a musical instrument like the electric guitar to come in to teach children a few chords.

Children can make musical instruments with common materials like wood, cans, plastic containers, dowelling, *papier-mâché,* and other recyclables. Music experiences give children a chance to become aware of different cultural traditions with dance, musical instruments, and songs.

Figure 11-5 ■ First Nations Duck Dance.

Activities

Purposes: *increase physical coordination*
develop listening skills
provide an outlet for expression of feelings
enhance appreciation of different cultures' contributions to the arts

Musical Styles

Play different kinds of music: classical, pop music, folk music, rap, country, rock, jazz, etc. Have the children identify each style, then ask them to compare two styles. How are they alike or different? Provide many opportunities to hear music, encouraging the children to really listen to how the music is formed. Place tapes or CDs in a listening corner for children to enjoy at their leisure.

Play selections of music from different countries and cultures. Select reggae from Jamaica, opera from Italy, a mariachi band from Mexico, sitar music from India, balalaika music from Russia, flute music from the Andes, or First Nations drum music. Ask the children to compare the sounds of the music. Why do they think the music is representative of the country?

Paint to Music

Play different kinds of music as children paint. Suggest they paint what they hear. Include music from different cultures.

Karaoke

Bring in a Karaoke machine or a microphone that can be plugged into a CD player. Add some costumes such as scarves, vests, and hats, and some music. Children will enjoy singing along and pretending to be their favourite musician. Children can make their own microphones, instruments, and costumes, and create their own musical band.

Dance Prop Box

Find an interesting trunk or box. Add props to enhance movement and dance: scarves, baton, hoops, coloured streamers, jackets, vests, skirts, pants, gloves, tutus, pompoms, boas, dance shoes, hats, masks, and musical instruments. Children could also make some of these items to add to the prop box. The "Dance Box" can be taken out any time. Children can choose some music and try out different dances such as ballet, folk, modern, hip-hop, jazz, or line dancing.

Tap Dancing

Collect three or four pennies or other coins. Assist the children with taping the coins to the bottom of their shoes with two-sided tape. Gather the children in a group on a hard floor surface (tile or other hard surface) and demonstrate a few tap-dance steps. Draw pictures of the steps and put them on a large poster so that the children can follow them. See http://www.tapdance.org/tap/steps/index.html.

Musical Limbo

All you need is a large open space, a long stick like a broomstick, and some Caribbean or Calypso music. Two volunteers hold the ends of the broom. Children form a line and go under the broom, without touching it, one at a time. The stick is lowered each time until only one child is left.

Figure 11-7 ■ Doing the Limbo

Folk Dances

Children may enjoy learning some simple dances like the Hora, which is a traditional Jewish folk dance; the Le Petit Train a Jonquière from Saguenay-St Jean, Quebec; the Farandole dance, popular in the Middle Ages; the Samba from Brazil; and line dancing, which is popular in country music circles.

Find information about different folk dances around the world at http://library.thinkquest.org/J002266F/folk_dance.htm.

Show children a video or DVD of dance segments (check your library). Discuss the kind of dance portrayed, then encourage children to dance to the video.

Musical Statues

Play a tape or CD while children dance. Instruct them to "freeze" when the music stops. Stop and start the music several times.

Mirroring

Provide a scarf for each child. Group them in pairs. Have one child act as leader, making movements using the scarf. A second child mirrors those movements. After a short period, change roles.

Instruments

Make a didgeridoo, a musical instrument used by aboriginal people in Australia. Use PVC pipe or cardboard wrapping-paper tubes. The length of the didgeridoo should match the height of the child. Use water-based acrylic paint and decorate the tubes with yarn, leather, and beads. Beeswax can be used to surround the mouthpiece for comfort, if desired. Provide pictures of didgeridoos and books about aboriginal people of Australia. See http://www.kinderart.com/multic/didgeridoo.shtml.

The drum is sacred to First Nations of North America. The drum stands for life, seasons, winds, and the north, south, east, and west. Drums come in different sizes and shapes and are used in ceremonies to accompany dancers.

Children can make drums or use pots, plastic containers, or boxes as drums. Thin dowels can be used for drumsticks. Experiment with different ways to communicate messages with the drum, such as "let's party," "there's a new baby in town," or "someone is moving away."

Musical Notes

Set up a keyboard with coloured sticker circles on each of the seven keys in a musical scale (CDEFGAB). Put together some simple songs on musical staff paper using similar coloured circles that match the notes of the song. The children will play each note by following the coloured circles on the lines and spaces and touching the corresponding colour on the keyboard. They can even make up their own songs with coloured circle stickers and blank sheets of musical staff paper.

Make up a Musical Instrument Bingo game by gluing pictures of musical instruments on bingo cards. Find a CD or tape of the different sounds of musical instruments on the bingo cards or make one up yourself. Use little bingo chips to cover the picture of the instrument when the musical instrument is heard on the CD. When a child gets a line filled with chips, she shouts "BINGO."

Equipment to Have Available

- keyboard
- karaoke machine
- blank tapes for recording
- books—song, poetry
- dance props—tap shoes, tutus, scarves, streamers, canes, hoops, ropes
- earphones for listening centre
- cultural musical instruments—maracas, bongo drums, Chinese temple blocks, didgeridoo
- guitar
- microphone

Figure 11-8 ■ Children working on a talent show.

- tape or CD player—assortment of tapes or CDs. Select all kinds of music including classical and modern pieces
- limbo stick
- selection of percussion instruments—drums, rhythm sticks, shakers, castanets, tambourines, bells
- television monitor and VCR or DVD player

Discussion

Some concepts to discuss with children to enhance their learning:

- musical terms: tempo, pitch, dynamics (loud/soft)
- movement: walking, running, swaying, balance
- dance forms: ballet, folk, tap, interpretive, jazz, hip-hop
- instruments: names, how they produce sound, care of instruments
- listening: differentiating sounds, following musical directions or beat
- traditional and cultural origins, and meanings
- musical notation, music scale

Dramatics and Story Making

From a very early age children engage in dramatic play. Toddlers charm their parents by imitating actions or situations they observe around them. Preschoolers use dramatic play to try out what it feels like to be a grownup; they play at being mom or dad, doctors, firefighters, teachers. As they get a little older, dramatic play becomes a way to conquer feelings of being scared or helpless. Four-year-olds and young "school-agers" play at being monsters, superheroes, or popular TV characters.

During the middle childhood years, children use dramatic play to consolidate and understand what they are learning in school and at home. Although they may still dress up and act out situations, they also use small toys, blocks, or other materials to replay a trip to the fire station or other community facilities. They may also reenact what they see happening on television news or familiar shows.

Older children take a more organized approach to dramatic play. They want to write their own scripts, assign parts, make costumes, and stage plays. This activity provides a variety of opportunities to practise skills that children are trying to develop during this period of their childhood. Writing a script entails listening to how people talk during conversations, writing words, and organizing a story line. Negotiations and compromise are necessary to be certain that all participants have an opportunity to contribute according to their own skills or interests. Drama experiences provide children with opportunities to practise a combination of different kinds of intelligences: including bodily/kinesthetic,

Figure 11-9 ■ Children use puppets to relive past experiences or express feelings.

interpersonal, intrapersonal and linguistic (Gardner, 1993). As children create and act out stories, situations, and ideas, they practise their expressive and receptive language (linguistic) skills. They often work cooperatively in groups to plan their plays and productions, developing interpersonal skills. Creative drama gives children an opportunity to develop intrapersonal intelligence by expressing themselves and releasing feelings and emotions as they replay situations that they have experienced in their own life.

The best kinds of dramatic play occur when children can play whatever they wish. Allow children many different opportunities to use their imaginations in both spontaneous and organized activities. Make materials available that allow for children's own creative ideas such as blankets, scarves, different types of materials, lace, tubes, tunnels, boxes, foam pieces, etc.

Activities

Purposes: *provide practice in negotiating and compromising during a group effort*
enhance the ability to set long-term goals and to postpone gratification
increase the ability to portray ideas, feelings, and experiences through either drama or using blocks

Puppets

Design and make different kinds of puppets. Try shadow, finger, hand, stick, *papier-mâché,* or sock puppets. Read about how puppets are constructed and used in other countries. (See Box 11-3 for ideas.)

Box 11-3 ▇ Puppets

Life-Size Puppets

Materials needed

dowelling, approximately 7–8 centimetres (3 inches) in length per child

newspaper

masking tape

cardboard, paper towel rolls, wool

paints

large paint brush

fabric (large enough to cover child's head)

glue gun with low-temperature glue sticks

Directions

Cut the dowelling. Wrap masking tape around a small ball of newspaper, then tape it around one end of the dowelling. Continue wrapping the newspaper around the dowelling with masking tape to make the head. Use cardboard pieces, paper towel rolls, etc. to tape features such as eyes, nose, mouth, and ears to the head. Cover with white paint and let dry. Paint head and features with coloured paints and let dry. Using a glue gun and low-temperature glue sticks, add extras like hair, moustache, or glasses. Glue fabric piece around the neck of the puppet to form a tent-like form. To operate the

---

puppet, children drape the material over their head and hold onto the dowelling. The puppet's head will be approximately 5 centimetres (2 inches) higher than the children.

Hand Puppets

Materials needed

hand

face paints/lipstick

black pencil/eyeliner

materials to make hair, hat, bows

Directions

Make a fist, with your thumb outside your fingers. Your thumb will move to look like a talking mouth. Use face paints and black pencil to make eyes, mouth, eyelashes, and eyebrows. Braid some yarn to make a wig to drape over the hand.

Shadow Puppets

Materials needed

craft sticks

construction paper

scissors

markers/pencils

stapler or masking tape

Directions

Have children draw a figure on the construction paper, then cut it out. Staple or tape the figure to the craft stick. Use an overhead projector or any light source and a blank wall to put puppets into action.

Puppet theatre. Older children can make a permanent theatre using carpentry tools and plywood or from a large appliance box. An impromptu stage can be as simple as a curtain, a wall of large blocks, or a table covered with a blanket.

Produce a puppet play. Have children write a simple script or use a favourite story. Let them make the puppets, have rehearsals, make props, hand out tickets, and present the play for families and friends.

Drama kits. Collect a variety of props children can use for dramatic play. Store them in related sets for different topics: kings/queens and knights, camping, wedding, fashion show, magic show, comedian. School-age children often love to tell jokes. Collect children's joke books and jokes from the following websites (listen for children's interests, then provide additional props for play): http://www.childrenlead.com/jokes.php; http://yahooligans.yahoo.com/content/jokes.

Makeup. Provide makeup (theatrical makeup, if possible) and mirrors. Allow children to try out ways to use makeup. Have tissues and cold cream for cleaning up when they are finished.

Homemade makeup: 5 mL (1 tsp) cornstarch, 2.5 mL (1/2 tsp) water, 2.5 mL (1/2 tsp) cold cream, food colouring, small covered containers for each colour of paint, and a small paintbrush.

Upside-down face painting. Children can work in groups of two or three. Ask the children to lie on their backs on the floor. Have each child draw a face on another child's chin with assorted colours of makeup. Place two tables side by side to form a stage. Children can take turns lying on the tables (on their backs) with their heads over the edge having conversations or singing songs as they perform for their peers. Faces can be covered with scarves to help bring focus to the painted faces on their chins.

Blocks. Provide both small and large blocks. Add accessories as children's interests dictate: cars, airplanes, boats, people, animals, trees, signs, boxes, packing forms, plywood, and cardboard tubes. Take pictures of the creations and display them in a photo album or on a bulletin board.

Play/skit. Have children write and produce a play. They can also adapt a book, use a published play, or make up their own skit based on a set of costumes. Folktales, fairytales, and favourite TV shows are popular choices for children to act out. They can make costumes, props, and stage settings. These projects can last for a number of weeks. Children may want to plan a small production and present it for their families and friends. Videotape the play so that the children can watch it themselves.

Write and tell stories. Encourage the children to tell their own stories that have a beginning, a middle, and an end. During group time, have one child start a story with a few sentences. The next child takes up the story line and continues with a few more sentences. Each child must listen to all the previous story tellers in order to remember the gist of the story before continuing. The last child has the most difficult part because he must bring closure to the story. As a variation, tape the story as the children tell it. Place the tape in the listening corner so that children can hear it again.

Read folktales. Folktales are stories that once were told by parents, grandparents, or community storytellers. Originally they were not written down but passed verbally from generation to generation. Read or tell folktales at group times or encourage small groups or pairs of children to read to one another. Ask the children to make up their own versions of fairy tales and make their own books. See the list of children's books at the end of the chapter.

Invite an adult storyteller to visit. Ask the adult to tell the children a story that was a favourite when she was a child. Encourage stories that have been part of a family tradition or culture.

Field trip. Look for professional performances at theatres or amateur performances of a puppet play or children's drama at schools, community centres, or libraries.

Equipment to Have Available

- blocks—wooden floor blocks, large hollow blocks, small coloured blocks
- block accessories—cars, boats, airplanes, people, animals, trees, signs
- boxes, shelves, racks for storing props
- carpentry tools—saw, measuring tape, yardstick, hammer, sander, nails
- dress-up clothes—skirts, dresses, capes, shoes, hats, wigs, scarves
- floor lights—standing lamps, spotlights, overhead projector
- mirrors—individual makeup mirrors, full-length mirrors

- puppet theatre or materials for construction
- sewing tools—needles, thread, pins, scissors
- tape recorder
- video camera

Discussion

Some concepts to discuss with children:

- imagination: new ways to tell a story or express feelings
- props: how to make props and costumes for their productions
- scripts: books, poems, movies, TV shows
- skills: skills needed to produce a drama
- puppets or marionettes: which one fits a particular character
- manipulating puppets to create a story

Summary

Not all children will grow up to be painters, sculptors, actors, musicians, or play-wrights. However, you want them to learn that when they go out into the sometimes harried world of adulthood, the arts will provide continuing pleasure and relaxation. By having a variety of art activities available, all children can find one that suits their own individual needs and abilities, whether working alone or in a group. So, make art of all kinds an integral part of your day. Both you and the children will reap boundless benefits. Creative activities satisfy children in a way no other experiences can because all participants can be successful; through the arts children can release emotions verbally and nonverbally, learn about themselves, and use their imaginations to relive or remake their own experiences.

The most effective art program will meet the needs of all ages of children in the program.

Very young children use all their senses to explore the properties of art materials. By kindergarten age, they learn that their feelings and experiences can be portrayed symbolically through art. By the end of middle childhood, children set goals for themselves and want recognition for their accomplishments.

Kindergarten children can sing simple songs and like to imitate rhythms they have heard or create their own. By the end of elementary school, most children have a good sense of rhythm and beat; they can remember many songs and even sing in harmony. Some can play instruments or compose music and it helps in other subject areas.

From an early age, children engage in dramatic play. Toddlers imitate what they see, preschoolers and young children try out adult roles, and older children want to write their own scripts and produce their own plays.

The arts will provide continuing pleasure for children into their adult years. Art of all kinds should be an integral part of the school-age program.

Key Terms

lateralization   convergent thinking   inquiry learning
divergent thinking

Student Activities

1. Visit a library, museum, community centre, or theatre in your community. Ask about programs or resources they might have that would interest school-age children. Prepare a list to share with your classmates.
2. Plan and implement one of the activities suggested in this chapter. Write an evaluation of the experience. Were there things you could have done differently? If so, how?
3. Talk to staff in three different school-age programs. Ask which creative activities their children most enjoy. Find out why they think those activities are so popular.

Review Questions

1. This chapter stated that "creative experiences satisfy children in a way few other experiences can." Give three reasons to support this statement.
2. In what way does a preschooler's use of art materials differ from that of a child approaching adolescence?
3. Give an example of how to promote inquiry learning through integrated art and dramatics experiences.
4. List three musical concepts to discuss with children in order to enhance their learning.
5. You want to encourage children in your school-age group to enjoy more music. What kinds of equipment should you have available?
6. Relate the developmental steps in children's dramatic play from toddlerhood to older middle childhood and identify three kinds of intelligences that are practised.
7. List some accessories children might use with blocks to expand their dramatic play.

Case Study

Hannah is a lively six-year-old. Her favourite activity is using whatever art materials are available each day, and she spends most of her inside time there. However, she constantly wants reassurance and praise for her efforts. She will finish an interesting collage, then run to Daria wanting her to look at it. She will ask, "Do you like my picture? Do you think those colours go together?"

1. How would you respond to Hannah's "Do you like my picture"? Explain your answer.
2. How would you react to her "Do these colours go together"?
3. Hannah spends most of her time at this one activity. Would you do anything to broaden her interests? If so, what?

References

Brooks, R. L. & Obrzut, J. E. (1981). Brain lateralization: Implications for infant stimulation and development. *Young Children, 36*(3), 9–16.

Gardner, H. (1993). *Multiple intelligences: The theory in practice.* New York: Basic Books.

Lamb, S. J. & Gregory, A. H. (1993). The relationship between music and reading in beginning readers. *Educational Psychology*, 13 (1), 21–26.

Ogu, U. & Reymond Schmidt, S. (2009). Investigating rocks and sand: Addressing learning styles through an inquiry-based approach. *Young Children*, vol. 64. No.2, 12–18.

Ontario Ministry of Education. (2010–2011). The full-day early learning–kindergarten program. Draft Version, 15.

Selected Further Reading

Anders, R. (1975). *Making musical instruments*. Minneapolis, MN: Lerner Publications.

Baker, W. (1990). *The dressing-up book*. Richmond Hill, ON: Scholastic Canada.

Bonica, D. & Devlin, K. (1997). *Cooperative quilts*. Torrance, CA: Fearon Teacher Aids.

Carlson, L. (1990). *Kids create!* Charlotte, VT: Williamson Publishing.

Carlson, L. (1993). *EcoArt*. Charlotte, VT: Williamson Publishing.

Cech, M. (1994). *Globalchild multicultural resources for young children*. Parsippany, NJ: Dale Seymour Publications.

Hart, A. & Mantell, P. (1993). *Kids make music*. Charlotte, VT: Williamson Publishing.

Haas-Foletta, C. & Cogley, C. (1990). *School-age ideas and activities for after school programs*. Nashville, TN: School-Age Notes.

Irons, J. & Parkes, S. (1998). *The Canadian Arctic Inuit*. Whitby, ON: S&S Learning Materials.

Kohl, M. (1999). *Making make-believe*. Beltsville, MD: Gryphon House.

Milford, S. (1990). *Adventures in art: Art and craft experiences for 7- to 14-year-olds*. Charlotte, VT: Williamson Publishing.

Milliken, L. (1996). *Medieval times activity book*. Dana Point, CA: Edupress.

Sadler, J. (2001). *Jumbo book of easy crafts*. Toronto: Kids Can Press.

Schecter, D. (1997). *Science art projects and activities*. Toronto: Scholastic Professional Books.

Sierra, J. (1991). *Fantastic theater, puppets and plays for young performers and young audiences*. New York: The H.W. Wilson Co.

Children's Books

Balliet, B. (2004). *Chasing Vermeer*. New York, NY: Scholastic.

Coulter, L. & English, S. J. (2001). *Secrets in stone*. Toronto: Madison Press Books.

Hayes, B. & Ingpen, R. (1994). *Folk tales and fables*. Broomall, PA: Chelsea House Publishers.

Muller, R. (2003). *The magic paintbrush*. New York, NY: Scholastic.

Munsch, R. & Martchenko, M. (2003). *Makeup mess*. Markham, ON: Scholastic Canada.

Norman, H., Dillan, L., & Dillan, D. (1997). *The girl who dreamed only geese and other tales of the Far North*. Harcourt Brace Children's Books.

O'Neal, S. & Evans, S. (2003). *Shaq and the bean stalk and other very tall tales*. New York: Cartwheel Books/Scholastic. Service, R. & Harrison, T. (1986). *The cremation of Sam McGee*. Toronto: Kids Can Press.

Service, R. & Harrison, T. (1986). *The cremation of Sam McGee*. Toronto: Kids Can Press.

Smucker, B., Wilson, J., & Holliday, L. (1998). *Selina and the bear paw quilt*. Toronto: Stoddart Kids.

Websites

Children's activities search engine
http://kids.yahoo.com/

Canadian Museum of Civilization
http://www.civilization.ca/childrens-museum

Child & Family Canada—Safety in the arts
http://www.cccf-fcsge.ca/docs/cccf/RS_21-e.pdf

Jan Brett's Books Site—stories and activities
http://www.janbrett.com

Nova Scotia Museum
http://museum.gov.ns.ca

McMichael Canadian Art Collection (Group of Seven artists)
http://www.mcmichael.com

Robert Munsch Books Site
http://robertmunsch.com

Chapter 12

Children as Natural Investigators

Objectives

After studying this chapter, the student should be able to:

- Discuss how inquiry learning enhances cognition: investigation, experimentation, problem solving, and reflection

- Recognize the scientific processes: coming up with a hypothesis, making predictions, observing, evaluating, and developing conclusions

- Discuss the facilitator's role in facilitating mathematical, scientific, and technology experiences

Profile

Mansura is a ECE student who is doing a placement in an extended-day program for children 4–10 years of age at one of the lab schools situated in an elementary school associated with Conestoga College in Kitchener, Ontario. She had been observing the children for many weeks and recorded observations of them building rocket ships and pretending to be astronauts in the block area. The children talked about how real rocket ships were built and asked many questions about their construction and how the astronauts were outfitted to go into space. They were very interested in space adventures, and wanted to know more about them. Mansura and the program staff helped the children to pursue those interests. They asked them what they wanted to do next. The children wanted to build a command centre and an astronaut suit so they found some plastic bottles to make helmets and used recycled keyboards, old clocks, and electronic equipment to form their space command centre.

They measured, counted, and engaged in lots of problem solving. The staff helped the children find some information on the Internet about famous Canadian astronauts such as Roberta Bondar and Mark Garneau. The children found some pictures of the Canadarm 2 and talked about Canadian astronaut Chris Hadfield and his role in installing the Canadarm 2 on the International Space Station.

Over the course of several weeks the children also gathered information about planets. Saturn was their favourite, so the staff encouraged critical thinking skills by asking questions such as "What do you think you would need to live on Saturn? How could we find out what the atmosphere is like there?" As they went along with their project, they recorded their adventures with stories in their program's monthly newsletter.

At the art centre the children created a model of Saturn, and chalked an area on the ground outside for their spaceship launching and landing pad. From their involvement in the Skydivers Club, the children had expanded their interests to explore the topic of "inventions."

Some high school students who may pursue careers in science and technology volunteered to assist the children with experiments and activities that would broaden their space horizons.

The children and high school volunteers have also been working together on a new invention called the "Ultimate Bubble Blowing Machine" after a volunteer told the story of Mary Spaeth. When Mary was a little girl, she always liked to play with tools and find new ways to solve old problems. She invented the "slit-and-tongue" design for the cereal box so the open box could be resealed and the cereal would not get stale (Inventive Kids, n.d.).

Children as Natural Investigators

Children enjoy investigating how things work: from how a clock keeps time to how a skateboard is constructed in order to keep the rider moving on it at an even pace. Children are also exposed to careers such as firefighter, teacher, doctor, scientist, or engineer, and some may consider these as potential career choices. All of these professions today require skills in the use of technology. Firefighters use sophisticated equipment such as oxygen tanks and masks with an alarm to let them know when their oxygen is running out. In the medical field, technology has provided machines and diagnostic tools to treat cancer, diabetes, and other serious diseases.

Scientists and those in the technological fields explore, investigate, observe, record data, make hypotheses, develop theories, and draw conclusions. Scientists use their mathematics knowledge as they measure, make quantitative and qualitative comparisons, classify information, and make charts and graphs of their findings. From very early ages, children naturally explore and investigate, observe, ask questions (hypothesize), and draw conclusions. They try to make sense out of what they see and to solve the problems they encounter. They develop their own theories of how the world works. According to Piaget, this is known as **constructing knowledge.** Children come to know concepts (construct knowledge) as a result of their own experiences and their own thinking about those experiences.

constructing knowledge
developing one's own theories about how the world works

During middle childhood, children's ability to develop more logical theories increases as they shift from preoperational thinking into more concrete thinking where they see cause-and-effect relationships more realistically. The five-year-old sees relationships and draws conclusions but has difficulty grasping concepts such as reversibility or recognizing that quantities of matter remain unchanged. As children's cognitive abilities mature, they realize that things can change physical form and be transformed again, such as water becoming ice and again becoming water.

Seven- or eight-year-olds are able to understand that something can change from one form to another, and they enjoy the process of doing so. They seem to investigate the world by asking, "How can I make it change?" or "How can I make it move?" As they actively engage with materials, they hone their observation and investigative skills. They continue to construct, test, and refine their theories. They are, in Piagetian terms, "constructing their own knowledge." Constructing personal knowledge about the world continues at all ages (even throughout adulthood). (You will construct your own knowledge about how children use scientific inquiry skills as you provide opportunities for children to make investigations.)

Both boys and girls should have equal opportunities to be involved in science and technology-related activities. Set up areas where all children can play with technical gadgets, scales, clocks, and pendulums, and experiment with physical phenomena such as sound, echo effects, and mirror effects. All children need to be exposed to female role models who have careers in scientific and technological fields, and staff should be comfortable with the process of investigating, problem solving, and discovering how things work. This gives both boys and girls the encouragement to take the time to ask questions and pose problems as they play and create with various tools and machines. In this way children will have the freedom to explore materials and carry through experiments in a nonthreatening atmosphere. Not only do they increase their scientific inquiry skills, but also gain confidence in seeking solutions to problems. This investigative environment allows children the opportunity to take risks. They try new things, make mistakes, learn from their mistakes, and continue trying new ideas.

Science activities also allow children to work together as they discover concepts of physics, chemistry, and biology. They share ideas, each bringing their personal experiences and knowledge to the investigative process, thereby helping one another as they brainstorm to develop theories, hypotheses, and strategies for experimentation and exploration.

Box 12-1 ▬ Is It Liquid or Solid?

Is it liquid or solid? (Messy but easy to clean up!)

Mix equal parts water and cornstarch on small trays. Encourage the children to investigate with their fingers. Provide utensils such as spoons, plastic knives, spatulas, etc., for further investigation. Discuss with the children the characteristics of a solid (holds its own shape) and characteristics of a liquid (pourable, wet, takes the shape of its container). Encourage children to hypothesize and form theories about the mixture.

Hint: It is both. The cornstarch remains a solid. It does not dissolve in the water, but its particles are suspended in the water.

Opportunities to explore areas of design and technology provide children with skills that may be necessary in their future careers. Children enjoy playing with machines and taking them apart to find out how things work. Children experiment with concepts of balance, form, motion, shape, scale, and symmetry as they create and build structures. They work with a variety of tools at the woodworking centre and learn about how axles, gears, pulleys, wheels, and wedges make everyday things like clocks, doors, microwaves, and cars work. Children also use tools in other areas of a school-age program, including the arts and crafts area, during cooking activities, and outdoors.

Children use the process of scientific inquiry to hypothesize, observe, problem solve, create, and evaluate. They can examine how different tools and machines have changed over the centuries and how inventions solved human needs or problems.

Children should have lots of experience with information technology as a means of recording, storing, and retrieving information. They can use computers to write stories and access the Internet to research topics of interest. Children can correspond with others around the world through e-mail. Other forms of technology, such as video and digital cameras, scanners, printers, CD players, and video and DVD players allow children to create photographs, record plays and music productions, and reproduce their work.

Figure 12-1 ■ Children can learn about science outdoors.

The Process of Inquiry and Content of Science

Children are incredibly curious about the world around them. Some children verbalize their thinking, whereas others simply act on their thoughts by experimenting as they search for answers. The *process* of science involves inquiry, experimentation, observation, and hypothesis testing. What if we raise the pendulum higher to try to knock down the block? How can we make the cars turn when they get to the end of the ramp? How can we make a river in the sandbox? Can we dig to China? What kind of magnet is the strongest? Why do some things float and others sink? What would happen if we mix all these colours of paint together? As children work to formulate answers to their questions, they are discovering the *content* of science—the scientific facts. Recall that learners must construct their own knowledge about the world (Chapter 5, Piagetian Theory). School-age children are concrete learners, meaning that they want to be active participants in the process. They are thinking of questions and manipulating materials to gain understanding of scientific principles. Although children can memorize facts, they do not gain a true understanding without having an actual hands-on experience.

The Mathematical, Scientific, and Technology Environment

Mathematics, science, and technology can be a part of outdoor play, a field trip, a guided small-group time, or an interactive display in an area of the room. Ideally, science-related materials are always available for children to explore in many areas of the program as they observe, inquire, and work to expand their knowledge. Children bring many found treasures to the school-age program and want to share them, whether they are insects, special rocks or shells, or the acorns that fell from their neighbour's tree. The outdoors is a natural place for children to explore and

Box 12-2 ■ Are You Ready to Absorb?

Provide the children with a tray lined with a piece of wax paper. Colour small amounts of water with food colouring. Use the three primary colours: red, blue, and yellow. Using eyedroppers, drip coloured water onto the wax paper. When the children have finished experimenting with dripping the colours, ask "Are you ready to absorb?" Have the children lay an absorbent paper towel onto the droplets. Listen to what the children say and watch as they investigate the materials. What are the processes that the children are engaged in? What is the science content they are learning as a result of their actions? What do you think they would have learned if you had demonstrated the process and not given them the materials to manipulate?

investigate how a praying mantis moves or what a walking-stick insect looks like. Providing tools such as magnifying glasses to look through and cameras for children to use to record their observations is a good plan.

Children should have opportunities to plan their own science/technology experiments, often as extensions of observations and other activities that they have taken part in each day. For example, if the children have heard that a local community has just experienced a tornado, talk to the children about setting up an experiment about making a "tornado in a jar." This gives children and parents the message that science and technology are important, and that the children's ideas and interests are an integral part of the curriculum. Displays, pictures, posters, and nonfiction and fiction books about science and technology add interest. The addition of tools and machines in areas of arts and crafts, woodworking, and cooking encourage lots of experimentation and exploration of the everyday use of technology. Having access to computers, cameras, and other forms of information technology provides enrichment to the curriculum.

It is not necessary to spend large amounts of money on expensive equipment; you can use a variety of recycled materials. For example, throwaway plastic containers can be used for collecting insects, and small water bottles with the bottom cut off make great funnels. Save old jars, batteries, wires, clocks, cardboard tubes, plastic bubble wrap, and so on. Shop in second-hand stores for old blenders and other cooking tools and find places where you can buy old overhead projectors and cameras. In fact, anything that is called junk may be of use in an experiment. Ask parents whether they have any tools they would be willing to donate to your program. As you read about the various areas of science and technology that follow, you will find that the activities suggested present many opportunities for children to investigate and that the materials used are often inexpensive.

Role of the Facilitator in Inquiry Learning

The most important component of the learning environment in science and technology activities is the program's staff. An adult who takes an interest in the children's science discoveries and explorations validates what they are learning. The leader can ask **divergent questions**, which are questions that have no specific answer and require the child to think critically. For example, in a pendulum activity a tennis ball is attached to the end of a hanging rope. The children experiment with placement of boxes and try to knock them down with the swinging ball. Some

divergent questions
questions that have no specific answer and require a child to think critically

divergent questions might be, "How can you stack these boxes so the ball can knock them down?" "What do you think would happen if you stacked them in a different way?" "What would happen if you put them in a different place?" This type of questioning encourages the children to think critically, to act on their thinking, to form their own questions, and, ultimately, to construct knowledge and develop theories and conclusions. Encourage children to ask each other these kinds of questions in the process of inquiry as well. Recall from Chapter 5 that children acquire new skills and knowledge via **scaffolding** and interactions with more skilled peers and/or adults. When the adults take an interest in the activities and interests of the children, children get the message that what they are doing is worthwhile. Remember that the children are in Erikson's stage of industry vs. inferiority (see Chapter 6). They are forming opinions about themselves as learners, critical thinkers, scientists, engineers, and mathematicians.

When facilitating mathematical, science, or technological explorations, school-age child care professionals and the children can investigate the possibilities and search for more knowledge about a particular interest together. At times a school-age child care professional may provide a "provocation," something of interest that he or she finds that might interest the children. Perhaps it is an old record player or typewriter that a staff member found at a garage sale. Piaget identifies three types of knowledge: social, physical, and mathematical. **Social knowledge** is the information children cannot construct for themselves: What is its name (e.g., magnet, iron)? What are the scientific terms (magnetism, repel, attract)? **Physical knowledge** refers to how objects behave as a result of their characteristics. This is information that the children learn as they explore: What does it do? How does it change? What does it feel or sound like? **Mathematical knowledge** includes number, geometry, measurement, algebra and data analysis. It involves the following areas of learning:

1. **Understanding and applying classification and seriation skills**
    This refers to how objects compare to one another. This is knowledge that children must construct as they discover likenesses and differences: How are these objects alike? This knowledge enables children to classify and categorize information.

2. **Understanding and using number concepts to solve problems**
    This may involve children figuring out how many blocks are needed to fill a particular space, including adding or subtracting the number of blocks needed to make a square.

3. **Understanding and applying size and measurement concepts**
    Provide measuring tapes, maps, charts, clocks, and other technological devices to record time, patterns, shapes, and sizes (Meisels et. al., 2001).

School-age child care professionals should have access to background information about an activity to guide children's thinking. Internet access can give some immediate information about many topics, and books are good sources. Often parents can be a resource for background information, or they may be willing to get involved in the information-discovery process through their own Internet search or exploration. See examples of websites at the end of the chapter.

It is important for school-age child care professionals to keep in touch with teachers in the school in order to support and extend on the children's school-curriculum topics. Plan for the exchange of resources like books and equipment and coordinate follow-up experiences like field trips so that there is no duplication.

scaffolding
the process of acquiring new skills and knowledge through interactions with peers and/or adults

social knowledge
information children cannot construct for themselves

physical knowledge
how objects behave as a result of their characteristics

mathematical knowledge
includes number, geometry, measurement, algebra, and data analysis

Figure 12-2 ■ Children experiment with everyday materials.

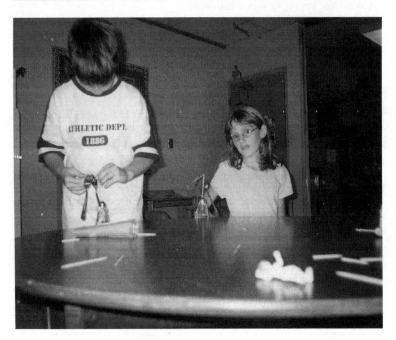

School-age child care professionals must also be careful observers. By observing children's interactions with their world, the staff can facilitate further learning by presenting additional materials and/or information. For example, a child working with a pendulum trying to knock down blocks may be unsuccessful because he consistently stacks the blocks out of reach of the pendulum. When asked "I wonder if there is another place to stack the blocks," the child will most likely rethink the situation and make changes in the blocks.

A final step to facilitating children's mathematical, science, and technology experiences is for the school-age child care professionals to help the children record their findings. Scientists record their findings, draw diagrams, and write about their experiments so they can share the information with others. In a school-age program, encourage children to draw pictures and write (or dictate) what they have learned. They can write about their strategies, observations, and new theories and hypotheses. These can be posted on a bulletin board so parents, other children, and guests will be able to see what children are learning. Drawings and written accounts can also be collected and made into a book for display. Incorporating reading and writing, along with science and technology, brings credibility to the school-age program. Documentation makes learning visible so that parents and others know what is going on in the program. Usually the only thing a parent has in order to judge what happens in the program is the piece of paper (i.e., artwork) that comes home in the child's hand. Parents do not always see the vast effort put into a block structure or the trial and error of a science and technology activity. This also gives parents something to talk to their child about. Rather than, "What did you do today?" the parent might say, "I see that you are experimenting with … Tell me about it."

There are additional ways to document children's experiences, as is often done in emergent-based curriculum approaches. The staff can use a large piece of easel paper to write comments the children made during the exploration process and create a web design of their experiences. This can also be done on the computer and posted for parents to see in the classroom, on your program's website, or in a monthly newsletter. Alternately, children can draw and write in personal journals.

Physical Science: How Can I Make It Move?

On an adult level, physics is defined as "the science of dealing with the properties, changes, and interactions of matter and energy." Children develop knowledge of physics by acting on the principle, "How can I make it move?" For example, a group of first-graders are playing with small cars on ramps that they have made from the blocks. They are experimenting with different heights of the ramps to see which ones make the cars go faster. To learn physics principles, they use actions such as pushing, sliding, rolling, tilting, pounding, and throwing, and materials such as sand, pendulums, magnets, balls, wheels, pulleys, ramps, marbles, paint, and water. As children create movement, they can observe the results of their actions, continue the action so as to gain mastery, formulate theories, make changes in actions, and refine their original theory or formulate additional theories.

Physical science activities tend to hold children's interest the longest and have a vast amount of learning possibilities. Children are actively involved with the materials and can vary the actions, and the results of those actions are immediate and comprehensible.

Activities

Physical Science

Purposes: *develop the scientific skills of observing, experimenting, and theorizing*
predict outcomes and formulate conclusions
interact with materials and develop theories about physical phenomena
develop a personal confidence as a scientist

Experiment with pendulums. Suspend from the ceiling, a doorway, or a swing set a cotton clothesline rope with a ball attached to the end of it. Children can stack plastic cups, cardboard boxes, or blocks and try to knock them down by swinging the pendulum. They will naturally experiment with placement of the blocks and the positioning of the pendulum. Various sizes and weights of balls can be provided for additional exploration. Children may discover the relationship between the length of the pendulum swing and its ultimate force as it collides (or fails to collide) with the blocks.

A variation on the pendulum is to attach other things to the end of the rope. For example, try attaching a paintbrush dipped in paint or water. Place a large piece of cardboard under the pendulum and discover what happens when the pendulum swings. Alternately, hang an empty milk bottle (with the bottom removed) upside down from the pendulum. Fill the bottle with sand, remove the cap, and let the pendulum swing. (It's best to do this outdoors.)

Explore inclined planes. Cut eavestroughs into lengths of 1 m (3 ft.), 1.5 m (5 ft.), or 3 m (10 ft.) to make ramps for balls, marbles, water, and toy cars. (Cover any sharp edges of eavestroughs with duct tape.) Children can discover the relationships between the height of the incline, its length, and the weight of the objects traveling down the plane. Provide other materials for children to discover concepts about things that slide and roll such as setting up plastic bottles for bowling pins and playing a game to knock them down. Use small blocks to build cars, and have a scale available for children to weigh the load of the cargo of their cars.

Cove moulding (available at a home-improvement store) cut in various lengths can be another staple addition to the block centre, and cardboard tubes from wrapping paper or mailing tubes can also be used as inclined planes. Large durable ones can be obtained from businesses that lay carpeting.

Discover propelled objects (target practice). Provide balls of different kinds and sizes, and materials for the target such as cardboard blocks, milk cartons, cardboard cylinders from paper rolls, and large juice cans. Children can work indoors or outdoors as they discover the relationship between the placement of target objects, the

Figure 12-3 ■ Girls investigate technology with tools.

kind and size of ball used, and the physical force with which it is propelled. Set up the containers in various patterns, then observe and describe how the arrangement affects the direction of the ball.

Additional discoveries can be made using Ping-Pong balls with Velcro® attached and a fabric target such as felt. Children learn best when they can clearly see where their propelled ball has landed.

Simple catapults can provide additional discoveries. Make them with a plastic spoon and a wooden ruler. Attach the handle of the spoon firmly to the end of the ruler using a rubber band. Place small pom-poms in the bowl of the spoon, pull back on the bowl of the spoon with one hand, holding the ruler with the other hand, and release the spoon.

Completing a circuit. Set out one D battery, two pieces of small-gauge electrical wire about 20 cm (8 in.) long, a flashlight light bulb, electrical tape, and modelling clay. Assist children with taping the exposed copper end of the electrical wire to the metal side of the light bulb. Place the exposed end of another wire on the surface of a 3-cm (1.25-in.) cube of clay. Assist children with taping the exposed copper end of the electrical wire to the metal side of the light bulb. Place the exposed end of another wire on the surface of a 3-cm (1.25-in.) cube of clay. Tape one end of the first wire to the metal bottom of the light bulb. Tape the other end to the flat, negative side of the battery. Place the second wire across the clay and press the bulb onto the wire and into the clay. Tape the other end of the second wire to the raised, positive side of the battery.

Explore magnetic force. Magnets should be another staple in your science centre. Wand and horseshoe magnets can be purchased from toy stores. Small, inexpensive (but not very durable) circular magnets are available at electronic stores. Strong internal magnets can be purchased from a store that sells products for large farm-animal care. (Internal magnets are used inside a cow to collect pieces of metal that the cow may ingest.) Encourage children to use the magnets to drag through the sand looking for particles of iron, to investigate a variety of metal-looking objects to determine which contain iron, or to use around the classroom, looking for metal containing iron. Develop a collection of items that are attracted to a magnet. Encourage children to build temporary sculptures held together by magnetism. For example, a collection of paper clips can be held together with a strong magnet, as the magnetic power passes through one paper clip to the next. Magnets can also be used to move objects. Place magnets under the table or a piece of clear plastic, and place objects to be moved on top of the table. Use the magnet to move the objects. Encourage children to see what happens when they place magnets on top of the table and move magnets underneath.

Technology: Past, Present, and Future

Technology refers to tools that humans make to help them succeed in their natural environment. This includes things like hammers that help people build houses, or coats that help people keep warm in cold weather. Most commonly, the term is used to refer to modern, complex inventions like computers, satellites, or artificial hearts (see http://collections.ic.gc.ca/science/english/science/tech.html).

Over the centuries, scientists and people from all walks of life have used creative thinking and problem-solving skills to come up with new inventions, ideas, and products for better ways of doing things. An invention used every day is the zipper, or the "separable fastener," which was invented by Gideon Sundback, from St. Catharines, Ontario, in 1913. A more complex invention is the invention of insulin for the treatment of diabetes by Dr. Frederick Banting and Charles Best at the University of Toronto in 1920. Inventions appear in many areas of our play and working day, from the clothes we wear and the food we eat to the sports equipment we use to play and the tools we use at work.

Children enjoy opportunities to design and build structures, to create and cook interesting foods, and to play and manipulate different kinds of machines. These activities provide a challenge for school-age children, who like to take on the role of inventor and find new and creative ways to solve everyday problems. Exploring the field of technology, in the past, present, and future gives them insight into future careers as web designers, computer animators, cosmetic chemists and forensic scientists.

Activities

Technology

Purposes: *develop problem-solving skills*
recognize the need for change and innovation
develop an understanding of how things work
increase knowledge of technology in the past, present, and in the future
develop awareness of careers in technology

Machines. Set up a table in the room and collect old clocks, cellphones, computer parts, radios, and other machines that children can take apart to explore how they work. Provide tools such as screwdrivers, pliers, goggles, hand drills, and other tools to assist them with their investigation, first discussing the safe use of tools.

Play with wheels, axles, and pulleys, and investigate other concepts related to physical science. Explore different kinds of levers: fishing poles, bottle-openers, scissors, tongs, tweezers, etc., and how they lift, pry, or pull up objects. Display pictures of parts of machines along with books about machines of all kinds.

Provide opportunities for children to explore old and present-day technology. Bring in an old turntable or record player and some old 45 and LP records. Let the children play the old records and compare the quality of sound to that of tape players and CD players used today. For the catapult activity discussed earlier, bring in information about their use in medieval times and how they are used today to launch airplanes from aircraft carriers. See http://www.catapults.info.

Talk about how various materials and equipment such as skateboards, snowboards, and surfboards are made and how principles of physics are used to make them work. (The pendulum effect, combined with concepts of gravity, speed, and balance, put the boards into action.) Research information about the first snowboards made and what may be in store for the future, such as mountain boards. Watch the television series *Popular Mechanics for Kids*.

Make a hovercraft. Collect old music CDs or computer discs, thread spools or 35-mm film canisters, balloons, and white glue. Help the children to make a pencil-size hole in the top and bottom of the film canister if they are using one instead of a spool. Have the children cover the top of the canister or spool with glue and attach it to the

CD by lining up the holes. Allow the glue to dry. The staff should blow up a balloon and twist the neck near the opening to keep the air from escaping. Keeping the balloon twisted, assist the children with stretching the neck of the balloon over the spool/canister. Set the hovercraft on a table. Release the balloon and give the hovercraft a flick. Measure and record the distance each one travels. See http://www.ceismc2.gatech.edu/bp/cars/hovrcrft/homepg.htm.

Invent a telephone. Ask children and their families to bring in clean, empty cans. Ensure that the edges are not sharp, then cover the edges with masking tape. Use art supplies to decorate the cans. Have the children cut 3 m (10 ft.) of string and help them hammer a nail through the bottom of each can to make a hole. Remove the nail and thread the string through the hole in the bottom of one can through to the bottom of another can. Tie a knot to the part of the string inside the cans to hold the string in place. Two children can have a conversation by speaking and listening through the tin cans. Discuss how when you talk into the can the sound waves move along the string, vibrate inside the other can, and make a sound. Do some research and talk about different kinds of phones from the past and in the present, and what may be in store for the future.

Make a windmill. Gather some coloured paper, a ruler, scissors, push pins, thin wooden dowelling, and pencils. Assist the children with cutting a piece of coloured paper into a perfect square about 15 cm (6 in.) by 15 cm (6 in.). Make a pencil mark in the centre of the square and draw two diagonal lines through the centre. Without cutting through the centre, cut along the lines to within 1 cm (½ in.) of the centre of the square. Fold each of the four triangle shapes into the centre. Press the push pin through the folded pieces and into the wooden dowel. Take the windmills outside and let them blow in the wind, or have the children blow on them to make them move. Research information about current and past wind-energy technology and how it can be used for a wide range of industrial purposes.

Thingamajigs. Provide lots of different materials including wood, dowelling, boxes, plastic containers, wheels, gears, axles, levers, string, white glue, glue guns and low-temperature glue sticks, tape, and other recycled items. Children can work individually or in groups to play with their materials in various ways, building and rebuilding inventions. Children can give their thingamajig a name and talk about their invention's purpose. Provide opportunities to draw and write about their invention on paper or at the computer. Give special "Inventor Awards" to each of the children, take pictures, and display their inventions. See Appendix E for an example of a "Patent Registration Form, My Invention." Talk about famous inventors, both past and present, e.g., Alexander Graham Bell, Frederick Banting, Armand Bombardier, and Elaine Thompson (who invented rubber asphalt).

Information technology (IT). Children should have lots of opportunities to freely manipulate and explore the use of computers. Choose software that is open ended, creative, nonviolent, and well integrated into other areas of the curriculum. Include a computer program in which children can make their own books, posters, banners, and cards, and set up a printer so that they can print them when they are completed. Provide opportunities for children to safely access the Internet and set up e-mail pals with children in other school and child care settings around the world. Encourage children to research topics using CD-ROMs and safe Internet websites. See Chapter 10 for more computer activities, games, and tips on safe Internet use.

Box 12-3 ■ Learn about Inclines and Velocity: Marble Rollways

Brief description: Children will work in teams to create a structure that they can roll marbles through.

Science/technology concepts explored: Children will learn about the relationship between the slope of a surface and the velocity of a rolling object. They will discover where a rolling object is propelled to.

Materials

thin cardboard in pieces of various sizes

paper cups

paper towel and/or toilet-tissue cardboard tubes

paper

masking tape

yarn or string

berry baskets, juice cans, or small plastic containers

marbles

other recycled materials as available

scissors, rulers, pencils, markers

Procedure

Display materials on a table. Entice the children by asking a divergent question: "How could you use these materials to create a structure that will let the marbles flow through it?" Divide children into teams to create their structure. (Hint: Create teams with a variety of ages. Older children can be leaders for the younger ones.)

Role of the Leader

- Set up the work environment.

- Give children adequate time (30 minutes or more).

- Provide children with a space to display their finished product.

- Make comments about what you see, and encourage children to verbalize what they are doing: "I notice that you decided to put this tube here. What do you think will happen?"

- Encourage further exploration by asking divergent questions or making comments. "How far do you think the marble will roll after it drops through the tube?"

- Guide children in writing and drawing about their structure and their discoveries.

- Guide children in creating a note to parents telling about the work they are doing.

Other physical science and technology activities could focus on:

- spatial awareness (fitting objects in, out, through, under, etc.)

- air (fans, blow dryers, homemade fans)

- construction (wood with hammers, nails, saws, screws, screwdrivers, and hand drills)

- kitchen tools (scoops, basting bulbs, sifters, beaters, gadgets, chopsticks)
- opticals (binocular, magnifying glasses, kaleidoscopes)
- making, listening to, and identifying sounds
- light and shadows
- different kinds of cameras (old and new): digital, video, Polaroid, underwater cameras
- inventions: finding a new use for something old and discarded
- building bridges with toothpicks, craft sticks, and wooden blocks

Chemistry: How Can I Make It Change?

Chemistry deals with the properties, composition, and transformation of substances. Although many chemical experiments require skills, equipment, and knowledge too advanced for the school-age child, chemical exploration opportunities can be provided that are age-appropriate. These will enable children to learn concepts of chemistry and further their scientific skills of theorizing, observing, and experimenting.

Keep in mind that school-age children are concrete learners (see Piagetian Theory, Chapter 5) and therefore must be able to act on their environment and see the results of their actions. Observations of the physical characteristics of substances and explorations that create transformations are very appropriate for this age group of children. For example, children can explore transformation by mixing substances such as vinegar and baking soda, baking cookies or scones, or adding water to sand. The child's natural tendencies are to respond to the internal question, "How can I make it change?"

Activities

Chemistry

Purposes: *further develop scientific skills of observation and theorizing*
observe physical characteristics of substances and phenomena that change those characteristics
acquire awareness of chemistry in our everyday lives

T-Shirt chromatography. Techniques of chromatography are used in scientific laboratories, including forensic labs where it is used to separate the components of "clue" substances such as blood, ink, and other mixtures found at a crime scene. Have the children bring a prewashed white T-shirt, boxer shorts, or other cotton material that parents know will not be returned.

Safety Caution: Do this activity in a well-ventilated area and put the rubbing alcohol in closed containers for each child.

Help children cut the centre out of the middle of a margarine container cover to resemble a hoop shape. Children will then stretch the material over the bottom of the container and put the hoop cover on top. Provide permanent markers to draw a picture, using dots and lines to outline the shape on the material. Have children place a small drop of rubbing alcohol in the centre of the hoop, which will move in outwards

Box 12-4 ■ Can You Mix Oil and Water?

Brief description: Children try to combine oil and coloured water in an attempt to make them mix.

Science concepts explored: Children can discover that oil and water do not mix and that paper absorbs oil differently than water.

Materials

small container of vegetable or corn oil

small container of water coloured with a small amount of tempera paint (preferably a colour such as blue that contrasts with the yellow of the oil)

spoons (one for each container)

construction paper, wax paper, tinfoil

tray to hold paper

spoons for mixing

craft feathers, cotton balls

Procedure

Children should first predict what they think will happen when they put the two liquids together. Place the construction paper, tinfoil, or wax paper on a tray. Drop a spoonful of oil and one of coloured water onto the paper. Notice how each liquid stands out on the paper. Tip the tray, causing the liquids to run toward each other on the paper, and try to get them to mix. Dip the cotton balls and feathers in the oil and water mixture and note what happens. After exploration, encourage the children to think of something they can use to mix the liquids. Allow the children to mix. Encourage them to wait and see what happens. Try other kinds of paper to observe any different actions that the liquid takes. Make up a chart to compare and describe the differences.

Divergent Questions

What do you think will happen when the two liquids meet? How could you make them mix without using a spoon? What happens when you use a different kind of paper for the liquids? What happens to the cotton balls and feathers when they are dipped in the oil and water?

Role of the Leader

- Set up the work environment. Be sure to test the liquids before presenting them to children to be sure the water isn't too thick with the added paint.

- Ask divergent questions, and be prepared to have materials ready to allow children to further explore to test their ideas.

- Talk about related topics such as what happens if an oil tanker has an oil spill in the ocean, what effects this has on the birds and water life. Find out what processes are used to clean up oil spills.

by capillary action. This is called "wicking." Repeat as desired to cover the material with design. See http://www.letstalkscience.uwo.ca/activities/html/chromatog.html.

Chemical energy. Assist children with filling a balloon with water from a small pitcher, using a small funnel if necessary. Put about 75 ml (¼ cup) of double-acting baking powder into a small bottle with a narrow neck (e.g., a water bottle or juice bottle). Cover the bottle with the balloon by stretching it over the mouth. When the baking soda and water meet, its causes a chemical energy reaction. The balloon fills up with carbon dioxide gas, and the chemical energy is converted to mechanical energy. See http://www.fi.edu/tfi/activity/energy/ener-4.html.

Rock crystals. Collect clear empty glass jars or drinking glasses. Help the children fill the jars or glasses with 75 mL (¼ cup) of hot tap water. Add 500 mL (2 cups) of white sugar and stir. The children will tie a string around a nail and tie the other end of the string to a pencil. Rest the pencil on the mouth of the jar and adjust the string so the nail hangs down into the sugar water without touching the bottom of the jar. Let it stand for a few days. As the water evaporates, the atoms in the sugar draw close together to form cubed crystals around the string.

Shine your pennies. Prepare four bowls of chemical mixtures: one with 30 mL (2 Tbsp) of vinegar; one with 5 mL (1 tsp) of salt; one with 5 mL (1 tsp) of salt and 30 mL (2 Tbsp) of water, and one with 3 mL (½ tsp) of salt and 30 mL (2 Tbsp) of vinegar. Set the bowls out on a table. Ask the children to bring in some pennies and add them to each bowl. Observe and record the reaction that the chemical mixtures have on the pennies in 5-, 10-, and 12-minute intervals. Try other coins to see if there are any changes when they are added to the chemical mixtures. Talk about corrosive components of chemicals, their effects on certain minerals like copper, and about the safe use of chemicals.

Investigate substances that make foods rise. Making things such as bread, scones, cookies, and pancakes gives children the opportunity to experience the effect of using substances such as yeast, baking soda, or baking powder. Additional benefits to cooking activities are the math and reading experiences that they provide as children read recipes and measure ingredients. Investigate heat as a means of transformation. Use blenders, food processors, bread machines, vegetable choppers, and other cooking tools.

Other chemistry transformations to explore include:

- condensation and evaporation (breathing on cold glass, investigating a puddle or melting ice over time)
- effects of freezing various liquids (salted water, frozen popsicles made of various substances)
- absorption (materials that do and do not absorb water)
- dissolving (substances that do and do not dissolve in water)
- colour mixing

Biological and Earth Science: How Do I Fit and What Is My Role?

Environmental science and biology involve the study of plants and animals. Earth science studies elements of the earth and the solar system beyond. Because all of these are intertwined, it is impossible to study one without investigating the others at least on some level, perhaps through an aspect of chemistry, physical science, and technology. When learning about plant life, it is also necessary to investigate soil, sun, and water. Earth science investigations involve phenomena such as shadows, weather, the heat of the sun, and properties of water. An investigation of shadows may also fall under the physical science section because it addresses the question "How can I make it move?" An investigation of weather that is interesting for children involves the children in learning how the weather affects them and how they can adapt to its impact on them.

The key to successful earth and biological activities is to develop them in such a way as to provide children opportunities to act on the materials, observe characteristics, make predictions, and develop theories. Investigations of the solar system and the formation of the planets encourages interest in space travel and the field of robotics.

Learning about the care of plants, animals, and the environment means experimentation without causing harm to living plants or creatures. The goal is to develop children's knowledge of environmental issues and an understanding about their role in the care of living creatures and their life-support systems (see Chapter 13). Learning about the human body and its functions and care, including nutrition, is also included in this aspect of science (see Chapter 14). Children have a natural sense of wonder about the world. Biology and some earth science discoveries are focused on answering the question, "How do I fit in and what is my role?"

Activities

Biological Science

Purposes: *develop an understanding of the natural environment*
acquire the ability to nurture and care for living creatures
observe the life cycles of plants and animals
cultivate awareness of endangered species and the need to preserve them

Let children care for live animals. Ask children to help choose an animal (gerbil, guinea pig, hamster, rabbit, snake, fish, salamander, lizard) to be added to the program. Be sure to review program policies regarding pets, confirm that the pet has the proper vaccinations, and check to see if there are any children who may have allergies to animals. Before introducing the animal, have children research (through the Internet, a local pet store, or a veterinarian) what the animal eats or drinks, what kind of environment it needs, and how to care for the animal. Construct a habitat appropriate for the animal.

Box 12-5 ■ Watch Worms at Work: Create a Worm Environment

Brief description: Children will create a temporary worm environment to learn about their worms' tunnelling behaviours.

Science concepts explored: Characteristics of worms such as their bodies, habitat, and diet.

Materials

tall, thin jar (preferably no more than five inches in diameter)

sand, soil, and water

ruler

magnifying glasses

worms (can be obtained from a bait shop)

½ apple

½ onion

knife and cutting board

two containers for mixing

factual books about worms such as *It Could Still Be a Worm* (Fowler, 1997)

Procedure

Place soil in container and mix with enough water to make the soil damp. In another container mix sand with water, making the sand damp enough to clump together. Layer the soil and sand in the tall, thin jar in one-inch layers. Place the worms on top of the top layer. Watch what the worms do. Cut onion and apple in very small pieces. Put on top of the soil. Place the container in a box, making sure no light can enter the box. Leave for four days. During that time, read about worms and predict what they will do while they are in the box. After four days, take the container out of the box and examine the tunnels. Use magnifying glasses before or after the activity to examine the structure of the worms. Be sure to keep the workspace moist. Worms don't like to be in the light, so examinations will have to be brief. Return worms to a safe place in a garden when finished with examination.

Divergent Questions

What do you think the worms will do when you put them on top of the soil? What will they do while they are in the jar in the box? What do you think worms like to eat? How could we find out?

Role of the Leader

• Set up the work environment. Be sure to have ample literature available for children to further their investigations.

• Use an Internet search engine to find information about worms.

• Investigate with the children.

• Encourage the children to draw and write about their experiment and findings. Help the children create a display for parents.

To stimulate scientific inquiry, encourage children to observe the animal. For instance, a hamster can generate questions about what kinds of vegetables the animal will eat. Let children predict, then test out various choices by offering a selection of lettuce, carrots, celery, and spinach. Note which the hamster prefers. Which will it not eat? Chart the results on paper or at the computer.

Let children observe the life cycle of frogs. Get some frog eggs or tadpoles from a stream, pond, or lake. Put them in an aquarium with plenty of pond water and a few pond plants. Feed the tadpoles extra food such as boiled spinach or other leafy green vegetables. Observe the growth.

Encourage children to predict how long it will take the tadpoles to turn into frogs. Let them chart the growth, noting the decrease in size of the tadpoles' tails and the appearance of legs. How close were the children in their predictions?

Cultivate a garden. Involve the children in a discussion of whether they want a vegetable or flower garden. Provide seed catalogues, books on plants, or gardening magazines. Take a trip to a local nursery.

Have children measure the amount of space that can be allotted to the garden, and research the type of plants that can be grown during different seasons of the year. Have the children draw a plot plan, spacing the various plants according to what they have learned about plant requirements. Plant the garden.

Invite further inquiry by asking the children to keep track of which plants come up first. If they have planted vegetables, which ones are ready for harvesting the earliest?

Play Twenty Questions to encourage children to use their senses in identifying fruits, vegetables, or parts of aromatic plants. Choose five or more examples that have distinctive odours. Punch holes in the sides of a corresponding number of paper bags. Place each item in a separate bag and fasten it. Code each bag with a number on the outside. Prepare a card with the code numbers and a space for naming the contents. Allow each child to smell the bags and write down what they think each is. When every child has had a turn, open the bags and let them check their answers.

Keep potted plants in the classroom. Include a variety of plants, including those grown from seeds, cuttings of mature plants, and pits or tubers (e.g., avocado pits or sweet potatoes). Research plant requirements in books or on the Internet. How much water do different kinds of plants need? What kind of food do plants require? Why do some plants grow better in shade than in bright sunlight? Ask children to prepare a bulletin board showing different plants that grow in the shade and those that require a lot of sunshine. Suggest that they draw pictures of the plants, use seed packets, or cut out pictures from magazines.

To further encourage scientific inquiry, tell the children they can perform an experiment to determine how much sunlight a plant

Figure 12-4 ■ A bulletin board shows children the steps for sprouting corn.

needs. Have them plant a bean seed in each of ten plastic cups filled with sterile potting soil. Place half of the cups at various distances from a window light source but not in direct sunlight. Cover the other cups or place them in complete darkness. Keep the soil in all the containers damp but not wet. Compare the growth of the two sets of plants once a week and chart their progress. Record the height and condition of the plants in each container. As a conclusion to the experiment, discuss what children have learned about plant requirements for sunlight.

Growing mould. Pour a thin layer of canned soup into a flat dish. Have children place bits of dirt, bread crumbs, or floor dust onto the soup. Cover with plastic wrap and put in a warm place. Within a few days mould spores will begin to grow. Provide a magnifying glass or microscope so children can examine the different "plants."

To stimulate further inquiry, do a second experiment to observe moulds growing on other materials. Rub a piece of bread on the kitchen floor, sprinkle it with a little water, and place it in a sealed jar. Place a piece of cheese in another jar and a fruit peel in a third jar. Seal the jars and place all three in a dark location. Observe the changes periodically, noting the different times it takes moulds to grow on the three media. Provide a microscope or magnifying glass so children can see the moulds. Are the moulds that grow on bread, cheese, and peels the same as or different from those on the soup? Talk about the invention of penicillin.

Make an egghead. Set up an area with some eggs, markers, potting soil, grass seed, construction paper, and tape. Invite the children to draw a funny face on an egg. Help them gently tap off the top of the egg (head) and shake out the contents. Use the eggs for scrambled eggs or for making cookies. Fill the shell with soil. Make a base for the egghead out of a 2.5-cm (1-in.) strip of construction paper wound into a 4-cm (1.5-in.) circle. Put some grass seed in the soil and mist it with water every day. Place the egghead in sunlight and, in about a week, you can give your egghead a haircut.

Activities

Earth Science

Purposes: cultivate curiosity about the Earth and the solar system
             encourage scientific inquiry
             provide practice in predicting outcomes
             increase knowledge of the principles of earth sciences

Explore the solar system. Obtain posters or photos taken during space explorations. The National Aeronautics and Space Administration (NASA) has views of Earth taken from outer space, pictures of astronauts at work, and photos from space probes of Mars, Venus, Mercury, and Jupiter. There are additional websites listed at the end of the chapter. Set up a bulletin board display. Your local library may have books, DVDs, or videos as well. Obtain books on space that children can read or browse through in the book corner.

Talk about famous Canadians such as Mark Garneau, naval commander and engineer, who was the first Canadian in space; and Roberta Bondar, astronaut and the first Canadian woman in space. Look up some information about the Canadarm 2, or the Space Station Remote Manipulator System (SSRMS) and the role that Colonel Chris Hadfield played in assembling the Canadarm 2 on-orbit. Look up further information at http://www.mdrobotics.ca.

To stimulate children's interest in space and space travel, ask them to draw or paint a picture of what they would find if they were on another planet. They could also draw another picture of things they would take with them on their trip. Display the pictures, and ask children to discuss their choices and explain why certain items would be necessary or desired.

Help children understand the principle that allows a spaceship to enter space by explaining that it is based on Isaac Newton's third law of motion (for every action there is an opposite and equal reaction). Provide each child with a balloon. Blow up the balloon and tell the children to hold their fingers tightly around the neck to keep air from escaping. Let the children release their balloons, one at a time. Do they know what happens? How does Newton's law apply? (The balloon pushes air backward as it is released through the neck. The escaping air pushes the balloon forward.) The children can also consider which balloons went the farthest and why. Is there any way they might control where the balloon-rocket goes?

Astronaut in space. Ask the children and their parents to collect plastic bottles of different sizes. These will be the spaceships. Decorate spaceships with signs, symbols, and flags of your country. Cut the bottles in half lengthwise. Provide raw eggs for each of the children taking part in the activity or for each group of children. These will be the astronauts. Draw faces, hair, etc. on the eggs with markers. Place the eggs in the spaceships and pack the spaceships with materials such as newspaper, bubble pack, etc. to keep the astronauts safe. Use masking tape to seal the two pieces of the spaceships together. Drop the spaceships from a height, standing safely on a sturdy chair or table. Have a contest to see which egg does not break in its spaceship when it is dropped. Talk about the force of gravity and about what astronauts do in training sessions before they go into space.

Constellation viewer. Children can collect shoeboxes or obtain them from a shoe store. Cut the end flaps open and have children paint the insides of their boxes with black paint. After the paint dries, cut a 2.5-cm (1-in.) hole at one end of the box so that a paper towel tube will fit in. Roll pieces of tinfoil into balls of different sizes to represent planets in the solar system and attach them to the underside of the cover with black thread and clear tape. Tape the flaps so a little light can enter the box. With the cover on the box, look at the constellations through the paper towel tube viewer. This is a project that can be done over a number of days. Children may wish to work at this on their own or in groups. Look at examples of constellations in books and on websites. Talk about myths and legends related to the constellations. Visit a planetarium in your community, if possible.

Chart the weather for a month. Provide a calendar form for each child or a large one for a bulletin board. Obtain an outdoor thermometer that records both temperature and barometer readings. Have children record daily temperatures, barometer readings, and weather conditions. Ask them to bring weather reports and predictions from daily newspapers. Have them keep track of how many times the predictions are correct. Can the children predict the weather based on a given day for the following day?

Have children find more information about weather prediction and tracking. Good sources are the Canadian Meteorological and Oceanographic Society (http://www.cmos.ca) and the National Climate Data and Information Archive (http://www.climate.weatheroffice.ec.gc.ca).

Egg in the bottle. Provide a bottle that has a narrow mouth or one that has an opening a little smaller than the circumference of an egg. Take one shelled hard-boiled egg and place it over the mouth of the bottle to show that it won't go in. Remove the egg and stuff some paper inside the bottle. Light the paper with a match. (**Caution**: The staff should do this part.) As soon as the fire goes out, have the children place the egg over the mouth of the bottle to see what happens. The air pressure created sucks the egg through the opening in the jar. Air pressure is the force of the atmosphere pushing on the earth. The layers of air around the earth are very heavy, weighing about 6 million billion tonnes.

Have children make a rain gauge. You will need a clear plastic tube that is sealed at one end (jewellery beads often come in this kind of tube), a ruler, masking tape, a pencil, and a piece of clay. Stick the tape along the length of the tube. Calibrate by placing the ruler against the tape, then (starting from the bottom) mark off one inch, two inches, etc., to the top of the tube. Set the tube into the clay, making sure it stands straight. Place the gauge outdoors where it will collect rain. Add rainfall records to the weather charts.

Figure 12-5 ■ A globe can help children understand world weather changes.

Tell children they can make "lightning." Provide each child with a balloon. Inflate the balloons, then darken the room. Tell children to rub their balloon on the carpet or on their wool clothing. Have pairs of children hold their balloons end to end, almost touching. If the room is dark enough, they will see an electrical spark jump between the balloons.

Tornado in a jar. Collect clear plastic bottles. Instruct the children to roll tinfoil into small balls and put them in a bottle. Fill the bottles with water and one or two drops of blue food colouring. When the children rotate the bottles a swirling effect will occur, which resembles the circular rotations of air in the atmosphere that form a tornado. You can also buy tubes from specialty toy stores that can be used to attach two bottles of water together to create a tornado.

Set out pictures and books about tornadoes and talk about what to do in case a tornado is coming.

Equipment to Have Available

- animal habitats, an incubator for hatching eggs
- ant farm with a supply of ants
- aquarium with books on tropical fish
- binoculars and bird identification books
- insect house, insect-capturing containers, butterfly net
- calculators, computers, software programs
- collections of shells, rocks, and fossils

- flashlights
- hair dryer, small vacuum, bicycle pump
- household scales or simple balance with weights
- levers, incline planes, pulleys, wheels
- magnets: bar and horseshoe, assorted sizes
- magnifying glasses, insect collections
- measuring cups
- microscope with prepared and blank slides
- mirrors
- bubbles, bubble blowers of different shapes— square, cylinder, round
- prisms, eyeglasses, gyroscopes, colour wheels
- PVC pipe lengths, rain gutters, wood planks, wood blocks
- rock-polishing equipment, jewellery tools
- rulers, metre stick, T-squares, tapes, and protractors
- tripod, video and digital cameras
- sun-sensitive papers and outlines
- telescope, and books on astronomy, a globe and compass
- terrarium, seeds, potting soil, small pots
- typewriter with plenty of inexpensive paper
- VCR, cassette tapes, CDs, CD player, tape player, earphones

Figure 12-6 ■ An incubator lets children watch eggs hatching.

Guidelines for Program Staff

Here are some guidelines to help you plan activities that allow children the maximum opportunity for learning.

- Give children many chances to explore and experiment on their own. Set up learning centres or have materials easily available for children to use when they wish.

- Provide enticing materials that will encourage them to participate. Listen to the children to find out what they are interested in, and then supply them with the means to pursue those interests. In addition, stimulate them to explore new interests.

- Do not give answers too readily. Ask questions that stimulate children to hypothesize, predict, or think of other possibilities. "What would happen if you . . . ?" "What can you do differently next time?" Encourage them to ask each other these kinds of questions.

- Listen to the children to find out what they already know or what they are thinking. Help them to correct any misinformation or add to the knowledge they already have. Design appropriate activities that will lead them to a higher level of understanding.

- Discuss connections between the children's experiments and activities to examples in the real world. Look up facts and information related to the activity.
- Encourage the enjoyment of mathematics, science, and technology for both females and males. Present male and female role models in the fields of science and technology. Talk about famous Canadian scientists such as Monique Frize, clinical engineer; James Gosling, computer programmer; David Levy, astronomer; and Dr. Elaine Thompson, inventor of rubber asphalt.
- Maintain a questioning attitude and a sense of wonder yourself. Be alert to any possibilities for exploration, and you will learn along with the children.
- Document children's work and learning. By making learning visible, administrators, parents, and the children themselves can readily see that the activities children engage in cause them to think critically and develop cognitively.

Summary

Children are incredibly curious about the world around them and consequently are natural investigators. They use scientific skills of observing, investigating, predicting, drawing conclusions, and developing theories about everything they encounter. The goal of a mathematics, science, and technology program is to provide opportunities for children to develop these scientific skills. Because they are concrete learners, school-age children need to have active involvement with materials. By directly working with materials, formulating their own questions, and developing their own ideas, they are constructing their own knowledge. It is this process of science that enhances cognitive development.

The mathematics, science, and technology environment and an interested school-age child care professional provide a setting for children to investigate their world. The staff, providing additional information and materials when needed, have an important role in providing children with divergent questions to encourage children's critical thinking. Suggested activities focus on the children's natural inclinations as they ask, How can I make it move? How can I make it change? How do I fit in and what is my role? Curriculum areas include physical science, technology, chemistry, biology, and earth sciences. The ideas and concepts in each of these areas are interrelated and provide program staff and children with a challenging approach to the exploration of the world around them.

A school-age child care program can provide children with many opportunities to use and reinforce concepts children learn at school. Guidelines for staff members to help in planning activities that allow children maximum opportunities for learning are:

- Give children lots of opportunities to explore freely.
- Provide enticing materials.
- Do not give answers too readily, but encourage children to find answers to their questions.
- Listen to children to find out what they already know, then help them to correct any misconceptions.
- Maintain a questioning attitude and a sense of wonder yourself.
- Make connections to the real world.
- Introduce male and female role models in the fields of mathematics, science, and technology.

- Identify how technological inventions have made changes in how we do things.
- Document the children's process of discovery.

Key Terms

constructing knowledge social knowledge mathematical knowledge

divergent questions physical knowledge scaffolding

Student Activities

1. Plan one of the activities described in this chapter and implement it with a group of school-age children. Record your observations of the children as they participate in the activity: What did they do and say? Bring the materials and your observations to class and share them with your fellow students.
2. Plan a field trip for a group of school children to a local site of scientific or technological interest. The power-generating station, the beach, an observatory, a nature reserve, a museum, and a radio or television station all provide insights into how science and technology are basic to our civilization. Follow up the trip with discussions about what the children learned. Describe the trip to your classmates. Were there things you would do differently next time?
3. Visit your local library to find some background information about an aspect of science or technology that can be easily understood by the children. Find at least two books on a subject, and develop an age-appropriate, exploratory activity for school-age children. Bring the books and an activity plan outlining an activity that you can share in class.

Review Questions

1. Children are natural investigators. Explain this statement.
2. What are the skills necessary for scientific inquiries?
3. Explain what it means to construct one's own knowledge.
4. Explain the difference between the *process* of inquiry in science and the *content* of science.
5. Explain why the program leader is considered an important component of a mathematical, science, and technology environment.
6. Briefly describe three physical science activities.
7. How can children learn about problem solving and divergent thinking by pretending to be inventors?
8. What kinds of activities can children engage in that help them answer the question, "How can I make it change?"
9. Explain how you can structure biological science activities to actively involve children.
10. List five inexpensive items of equipment that can be used for science experiments.
11. Describe experiences that children might explore that focus on an interest in space.

12. Who are some of the famous Canadians in the field of science and technology mentioned in the chapter?
13. List eight guidelines for staff members when facilitating experiences with mathematics, science, and technology.

Case Study

Olivia and Juanita, both aged eight, have been watching two slightly older boys work with a combination of rain gutters and blocks to create a raceway for their cars. The boys abandoned their work to play a game with some other friends. Nicole, one of the staff members, noticed that the girls appeared interested in the boys' exploration.

1. What questions could Nicole ask that would cause the girls to think about the inclined-plane exploration and ultimately entice the girls to explore the gutters?
2. What mathematical, science, and technology concepts could the girls learn from working with gutters and cars?
3. How could the girls document the concepts they learned? How could Nicole document their work?

References

Inventive Kids. (n.d.). Retrieved April 1, 2005, from http://www.inventivekids.com

Meisels, S. & McMahon, P. (2001). *Thinking like a teacher: Using observational assessment to improve teaching and learning.* Boston, M.A. Allyn and Bacon.

Selected Further Reading

General Science

Chickadee and *Owl Magazine*, 49 Front St., E. #200, Toronto, ON, M5E 1B3; http://www.owlkids.com

Churchill, E. R. (1991). *Amazing science experiments with everyday materials.* New York: Sterling Publishing Company.

Friedhoffer, R. (1990). *Magic tricks, science facts.* New York: Franklin Watts.

Gold, C. Donev. M., & Westrup, H. (1994). *The jumbo book of science.* Toronto: Kids Can Press.

Hirschfeld, R. & White, N. (1995). *The kids science book—Creative experiences for hands-on fun.* Charlotte, VT: William Publishing Co.

Lind, K. K. (2000). *Exploring science in early childhood education.* Albany, NY: Delmar.

Van Cleave, J. (1996). *202 oozing, bubbling, dripping and bouncing experiments.* Mississauga, ON: John Wiley & Sons Canada.

Wheeler, R. (1997). *Creative resources for elementary classrooms and school-age programs.* Albany, NY: Delmar Publishers.

Wings of Discovery Science. (2004). GTK Press Kit, 18 Wynford Dr., Unit 109, Toronto, ON, M3C 3S2.

Physical Science

Ardley, N. (1991). *The science book of electricity*. Orlando, FL: Harcourt Brace Jovanovich.

Sabbeth, A. (1997). *Rubber-band banjo's and a java jive bass: Projects & activities on the science of music and sound*. Mississauga, ON: John Wiley & Sons Canada.

Vancleave, J. P. (1991). *Physics for every kid: One hundred one experiments in motion, heat, light, machines & sound*. Mississauga, ON: John Wiley & Sons Canada.

Biological Science

Brooks, S. (2004). *Reptiles interfact: The book and CD ROM that work together*. Chamhassem, MN: Creative Publishing.

Esposito, A. & Berg, J. (1997). *A-maze-ing human body adventure*. Montreal: Readers Digest Association of Canada.

Fowler, A. (1997). *It could still be a worm*. New York: Children's Press.

Macmillan, U.K. (1998). *In the deep*. New York: Alfred A. Knopf.

Strauss, R. & Thompson, M. (2004). *Tree of life*. Toronto: Kids Can Press

Suzuki, D. (1992). *Looking at plants*. Mississauga, ON: John Wiley & Sons Canada.

Earth Science

Clarke, V. & Melnyk, L. (1991). *Weather*. Ontario: S&S Learning Materials.

Factfinders: Bugs, dinosaurs, outer space, the sea, weather with CD-ROM. (2000). New York: McGraw Hill/W. C. Brown.

Firth, R. (2004). *Astronomy*. Usborne Publishing.

Kahn, J. (1999). *Women in earth science careers*. Minneapolis, MN: Capstone Press.

Weiner, W. (1994). *Hands-on minds-on science: Space*. Huntington Beach, CA: Teacher Created Materials.

Zike, D. (1993). *The earth science book, activities for kids*. Mississauga, ON: John Wiley & Sons Canada.

Technology

Jefferis, D. (1998). *Artificial intelligence*. New York: Crabtree Publishing Co.

Kassinger, R. (2002). *Build a better mousetrap: Make classic inventions, discover your problem-solving genius, and take the inventor's challenge*. Mississauga, ON: John Wiley & Sons Canada.

Levine, S. (2004). *First science experiments: Mighty machines*. New York: Sterling Press.

Mason, J. (2004). *Modern marvels: Inventions that rocked the world*. Richmond Hill, ON: Scholastic Canada.

Oxlade, C. (1998). *Machines*. New York: Gareth Stevens.

Thimmesh, C. (2002). *Girls think of everything: Stories of ingenious inventions by women*. Boston: Houghton Mifflin Press.

Vancleave, J. P. (1993). *Janice VanCleave's machines*. Mississauga, ON: John Wiley and Sons Canada.

Wheatley, A. & Reid, S. (2004). *Introduction to archaeology*. Usborne Publishing.

Chemistry

Heiseman, D. L. (1991). *Exploring chemical elements*. New York: McGraw-Hill.

Vancleave, J. P. *Janice Van Cleave's molecules*. Mississauga, ON: John Wiley and Sons Canada.

Websites

Kids' search engine: science, technology, nature
http://yahooligans.com

Bill Nye—the Science Guy
http://www.billnye.com

Canadian Scientists
http://collections.ic.gc.ca/science/english/canadian/index.html

Cool Science for Curious Kids
http://www.hhmi.org/coolscience

Earth Science Enterprise
http://kids.earth.nasa.gov

Guinness World Records
http://www.guinnessworldrecords.com

Inventions: games, contests, female inventors, parent and teacher section
http://www.kidsinventive.com

Kidzone, Fun Facts for Kids: science, magic tricks, lesson plans, math
http://www.kidzone.ws

Let's Talk Science: science curriculum and activity ideas
http://www.letstalkscience.ca

Science News for Kids: stories, games, puzzles
http://www.sciencenewsforkids.org

4000 Years of Women in Science
http://www.astr.ua.edu/4000WS/4000WS.html

Technology-related Topics: drafting, design, encryption, computer history
http://www.tekmom.com/students

WeatherEye: children's section, resources, lesson plans and parents centre
http://weathereye.kgan.com

Kidstorm: facts about tornadoes, lightning, hurricanes
http://skydiary.com/kids

NASA Spaceplace: games, projects, animations and fun facts about earth, space, and technology
http://spaceplace.jpl.nasa.gov/en/kids

Free Kids Stuff in Canada
http://www.canadianfreestuff.com/kids.html

Museums, Science Centres, and Planetariums

Canadian Association of Science Centres, such as the Ontario Science Centre, Science North, Okanagan Science Centre, Calgary Science Centre; and museums such as the Royal Ontario Museum, nature museums, and planetariums
http://www.canadiansciencecentres.ca/members.htm

The Tech Museum of Innovation, San Jose, CA
http://www.thetech.org

Museums of the World: 5 CD-ROM set. Topics Entertainment.
http://www.topics-ent.com

Chapter 13

Community Awareness and Citizenship

Objectives

After studying this chapter, the student should be able to:

- Plan and implement experiences that help children learn about their community and the world around them
- Describe different ways that children can explore the meaning of culture
- Explain the importance of preparing children to become good citizens

 Profile

The school-age program is part of the Bkejwanong Children's Centre on Walpole Island First Nation in Ontario. Walpole Island was the first reserve in Canada to build a child care centre. Staff at the centre are a mix of both native and non-native early childhood educators. In 1996, Teresa Altiman joined the staff as a "cultural enrichment instructor." As an artist and educator, she has brought much of her cultural knowledge and artistic talents into the program to enrich the curriculum and celebrate the uniqueness of the native community and culture. This allows for the development of positive self-esteem and self-identity for the children and their families.

Even though the program is culturally homogeneous, diversity exists within this like population. There are variations in family makeup, economic status, abilities, religion, and values.

Children of all ages from the Centre take part in an annual Mini Pow Wow in the summer. Children from other programs and people from the community are also invited to attend.

They have developed a manual and video, entitled *Celebrating the Diversity of Mother Earth,* which focus on the general principles of anti-bias education, self-awareness, and diversity awareness in curriculum planning for all age groups of children. Suggestions for professional development of staff and involvement of parents are also included.

From "Celebrating the diversity of Mother Earth: First Nations child care project, Bkejwanong Children's Centre," by T. Perron & J. Woehl, 1998, *Interaction,* CCCF, pp. 32–34.

Importance of Preparing Children for Developing a Sense of Community and Citizenship

There are many influences on children, although family is still the strongest influence for the child between the ages of 6 and 12 (Craig, Kermis, & Digdon, 2001, p. 432). Understanding of their community and the world around them is related to their own experiences and is somewhat limited by their cognitive abilities. Between the ages of five and seven, children are still somewhat egocentric, and the knowledge of their community is related to themselves. As they have more experiences in their community relating to different cultural groups, ages of people, people with different abilities, individuals in non-gender-specific roles, and with those who are concerned about their environment and community, children begin to "decentre" and are able to explore a variety of viewpoints. As children move into the stage of concrete operational thinking, they become more flexible and multidimensional in their thinking. They also are more "sociocentric" and can share different interpretations of a social situation (Craig, Kermis, & Digdon, 2001, p. 401).

Social learning takes place in the context of relationships children have with their parents, members of their extended family, friends, and people who are part of their school and their community. Children learn about how to get along with others; the differences and similarities between people; peace, justice, empathy, and compassion; taking care of others; and respecting themselves, others, and their world around them.

In Canada, we celebrate the diversity of families and cultures in our communities. All people in Canada have the right to retain their heritage including their religion, language, schools, clubs, associations, etc. (Murphy Kilbride, 1997, p. iv). This allows families to provide a secure and familiar framework within which children can develop a positive self-image and a feeling of "being competent in an otherwise bewildering world" (Craig, Kermis, & Digdon, 2001, p. 431).

The diversity of children and families in our communities across Canada provides enriching experiences that everyone in the school-age program can draw upon. Kunderman (1998) states, "Every center should have a multicultural program because all children need to see that cultural diversity exists. Children need to understand the

Figure 13-1 ■ School-age children building a town.

similarities we share as humans." Children should have opportunities to explore cultures beyond those of families represented in their own programs and their specific community.

Exploring the Options of Community

community

rural, urban, suburban settings; buildings; diversity of people, families and cultures; citizenship and caring for the environment

The following activities will give the children an opportunity to explore what makes up their **community** and how to be a good citizen. These activities can be set up based on themes related to the topic of community, developed as projects or be implemented in an emergent based–curriculum approach. Most of the activities can be set up in traditional curriculum areas such as block play, arts and crafts, and drama. Curriculum goals should be child centred, focusing on the children's interests and their individual levels of development.

Exploring the community would include:

- looking at different buildings, including homes, schools, recreation facilities, stores, offices
- examining urban, suburban, and rural communities
- talking about the people in our communities, including the variety of jobs and professions
- finding out about the various modes of transportation that are used in communities
- exploring characteristics of a good citizen
- looking at the qualities of a good citizen: respect, trust, honesty, fairness, integrity, compassion, self-discipline, cooperation, and friendship
- talking about the diversity of families, cultures, abilities/special needs, age groups, and gender roles
- discovering ways in which individuals can take care of their environment and deal with global concerns

Our Neighbourhood

Activities

Purposes:　*provide practice in portraying concrete objects as symbols on a map*
　　　　　encourage cooperative problem solving
　　　　　increase awareness of spatial relationships
　　　　　reinforce math concepts of area, distance
　　　　　practise literacy skills of reading and writing

Set up an interest centre. Ask for the children's help in setting up an interest centre with a globe, an atlas, and maps of the area surrounding your school-age program. Display pictures of different communities around the country that include mining, fishing, farming, and other industries. Ask the children to bring in items from home that represent something unique about their particular community, such as different rocks and minerals from a mining community. Include pictures of a variety of homes such as bungalows, duplexes, townhouses, two-storey homes, mobile homes, apartments, split-level homes, and semi-detached homes in rural, urban, and suburban neighbourhoods. Prepare activity cards asking the children to find specific places on the globe or map. Sample directions might include:

- Find the country we live in.
- Outline the province where our city is situated.
- Find out what kind of community you live in: urban, suburban, or rural.
- Find our school-age program on the map.
- Find your street on the map.
- What kind of home do you live in?
- Mark a route from your home to school.
- How many blocks is it from your house to school? How many miles?
- How long does it take to drive from home to school? How long does it take to walk?
- Where do your grandparents live? How many miles is that from your house?
- How long would it take to get to your grandparents' house by car? By airplane?

Map the neighbourhood. Provide children with notepads and a pencil. Take them on a walk around the school neighbourhood. Instruct them to write down distances in blocks. Tell them to note where buildings are located. When you return, have the children draw a map of the neighbourhood on a large piece of paper.

The children may like to construct models of the buildings in the neighbourhood to place on the map.

Build a paper-bag city or town. Using various sizes of paper bags, the children can create a village or street. Use markers and paints to draw windows, doors, shutters, signs, and other parts of buildings. Stuff undecorated bags with crumpled newspaper and put the decorated bag over the top of the stuffed bag. Display the bags vertically or horizontally. This could be a project that they develop over a number of days or weeks.

Twig architecture. Go for a walk and collect sticks and twigs of manageable sizes from the ground. Bring them back to the play yard and discuss different kinds of homes and shelters that can be made from them, such as tent style, pole-tepee, longhouse, or log home. Ask the children to work together to build their structure. Many children in First Nations communities continue to learn how to build a tepee, keeping up the traditions of their ancestors.

> In the 1500's, the Iroquois Nations people lived in long houses made from elm trees. A long house was 15–30 m long. Many families lived in separate parts of the same long house. (Nordgaarden & Armstrong, 1995, p. 24)

Make a community flag. Display the Canadian flag and flags of each of the provinces, as well as those of your city or town and other cities and towns in Canada. Provide pieces of paper for the children to create their own flag or that of their province, city, or town. Hang their flags on a string stretched across the room.

Make a community phonebook. Collect pictures of different places in their community. Ask the children and parents, as well, to bring some pictures of various community attractions, such as museums, recreation facilities, and libraries. These pictures may come from brochures, newspapers, or photos taken on a field trip around the

Figure 13-2 ■ Setting up a tepee.

community. Provide construction paper, markers, pens, paper punch, ribbon, and string. Put one picture on each page. Write a description of the facility and include the phone number. Tie the pages with ribbon or string, decorate the cover, write "Fun Activities in My Community" on the front, and display it for families to see.

Equipment to Have Available

- atlas, maps, globe
- cardboard
- compass
- glue
- map maker
- marking pens, pencils
- paper (variety of sizes)
- pencils
- rulers, measuring tape
- scissors
- tape
- paint
- string, ribbon

Materials to Collect Ahead of Time

- wood blocks/pieces
- milk cartons
- paper bags
- empty cans of various sizes
- craft sticks
- twigs
- boxes of various sizes

Place the neighbourhood map in the block area. Encourage children to use blocks to construct buildings. Add small cars, trucks, trains, airplanes, boats, street signs, trees, and toy people (different races and ages).

Obtain a city/town plan of the area around your facility from the planning office at your city or town hall. Discuss the kinds of information shown on the plan and how it is used.

Provide map puzzles. There are wooden and jigsaw puzzles of Canada. Look for them in toy stores and at school equipment-supply companies.

Make a replica of a construction project. Discuss different kinds of construction projects that children might be seeing in their neighbourhood: home building, office complexes, or highway construction. Collect and display pictures of construction projects in progress and of finished buildings. Provide toy replicas of equipment needed to construct areas of a city: earth movers, trucks, cement mixers, etc. Children may wish to create their town or city in the sandbox using houses and other things they have made from their woodworking projects.

Invite a carpenter to visit your class. Ask him or her to bring tools used on construction projects. Discuss the use of each of the tools. Allow children to ask questions. They might ask: What do you have to know to be able to do the job? What do you like about your job? What do you do each day?

Box 13-1 ■ Make an Inukshuk

Figure 13-3 ■ Make an inukshuk.

Brief description: Children will work individually or in groups to create a stone structure called an inukshuk.

Concepts explored: Children will learn what an inukshuk ("in-ook-shook") is and how these lifelike rock figures are used by Inuit as markers or signposts to guide them safely across the treeless tundra of the Canadian Arctic.

Materials

small stones

small amount of vegetable oil

bowl, small rag

craft clay or Plasticine

twigs

string

Procedure

Have tables set out with different shapes and sizes of washed stones. Set out a rag and small bowl of oil to polish the stones. Also have craft clay or Plasticine on the tables, along with twigs and string. Display picture books about inukshuks and Inuit culture. The children should polish the stones first and wipe off any excess oil. They will use the craft clay or plastecine to hold the stones together. Twigs can also be added to the structure for arms or other decoration.

Role of Program Staff

• Set up the work environment and displays.

• Look up information about inukshuks, what they look like and how they were used by Inuit.

• Provide space to display the children's finished products.

• Take pictures of their stone structures.

• Encourage the children to look at similarities and differences in their designs.

• Talk about where the children might have seen other stone structures in their travels.

• Ask the children to think of other guidelines, signs, and markers that are used in our communities to help us find our way to various destinations.

In the winter inukshuks can be made out of snow blocks instead of rocks.

Exploring the Concept of Culture

Culture is a way of living, shared with other members of the same group. This includes ways of thinking, beliefs, languages spoken, holidays and celebrations, and customs that reflect integral aspects of behaviour toward others. Each of us

Figure 13-4 ■ Documentation of children's play experiences on the topic of "Canada."

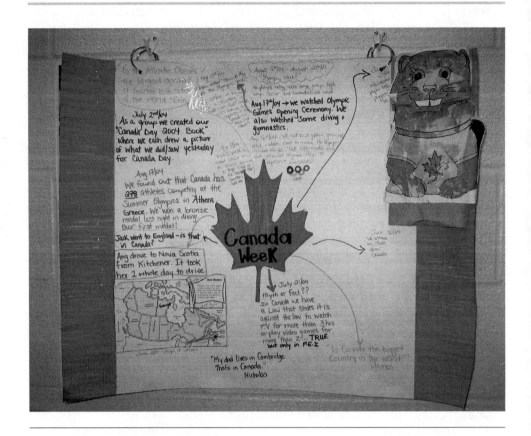

belongs to different cultures found within the family, ethnic group and society. The Canadian federal government's policy on multiculturalism (1971) and its Bill C-93 (1988) firmly roots cultural and linguistic diversity as a strongly held value in Canadian society. (Saderman Hall & Rhomberg, (1995) p. 38)

culture

way of living, shared with other members of the same group, which includes ways of thinking, beliefs, languages spoken, holidays, celebrations, and customs

Multicultural education should not just focus on the exotic aspects of various **cultures** but should emphasize an ability to identify, empathize, and relate to various groups of people. As discussed in the section on antibiased curriculum in Chapter 8, be cautious of the "tourist approach" to planning activities and be sure that they are well integrated, meaningful, and based on the interests of the children. Activities should allow children to examine and appreciate the similarities and differences of all people.

Be aware of any activities that are reserved for ceremonial or religious use only and that do not have a place in program curriculum. One example would be the importance of talking with the children about the spiritual aspects of First Nations drums and about how they are made and used by First Nations. Also be aware of any activities that may inadvertently stereotype a particular culture and give a biased view. For example, children should not make aboriginal head dresses, because they are sacred to aboriginal ceremonies. Making aboriginal head dresses tends to perpetuate a stereotype of First Nations people wearing these when they are at war.

Activities

Purposes: *increase cultural awareness*
develop literacy skills
enhance appreciation of differences in communication

Celebrations and holidays. Talk with the children about the different holidays and celebrations that take part in their family and community. Plan parties that focus on these various celebrations with the inclusion of food, music, crafts, games, and dance. Some holidays to celebrate are Kwanzaa, Diwali, Hanukkah, Chinese New Year, Canada Day, Rosh Hashanah, Easter, Ramadan, Christmas, May Day, and other various spring festivals. Many families celebrate a combination of holidays. For example, some children will celebrate both Christmas and Hanukkah based on the traditional beliefs of each parent. It is especially important to recognize the celebrations and holidays that the children in the program celebrate at home.

> For example, in Newfoundland people dress up in disguises at Christmas and go mummering starting on Boxing Day. They sing, dance and play music as they go door to door and people try to guess who they are

Sing Happy New Year in Chinese. Chinese New Year is also known as Lunar New Year and is celebrated sometime between January 21 and February 20 each year—it does not have a fixed date. Assist the children with researching the celebration of Chinese New Year. Celebrations include spring cleaning a month prior to the new year, gathering of family, enjoyment of food, exchange of gifts, and passing on of good wishes and fortune for the following year.

Happy New Year

Happy New Year, Happy New Year

Happy New Year to You All

We Are Singing, We Are Dancing

Happy New Year to You All

Xin Nian Hao, Xin Nian Hao

Zhu Fu Da Jia, Xin Nian Hao

Wo Men Chang Ge, Wo Men Tiao Wu

Zhu Fu Da Jia Xin Nian Hao

Languages and greetings. Provide a list of greetings from different languages around the world. Invite the children to talk about how people greet each other in their family. Set out paints, stencils, and stamps so that the children can create a "hello" greeting. Make up word searches and crossword puzzles, or find word puzzles in books. (See http://www.factmonster.com—go to Word Wise.)

Splatter box greetings. In the art area, provide shoeboxes that have had the opening covered securely with window screening. Set out foam shapes of various letters, tempera paints, toothbrushes, and white paper that the children can use to create greetings in different languages. Children can place the letters of their chosen greeting on a white sheet of paper, hold the shoe box over the top of the paper, and brush the paint across the screen, flicking paint over the foam letters. When they remove the box, an imprint of the greeting will emerge.

"ALO" "HOLA" "BONJOUR" "KANNICHIWA" "AHNEE"

Miming greetings. People around the world use different gestures to greet one another. For example, it is customary in Italy for individuals to kiss each cheek when they meet; North Americans shake hands or hug when they greet each other. Other gestures such as "hooking pinkie fingers together" to show that you intend to keep a promise, is common in Japan. Children in Italy will trace the sign of the cross on their chests to show this same gesture (Milord, 1992, p. 33). Have children role-play various greetings through mime or mirroring of gestures.

Equipment to Have Available

- books and pictures about different cultural holidays and celebrations
- music from different cultural celebrations
- foam letters
- shoe boxes
- window screening
- white paper
- tempera paint
- toothbrushes
- stencils
- stamps
- tape

Concepts of Citizenship and Friendship

As children explore their place in the world, they see that they are part of many groups in their community: family, school, class, clubs, teams, and the school-age program. They begin to develop character attributes that can be encouraged and reinforced through interactions and activities in their school-age programs. While children interact with one another in a school-age program, they develop **friendships** that may last a lifetime. They learn about **citizenship** and what it means to care for themselves and others in their family and community, and to respect their environment. Being a good citizen and a good friend involve qualities of fairness, honesty, trust, respect, compassion, responsibility, and integrity. (For further reference, see "Character Education, Ideas and Activities for the Classroom," 1998; Goodcharacter.com, n.d., http://www.goodcharacter.com/pp/citizenship.html; and Parenting.org, n.d., http://www.parenting.org/archive/discovery/life_lessons/2001-02/Nov02_good_citizen.asp).

Activities

Purposes: *enhance awareness of the qualities of friendship and citizenship*
              explore the value of getting along with others and of world peace
              provide opportunities to work in groups on a long-term project

Friendship rainbow. Children trace their hand on a piece of coloured construction paper. They then decorate their paper hands with unique characteristics, using various materials to make nails, rings, or bracelets. Talk about how hands look the same or different from one another.

Make a rainbow from coloured construction paper and staple it to a bulletin board. Work together with the children to design the bulletin board. Talk about the different

friendship

relationship between people that involves qualities of fairness, honesty, trust, respect, compassion, integrity, and caring

citizenship

being part of a community; being responsible for one's own property; respecting the property of others; caring for others and doing good deeds for them; following rules and valuing oneself and the environment

Box 13-2 ■ A Good Citizen Is ...

- someone who cares for his own property and the property of others
- someone who takes responsibility for her actions and apologizes for wrong doings
- someone who is caring and does good deeds for others, even when no one is watching
- someone who takes turns
- someone who shares
- someone who listens to what others have to say without interrupting them
- someone who recognizes the importance of making and following rules
- someone who tells the truth
- someone who is considerate of other people's feelings
- someone who values oneself and the environment and its inhabitants
- someone who reuses, reduces, and recycles to protect the environment
- someone who helps in the community
- someone who accepts the differences in people (race, culture, age, gender, ability, lifestyle)
- someone who states one's rights without putting someone down
- someone who knows the difference between right and wrong

colours of the rainbow and how they come together to make a beautiful collection. Staple the hands around the rainbow in an attractive display. Use this activity as a way to discuss similarities and differences of people in our communities and around the world, and how this collection provides an interesting and diverse perspective.

World globes. Children often show interest in places around the world. Develop a project that is based on their interest. Provide examples of what a world globe would look like. Set out balloons that have been blown up, along with a *papier-mâché* mix of flour, water, and newspaper strips (see page 190). Children cover the balloons with 2–3 layers of *papier-mâché* strips. Leave an opening at the top so that the balloon can be popped and removed after it has dried. The globes will need to dry overnight. The next day, the children can paint the world, with landforms and oceans, on their *papier-mâché* globe. The balloon can be popped with a sharp pencil, then removed, and the opening covered with more *papier-mâché* strips. After allowing the globes to dry again overnight, the children can attach a string or yarn to the top of their globe and hang it from the ceiling.

Friendship bracelets, anklets, rings, and key chains. Provide various materials, such as leather strips, yarn, fishing line, and beads to make and exchange bracelets, anklets, rings, or key chains. Collect old zippers and ask parents to collect them as well. Assist the children with separating the zipper into two separate halves. They can decorate each half of the zipper with acrylic paints and glue a fastener to each end, forming a bracelet. The children may like to give one half of the zipper to a friend.

Figure 13-5 ■ A friendship rainbow.

E-mail or pen pals. Ask the children if they would like to write to someone in another city, town, province, or country. With written parental permission, children could talk about how old they are, their family, and their hobbies and interests. Safe practice and use of the internet for e-mail exchanges would need to be carefully monitored. Contacts can be made to organizations that promote world peace and friendship such as UNICEF at http://www.unicef.ca.

Equipment to Have Available

- construction paper of various colours, including different skin tones— brown, tan, white, black
- scissors
- markers, pencils
- glitter, sequins
- maps, globes
- paints
- paint brushes
- strips of newspaper
- large balloons
- flour, water, bowl
- string, yarn
- beads

Discussion

- Talk about what makes a good friend (qualities of trust, honesty, integrity, compassion, caring).
- Consider the similarities and differences of each other in terms of physical appearance, likes and dislikes, and cultural backgrounds.
- Discuss different countries in which the children are interested, including perhaps those that members of their family have come from.
- Celebrate International Friendship Day, which occurs on the first Sunday of August, and its importance in bringing awareness to the value of world peace.

Understanding Differing Abilities: Special Needs

differing abilities/special needs individuals with different physical and cognitive limitations

Children also need to develop awareness, understanding, and an appreciation for people's **differing abilities.** In this way, children will be able to identify, empathize with, and relate to a variety of individuals in positive ways. The concept of inclusion is important in all communities today; it provides all people with the opportunity to be fully active participants, regardless of physical or cognitive abilities. Inclusion can be defined as "no one being left out" or "helping everyone to feel a part of an activity or situation" (Saderman Hall & Rhomberg, 1995, p. 4).

Activities that promote the awareness and acceptance of all individuals allow for the development of positive self-esteem and a healthy, responsive, and nurturing social setting or community.

Activities

Figure 13-6 ■ Children with differing abilities.

Purposes: develop an awareness of a variety of ways to communicate
develop a respect for people with different abilities
practise literacy skills

Sign-language charades. Invite the children to play a different version of the game Charades. Divide the group into two teams and provide signing alphabet charts. Children will take turns, alternating between teams, to pick a card with a word on it from a hat. (Use the names of the children in the program or words from a simple category like animals.) Children on each team take turns to sign the word and the other team tries to identify it.

Trust walk. Ask the children if they ever considered what it would be like to be blind. Pair children up and blindfold one child. The child who is not blindfolded leads the other child around a simple obstacle course or around the room.

Collect old eye glasses. Plan a collection drive for old glasses. Local optometrists and pharmacists often have connections with worldwide relief organizations to help people in some other countries who do not have the means to get eye glasses that they need.

Braille name cards. Set up a table with stiff paper, pen, and thumbtacks. Ask the children to print their names with a black marker on the cards and draw dots on the back along the letters, which will show through. Children can punch out the dots with the tacks. When they turn over the card with the dots raised, they can feel each of the letters with their fingers. Set out examples of books that are written in Braille. Talk about places in the community where Braille signs are found, such as in elevators (Saderman Hall & Rhomberg, 1995, p. 142).

Robert Munsch's Book Zoom. Invite the children to listen to the story *Zoom* and talk about places in the community that are accessible to people with different physical disabilities. Provide a variety of play toys like dolls, ramps, and wheelchairs for children to use in their dramatic play.

Heroes. Set up a display table of information, books, and pictures about heroes such as Terry Fox, Rick Hansen, Lise Thebault, and Joanne McDonald, who have endured great physical challenges. Rick Hansen has a website of curriculum ideas related to his Man in Motion World Tour that can be downloaded. This would be a suitable topic to explore during the time that the Wheels in Motion Fundraising Event comes to your area. See http://www.rickhansen.com/Youth/ youth_resources_ lessons.htm.

Invite guests to come and talk about themselves or about charities who raise funds to support those with disabilities. Contact various organizations such as the Canadian National Institute for the Blind, Canadian Hard of Hearing Association, Canadian Abilities Foundation, Association for Community Living, and the Canadian Paraplegic Association.

Walking sticks. Collect different materials such as tree branches, discarded sticks, or mop handles. Bring in real canes and walking sticks and talk about the materials they are made from—wood, plastic, or aluminum. Experiment with different lengths of the stick to determine which would best assist someone when they are walking. Try out the walking sticks on different land surfaces such as paved walkways, dirt pathways, rocky areas, sand piles, muddy fields, and hills (School-Age Notes, 1989).

Equipment to Have Available

- alphabet signing chart
- signing cards
- blindfold
- stiff paper
- pens
- thumbtacks
- Braille charts and books
- dolls of various sizes and abilities
- toy wheelchairs for dolls
- blocks to make ramps
- play house, farm, town
- branches
- discarded broom or mop handles

Environmental Awareness

An important part of helping children understand what it means to be a good citizen is learning about how we take responsibility for maintaining a safe and healthy environment, both with respect to our local communities and throughout the world as a whole. Taking care of the **environment** includes protecting animals, habitats, forests, lakes, oceans, and rivers; reducing pollution and waste; conserving energy; and reusing and recycling items. This is often referred to as our ecosystem and involves the study of **ecology.**

Activities

Purposes: *develop awareness of environmental issues*
strengthen ability to plan and carry through a long-term project
practise cooperative problem solving
increase ability to communicate ideas

Earth Day. Canadians from coast to coast join over 500 million people worldwide to celebrate International Earth Day every April 22. Events take place in various communities to raise awareness about environmental issues. Children can take part in these events in their school-age program by:

- planting trees
- adopting a tree
- cleaning up their play yard
- collecting old items and recycling them
- researching on the Internet, and through books, about various animals and their habitats
- writing to various environmental awareness organizations to identify and support their concerns, such as the World Wildlife Fund
- having a garage/yard sale
- coordinating an exchange program for items like skates, skis, ski boots, roller blades, and skateboards

environment

preservation of animals and their habitats; sustainable use of natural resources and the reduction of pollution and waste

ecology

study of life forms (living and nonliving) as they relate to each other and their environment

Box 13-3 ▦ Eco Fact

Did you know... that frogs not only breathe through their lungs, but through their skin as well? (Eco Kids, n.d.)

Box 13-4 ▦ World Wildlife Federation

"WWF has effectively safeguarded hundreds of species and millions of acres of wildlife habitat in pursuit of three goals: the preservation of the Earth's rich biodiversity; the sustainable use of natural resources; and the reduction of pollution and waste." (WWF Kids' Treehouse, n.d.)

Create a bulletin board showing people's misuse of the environment. Display burning rain forests, soil erosion because of logging, and polluted streams and lakes. In conjunction with a study of weather, investigate how these practices affect not only the immediate environment but also the global environment. Ask children to brainstorm alternatives to these harmful practices. Write down their responses and include that information on the bulletin board.

Increase pollution awareness. Have children write to companies that have the potential for polluting their communities. What are the companies currently doing to eliminate pollution? Do they have additional plans as information becomes available and technology advances? What would the children do when they are adults to prevent environmental pollution?

Start an ecology club. Let the children choose interest areas concerning the environment—for example, ozone layer, smog, greenhouse effect, nuclear waste, solar energy, lasers, and sound waves. Have them research what these might be doing to the environment and what is being done to prevent further damage.

Compile a scrapbook. Have children collect newspaper or magazine articles on the destruction of our natural resources—rivers, forests, lakes, wilderness areas, and animal habitats. Classify the information according to the kind of resource. Compile a large scrapbook of the articles, and leave it in the reading corner for children to browse at leisure.

Analyze food packaging for potential harm to the environment. Examples include candy wrappings that contain a plastic wrap inside a cardboard box, and food sold or packaged in styrofoam, which does not biodegrade. When the styrofoam breaks up, it can be eaten by wildlife. Plastic rings that hold six-packs of drinks can strangle birds and fish. Have children write to companies that make the products or publish an article in the program's newspaper.

Figure 13-7 ▦ Building an appreciation for nature.

Concerned Consumers

Purposes: *increase ability to infer results based on previous information*

              think creatively when finding new uses for household objects

              communicate information and ideas to others

biodegradable

objects that disintegrate over time

nonbiodegradable

objects that will not disintegrate over time

Survey packaging materials to determine whether they are biodegradable or non-biodegradable. Explain to the children the meaning of the words "biodegradable" and "nonbiodegradable." **Biodegradable** refers to those objects that will disintegrate over time, such as paper, food scraps, and garden clippings. **Nonbiodegradable** refers to objects that will not disintegrate, such as plastic, metal, and styrofoam. Ask the children to think of things they have at home that fit the two categories.

Take a trip to a nearby store. Group the children in twos or threes and tell them that each group will survey an aisle in the grocery store. Provide children with paper, pencils, and clipboards or a book to write on. Assign each group an aisle of the store. Tell them to go slowly through the items on the shelves, noting things that are packaged in biodegradable and nonbiodegradable packaging. Discuss the information they have gathered when they are back at the centre. Can they think of better ways to avoid filling the environment with garbage that will still be there many years into the future?

Sort items into biodegradable and nonbiodegradable. Collect items and ask children to bring in empty boxes, bags, or other materials that were used to package goods. Have the children sort them into piles according to their degradability.

Test the biodegradability of several items. Have children dig one hole for each item in an unused part of the playground. Pour some water in the hole and let it soak into the ground. Place one object in each hole, then cover it with dirt. Mark the places with small signs to show what is buried there. Some suggestions for items to bury are a newspaper, an egg carton, a tin can, a plastic food carton, and a paper bag. Have the children predict which items will deteriorate. Dig up the objects at the end of 30 days. How accurate were the predictions? Would some of the items degrade if left longer?

Recycle household objects. Ask children to bring one object from home that would have been thrown in the garbage. Place all the objects on a table, and ask children to think of things that could be done with each. Provide any additional materials they need to make useful items from the objects. Some things children might make are sand shovels from plastic bottles; a paint applicator from roll-on deodorant bottles; a rocket from an oatmeal box; and towers from painted cans of all sizes to add interest to block buildings. A large variety of objects can also be used to create sculptures or other art projects.

Equipment to Have Available

- bulletin board
- computer
- cups, bowls
- glue
- newspapers, magazines
- paper, pencils
- scale (balance or digital)
- scissors
- scrapbooks
- shovels, buckets
- tape (masking, duct, or sticky)
- tape recorder

Summary

In order for school-age children to develop positive social attributes and positive images of themselves, they need opportunities to learn about their community, how to be a good citizen, and how to acquire understanding and acceptance of the diverse aspects of people's neighbourhoods, culture, languages, abilities, and family composition. They also need opportunities to develop an appreciation for their environment and all that nature can provide: the land, waterways, and animals and their habitats.

Activities that allow children to become familiar with their community are outlined. These include topics about different kinds of homes, learning about other similarities and differences between communities, and making maps.

Exploration of culture is presented with experiences that revolve around celebrations, languages, and greetings. These activities assist the school-age child care professional in talking with the children about similarities and differences between cultures.

Activities that help children to understand the importance of friendship and citizenship are presented; children are encouraged to view these from both a local community and worldwide perspective. In promoting the importance of being a good citizen, activities discussed will help children gain awareness of people of differing abilities or special needs, the importance of inclusion, and the value of friendship.

Part of being a good citizen means learning ways to take care of the environment. Activities mentioned provide opportunities to talk about such concepts as reducing waste, recycling, pollution, and conserving energy.

Key Terms

community	differing abilities/special needs	biodegradable
culture		nonbiodegradable
friendship	environment	
citizenship	ecology	

Student Activities

1. Examine the different parts of your community and talk about what makes them the same or different from your friends' and classmates' communities.
2. Make a list of the aspects of your culture or family celebrations that you could share with children. Include music, dance, arts and crafts, food, and games.
3. Research different organizations that promote awareness of diverse abilities and identify some noted Canadian heroes (see the list of websites below).
4. Identify the environmental issues that are important to you, and then write a letter or send an e-mail to an organization that promotes environmental awareness in Canada (see the list of websites below).

Review Questions

1. Why is it important for children to learn about their community?
2. How does Canada's policy on multiculturalism relate to curriculum planning?
3. What are the qualities of a good citizen?
4. List activities that may help children understand the value of friendship.
5. Describe how and why you would plan activities to promote understanding about differing abilities.

6. Outline a plan of activities for Earth Day.
7. Name two activities that will help children decrease the amount of waste they discard.

Case Study

A group of children are playing with small toy dolls and small blocks. Samara says "I'm making an apartment building for my doll family just like the one I live in." Tara says "I wouldn't live in an apartment. That would be yucky! Only poor people live in apartments. There would be no place to play outside. You should build a house like the one I live in. It has an upstairs where I have my bedroom and a big back yard."

1. Would you respond in any way to Tara's comment about living in a house vs. an apartment? If so, what would you say?
2. How could you help these children broaden their thinking about their community?
3. How could you help each of these children understand that it is okay to be different?

References

Craig, G., Kermis, M., & Digdon, N. (2001). *Children today* (2nd Canadian ed.). (2001), Toronto: Prentice Hall, Canada.

Eco Kids. (n.d.). *Eco Fact.* Retrieved June 2004 from http://www.ecokids.ca/pub/index.cfm

Goodcharacter.com (n.d.). How to be a good citizen. *Teaching Guide: Citizenship for Grades K–5.* Retrieved March 21, 2005, from http://www.goodcharacter.com/pp/citizenship.html

Hall, A., Holder, B., Matthews, E., McDowell, M., Pyne, L., Walker, S., Welch, R., & White, K. *Character Education, Ideas and Activities for the Classroom.* (1998). Greensboro, NC: Carson-Dellosa Publishing Co., USA.

Kunderman, J. (1998). Celebrating the diversity of Mother Earth: First Nations child care Project, Bkejwanong Children's Centre. *Interaction, CCCF,* 32.

Milord, S. (1992). *Hands around the world: 365 creative ways to build cultural awareness & global respect.* Charlotte, VT: Williamson Publishing, USA.

Murphy Kilbride, K. (1997). *Include me too! Human diversity in early childhood.* Toronto: Harcourt Brace.

Nordgaarden, C. & Armstrong, B. (1995). *Create a culture.* Huntington Beach, CA: Creative Teaching Press.

Parenting.org (n.d.). The mark of a good citizen. Retrieved March 21, 2005, from http://www.parenting.org/archive/discovery/life_lessons/2001-02/Nov02_good_citizen.asp

Perron, T. & Woehl, J. (1998). Celebrating the diversity of Mother Earth: First Nations child care project, Bkejwanong Children's Centre. *Interaction, CCCF,* 32–34.

Saderman Hall, N. & Rhomberg, V. (1995) *The affective curriculum: Teaching the anti-bias approach to young children.* Toronto: Nelson, Canada.

School-Age Notes. (1989). Vol. IX, No. 6, Nashville, TN: School-Age Notes.

WWF Kids' Treehouse. (n.d.). Retrieved June 2004 from http://www.wwf.ca/satellite/wwfkids/index.html

Selected Further Reading

Bkejwanong Children's Centre. *Celebrating the diversity of Mother Earth.* Walpole Island First Nation, R.R. #3 Wallaceburg, ON, N8A 4K9, 519-627-1475.

Everix, N. (1991). *Ethnic celebrations around the world—Festivals, holidays and celebrations.* Redding, CA, Good Apple.

Kalman, B. (1991). *Reducing, reusing, and recycling.* St. Catharine's, ON: Crabtree Publishing Company.

Needham, B. (1999). *Ecology crafts for kids.* New York: Sterling Publishing Co.

Solski Group (1990). *Famous Canadians.* Napanee, ON: S&S Learning Materials.

Solski, R. & Hill, B. (1999). *What is a community*. Napanee, ON: S&S Learning Materials.

Parry, C. (1987). *Let's celebrate! Canada's special days*. Toronto: Kids Can Press.

Wheeler, R. (1997). *Creative resources for elementary classrooms and school-age programs*. Albany, NY: Delmar.

Wood, L. (1991) *Canadian Native People*. Napanee, Ontario, S&S Learning Materials.

Computer Software

Mia's Language Adventure: The Kidnap Caper. (n.d.) CD-ROM. http://www.smartkidssoftware.com

Sim City, Sim Farm. (1996). CD-ROM. Walnut Creek, CA: Maxis, USA.

Webster's Encyclopedia World Wildlife. (2000). CD-ROM. Marshmallow Interactive.

Websites

Canadian National Institute for the Blind
http://www.cnib.ca

Canadian Hearing Society
http://www.chs.ca

Easter Seals
http://www.easterseals.ca

Helping Hands Monkey Helpers for the Disabled
http://www.helpinghandsmonkeys.org

Family Fun
http://familyfun.go.com/arts-and-crafts

Kids' Turn Central: holidays and occasions
http://www.kidsturncentral.com/holidays.htm

Habitat for Humanity Canada
http://www.habitat.ca

Earth Day Canada
http://www.earthday.ca

Recycle City: games, activities, and facts about recycling
http://www.epa.gov/recyclecity

Ecology Action Centre
http://www.ecologyaction.ca

Friends of the Earth Canada
http://www.foecanada.org

Canadian Environmental Network
http://rcen.ca

Education Division of the Canadian Wildlife Federation
http://www.cwf-fcf.org/en/educate

Greenpeace Foundation
http://www.greenpeacefoundation.org

Pollution Probe
http://www.pollutionprobe.org

Chapter 14

Getting Physically Active; Staying Healthy and Fit

Objectives

After studying this chapter, the student should be able to:

- Discuss the health of children in Canada
- Facilitate opportunities to engage in nutritional experiences
- Facilitate active play experiences, both indoors and outdoors
- State suggestions for implementing activities that promote fitness

 Profile

4-H is a nationwide program for children in rural communities across Canada. The age range of children that belong to 4-H varies between provinces, usually beginning at age 7 or 8. These are community-based programs that focus on "learning to do by doing."

Children learn new skills and increase knowledge about various topics that are related to their daily lives. They learn how to work effectively in a group and acquire positive attitudes towards learning. They make friends and take part in club and community activities, sports and games, picnics and campouts. In the process, they broaden their interests, discover their talents, increase pride in their community, and have fun.

The 4-H emblem symbolizes the head, heart, hands, and health.

At the beginning of each year the children talk about different interests and hobbies they have with their leader. They then decide on a project that they will work on for the year.

The children in one rural community, who usually attend a home-based school-age program after school each day, attend 4-H club once a week. They have written permission from their parents to take the bus to the local community centre where the 4-H club meets from 3:30 p.m. to 5:30 p.m. every Tuesday.

The topic that they decided to work on for the year was "foods." With this topic, they learn about the food groups, nutrition, cooking techniques, and preparation of a variety of foods. The children enjoy various cooking projects, from how to make an egg salad sandwich to making ice cream in a bucket.

Many of the experiences they have with learning about foods and food preparation help prepare them for the time when they will be in self-care. They learn about healthy restaurant eating, how to make good food choices, and about a healthy body image. The emphasis is placed on developing a positive self-image and healthy life style. They talk about different cultures and the various foods that they enjoy. Many of the basic foods that are used such as bread, rice, potatoes, beans, eggs, corn, and nuts are common in a number of cultures around the world. For example, corn is popular all over the world. The children learn that First Nations peoples first discovered corn and that it is part of harvest festivals and holiday celebrations. They talk about how corn on the cob is commonly eaten at family gatherings around the barbecue in the summer.

One of the children in the group is African-Canadian. She tells the children about Kwanzaa and about the Karamu (kah-rah-mu) feast. Kwanzaa is an African-American harvest festival that lasts for seven days. Corn is one of the seven holiday symbols and is used to represent the number of children in each family. Over the course of a month, they try out different corn recipes: tortillas, tacos, corn pudding, cornbread, and popcorn.

The children are creating a recipe book that will include recipes of different foods that they have tried. They will be able to take it home and try out some of the recipes with their families.

From Nova Scotia Agriculture and Fisheries (2004). *What is 4-H? The basics.* Retrieved April 25, 2005, from http://www.gov.ns.ca/nsaf/4h/awareness/whatis4h.htm

How Healthy Are Our Kids?

Positive health is measured by the degree of physical fitness because the human body was built to move and vigorous physical activity is required for the development of a healthy body. Engaging in regular physical exercise and active play helps children build positive attitudes toward maintaining an active lifestyle throughout their adolescent and adult years.

According to studies by the Canadian Fitness and Lifestyle Research Institute's Canadian Physical Activity Levels Among Youth (CANPLAY), 87 percent of children and youth do not accumulate enough daily steps to meet Canadian Physical Activity Guidelines (CPAG). These guidelines suggest that children add 90 minutes of moderate-to-vigorous activity to general day-to-day activities (about 16,500 steps). Boys take more daily steps than girls, and younger children ages 5–10 take more steps than those ages 11–14 (Canadian Fitness and Lifestyle Research Institute, 2005–2008).

As mentioned in Chapter 4, the percentage of Canadian children who are overweight or obese continues to climb. In 2004, 26 percent of children and adolescents aged 2–17 were overweight or obese compared to 15 percent in a 1978/79 survey (Statistics Canada, 2006). The increase in childhood obesity and low levels of activity is a common phenomenon in developed countries. Obesity and inactivity has been linked to greater health risks such as coronary disease and type 2 diabetes. Concerns and causes of obesity were discussed in Chapter 4.

During the school-age years, children become very concerned about their body image in view of society's perceptions. Some children will be either below or above the average range of body mass by age, gender, and height. School-age child care professionals should be aware of the physical and emotional effects of being overweight or underweight. They should ensure that children get the proper nutrients and that they understand what it means to have a healthy image of their bodies. School-age child care professionals need to promote the acceptance of differences in our physical body makeup and work to break down stereotypes about thin bodies, muscular bodies, and bodies with large breasts that are perpetuated by the media. Promotion of healthy eating habits and healthy food choices should be encouraged. Providing a healthy menu plan of lunches and snacks will help to provide a good model for families and should give children opportunities to be involved in planning and preparing healthy foods.

Children aged 5–14 from various communities in Nova Scotia were asked six questions about the barriers and enablers to physical activity and healthy eating. Enablers to physical activity for girls and boys included access to facilities, equipment, friends, having fun, and participating in physical education classes. Watching television and playing computer games and video games were some of the barriers to physical activity mentioned by boys and girls. Boys also said that not having enough time or having other chores and homework to do were barriers to physical activity. Girls identified being out of shape or not feeling comfortable about participating as barriers to taking part in physical activity (Canadian Diabetes Association, Nova Scotia Division).

As you read in Chapter 3, even though the rate of child poverty is slowly declining, from 11.9 percent in 1989 to 9.5 percent in 2009, there are still nearly 639,000 children (1 in 10 children), who remain in poverty in Canada (Campaign 2000 Report Card, 2011). "Poverty means having little money to get through the month and buy even life's necessities: shelter, food and clothing. Poor families may find that they have to buy the cheapest food in order to get through the month, and go hungry when that has run out" (Mandell & Duffy, 1995, p. 259). This food often lacks the nutritional value necessary for optimum growth. The Canadian Council on Social Development (1998) identifies other needs that are necessary for families in order to equalize the chances for children to become healthy, competent adults. They include developing good health; social, learning, and earning skills; and having access to public services such as public education, quality child care, health care, and recreation (CCSC, 1998). In recent years, a number of studies have reported on the relationship between the physical development of the brain and its connection with health, learning, and behaviour. "The brain is the master control of our health and well-being, competencies and coping skills. It directs all aspects of bodily functions through established biological pathways (Bertrand, 2001, pp. 8–9).

The foundation of brain development begins in early childhood; the middle childhood years from 6–12 continue to

Figure 14-1 ■ **Children can chart changes in their height to measure growth.**

allow for continued development, as long as optimal conditions for physical, emotional, and social health are present (Bertrand, 2001, p. 16).

Many health benefits of outdoor play are discussed in Chapter 9. The National Wildlife Federation report "Whole Child: Developing Mind, Body and Spirit through Outdoor Play" identifies studies that found that outdoor time has a dramatic impact on children's attentiveness in school along with a reduction in ADHD symptoms, particularly when the children are immersed in natural settings. A new alliance group called the Outdoors Alliance for Kids (OAK) in the United States advocates for new legislation called the "Moving Outdoors in Nature Act"(National Wildlife Association, 2010).

More can be done for children and families by advocating for better health care and recreational resources in your community. You can also have a large impact on the small group of children in your group. Provide them with experiences that foster attitudes and practices that will improve their well-being. You can give them knowledge that will enable them to continue these throughout their lifetimes.

Research compiled by the Canadian Fitness and Lifestyle Research Institute found that a lack of environments that support organized sport and physical activity at school was associated with minimal levels of student physical activity. With the large number of children in after-school programs, there are more opportunities to engage in active play indoors and outdoors. Unfortunately, costs and transportation issues are reported barriers for these programs, particularly for those from low-income families (Canadian Fitness and Lifestyle Research Institute, 2005–2008).

Since snack time is already a part of every session in a school-age program, it is a good place to start. Teach children what their bodies need to stay healthy. Help children plan to make changes in their food habits. Ask them to decide upon one change, making it as specific as possible. They may decide to change the kinds of snacks they consume rather than eliminating all snacks. Take responsibility for providing nutritious snacks each day that are not high in fat, sugar, or salt. This may involve being creative at times but will be worth the effort. Fruits, vegetables, whole-grain breads, cottage cheese or yogurt, whole-grain cereals, and nuts or nut butters can all make flavourful and nutritious snacks.

Activities

Good Food, Good Health

Purposes: *increase ability to make informed decisions about food choices*
expand knowledge of nutritional requirements
encourage participation in planning food for snacks

Talk to children about what their bodies need to stay healthy. Prepare a bulletin board that shows the *Eating Well with Canada's Food Guide—Rainbow* recommended by Health Canada. Encourage the children to consider their own diet. How many food groups did they have for breakfast? How many are in today's snack? What are some ideas for nutritious snacks? **Eating Well with Canada's Food Guide** is shown in Figure 14-2, and the Office of Nutrition Policy and Promotion offers numerous other resources. Cultural adaptations to *Eating Well with Canada's Food Guide* are also available through the Nutrition Resource Centre. Each adaptation has been produced in the language of the cultural group and features culturally specific foods. See the list of websites at the end of the chapter.

Eating Well with Canada's Food Guide
guideline for planning healthy, nutritionally balanced snacks and meals based on four food groups, including cultural adaptations

Figure 14-2 ■ Eating Well with Canada's Food Guide.

Eating Well with Canada's Food Guide Excerpts. *Canada's Food Guide.* Health Canada, 2011. Reproduced with the permission of the Minister of Health, 2012.

■ Bannock Bread

Purposes: *increase cultural awareness*
         practise math concepts by measuring ingredients
         foster cooperation

Involve the children in preparing a snack of bannock bread, which is a snack representative of our First Nations culture. Assign two or three children to do the initial measuring and mixing. Divide the dough in half, allowing two more children to roll

Recommended Number of *Food Guide Servings* per Day

	Children			Teens		Adults			
Age in Years	2-3	4-8	9-13	14-18		19-50		51+	
Sex	Girls and Boys			Females	Males	Females	Males	Females	Males
Vegetables and Fruit	4	5	6	7	8	7-8	8-10	7	7
Grain Products	3	4	6	6	7	6-7	8	6	7
Milk and Alternatives	2	2	3-4	3-4	3-4	2	2	3	3
Meat and Alternatives	1	1	1-2	2	3	2	3	2	3

The chart above shows how many Food Guide Servings you need from each of the four food groups every day.

Having the amount and type of food recommended and following the tips in *Canada's Food Guide* will help:

- Meet your needs for vitamins, minerals and other nutrients.
- Reduce your risk of obesity, type 2 diabetes, heart disease, certain types of cancer and osteoporosis.
- Contribute to your overall health and vitality.

it out and cut it. Two more children can be assigned to assist with baking the finished squares. See Table 14-1 for the recipe.

■ Taste Trip

Purposes: *increase cultural awareness and appreciation*
            expand food preferences

Table 14-1 ■ Bannock Bread

1.5 L (6 cups) flour
250 mL (1 cup) lard
45 mL (3 tbsp) baking powder
15 mL (1 tbsp) salt
500 mL (2 cups) currants or raisins
850 mL water

In a medium-size mixing bowl, mix the flour and lard together by hand. Then add the baking powder, salt and the currants or raisins. Next add the water and work the ingredients into a dough. Spread the dough out into two 22.5 cm × 22.5 cm (9 in. × 9 in.) square cake pans.

Bake at 225°C (425°F) for about 20 minutes or until golden brown.

Bannock bread can also be cooked over a campfire. Divide the dough into four lumps and firmly wrap each lump around the end of a 1.25 m (4 ft.) stick and prop securely over the fire until golden brown and cooked through.

Caution: If you are building a campfire, be sure to check with the appropriate provincial/territorial ministry to see if there are any campfire bans in place, and be sure to build the campfire in a suitable spot, away from flammable materials. Ensure that the children use extreme caution when they are cooking their bannock bread; they must stand at a safe distance from the campfire and have a bucket of water close by to put out the fire. Before leaving the campfire site, pour water over the fire, then stir up the ashes and be sure the fire is out.

Select fruits from different countries. Set them out on trays with labels indicating the country of origin. Encourage children to taste several items, then write their reactions. The following are suggested foods, but visit your local supermarket to find others.

- Haiti, East Indies, or Mexico: mango—peel, slice, and add to fruit cups
- Central and South America: burro banana—add to salads or fruit cups
- Hawaii: papaya—cut in half, seed, peel, and slice
- Japan: Asian pear—eat raw or bake
- Mexico: cactus pears—peel and eat or add to salads
- New Zealand: feijoa, also called pineapple guava—peel and slice
- New Zealand: kiwi fruit—serve in thin slices peeled or unpeeled
- New Zealand: passion fruit—scoop out pulp and serve over yogurt
- China: lichee fruit—cut into pieces and add to a fruit salad
- Mexico: jicama—peel and slice, serve with a seasoned cottage-cheese dip
- South America or Hawaii: pineapple—peel, core, and cut into chunks

■ *Menu Planning*

Purposes: *expand ability to make cooperative decisions*
practise mathematical calculations when determining how much to buy
use Eating Well with Canada's Food Guide *to make food choices*

Appoint a group of interested children to plan nutritious snacks for a week. Ask them to include items from at least two food groups for each snack and ensure that all four food groups are represented during the week. Take into consideration any food allergies or food restrictions. When they have completed their menu, ask them to make a shopping list of required ingredients. They may have to consult cookbooks or ask someone to help them determine quantities. If you have a cook at your centre, he or she would be a good resource person. Schedule a trip to the supermarket to purchase the food. See the Suggested Readings for books with recipe ideas, and Table 14-2 for snack ideas.

▦ *Ice Cream in a Bucket*

Purposes: *observe the physical changes that take place when the mixture freezes*
participate in a group effort to achieve a goal

Make ice cream in a bucket. Most children have never had the opportunity to make homemade ice cream and will remember this unique experience. The recipe in Table 14-3 gives the directions.

As a variation, use a commercial ice-cream maker. To make frozen yogurt, merely mix crushed fresh fruit with plain yogurt. Add a small amount of sugar or honey, then pour into the container. Freeze according to the machine's directions.

Table 14-2 ▦ Scrumptious Snacks

- Apple slices, cream cheese, raisins
- Assorted raw vegetables with seasoned cottage-cheese dip
- Banana slices dipped in honey and rolled in nuts
- Celery stuffed with peanut butter or cheese spread
- Balls of soft cheese rolled in chopped nuts
- Cottage cheese with fruit
- Devilled eggs—mix yogurt, mustard, salt, and paper with the yolks
- Fresh fruit gelatine served with any seasonal fruit
- Fruit kabobs—banana wheels, pineapple chunks, cherries, strawberries, orange wedges on a skewer
- Fruit shakes—blend fruit and nonfat dry milk in blender with a few ice cubes
- Graham crackers, peanut butter, and applesauce
- Granola or bran cereal sprinkled with yogurt
- Ice cream with fruit in milk shakes or in make-your-own sundaes
- Nachos—tortilla wedges, refried beans, cheddar cheese; heat in microwave oven until cheese melts
- Nut bread with cheese spread
- Pizza—use pizza dough or English muffins and top with pizza sauce, cooked ground meat, cheese, tomatoes, mushrooms, chopped bell peppers, and olives
- Tacos or burritos—fill with cheese, leftover meat, and sliced tomatoes
- Tiny meatballs made with ground meat, rice, and seasoning
- Wheat toast with tuna salad or cheese, broiled to melt cheese
- Yogurt with fruit

Table 14-3 ■ Ice Cream in a Bucket

a large plastic bucket

a 500g (1 lb) coffee can with a plastic lid

500 mL (2 cups) rock salt

Beat together in the coffee can:

1 egg (see note)

75 mL (1/4 cup) honey

Add 250 mL (1 cup) milk

125 mL (1/2 cup) cream

5 mL (1 tsp) vanilla

dash of salt

Be sure the coffee can is only half full or the ice cream may spill over the sides as it freezes.

Put a layer of ice in the bottom of the pail. Crushed ice is more effective for freezing ice cream, but cubes will work also. Sprinkle the ice with some of the salt.

Put the lid on the coffee can and set the can on top of the ice. Pack more salt and ice in the pail around the sides of the can. Sprinkle layers of ice with salt as you fill the bucket. When the ice is almost to the top of the can, take off the plastic lid.

Stir the ice-cream mixture with a wooden spoon, letting the can turn too. Let the children take turns stirring because it will take from 15 to 30 minutes for the ice cream to freeze. The children will likely want to eat it right away, while it is still soft.

This recipe will serve four to five children, so you may need to make more than one batch.

Note: If you are concerned about possible salmonella bacteria in the raw egg, you can coddle it. (Heat water to 115°C (240°F). Pour enough water into a cup to completely cover the egg. Let stand for one minute. Any bacteria will be killed, but the egg will not cook.)

Figure 14-3 ■ A chef's club can prepare snacks for the entire group.

■ A Guest Chef

Purposes: increase awareness of cultural meanings of food preferences
expand food experiences to include those from other countries

Invite a guest chef to demonstrate how a favourite recipe that is representative of her culture is prepared and cooked. Let children take part in preparing items from the recipe and then taste the final product. Note: Discuss the recipe with the chef before the presentation and consider any constraints of your facility. Where will the food be prepared? Can the recipe be prepared safely? Do you all the equipment she will require? Let the chef know if any children have food allergies or food restrictions.

For an alternative, ask a parent from the program to demonstrate a dish that is specific to his culture. Have the parent and his child explain whether this is a dish the family might eat frequently or if it is served on special occasions. Some possibilities are:

- An Asian stir-fry dish. Provide chopsticks and ask the parent to demonstrate how to use them.
- Mexican burritos with homemade salsa
- Japanese noodles and vegetables

- Jewish potato latkes or cheese blintzes
- Indian puri
- Spanish sopapillas

■ Cookbook

Purposes: *cooperative effort to achieve a goal*
increase reading and writing skills
plan and carry out a long-term project

Plan a project with the children that involves compiling a book of their favourite recipes, which may be used as a fundraiser. The children may have to consult a cookbook or ask their parents for help with this. Use a computer or typewriter to type the recipes; older children or parents may volunteer to help. Make copies for each of the children in your group. Let each of them make a cover for their book.

■ Cook, Cook, Cook

Purposes: *reinforce knowledge of nutritional requirements for health and fitness*
practise decision-making skills
experience foods from different cultures

Set up a chefs' club with the children and plan cooking projects together. Each experience is an opportunity to reinforce good nutrition and the importance of making appropriate food choices. It is also an opportunity for children to broaden their tastes and to experience foods from different cultures.

Japanese Rice Balls
250 mL (1 cup) short-grain white rice

375 mL (1 1/2 cups) water

salt to taste

Put rice in a saucepan and add water. Soak for 30 minutes, then cook covered until all the water is absorbed. Let the rice cool with the pan covered for about 5 minutes or until it is cool enough to handle (already cooked, cold rice can be used if no stove is available). Children should wet their hands, take a scoop of rice, form the rice into a ball with a hole in the middle, then place a pickled Japanese plum in the hole. If desired, the ball can be wrapped with a piece of nori (seaweed). Wet the ends of the nori so it will seal.

Flour Tortillas
1 L (4 cups) whole-wheat flour

5 mL (1 tsp) salt

75 mL (1/3 cup) vegetable oil

approximately 250 mL (1 cup) warm water

Mix the flour and salt: add oil, mix together with fingers. Stir in enough water to make a firm ball. Knead the dough until it is smooth, then let it rest for 20 minutes. Pinch off a golf-ball size piece of the dough. Roll it out on a floured board until it is 10 cm (4 in.) in diameter. Cook on an unoiled griddle for about two minutes on each side.

Equipment to Have Available

You will need some equipment for food preparation or cooking. If your centre has a kitchen, most items will be available there. If not, accumulate the basics, then add to them as your children become more involved in their culinary projects. The number of each item will depend upon the size of your group of children.

- bottle and can opener
- bowls—several sizes for mixing ingredients
- cake pans—both sheet pans and layer pans, muffin tins
- colander, strainer, flour sifter
- cookie cutter, cookie sheets
- cutting boards—plastic or wooden, large boards and individual sizes
- eggbeaters, scrapers
- fork, tongs—both long handled
- gelatin moulds—both single and individual
- grater—four-sided is best for children to hold
- hot plate
- knives, serrated for greater safety (if ends are pointed, round them with a tool grinder)
- measuring spoons, liquid and dry measuring cups
- pancake turner, spatula, wooden and slotted spoons
- pastry brushes
- potato masher
- saucepans
- rolling pin (you can also use pieces of dowel)
- frying pan
- timer
- vegetable peeler, apple corer

The following are optional:

- popcorn popper
- electric blender and mixer
- electric food processor
- ice-cream freezer
- toaster oven

Getting Physically Active, Staying Fit

fitness

physical state of well-being that allows people to perform daily tasks with vigor, reduces risks of health problems, and establishes a performance base of physical activity

The kinds of outdoor play experiences children have today are vastly different from the past. Many children today live in urban areas in apartments where there is no space to play. Even in residential areas where there are yards, many children do not go outdoors because of fear for their safety or because they would rather sit indoors watching television. Even when children are outdoors, studies show they are not active enough to raise their heart rates for very long periods of time (Gilliam et al., 1981, 1982). Increased heart rate is one indicator of **fitness.**

Although a school-age program provides a safe place where children can play outdoors, it is necessary to incorporate an exercise regimen in the program. The fitness statistics described at the beginning of this chapter indicate that children need much more time for active play and fitness. For health benefits, children (ages 5–11) need 60 minutes of active, vigorous physical activity per day and at least 3 days per week that strengthens muscle and bone structure (Active Healthy Kids Canada Report Card, 2012).

The **Canadian Association for Health, Physical Education, Recreation, and Dance (CAHPERD)** advocates that all Canadian children (5–18 years of age) participate in 150 minutes of physical education per week (i.e., 30 minutes per day) (Anderson, 2000). CAHPERD describes fitness as a physical state of well-being that allows people to

1. perform daily activities with vigour
2. reduce their risk of health problems related to lack of exercise
3. establish a fitness base for participation in a variety of physical activities

CAHPERD's standards address several components: aerobic endurance, body composition (proportion of fat and lean), muscular strength, and flexibility. A good fitness program will address all of these. Exercise can also relieve some of the tensions children feel because of the pressures of school or family problems, and provide cognitive as well as physical benefits. A study done with children at an elementary school in Trois-Rivières, Quebec, found that when children spent extra time in physical education, they were more alert and their academic performance increased (Shepard, as cited in Craig, Kermis, & Didgon, 2001). Physical activity improves self-esteem, enhances psychological well-being, overcomes boredom, and provides leisure pursuits (Canadian Fitness and Lifestyle Research Institute, 2000).

Ensure that there are many opportunities for children to be active, both indoors and outdoors. Incorporate some of the exercises listed here, whether spontaneously or at a preplanned time.

Many of these exercises can be done in any kind of space with small groups of children; however, access to a gymnasium often provides extra space and equipment. Always begin with warm-up activities to limber up the muscles in preparation for exercise, minimizing the chance of injuries or strains. The following lists of exercises are presented in order of difficulty. Start with a few exercises from each category, at the easiest level, then gradually add others or move on to more difficult exercises when the children have increased their fitness. Above all, make the sessions fun. Adding music helps to keep the pace and increases children's enjoyment. Yoga and junior versions of Tae Bo are good ways to develop a routine of fitness exercises, as well as developing muscle strength and endurance. You may also use one of the videos or DVDs listed at the end of the chapter.

In all of the exercises, a staff member should demonstrate the moves if they are unfamiliar to the children. The school-age child care professional can ask the children to come up with other examples of suitable exercises as well. Display pictures of stick figures doing these exercises, so the children can practise on their own.

When children exercise in pairs or groups, use different ways to bring them together. For example, you could number them from 1 to 5 and ask all the 1s to make a group, 2s to make a group, etc. Alternatively, children can find partners who are wearing something similar, or share a birthday month. If there are an uneven number of children in the group, propose a challenge to one group to try the exercise with three children instead of two. These strategies eliminate the possibility of anyone feeling left out.

Canadian Association for Health, Physical Education, Recreation, and Dance (CAHPERD) advocates daily physical activity and more extensive physical education in schools

Figure 14-4 ■ **Healthy children have lots of energy.**

Activities

■ Warm-up

Purposes: prepare for exercise in order to prevent injuries or strain

foster a sense of well-being that will increase the likelihood of continuing a fitness regimen

Start exercises with a warm-up. The children may wish to take turns being the leader. Do 10 reps of the following:

1. *Head tilt.* Stand with feet apart, hands on sides. Drop head forward, then arch head back as far as possible.
2. *Head tilt, side to side.* Stand with feet apart, hands at sides. Keeping shoulders stationary, drop head to one side then the other. Touch ear to shoulder.
3. *Head turn.* Stand with feet apart, hands at sides. Turn head to right as far as possible, then to the left.
4. *Shoulder shrugs.* Stand with feet apart, arms at sides. Tighten abdominal muscles while raising shoulders up to ears. Lower them and repeat.
5. *Side lunges.* Stand with feet apart and arms outstretched at shoulder height. Tighten abdominal muscles. Bend right knee and lunge to the right while keeping the left leg straight. Reverse, bending left knee.
6. *Torso bend.* Stand with feet apart, hands at side. Keep legs straight while sliding right hand down thigh, toward knee. Stand straight, then repeat with left hand.

■ Arm and Hand Exercises

Purposes: Increase strength in arms and hands

Develop awareness of muscle action

1. Stand with legs together. Bring left arm forward and up, and swing right arm backward. Repeat, changing arms.
2. Stand with legs apart. Clasp hands together and swing them all the around in a circle. Go from left to right, then reverse.
3. Stand with legs apart, arms stretched out at shoulder level. Rotate arms in small circles, first forward, then backward.
4. Stand with legs apart. Grasp a yardstick or 1-m (3-ft.) piece of dowel at each end. Keep legs straight while twisting at the waist from side to side.
5. Keeping upper arm close to the body, raise one hand. Place a small rubber ball in the extended hand. Squeeze as hard as possible while counting to four. Change to other hand and repeat. As strength increases, continue the count up to eight.

■ Leg Exercises

Purposes: increase strength in leg muscles

cooperate with a partner

develop group cohesiveness

1. Squat with feet flat and palms touching the floor. Push one leg straight back. Hold for a few seconds, then change legs.
2. Run in place, raising knees as far off the floor as possible. Vary this exercise by telling the children to jump, then land in a squat when they hear you clap. Another clap is a signal to jump and continue running in place.
3. Stand with feet together, hands extended to the front at shoulder height. Raise one leg at a time, trying to touch each hand.

4. Sit on the floor cross-legged. Grasp right foot with both hands and pull it up to the nose. Repeat with left foot.

5. Lie on the floor on right side. Rest on the elbow and forearm with legs outstretched. Lift and lower left leg, keeping toes pointed straight. Roll over on the left side and repeat with right leg.

6. Lie on right side, body propped up by right elbow. Put left hand on the floor in front of body. Lift left leg a few inches, then swing it forward then back to align with torso. Repeat several times. Roll over on the left side and repeat with right leg.

7. Squat on floor, with hands flat on the floor. Jump with both legs, extending feet straight back. Return to a squatting position.

8. Sit on floor with legs straight and apart. Point toes toward floor while clasping right knee with both hands. Bend torso forward toward knee as far as possible. Hold position for three seconds, then return to sitting position. Repeat with left leg.

Group Exercises

1. Ask children to do this exercise in pairs. Each player places a ball on the ground or floor behind her. Partners face each other and join hands. One player in each pair sits on her ball while the other remains standing. As the seated player stands up, the partner lowers herself onto her ball. Alternate several times.

2. Try this exercise with a group of five. Players stand in a circle, all facing in the same direction. The first player passes a ball over his head to the player behind him. The second player has to reach up for the ball, then pass it through her legs to the next player. Continue this alternation several times around the circle. You can also use two balls so each player has more turns to reach or bend.

▨ Torso Exercises

Purposes: *increase torso flexibility and strength*
work with a partner to achieve a goal

1. Lie on the stomach with hands outstretched to the side. At the same time, raise legs and hands while arching back. Hold for a few seconds, then lie flat again.

2. Stand with feet apart. Stretch arms out to the side at shoulder height. Bend at the waist and touch right foot with left hand. Keep right arm stretched up in the air. Return to standing position, then repeat with the right arm.

Pair Exercise

1. Two children can work together on this one. One child lies on the floor with hands clasped behind her head and her knees bent. The second child holds her partner's feet firmly on the floor. The first child tightens her abdominal muscles,

Figure 14-5 ▨ Playground equipment can help children stay physically fit.

pulls to a sitting position, holds for a count of five, then slowly lowers to a lying position. Try six to eight sit-ups and change places.

■ *Yoga*

Purposes: *strengthen upper torso muscles*
develop balance and coordination
learn effective breathing and relaxation techniques

A carpeted area works well for yoga, or the children can use gym mats. Children can practise simple yoga moves like "downward dog," "cat pose," or "cobra." Find pictures of simple yoga poses and post them on the wall. Start with only one or two poses. Demonstrate the poses for the children and then allow them to experiment with different moves.

Show the children various ways to relax as they try the yoga poses, such as lying on the floor in a supine position with their legs and arms stretched out at the sides for a few minutes. Show children how to breathe properly by filling their bellies with air and releasing the air as they pull their bellies in.

Equipment to Have Available

active physical play
opportunities for children to plan their activities, experiment with new skills, and learn by trial and error, benefiting all areas of development

In addition to exercises, there are some simple pieces of equipment that will encourage children to participate in **active physical play**. This equipment is not expensive and in fact may already be in your school.

1. *Jump ropes.* Have several so more than one child can jump at a time. Have at least one that is long enough for two children to turn while others jump.
2. *Balls.* Have beach balls, exercise balls, tennis balls, etc. Children can throw or roll on balls.
3. *Nerf® balls.* Use with paddles to play Pom-Pom Paddle Ball (Chapter 10).
4. *Hoops.* Children can use them as hula hoops, or jump in and out of the hoops. Lay hoops in patterns on the floor so that children have to hop or jump from one to the other.
5. *Plastic field hockey sticks.* Play floor hockey.
6. *Balance beam.* You can find a low beam in many school equipment catalogues; however, they are also simple to make. Children can walk across with eyes open or closed or holding a plastic or wooden egg in a spoon.

Guidelines for School-Age Child Care Professionals

Cooking and eating should be fun. Do not pressure children to taste unfamiliar foods; if you continue to offer interesting varieties, their curiosity will probably get the better of them. Also, they will see that others try out unfamiliar foods, and they may want to get involved.

Set up a cooking environment with maximum safety in mind. Position the cooking table against a wall, with electrical cords behind the table and out of the way. Teach children safety rules and realize that with assistance they can cut up vegetables without getting hurt and can use an electric frying pan. Supervise closely and never leave an area where children are cooking or a cooking appliance is turned on.

Try not to impose your own food likes and dislikes on children. If you really hate a particular food, then do not include it. You may think you will be able to hide your dislike from the children, but they will sense it.

Be a good role model. Do everything you can to be healthy yourself. Demonstrate good eating habits by bringing only healthful foods and drinks to school.

Provide a variety of activities and materials that encourage active play. Tag games, ball games, jump rope, follow-the-leader, and obstacle course are all possible physical activities that can be incorporated into the daily program.

Allow children to choose an activity according to their developmental capabilities or fitness level. A vertical ladder leading to a high piece of climbing equipment may be too difficult or intimidating to the youngest children. Nevertheless, they might be able to master a short ladder leading to a low platform. Young children can hit a ball on a support, while older children may be ready to hit a pitched ball.

Set up active play stations indoors and outdoors. Chapter 10 includes suggestions for active games to be played indoors. Begin with those and then add others of your own design. Install basketball hoops outdoors at different heights, and provide places to toss balls at a target, a place to jump from, or hard surface areas for in-line skating.

Allow ample opportunities for children to practise skills. This means having more than one ball or that group activities should be organized for a small number of children. Having just one ball or playing large-team games entail waiting idly for a turn with little chance to participate and practise.

Enjoy exercising yourself and children will enjoy it. Avoid any comparisons or competition; this is not a time to see who can do the most sit-ups or jump the highest. Be careful not to use phrases such as "Let's see who can keep the ball in the air the longest"; simply say "Keep the ball in the air as long as possible."

Encourage parents to use health care resources for themselves and their children. Find out what is available in your community, then share this information with parents.

Be an advocate for good health programs and policies for children, and join professional organizations to further these causes. Speak or write to local government officials about the need to protect children.

Volunteer for health-related events in your community, and include your school-age group when you can. Health fairs, running, or bicycling events are some examples.

The health of children is too important to be overlooked.

Summary

School-age children need to be part of programs that allow them to continue to develop healthy concepts of themselves. They need to have opportunities to be involved in physical activity on a regular basis. In Canada, health concerns for children include issues of obesity, poverty, and inactivity. Awareness of the need to provide children with settings and community services that will provide for optimal growth and development—physically, emotionally, and socially—are critical.

As a school-age child care professional you can provide children with experiences that foster attitudes and practices to improve their health. You can also give them knowledge that will enable them to continue to be healthy throughout their lifetimes.

Research compiled by the Canadian Fitness and Lifestyle Research Institute found that a lack of environments that support organized sport and physical activity at school was associated with minimal levels of student physical activity. With the large number of children in after-school programs, the potential for ensuring that children have these opportunities is reported to be appealing. Costs and transportation issues are reported barriers for these programs, particularly for those from low-income families (CFLRI, 2008).

One way to develop health consciousness is to begin with the foods children eat. Introduce the children to *Eating Well with Canada's Food Guide*, then help them plan and prepare nutritious snacks. Expose them to new foods and different methods of cooking.

School-age children spend a lot of their time in sedentary kinds of activity each day and, although they do play outdoors, there is still a need to focus on fitness. The CAHPERD definition of fitness includes performing daily activity with vigour, reducing the risk of health problems related to lack of exercise, and establishing a fitness base for participation in physical activities. In order to achieve this degree of fitness, children and adults need to exercise.

The chapter describes a variety of exercises for specific parts of the body. Yoga is discussed as a good activity to build muscle strength and develop skills of balance and coordination. Purchasing some simple pieces of equipment encourages children to engage in physical activity.

The chapter provides some suggestions for school-age child care professionals about instituting a good food program. Cooking and eating should be fun, so do not pressure children. Do not impose your own food likes or dislikes on children; be a good role model by eating only healthful foods.

To help children achieve fitness, enjoy exercising yourself. Encourage parents to use health care resources for themselves and their children. Be an advocate for good health programs in your community, and participate in health-related community events.

Key Terms

Eating Well with Canada's Food Guide

fitness

Canadian Association for Health, Physical Education, Recreation, and Dance (CAHPERD)

active physical play

Student Activities

1. Make either bannock bread or ice cream in a bucket at home. Invite your family or friends to taste-test the results. Did they like the food? If not, why not? Were there any difficulties you encountered that were not addressed in the recipe? If so, how can you change the procedure to eliminate the problem?
2. Make a list of your own favourite foods. How many are healthful and how many might be considered junk foods?
3. Buy or borrow one of the pieces of equipment listed in this chapter. Try it out. How many physical activities can you think of to use this equipment?

Review Questions

1. Name two agencies that have done studies on the fitness of Canadian children. What were their conclusions?
2. Name the food groups in *Eating Well with Canada's Food Guide*. State the recommended daily servings of each.
3. Describe an activity a guest visitor might be invited to conduct in a school-age program.
4. Describe two activities that encourage children to try new foods.
5. Name 10 pieces of equipment that you could use for food preparation in a school-age program.
6. Define fitness.
7. Describe three exercises that strengthen leg muscles.
8. List four pieces of equipment that will encourage children to be physically active.

Case Study

Holly and Louisa are 11 years old and are beginning to look and act like teenagers. They sit together for long periods of time looking at teen magazines that Holly brings in her school backpack. They talk about the clothes, the models, and the celebrities featured in the magazines. At snack time, they often refuse the food, saying that it will make them fat. One of the staff members in their group thinks the magazines should be banned from the program.

1. Do you agree or disagree with the position of the staff member? Explain your reasoning.
2. What would you say to the girls?
3. Can you think of some activities to include in your program that might help Holly and Louisa have a more realistic image of young girls and women than is portrayed in teen publications?

References

Active, Healthy Kids Canada. (2012). *Report card on physical activity for children and youth*. Retrieved June 24, 2012, from http://dvqdas9jty7g6.cloudfront.net/reportcards2012/AHKC%202012%20-%20Report%20Card%20Long%20Form%20-%20FINAL.pdf

Bertrand, J. (2001). *Summary of research findings on children's developmental health*. Ottawa: Canadian Institute of Child Health and Canadian Child Care Federation.

Campaign 2000 Report Card on Child and Family Poverty in Canada. (2011). Retrieved June 27, 2012, from http://www.campaign2000.ca/reportCards/national/2011EnglishRreportCard.pdf

Canadian Association for Health, Physical Education, Recreation, and Dance. *Facts and stats*. Retrieved April 4, 2005, from http://www.cahperd.ca/eng/advocacy/facts/facts_stats.cfm

Canadian Council on Social Development. (1998). Child poverty in Canada: Recasting the issue. Retrieved April 4, 2005, from http://www.ccsd.ca/pubs/recastin.htm

Canadian Diabetes Association, Nova Scotia Region. (n.d.). *Barriers and enablers to healthy and active living in children: Key findings in six Nova Scotia communities*. Halifax, NS.

Canadian Fitness and Lifestyle Research Institute. (2005–2008). Kids can play! Encouraging children to be active at home, at school, and in their communities. http://www.cflri.ca/media/node/577/files/CANPLAY_2008_b1.pdf

Gilliam, T. B., Freedson, P. S., Greenen, D. L., & Shahraray, B. (1981). Physical activity patterns determined by heart rate monitoring in six- to-seven-year-old children. *Medicine and Science in Sport, 13*(1), 65–67.

Gilliam, T. B., MacConnie, S. E., Greenen, D. L., Pels, A. F., & Freedson, P. S. (1982). Exercise programs for children: A way to prevent heart disease? *The Physician and Sports Medicine, 10*(9), 96–108.

Mandell, N. & Duffy, A. (1995) *Canadian families: Diversity, conflict and change.* Toronto: Harcourt Brace.

National Wildlife Federation, Be Out There. (2010). *Whole child: Developing mind, body and spirit through outdoor play.* Retrieved June 27, 2012, from http://www.nwf.org/~/media/PDFs/Be%20Out%20There/BeOutThere_WholeChild_V2.ashx

Nova Scotia Agriculture and Fisheries (2004). What is 4-H? The basics. Retrieved April 25, 2005, from http://www.gov.ns.ca/nsaf/4h/awareness/whatis4h.htmCraig, G., Kermis, M. & Didgon, N. (2001). *Children Today* (3rd ed.). Toronto: Prentice Hall.

Statistics Canada. (2006). Childhood obesity: A troubling situation. Retrieved June 24, 2012, from http://www41.statcan.ca/2006/2966/ceb2966_004-eng.htm

Selected Further Reading

Bersma, D., Visscher, M., Marix Evans, A., & Kooistra, A. (2003). *Yoga games for children: Fun and fitness with postures, movements and breath.* Alameda, CA: Hunter House Smartfun Books.

Canadian Paediatric Society. (n.d.). Healthy active living for children and youth. http://www.caringforkids.cps.ca

Cook, D. (1995). *Kids' multicultural cookbook.* Charlotte, VT: Williamson Publishing.

Dairy Farmers of Ontario. (n.d.). *Nutrition: Primary ideas for active learning, nutrition education.* http://www.teachnutrition.org

Gavin, M., Dowshen, S., & Izenberg, N. (2004). *Fit kids.* Toronto: Darling Kindersley Publishing. Harrison, J. (1993). *Hooked on fitness—Physical conditioning games and activities for grades K-8.* West Nyack, NY: Parker Publishing Company.

Health Canada. (n.d.). *Canada's food guide to healthy eating: A rainbow approach—Books, snacks, kids' links.* http://www.nms.on.ca/Elementary/canada.htm

Health Canada. (n.d.). *Canada's physical activity guide to healthy active living.* http://www.paguide.com

Health Canada. (2002). *Canada's food guide to healthy eating.* Retrieved April 25, 2005, from http://www.hc-sc.gc.ca/hpfb-dgpsa/onpp-bppn/food_guide_rainbow_e.html

Lesser Rothstein, G. (1994). *From soup to nuts multicultural cooking activities and recipes.* Toronto: Scholastic Professional Books.

National Wildlife Association. (2010). Whole child: Developing mind, body and spirit through outdoor play. Retrieved June 24, 2012, from http://www.nwf.org/~/media/PDFs/Be%20Out%20There/BeOutThere_WholeChild_V2.ashx

Nutrition Resource Project—Food Guide: Cultural Adaptations to Canada's Food Guide to Healthy Eating. Retrieved May 4, 2005, from http://www.nutritionrc.ca/guide.html

Rowland, T. W. (1990). Exercise and children's health. Champaign, IL: Human Kinetics Books.

Stretch-n-Grow—The Fabulously Fun Fitness Program. http://www.stretch-n-grow.com

Warren, J. (1992). *Super snacks.* Everett, WA: Warren Publishing House.

Visual Media

Fitness, dance, and yoga videos and CDs can be found at
http://www.fitnessbeginnings.com

Partnerships: Quality and Standards

Chapter 15

Creating Community Partnerships

Objectives

After studying this chapter, the student should be able to:

- Discuss the advantages of developing partnerships within the community
- Describe the benefits of intergenerational programs
- List activities appropriate for volunteers and children
- Describe ways to use resources in the community
- State ways to make a volunteer program effective

 Profile

Tamerak school-age program is located in a community development that houses a child care centre, a school-age program, and a senior's centre in the same facility. The people who come to the seniors' centre are very active older people who have a continued interest in working within their community to share their skills and learn something new as well. The school-age program has a group of 25 children aged 6 to 10, and two staff. It operates after school each day and on school holidays.

Bob is a grandfather of 10 children who all live far away from him and his wife. He sees them only a couple of times a year, at Christmas and for a week in the summer. Bob has been retired for 15 years and had worked as a television sports reporter for 30 years. Bob visits the seniors' centre frequently and is involved in several centre activities. There is a wood-working workshop at the seniors' centre where he spends a great deal of time on his favourite hobby, making wooden birdhouses.

Bob knows some of the children as well as one of the school-age child care staff, Takeshi, who lives in Bob's neighbourhood. One day Bob invited the school-age children and Takeshi to come and visit the woodworking workshop. The children went in small groups and had a chance to see the various tools, machinery, and projects. Bob showed the children how to make a birdhouse and gave some leftover wood to the children.

Back at the school-age program, Takeshi and the children talked about various ways to use the wood and planned projects that they could work on every day after school. Takeshi found that the children looked forward to coming each day so that they could work on their projects with wood-working tools, glue, paints, and other craft materials. Bob dropped by the program from time to time to see how the children were progressing and offered a few tips to assist them. Sometimes he would bring a friend along to visit the children as well. As the children worked on their projects, they talked with Bob and his friends. Bob talked about his job as a television sports news reporter and about different sports and games he played as a youth. This was a big hit with the children as they also talked about their interests in hockey, basketball, and soccer. One of the girls shared her goal of becoming an Olympic hockey player for Canada.

The visits by Bob and his friends have developed into an intergenerational program with the school-age children after school. Volunteers from the seniors' centre come on a weekly basis to share their interests and hobbies, play games, help with homework, or just spend time talking with the children.

How Community Partnerships Can Support School-Age Programs

School-age child care professionals may greet the idea of developing partnerships and using community resources to enrich their curriculum with mixed reactions. Some cite the general hassle involved in recruiting and training volunteers. Others say they cannot get out into the community because of transportation problems. Some point to the fact that except for summers, the time children spend at the program is too limited. Some people say it is difficult because of the wide age differences of the children they serve. All these are valid reasons but should not deter you. The problems can be resolved, and you may find the benefits to the children will be well worth the effort.

School-age children are ready and eager to learn about the world outside their immediate environment. When they take that first step away from their home and out into the community, most find it a fascinating place and are eager to find their own place out in the world. Developmentally they are ready; they have good muscular control and want to try out their skills in new ways. Cognitively, they have a good memory and a much longer interest span than younger children. Coupled with this, they can postpone rewards, allowing them to work on projects that take a long time to complete. They are ready to consider different ways of thinking or doing things. They find that not everyone lives or thinks as they do. When presented with alternatives, they like to consider the options. In addition to all these characteristics, school-age children have a high energy level. They need lots to do and challenges to meet.

One way to involve your children in the community and develop partnerships is by inviting representatives from agencies and organizations to participate in activities at your facility. This method has a distinct advantage in that it eliminates transportation problems and does not entail travel time for the children. An added advantage

Figure 15-1 ■ **Both children and adults benefit from an intergenerational program.**

is that your program becomes known in the community, which may be helpful if you have to fundraise in the future. What is most important, however, is that both children and outside adults benefit from this relationship.

Intergenerational Programs

intergenerational program
planned, intentional interaction between different age groups in a variety of situations at a level that provides close communication, sharing of feelings and ideas, and cooperative activity

Intergenerational programs are one way to bring the community into the school-age program.

Intergenerational programs support the use of older people and young adults or teens as volunteers. Older persons especially are often looking for meaningful ways to share their lives and knowledge. At the same time, some children either do not know or do not live close to grandparents. Both can benefit from the relationship.

Many secondary school students are required to take part in community volunteer experiences as part of their course curriculum requirements. Some may be interested in working with children in their future career and would welcome the opportunity to spend some time with school-age children.

College and university students may also be interested in volunteering with children in a school-age program. Many of these young adults have skills in coaching sports, music, and dance and may have other special talents to share.

Older people will feel they can make a difference in someone else's life by sharing their interests, talents, or by just being a friendly person to talk to. The children will enjoy increased self-esteem because there is someone who listens to and cares about them. Both can learn to appreciate the similarities and differences that exist between the generations.

Children need to see older people working and playing in active, meaningful, and fulfilling ways to break down preconceived notions they may have of older adults.

Children also need to see teens and young adults taking part in meaningful activities in their community; this presents a good role model for them when they become teens.

Teens and young adults will also feel like they are making a contribution to their community and will refine skills and develop more confidence in themselves. The children will enjoy being with male and female role models who are a little older than they are, but have similar interests in music, movies, sports, and games.

Organizations That Support Intergenerational Projects with Older Adults

Intergenerational programs can be found in many communities throughout Canada. In British Columbia, the Volunteer Grandparents Society has been in operation for 25 years, bringing surrogate grandparents into children's lives. These programs and other similar ones are also available in other provinces across the country. United

---

Box 15-1 Every Day Millions of School-Age Children . . .

Every day millions of school-age children are asked, "What did you learn at school today?" The same answer is given—"Oh, nothing." Volunteer Grandparents learn how to ask the right questions about things that the children are interested in. They come to know that children often express their emotional feelings in a "code." (Kembar, 1984)

Box 15-3 ■ Recruiting Older Persons

Recruit older persons through the following:

- community centres
- groups for active seniors
- parks and recreation departments
- seniors' centres
- retirement communities
- churches
- special-interest groups: hobby clubs or environmental advocates
- local service clubs such as the Kiwanis or Rotary clubs
- senior citizens' service agencies (county or city)
- notices in volunteer information columns of newspapers

Generations Ontario is the province's "official voice" and coordinating centre for intergenerational programming. Its mission statement declares that "United Generations Ontario (UGO) is ... dedicated to promoting programs that bring young and old together in a spirit of cooperation, mutual support, and shared affection and regard. Our commitment is to empower people to create a vital volunteer exchange in caring and sharing" (Shipman, 2003, p. 6).

One of the most successful programs promoted by UGO is called Knitting Generations Together, in which seniors teach children how to knit. This program has the support of several business partners, including some major Canadian yarn companies. The program is inexpensive, promotes volunteering, and helps to break down age stereotyping (Andrew, 2002, p. 2). In aboriginal communities across Canada, young and old come together, providing opportunities for elders to pass on native traditions and languages that have been lost in previous years.

School-age programs can use the talents of older adults who come from a variety of jobs and professions. Artists, teachers, musicians, scientists, gardeners, veterinarians, and cooks are just a few who have knowledge and skills that can be shared with children. These people can do what grandparents do: plan special activities, demonstrate how to do things, go on outings together, and celebrate holidays and special occasions.

Activities for Volunteers and Children

The following is a list of just a few things volunteers can do with children. You can develop others based upon the needs of your particular program or the talents of the volunteers available to you.

Tutoring

- Assist individual children with math, English as a second language, or homework in general.

- Many retired teachers want to maintain contact with children but do not want the structure of a classroom setting. Teens and young adults are studying similar subjects such as English literature, science, and math and can assist children with their homework in these areas. Children will appreciate help with either homework or practising their English.

Science Experiences

- Demonstrate scientific phenomena such as electricity, chemistry, and weather through watching and participating in demonstrations.

- Plan and conduct hands-on science activities for the children following a demonstration (see the activities described in Chapter 12 or contained in that chapter's Selected Further Reading).

- Share an interest in exotic plants (orchids, cacti, tropical plants, etc.).

- Work with children to make exhibits for a school science fair, and invite other school groups and parents to see the results.

Cultural Awareness

- Demonstrate musical instruments specific to a culture. Let children play them.

- Cook and taste traditional foods. Use traditional cooking pots and implements.

- Teach dances of aboriginal peoples. Display pictures of or show examples of "traditional dress" or watch a video of some traditional dances.

- Display toys and games used by children in different cultures. Tell how they are used and let children try them.

- Read children's books from different countries in the native language, then translate. Discuss how the stories reflect life in that country.

- Show folk arts or crafts. Teach children how to create some typical folk objects.

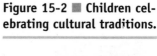

Figure 15-2 ■ Children celebrating cultural traditions.

- Share with children how holidays and special occasions are celebrated in the volunteer's native country.

- Develop a network of e-mail or pen pals from different countries. Help children write letters to a pen pal or send them an e-mail. Remember security measures regarding safe use of the Internet, discussed in Chapter 10.

Collections

- Share special collections: rocks, shells, fossils, insects, stamps. Work with children to classify and organize their own collection.

- Act as an adviser to a club based on collections.

Games

- Play table games with children. Canadian Monopoly®, Clue®, Trivial Pursuit®, Scrabble®, Life®, Crokinole, or card games can be enjoyed by children, teens, and older adults. Other group games include Telephone, Taking a Trip, Twenty Questions, or Charades.

Drama

- Work with children to write, produce, and perform a play. Children can make their own costumes, design and construct scenery, and set up proper lighting.

Music and Dance

- Bring in guitars, keyboards, and other musical instruments, and show the children how to play a simple tune.
- Demonstrate some simple dance steps in ballet, tap, clogging, and other current popular dances. Many teens and older adults are involved in dance groups and can share their techniques.
- Help children choreograph a dance. Perform for other children or parents.

Conversation

- Talk with and listen to children. Teens may be able to help children express their worries or fears or to discuss their problems.

Life Stories

- Older adults can tell children about their own childhood. Many children cannot conceive of a world without the modern conveniences they take for granted. A good storyteller can paint a picture of life in "the old days."
- Share photo albums of their own childhood with children. Show themselves as babies, as "school-agers," and as teens.
- Help children compile their own life story. Older children will be able to write theirs. Younger children can portray their history through photographs and drawings or collages.

Art Projects

- Work on special art projects. Try some new techniques for creating art: airbrush painting, mould making, using charcoal for drawing. Accompany staff and children on a tour of the studio of an artist who uses one of these techniques.

Figure 15-3 ■ A game of chess with a volunteer sharpens the ability to analyze problems and plan strategies.

Figure 15-4 ■ Volunteers can read a story and lead music time.

Chapter 15   Creating Community Partnerships

- Help children plan and paint a mural. This can either be a child-only project or a joint project between adults and children. Each could contribute something to the finished product.

Needlework and Crafts

- Share patterns with children and show them how to knit, cork, or crochet. Help them create simple garments: a scarf, hat, or small blanket.
- Demonstrate some embroidery stitches. Help children create a pillow cover, placemat, or wall hanging.
- Help children make a simple hand loom. Work together to weave placemats or make wall hangings or a simple quilt. Many traditions such as quilting are passed down from generation to generation in Mennonite and other rural communities.

Woodworking

- Assist children with the proper use of power tools and hand tools. Supervise woodworking projects.
- Accompany children to a furniture-manufacturing site.

Computers

- Work with children at the computer. Play games with children, and help them write stories or letters to a pen-pal or e-mail pal.
- All generations benefit by learning from each other by keeping up with new software and computer technology.
- Help children produce a monthly newspaper. Show them how to gather news, and go with them to interview interesting community people. Use a word-processing program to write the stories. Use a desktop publishing program to arrange the stories into a newspaper layout. Print the paper and distribute it to parents and staff.

Figure 15-5 ■ **Summer Games day.**

Gardening

- Talk with the children about the basic needs of plants. Help them to prepare, plant, and maintain a garden.
- Assist the children with planting a vegetable garden and harvest vegetables. Plan and prepare vegetables for a snack together (e.g., raw vegetables and a dip, or zucchini bread).

Photography

- Demonstrate the basics of using a camera for the children. If possible, help children to develop their own pictures, using computer software for digital cameras.
- Help children put together an exhibit of their photographs for a parent bulletin board.

Field Trips

- Assist staff and accompany children on field trips (e.g., park, zoo, beach, nature walk).

Sports

- Show the children proper techniques for playing popular sports, such as tennis, basketball, baseball, soccer, golf, and hockey. Practise with individual children who need help in perfecting their skills. Organize a game of fun and recreational sport.

Community Agencies, Organizations, and Businesses

You may decide you do not want volunteers to come to your school but would rather schedule periodic activities that use facilities in your community. Nearly every area will have some resources that would interest children. Check your neighbourhood, call government offices, and talk to people working with children in other programs. If you have lived in the area for a long time, where did your parents take you when you were a child?

Museums

Local history museums usually provide presentations or tours at the museum. Consider presentations on local history, plants, or animals indigenous to the area.

Children's discovery museums are marvellous places for a field trip; children can touch, manipulate, and participate in a variety of activities.

Art museums may conduct tours especially designed for children. Most large museums have a docents program, which comprises volunteers who know a great deal about the art in the galleries. Sometimes a tour is followed by a session in which the children can create their own art.

Library

Many libraries have a children's librarian who will help children choose books, and often have videos suitable for young children. Libraries may also have reading incentive programs: a reward for children who read a specified number of books.

Ask whether the library can supply or recommend storytellers. Ask the storyteller to visit the program to explain the art of storytelling and then tell a story.

Businesses

Some businesspeople may be willing to conduct a tour of their facility and then answer questions or tell children how to prepare themselves for that line of work. A newspaper office, dairy, radio or television station, restaurant, and a spa might interest children.

Fire Station

Take a tour of the facility, and discuss requirements for becoming a firefighter. Some departments have fire-prevention programs such as the Learn Not to Burn Program featuring Sparky the Dog, and could do a presentation.

Police Station

Take a tour of the facility, and discuss requirements for qualifying to be a member of law enforcement. Some departments have drug prevention programs and could give a presentation to the children.

Figure 15-6 ■ **Local businesses may be willing to conduct tours of their facilities.**

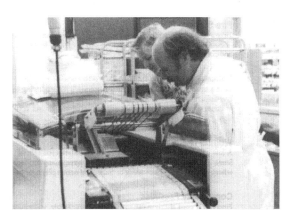

Wildlife Refuge, Conservation Areas, or Farms

Some communities have areas set aside for endangered animal species or plants. Some conduct nature walks; others may have plant propagation workshops where children help plant seeds or transplant native plants or trees. Many of these organizations can also plan a visit to school-age programs and will bring some of their animals.

Community Facilities

Take the children to a local riding stable, swimming pool, bowling alley, skating arena, or public tennis courts. These are excellent recreational activities that the children would particularly enjoy when they are scheduled to be at the school-age program all day.

Guest Visits

Periodic planned visits of people from various service organizations and businesses would also be a valuable asset to the school-age program. School-age child staff should meet with the presenter well ahead of time to arrange a date and time, and to discuss what will be included in the presentation. Children should be actively involved in the presentation as much as possible, either by viewing and examining items that the guest brings with them or by practising specific skills that the guest has taught them.

Parents are often good resources to either be a guest presenter themselves or to offer suggestions about other people in the community who might be of interest to the children.

Possible guest visits and presentations:

- exotic pet owner—iguanas, geckos, chameleons
- professional entertainer—storyteller, magician, dancer, musician
- professional or amateur athlete—teach specific skills and play a popular sport
- people in unique jobs—detective, film director, diver, weaver, animal trainer, earthworm farmer, actor, consumer-product-odour judge

Be sure to prepare the children ahead of time, connect the topic that the guest is focusing on with the curriculum, and talk with the guest ahead of time to be sure you know what sort of presentation will occur. The more hands-on the presentation is for the children, the more interested they will be. Have one of the children thank the guest at the end of the presentation or get the children to put together a thank-you letter and mail it after the presentation.

Developing these community partnerships and taking part in such activities will enhance your curriculum immeasurably. However, you may still be thinking that it is all too much trouble. Below are some ways to resolve problems that may arise.

Guidelines for Using Volunteers

It is important to have an organized method of managing your volunteers. They should see themselves as an integral part of what you are trying to achieve. To begin with, they will be more valuable if they know what they are expected to do, if they are trained and supported as they work with you, and if they know they are appreciated. Time and effort spent in setting up this kind of program will pay off in the long run. Your volunteers are more likely to stay with you longer, and will contribute to your curriculum.

Prepare a booklet of information that clearly states expectations for volunteers. Talk with them about the volunteer job and discuss their hours. Let them know who will be supervising them and to whom they can go when problems arise.

Check your local licensing requirements regarding criminal checks for volunteers. If necessary, tell volunteers where criminal checks can be done and how much a criminal check will cost.

Ask for a specific time commitment from each volunteer. Because a lot of effort goes into making a volunteer program successful, it is important to avoid constant change in its members. Have each volunteer say how much time and for how long a period he can commit to your program.

Plan and conduct an orientation for each volunteer. Develop a program that gives a general overview of your centre and its goals and philosophy. Suggest ways of interacting with children. Help them become familiar with policies and procedures for your program such as policies for guiding children's behaviour and procedures for serious occurrences. These are often found in a program handbook that can be given to the volunteer.

Provide ongoing supervision and training. Additional training as volunteers become more familiar with your program will enhance their self-esteem and make them more committed.

Have realistic expectations for your volunteers. Remember that they may not always be available when you need them. Older people sometimes have health problems, and teens and young adults have many other demands on their time.

Assign volunteers to simple, specific tasks at first. Start with having them work with one child at an activity. Be available to help them out when needed. As you learn more about each person's abilities and strengths, you can gradually allow greater responsibility.

Evaluate and provide feedback periodically. Remember that volunteers are not getting paid for their time. To make it worthwhile, they must feel they are appreciated and that they are learning.

You may have to make some adaptations to your environment in order to foster an effective intergenerational program. Consider the following changes to accommodate individuals from different generations in your setting:

- Place small sofas or wide armchairs in a quiet corner. This will invite opportunities for one or two children to sit together to read or talk with a volunteer.

- Set up a picnic table in the playground. A favourite place for many children is sitting at a picnic table with grandpa or grandma and other family members. This would provide opportunities for conversation and working on projects together.

- Provide at least one table indoors that is high enough for an adult, a young adult, or teen. Let children sit on stools so they can work with the volunteer at this table on art projects, science experiments, writing, or whatever they wish.

- Provide a place where children can leave a message for the volunteer. Because they are not there on a daily basis, the children may want to write them a note about something that happened or just leave a special drawing. This can be an important avenue for developing a relationship.

- Provide a place where volunteers can keep their own belongings secure and private.

- Plan a means for thanking volunteers. Write a letter at the end of a specified period of time or give an award. You can also have a special meeting or dinner to recognize the contribution that volunteers have made to your program.

Removing Barriers to Community Participation and Partnerships

At the beginning of this chapter, we indicated that many school-age child care professionals have mixed reactions to developing partnerships and using community resources. They cite a variety of reasons. Here are some solutions that other programs have found successful:

- Use public transportation—buses or trains.
- Walk to places that are close to the school-age program.
- Rent a bus or van.
- Take small groups at a time, using public transportation.
- Divide groups according to age levels of children and take trips to different sites.
- Use volunteers to assist staff with small groups on trips.
- Check licensing requirements regarding ratios of adults to children when on trips.
- Have parents pick up their children at the place being visited—park, swimming pool, library.
- Raise money for field trips by planning fundraising events that the children can be involved in. Get donations from local businesses and companies.

Box 15-4 ■ Reminder

Taking children on a field trip requires careful planning. Written permission from parents must be obtained. You should also check with your insurance agent to be certain that the form of transportation you will use is covered by your policy. See Appendices C and D for guidelines for planning a field trip and a sample permission form.

Intergenerational contact is not a new concept. In past generations young children were often cared for by older brothers and sisters, aunts, uncles, and grandparents. Each age level contributed to the child's knowledge of what growing up means, and was a model that children could imitate. Today's children who live in nuclear and mobile families miss that experience. Using older people, teens, or young people as volunteers can re-create that environment. It is well worth the effort in terms of benefits to the children and to the volunteers themselves.

Summary

Staff working in a school-age program are sometimes reluctant to use resources and build partnerships in the community. They say the problems are difficulty in recruiting and training volunteers, transportation problems, the short time children spend at the program, and the fact that children are at different age levels.

One way to involve children in the community is to invite individuals or representatives of agencies to visit the program. Using older people, teens, or young people as volunteers is one method that has been successful in some programs.

Older adults and volunteers from secondary schools, colleges, and universities have many talents and interests that they can share with children—anything from learning new soccer or golf tips to learning about quilting and how to play chess.

It is important to build partnerships with community agencies, organizations, and businesses that will interest children. Museums, libraries, and police and fire departments may have programs designed specifically for children. Businesses might be willing to conduct tours of their facilities or send a representative to the program.

An organized method of managing volunteers will make the program more effective. Prepare an information manual of information, have an orientation, provide ongoing supervision, and give volunteers feedback about performance. Start volunteers doing simple activities with the children. It is important to have realistic expectations for your volunteers and to thank them for the work they do.

You may have to alter your physical environment to make the most effective use of volunteers. Have places where a volunteer and child can sit together and a high table that is comfortable for them to sit at. Provide a place where children can leave messages for volunteers and where they can keep their belongings.

Remove barriers to community participation by using public transportation or walking to nearby sites. Be sure to check requirements regarding insurance to cover the children in your program when they are on trips, and the insurance requirements if you take a bus or van. Take small groups at a time. Check the licensing requirements for your province/territory regarding volunteers taking children outside the program. Ensure requirements about proper ratios of adults to children are being followed as well. Use volunteers to assist school-age child care professionals with individual children on trips. Plan ahead to let parents know that they can pick up children at the place being visited if that is convenient for them.

Key Term

intergenerational program

Student Activities

1. Talk to an older person in your family about her childhood. How different was it from your own growing years? In what ways might this information help you to understand that older person better?
2. Visit a seniors' centre in your community. Find out whether any of the seniors are involved in an intergenerational program. If they are, ask what they like to do and what they like about working with the younger generation. Ask them if they were involved in an orientation before they started to volunteer in the program and, if they were, what they did.
3. Plan one activity that a young person or teen could do with a group of nine-year-olds. List the materials required and describe any special procedures.

Review Questions

1. List the three reasons school-age child care professionals are hesitant about using resources in the community and building partnerships, and list three benefits.
2. State five places to recruit older persons as volunteers.
3. Describe five activities in which volunteers can share their cultural traditions with children.

4. Name an activity through which volunteers can share their life stories.
5. State the resources that are often available through museums.
6. List seven things you can do to make a volunteer program more effective.
7. In what ways can you change the environment in your program to make it easier for volunteers to interact with the children?
8. This chapter stated nine ways to remove barriers to community participation and partnership. What are they?

Case Study

Melinda is 65 years old, and she lives in a Mennonite community. She has seven grandchildren, and two of her grandchildren are in the after-school program at their school. One of her grandchildren asked her to come and visit the program. Now Melinda comes once a week and shows the children quilting stitches. She is planning to make a quilt with the children. Melinda wears traditional Mennonite clothing: netted cap, patterned dress, apron, and leather boots. Most of the children look forward to the days that Melinda comes to the program, but three boys never participate in the quilting activity. When she isn't there they make comments about her white hair and wrinkles and about her clothing. They say that quilting was "dumb" and that it is only for old people.

1. What should be done about the attitude that the three boys have towards Melinda?
2. Is there something Melinda could do to help the boys feel more comfortable with her?
3. Can you think of a way that the children can learn about and become more appreciative of older people and about traditions and culture?

References

Andrew, C. (2002, Fall). Parent's corner: Intergenerational programming. *Education Today*. Retrieved April 7, 2005, from http://www.opsba.org/pubs/et/articles/Fall_2002_Andrew.html

Kembar, N. (1984). *Volunteer Grandparents Society of BC start-up manual*. Vancouver: Volunteer Grandparents Society of British Columbia.

Shipman, M. (2003). *An Intergenerational Approach to Child Care: A Challenge During the International Year of Older Persons*. Retrieved April 7, 2005, from http://www.cccf-fcsge.ca/practice/programming/intergenerationalapproach_en.htm

Vanier Institute of the Family. (2000). A Society of All Ages: Those Who Know: Profiles of Alberta's Native Elders. *Transition Magazine*, pp. 1–2.

Young & old together: A resource manual for developing intergenerational programs. (n.d). Toronto: Ministry of Community and Social Services.

Selected Further Reading

Bogart, J., Fernandez, L., & Jacobson, R. (1997). *Jeremiah learns to read*. Toronto: Scholastic, Canada.

Community involvement. (1982, September–October). *School-Age Notes, 3*(1).

Horsfall, J. (1999). Welcoming volunteers to your child care center. *Young Children 54*(6), 35–36.

Lyons, C. (1985, Spring). Older adults in intergenerational programs: The other side of the story. *Beginnings, 2*(1), 3–5.

MacLeod, E. & Mantha, J. (2004). *The kids' book of great Canadians*. Toronto: Kids Can Press.

Munsch, R. & McGraw, S. (1986). *Love you forever.* Scarborough, ON: Firefly Books.

Schine, J. & Campbell, P. (1989). Young teens help young children for the benefit of both. *Young Children, 44*(3), 65–69.

Seefeldt, C., Warman, B., Jantz, R., & Galper, A. (1990). *Young and old together.* Washington, DC: National Association for the Education of Young Children.

Silverstein, S. (1964). *The Giving Tree.* New York: Harper Collins.

Wolf, D. (1985, Spring). Creating settings for multi-age caregiving. *Beginnings, 2*(1), 27–30.

Resource Organizations

BC Council for Families
#204–2590 Granville St.
Vancouver, BC, V6H 3H1
http://www.bccf.bc.ca

United Generations Ontario
1185 Eglinton Ave. East, Suite 604B
Toronto, ON, M3C 3C6
http://www.ohpe.ca/node/4902

Volunteer Grandparent's Society
203-2101 Holden Ave.
Burnaby, BC V5B 0A4
http://www.volunteergrandparents.ca

Websites

Fire Prevention Canada: Learn Not to Burn Program
http://www.firesafetycouncil.com/english/lntb.htm

Legacy Project—Planning a Grandparents Day
http://www.legacyproject.org/guides/gpday.html

Chapter 16

Quality and Standards

Objectives

After studying this chapter, the student should be able to:

- Discuss trends in school-age child care
- Explain the implementation of full-day early learning–kindergarten programs
- Identify components of quality school-age programs
- Identify standards and regulation requirements
- Discuss evaluation methods of school-age programs

 Profile

Parkdale Public School in Toronto, Ontario, supports partnerships between home, school, child care, and community, and offers a number of community-based programs that families can choose from. [The school has] an after-school international languages program, a healthy breakfast and lunch program, an intergenerational program, a school child care program, and a full-day kindergarten program. It shares the building with the Parkdale Community Centre, which operates various recreation programs in fitness, organized sports, swimming, and the arts.

Parkdale P.S. Child Care Centre is a licensed, nonprofit child care centre operated by the Toronto District School Board on the first floor of the school. It offers quality programs for children ages 3.8–12 years of age before and after school, and on PD days and holidays. The program focuses on all areas of child development, and play is an integral part of the curriculum. Encouraging children's self-esteem, independence, and self-motivation are key goals of the program.

Its seamless day approach with the kindergarten classes in the school offers an easy transition for 4- and 5-year-olds, and provides a more stable, comfortable, and supportive atmosphere for the children. The kindergarten and child care programs are established on an equal partnership basis and complement each other. They share facilities and the expertise of different personnel in the school community.

Common curriculum areas that are coordinated by the child care and the kindergarten include Language Experiences: listening centre and books; Arts: dramatic play, music, and visual art; Self and Society: nutrition and active play; and Math, Science, and Technology: water, sand, blocks, and construction. Their common philosophy is based on five areas: Literacy: applying language skills in all areas; Creativity and Aesthetic Expression: appreciation and imagination; Responsible Citizenship: values of peace, responsibility, and environment; Communication and Collaboration: working together cooperatively; and Information Management: making decisions and solving problems.

From Toronto District School Board, (n.d.), retrieved October 2004, from http://schools.tdsb.on.ca/parkdaleps.

Trends in School-Age Child Care

Over the last 15 to 20 years, school-age child care has expanded across the country. Young (1994) states that children between the ages of 4 and 12 spend an average of 18,000 hours in out-of-school programs. The time that school-age children spend outside school has become recognized as valuable time for the continued nurturance and development of the child socially, emotionally, physically, and intellectually through play. According to figures published by the Canadian National Child Care Study, for families where the lone parent or both parents are in the paid workforce, 40 percent of school-age children spend time out of school without any adult supervision (cited in Park, 1993). In a 1992 Canadian study, 67 percent of families with children 6 to 9 years of age were in school-age care either full time or part time (Lero, Pence, Shields, Brockman, and Goelman).

Achieving balance between child care and work can pose challenges for parents: 66 percent of employees surveyed by the Conference Board of Canada (1994) found that they had difficulty balancing their family and work lives (cited in Ontario Coalition for Better Child Care, 2000). This need for school-age child care has been confirmed in recent studies, as reported to the National Children's Alliance by the Canadian Child Care Federation (CCCF, 2006). This rapid proliferation of programs continues to be accompanied by attention to quality.

Research studies show that children who attend quality programs benefit in other aspects of their life. Studies by Vandell and Corasaniti (1988) at the University of Wisconsin and surveys by the California Department of Education (1996) found that children in quality programs were more self-assured, were less likely to be retained in a grade or placed in special education programs, had better social skills, and were less likely to have behaviour problems or become involved in vandalism around their school. Canadian and American cost-benefit analysis shows that the benefits of public spending on child care services provide savings in crime reduction and health, special education, and welfare costs (Ontario Coalition for Better Child Care, 2000; CCCF,

2006). Public perception of school-age child care has also changed since a 1993 Canadian study reported overwhelming parental support for school-age child care in schools (Cadden, 1993).

Progress of School-Age Care

Early generations of out-of-school programs were found in each province's child care and playground movements; their original purpose was to provide care for the children of working mothers and to "keep children off the street" during the times that they were not in school. In the early 1900s, some cities like Toronto (Victoria Creche) and Vancouver (City Creche), established child care for preschool and school-age children (Griffin et al., 1992, as cited in Jacobs and Mill, 2000). In these centres, children were served a hot lunch and received somewhat custodial care after school.

Early models for the school-age programs' curriculum were the traditional day camp, club, or recreational prototype. Within the province of Ontario, parks and recreation departments in larger cities like Toronto, Hamilton, London, and Ottawa provided supervised playground facilities where children could "exercise their bodies and limbs" (Kelso, as cited in Young, 1994, p. 29). Other types of out-of-school programs, sponsored by various clubs, settlement houses, and religious institutions, began to emerge.

During World War II, centres were set up to provide care for children of families who were working in the war industries. In British Columbia, child care services and licensed care emerged in 1943 in Vancouver, Victoria, Ocean Falls, and Port Alberni (Griffin et al., 1992, as cited in Jacobs and Mill, 2000). In 1946, many of the out-of-school programs across the country closed as soldiers returned from the war and women were discouraged from participating in the workforce.

The 1960s to 1980s brought many changes to out-of-school programs as women entered the workforce in greater numbers. Parents had to scramble to find ways to provide out-of-school care for their children. Sometimes this was done with a patchwork of various recreational programs, visits to friends' homes, or informal supervision by a neighbour (Jacobs and Mill, 2000). In Ontario, in 1966, the Day Nurseries Act was amended to allow school-age children to participate in licensed group care (Young, 1994). Also in 1966, the municipal government of the City of Edmonton, Alberta, played a large role in the establishment of school-age programs in cooperation with churches, schools, and other community groups (Jacobs and Mill, 2000).

If access and quality were to be promoted and maintained, the involvement of all those concerned with the education and care of children in a community was needed. This meant communication between parents and programs and between programs and community agencies. There needed to also be some coordination between the various types of programs.

In 1987, the release of the New Directions in Child Care in Ontario report identified that school boards and the child care community would work together to meet the needs of their families for child care, including school-age care. At this time, it was legislated that every new elementary school built in Ontario would house a child care centre that would provide school-age care (Ontario Ministry of Education & Ministry of Community Services, 1988–1989). This initiative lasted until the mid-1990s, when the provincial government was defeated.

During this time in Quebec, school boards began to recognize the success of school-age programs initiated by parents and assumed responsibility for the operation of these programs, as well as opening others in schools that didn't have a school-age program (Archambault, cited in Jacobs and Mill, 2000).

Over the years, the issue of children in self-care has been a great social concern. In many communities, formal school-age programs are nonexistent, and parents have to resort to the children coming home after school and letting themselves in. These **latch-key children** stay in their homes unsupervised until their parents return at the end of their work day. Early studies by Long and Long (1982) found that children who were in latch-key situations experienced an increase in fear, a heightened sense of social isolation, and a lower sense of self-worth. Other studies contradict some of these results, depending on the age and the readiness of the children to be in self-care.

Studies by Posner and Vandell (1994) found that low-income children who attended a formal school-age program were better adjusted emotionally and socially. They got along better with their peers and had better work habits and grades as compared to those who were in other more informal kinds of after-school arrangements. On measures of self-esteem, social adjustment, academic achievement, and peer relations, children who were in self-care did not differ from those who were supervised by an adult (Galambos & Garbarino, 1983; Rodman, Pratto, & Nelson, 1985; Vandell & Corasaniti, 1988).

Since the 1980s, school-age care has been recognized as an important part of services for children. It is now seen as a place for growth, nurturing, and development of life skills. The role of the adult is as a facilitator of positive development through healthy interactions, and issues of quality focus on the kinds of adult–child interactions that promote growth. To meet these needs, various training programs in school-age care emerged during the 1990s in postsecondary educational institutions across the country. Models such the **seamless day** for junior and senior kindergarten (as outlined in this chapter's opening Profile) and other approaches were established within the coordination of services between schools, child care, and recreation. Coplan (n.d.) reports that the Ottawa–Carleton District School Board (1997–1998) did a pilot study on junior kindergarten differentiated staffing where staff with early childhood diplomas led junior kindergarten classes. Findings showed that there was little difference between classes led by ECEs and traditional teacher-led classes on measures of children's skill development and abilities, parental satisfaction, and overall attitudes of parents toward junior kindergarten.

latch-key children
children who let themselves into their homes with a key and are unsupervised during out-of-school time until their parent(s) or guardian comes home

seamless day
concept that provides a link between junior and senior kindergarten and before and after kindergarten in child care; allows for the coordination of services, resources, and curriculum planning between qualified professionals, and ensures limited transitions for the children

Figure 16-1 ■ Before- and after-kindergarten group in child care.

Child Care in the 21st Century

In the June 2004 election, the federal Liberal Party made a commitment to develop a pan-Canadian child care system (for children from birth to 12 years of age) based on four principles—Quality, Universality, Accessibility, and Developmentally Appropriate Programming. This set of principles is referred to as QUAD and also includes the principle of Inclusion (see Child Care Advocacy Association of Canada, n.d.).

For over 20 years the **Child Care Advocacy Association of Canada (CCAAC)** has advocated for strong federal, provincial, and territorial policies that entitle all families in Canada to a publicly funded, nonprofit, quality, inclusive child care system. Research shows that publicly funded systems with low, affordable user fees are the most effective way of achieving the four principles of QUAD. Quebec has been the only province with a universal, publicly funded child care system that also includes before- and after-school care in every school for $7.00 a day. In spring 2000, British Columbia announced a $7.00 initiative for regulated school-based child care programs, while similar models were being discussed in Saskatchewan and Manitoba (Ontario Coalition for Better Child Care, 2000).

In October 2004, the Paris-based **Organisation for Economic Cooperation and Development (OECD)** reviewed 20 countries and their child care systems. Samplings of provinces included in the report were Prince Edward Island, Manitoba, Saskatchewan, and British Columbia. As compared to many European countries, Canada's system of child care was identified as being fragmented and chronically underfunded, with marginalized services of quality care and accessibility for all children. The report recommended that federal and provincial governments each pay 40 percent of daycare costs, with parents making up the remaining 20 percent and thus increase regulated child care spaces. This is more in keeping with high-quality child care systems in countries like the United Kingdom and Denmark. The report also recommended that child care be more integrated with kindergarten and that recruitment and training be improved (CBC, 2004). This may bring about another look at the "seamless day" JK/SK and child care approach, which would provide better coordination of services, resources, and curriculum between qualified professionals in child care and education. In November 2004, the Ontario Minister of Children and Youth Services announced the government's "Best Start Plan," which would provide combined kindergarten and child care programs in schools for four- and five-year olds. The government plans to expand on a pilot project called "First Duty," which is a blend of kindergarten, child care, and parenting centres that has been tested in five Toronto schools. Preliminary findings have shown that children entering grade 1 from the combined program are more prepared for classroom learning (www.childcareontario.org, n.d.).

A document entitled "Early Learning for Every Child Today: A Framework for Ontario Early Childhood Settings" was developed by the Best Start Expert Panel on Early Learning in 2006. It is a guide to support curriculum and pedagogy in Ontario's early childhood settings, including kindergarten classrooms and child care centres (focus up to age 8) and was based on the recommendations of the Early Years Study by McCain and Mustard in 1999. Included are six statements of principles reflecting important beliefs, values, experiences, and current research findings that support effective practices. The document also has a section about understanding children's continuum of development that assists staff with the processes of observing, documenting, and planning curriculum. Examples illustrating how to

Child Care Advocacy Association of Canada (CCAAC)

advocates for strong federal and provincial/territorial policies that entitle all families in Canada to a publicly funded, nonprofit, quality, inclusive child care system

Organisation for Economic Co-operation and Development (OECD)

a forum in which governments can work together to solve social, economic, and environmental issues put the statements of principles into practice are provided, along with approaches to assessment and evaluation. A glossary of research-based definitions and an international review of early childhood programs completes the document (Best Start, 2006).

Full-Day Early Learning–Kindergarten Programs and Extended-Day Programs

As a result of much research about the value and importance of early learning (discussed above), the seamless day, and quality programs for children in their early years, Full Day Kindergarten began its implementation in Ontario and British Columbia by the fall of 2010. These provinces have planned to initiate these systems of integrating early care and learning kindergarten programs over a period of 2–5 years. PEI began this process in 2008.

In Ontario, responsibilities for child care policy and programs for children from birth to age 12 were moved from the Ministry of Children and Youth Services to the Ministry of Education in 2010. Bill 242 was passed, amending the Education Act to allow for the implementation of a plan for a seamless, integrated service delivery of early learning programs. This bill mandates school boards to provide early learning programs for 4- and 5-year-olds and to provide fee-based extended-day, before- and after-school programs. Legislation establishes expectations for teachers and registered early childhood educators to work together in the planning and delivery of JK/K programs, to be involved in the assessment and observation of children, to communicate with families, and to be responsible for maintaining a healthy, social, emotional learning environment.

Registered ECEs are responsible for leading extended-day (fee-based) programs. The program is play based and complements the core kindergarten day. As with the full-day JK/K, the ratio of staff to children during the extended day is 2:26. The extended-day component, if operated by the school board, will not be subject to the Day Nurseries Act or its licensing requirements. Further amendments also allow for third-party agreements with community agencies/partners for the provision of extended-day programs. This is often dependent on the individual schools' projected enrolments of JK/K children and can also include children in grades 1 and 2 (MOE Memorandum, 2010). Program guidelines for the kindergarten day and extended day are identified at the end of the chapter under "Further Resources."

In September 2010, the Ministry of Education in British Columbia also began phasing in universal access to full-day kindergarten for 5-year-olds over two years. The BC Government's vision of a high-quality, play-based kindergarten program supports research about the long-term benefits for children's academic and social skills, including building a strong foundation for lifelong learning. It provides parents with an opportunity to make connections with their local community school and provides more economic benefits related to child care (British Columbia Ministry of Education, 2010).

Prince Edward Island has offered a full-day kindergarten program since 2008. Responsibility for early childhood education moved from the Department of Social Services to the Department of Education and Early Childhood Development. At this time, a play-based integrated curriculum was implemented in all kindergartens. Each kindergarten has a maximum of 15 students, and the focus is on learning skills and concepts through exploration, discovery, and hands-on involvement.

Quebec has offered full-day kindergarten programs for 5-year-olds since 1997, with (fee based) after-school care offered in every school.

Other provinces may have some variations of full-day kindergarten programs; sometimes operating every other day, for shortened hours in the day, or under a different model. Some provinces are looking at implementing a model similar to those in Ontario, British Columbia, and Prince Edward Island in the near future (Alberta Teachers Association, 2010).

The Ontario Coalition for Better Child Care and Jacobs and Mill (2000) identified the following components of a quality program for school-age children:

1. *Low ratios:* Smaller groups and ratios between children and staff provide more opportunities to develop meaningful and warm interactions. The Policy Research on Children, Youth and Families School-Age Care Workshop (as cited in Jacobs, 2000) recommended ratios of 1:12 after school for children five years and older; 1:24 at lunch time (the school-age child care professional being a trained person); 1:8 for full-day programs on professional development days and holidays; and 1:10 for junior and senior kindergarten programs. Maximum group size was 24 for grades 1 to 6 and 20 for four- and five-year-olds. A 1990 survey of licensed school-age programs in Ontario (Jacobs and Mill, 2000, p. 12; ARA Consulting Group, 1990) indicated that many schools held child–staff ratios similar to these recommendations.

2. *Qualified staff and training:* Postsecondary early childhood training with an emphasis on learning about child development, learning how to communicate with other adults working with the children, and developing the ability to understand preadolescent needs were seen as important. Staff with postsecondary training provide more developmentally appropriate activities and higher levels of language stimulation. Continuity of staff–child relationships is also essential to the child's overall well-being and development.

3. *Well-compensated staff:* Staff need better wages and work conditions in order to stay with their jobs and to maintain consistency.

4. *Appropriate physical environment:* Adequate space for a minimum of 2.8 usable square m (25 square ft.) of space per child in a room is necessary in order to avoid potential behaviour problems that result from overcrowding.

5. *Nonprofit delivery:* Better conditions of health, safety, trained and consistent staff, and a developmentally appropriate program provide greater public accountability.

6. *Regulatory standards:* Regulations ensure that minimum standards of quality care are established, enforced, and monitored regularly.

7. *Curriculum:* Program flexibility and the willingness of the staff to meet the needs and interests of the children enrolled in the program are crucial in terms of each child's willingness to attend a school-age program. The program's affiliation and its location (for example, whether in a school or recreational setting) would determine the activities offered. Focus should be on play with friends, development of leisure skills, and the provision of a variety of activities that encourage children's sense of industry, adventure, and imagination.

8. *Teacher–staff communication:* The researchers recommend that teacher–staff communication needs to be addressed in order to achieve a quality program. Messages about general health are communicated between the classroom teacher and the school-age child care professionals; however, information about the

child's day or about any problems the child may have experienced will require parental permission. The types of curriculum activities, such as crafts, done in the classroom vs. in the after-school program need better coordination. As discussed in Chapter 3, a permission form signed by the parent will allow for more detailed communication (see Appendix D).

9. *Preadolescents:* Curriculum activities for children in the age group of 9 to 12 need to be developmentally appropriate and provide challenges that meet preadolescent interests and abilities.

These findings were based on a combination of research studies that used several different quality measurement rating scales developed by school-age child care associations, such as the NSACA Standards for Quality School Age Care (mentioned later in this chapter) in the United States and other quality assurance instruments from children's recreation and sports activities. The most common quality rating scale used in Canada is the School-Age Care Environmental Rating Scale (SACERS), which was developed by a team of Canadians and Americans. It will be discussed later in this chapter as well. Other findings came from interviews about general practices that people had when working in school-age programs.

Standards, Regulations, and Accreditation

Currently, the agencies responsible for the licensing of school-age care in Canada differ from one province to another, meaning that some family-home child care and recreation and parks programs are not regulated. In some provinces, the responsibility for licensing falls under the provincial Ministry of Health, whereas in others it falls under the Department of Education.

Variations, associated problems, and inconsistencies are often due to a school-age program being with a different agency and host. Some programs may be in a school setting but be operated by a social service agency and be licensed by a ministry other than the one that regulates classroom education for the children during the day.

Table 16-1 summarizes the current governance for early childhood education (ECE) by province/territory, with particular reference to the integration of early-learning kindergarten programs. Manitoba has developed a policy to support partnerships between the school system and child care centres. Quebec has integrated school-age child care into its family policy up to age 12. It is funded at $7/day and is administered by the Department of Education (Canadian Child Care Federation, 2006). As mentioned above, in Ontario, responsibility for child care has moved from the Ministry of Children and Youth Services to the Ministry of Education. Child care programs, including school-age programs, follow regulations set out by the Day Nurseries Act, which is currently under review. Full-day kindergarten and extended-day school-age programs operated by school boards have their own regulations.

Licensing requirements often reflect only minimal standards that are mainly focused on health and safety provisions—basically ensuring that the service does not harm a child. In an informal survey conducted by the Canadian Child Care Federation, 68 percent of child care respondents said the monitoring of child care programs in their province/territory was inadequate (Child and Family Canada, 1994). Government reports from Ontario (1990) and Alberta (1994) reported similar concerns (Andrew, 2002). A more specific concern related to school-age programs in child care is that the regulations in many provinces/territories are not specific to

Table 16-1 ■ Governance for Early Childhood Education by Province/Territory

	Single ECE Department	Common ECE Supervisory Unit	Integrated ECE Framework	Local Authority	Public Oversight/Advisory
NL			Under discussion: *Developing a Provincial Early Learning Strategy: What We Heard* (September 2011)	Kindergarten: 5 school districts. Child care fee subsidies: 4 regional health authorities. Child care licensing: Department of Child, Youth and Family Services	
PE	Department of Education and Early Childhood Development	Early Childhood Development Section except kindergarten	*Securing The Future For Our Children: Preschool Excellence Initiative* (May 2010)	Kindergarten: English and French Program Divisions. Child care: Child Care Facilities Board. Child care fee subsidies: Department of Community Services, Seniors and Labour	Children's Secretariat, Early Years Steering Committee, Child Care Facilities Board
NS				Pre-primary: 8 regional school boards. Child care: 4 regional social service sectors	Child and Youth Strategy
NB	Department of Education and Early Childhood Development	Early Childhood Development Division responsible for all ECE and related programs except kindergarten	Under discussion: *Government Renewal: Discussion Paper* (September, 2011)	Kindergarten: 18 school districts. Child care: Regional Early Childhood Service Coordinators responsible for child care licensing. Child care fee subsidies. 8 Social Development regional offices	Ministerial Advisory Committee on Early Learning and Child Care
QC			*Québec Family Policy*	Kindergarten: 17 school districts. Child care: 165 regional coordinating offices of the Ministère de la Famille et des Aînés	Conseil de la famille et de l'enfance, replaced in 2011 with regional advisory committees
ON	Ministry of Education	Early Learning Division		Kindergarten: 72 school boards. Child care: 47 Consolidated Municipal Service Managers and District Social Services Administration Boards. Education to take over child care licensing in Jan. 2012.	

	Department	Division / Notes	Strategic Plan	Kindergarten / Child Care	Council / Committee
MB			Family Choices: Manitoba's Five-Year Agenda for Early Learning and Child Care (2008)	Kindergarten: 37 school districts Child care: regional offices	Child Care Regulatory Review Committee and Provincial Healthy Child Advisory Committee
SK	Department of Education	Early Years Branch includes all ECE and related programs except kindergarten		Kindergarten: 28 school divisions Child care: 3 regional offices	
AB				Kindergarten: Over 300 school authorities offer Early Childhood Services (kindergarten, pre-kindergarten and early intervention programs) Child care: 10 regional Child and Family Services Authorities	Alberta Association for the Accreditation of Early Learning and Care Services
BC				Kindergarten and StrongStart: 57 school districts Child care fee subsidies: Ministry of Children and Family Development Child care licensing: 5 regional health authorities	Provincial Child Care Council
YK				Kindergarten: 1 French school board and the Assistant Deputy Minister of Public Schools Child care: Child Care Services Unit in the Department of Health and Social Services	
NT	Department of Education, Culture and Employment	Division of Early Childhood and School Services	Building on our Success: Strategic Plan 2005–2015	Kindergarten: Early Childhood and Schools Services Child care: Early Childhood Program	
NU	Department of Education	Early Childhood Division/School Services Division	In development	Kindergarten: 3 regional School Operations Child care: 3 regional education officers oversee child care licensing and subsidies	

Source: Provincial/territorial profiles www.earlyyearsstudy.ca.

Figure 16-2 ■ Indoor space should meet the needs of the children served and be arranged so that a variety of activities can take place.

school-age children. For example, in many provinces/territories, space requirements for preschool children are the same as those for school-age children regardless of the latter's increased physical size (Jacobs and Mill, 2000; Canadian Child Care Federation, 2006). Some provinces have amended their legislation to include specific requirements for school-age care. Table 16-2 shows additional regulations across Canada regarding licensing procedures, specific school-age training and requirements for space and furnishings that are specific to school-age children and that address their different needs.

Professional Associations in Canada

Across Canada, there are a number of professional associations in the fields of child care and recreation. A few of them will be discussed here. Many other child care associations can be accessed through the Canadian Child Care Federation Website listed at the end of the chapter.

Canadian Child Care Federation (CCCF)

Canadian Child Care Federation (CCCF)

professional organization that promotes the recognition of quality care for children from infancy to age 12; CCCF advocates for professionals in the field of child care, building credibility through an accreditation system

accreditation

process by which a representative body recognized by the service community and the community in general establishes standards that are above minimum regulatory requirements of the government; programs apply for evaluation and receive a certificate when they meet the standards

The **Canadian Child Care Federation (CCCF)** promotes the recognition of quality care for children from infancy to age 12. The Federation is an advocate for professionals in the field of child care and works toward building credibility and an accreditation system for operators of child care centres. The guiding principles of the **accreditation** process include assessing the facility, funding, policy and procedural guidelines, strategic planning, management information systems, public relations, and hiring practices (Ferguson, 1995; Doherty, 1991). Accreditation is

> a process by which a representative body, recognized by both the service community and the community in general, establishes standards for services. The standards are above the minimum regulatory requirements of the government. Programs apply on a voluntary basis for evaluation against the standards and, if found to meet or surpass them, are granted a certificate which recognizes this fact (Doherty, 1991, p. 1).

Various municipalities in Ontario, such as Hamilton, Kitchener-Waterloo, and London, have implemented community accreditation programs for licensed child care centres, including school-age programs. The initiative is called "Raising the Bar on Quality." It is a voluntary process that builds on the strengths and supports the quality of child care programs. The initiative involves many aspects of the community including social planning councils, government departments, training institutions, various types of child care service programs, and child and family resources. Training sessions in the use of the School-Age Environmental Rating Scale (SACERS), along with other age-specific rating scales, have been offered to community school-age child care professionals as part of this accreditation process.

Table 16-2 ■ Regulations Specific to School-Age Children

Note: The checkmarks in PEI relate to that province's application process; checkmarks in B.C. relate to a checklist on school-age care. Yukon has separate regulations for school-age programs; Quebec doesn't have guidelines.

Specific School-Age Needs	NL	NS	NB	PEI	ON	MB	SK	AB	BC	NT/NU
Discipline				✔				✔		
Furnishings				✔				✔		
Licensing procedures				✔	✔					
Program design; provisions		✔		✔		✔	✔	✔	✔	
Sleeping arrangements					✔					
Specific school-age training								✔		
Staffing	✔			✔	✔	✔		✔		
Subsidy age extensions					✔	✔		✔		
Supervision	✔					✔	✔	✔		
Usable floor space; physical space				✔	✔		✔	✔	✔	
Washroom facilities (privacy)						✔	✔	✔	✔	

Governance for ECE by province/territory. Reprinted with permission from the Early Years Study/Margaret Wallace and McCain Family Foundation. www.earlyyearsstudy.ca.

College of Early Childhood Educators in Ontario

The **College of Early Childhood Educators** is a self-regulating body that identifies standards of practice and supports the promotion of advocacy. The Early Childhood Educators Act, 2007 sets out how the College regulates the profession, defines the qualifications and requirements for those working as early childhood educators, and accredits those who meet them. Members are held accountable to practise according to the act, which includes a code of ethics and standards of practice. This provides confidence that those who work as early childhood educators are qualified, competent, and ethical. The college also acts in an advocacy role for the profession, promoting and supporting the economic and professional interests of its members. This may include raising awareness of the value of the work of ECEs, responding to government and policy makers, and providing current research and educational resources (College of Early Childhood Educators, 2012).

College of Early Childhood Educators
Ontario's self-regulating body identifying standards of practice, qualifications, and requirements for those working as early childhood educators; accredits those who meet the standards

Association of Early Childhood Educators in Ontario (AECEO)
professional organization of individuals who work in early childhood and child care settings; advocates for quality programs; provides leadership between professionals

Child and Youth Care Association of Alberta (CYCAA)
organization of child care professionals who have common interests, concerns, and objectives in providing quality services to children and youth

The **Association of Early Childhood Educators in Ontario (AECEO)** is a professional association of early childhood educators. Its mission is to serve and act on behalf of ECEs, advocate on behalf of the profession, promote quality early learning and care, and provide leadership between professionals. The association supports the professional growth of ECEs by providing ongoing professional development, current research, and resources about early childhood education and care.

The **Child and Youth Care Association of Alberta (CYCAA)** is an organization of child care professionals who have common interests, concerns, and objectives in providing quality services to children and youth. The objectives of this association are

- to promote, improve, and maintain progressive standards of child and care services
- to provide a democratic organization which will unite all persons involved with child and youth care and provide a forum for discussion of ideas and concerns
- to promote child and youth care as a profession
- to act as an educational forum for the exchange of ideas and information
- to form liaisons with other child and youth care associations
- to promote and oversee the certification of child and youth care workers

Child and Youth Care Association of Alberta.

Association for the Accreditation of Early Learning and Care Services (AELCS)
manages the accreditation process in child care centres and contracted family child care agencies in Alberta

School-Age Child Care Association of British Columbia (SACCA B.C.)
province-wide nonprofit organization that is open to professionals and students working or studying in the school-age child care field; its goal is to improve the availability, quality, and affordability of school-age child care

The **Association for the Accreditation of Early Learning and Care Services (AELCS),** in partnership with the Alberta Child Care Network Association and the Canadian Child Care Federation, manage the accreditation process in child care centres and contracted family child care agencies in Alberta. The accreditation model was developed with the participation and consultation of the child care community. The process is voluntary and goes beyond the minimum standards set by the province to attain a higher standard of practice and quality care (Alberta Association for the Accreditation of Early Learning and Care Services, n.d.).

The **School-Age Child Care Association of British Columbia (SACCA B.C.)** is a province-wide, nonprofit organization open to professionals and students working or studying in the school-age child care field. The association's goal is to improve the availability of quality, affordable school-age child care by providing programs and services to professionals in this field. SACCA's objectives focus on the following:

- to increase public awareness through lobbying, workshops and forums
- to provide professional networking through a province-wide newsletter, directories, and other professional events
- to develop educational services through a program of guest speakers, seminars, and workshops
- to promote the development and advancement of a province-wide voluntary set of standards for school-age child care

School-Age Child Care Association of British Columbia.

Canadian Parks and Recreation Association (CPRA)
national voice for a network of people who are in partnership with communities to build a healthy, active quality of life and support social-recreation programs out of school hours

The **Canadian Parks and Recreation Association (CPRA)** is a national voice for a network of people who are in partnerships with communities to build a healthy, active quality of life. Their values place emphasis on inclusion, accountability, partnerships, diversity, teamwork, collaboration, and equity (Canadian Parks and Recreation Association, n.d.).

Some social-recreation programs during out-of-school hours are operated by municipal recreation departments and community organizations. These programs are offered on specific days for a designated period of time, often during school breaks and during the summer months. This is generally an unregulated system, but one that offers some interest, particularly for older school-age children. Young (1994) recommends a better link between school-age child care services and recreation programs. This would result in improved coordination of services and families having easier access.

In 1994, **Parks and Recreation Ontario (PRO)** launched the Quality Assurance in Children's Recreation and Sport Initiative in order to establish a consistent standard of quality for their programs. The Quality Assurance Measurement Tool gave providers a way to evaluate their program through a set of criteria focused on developmental outcomes. From this evaluation process, providers could identify both strengths and areas where they could improve. By implementing this process, parks and recreation programs would become more accountable to parents, increase knowledge and expertise in child development amongst staff, provide a necessary basis for further training of staff, and develop a collection of resources for parents and staff (De Vaal, 1998).

Figure 16-3 ■ **Staff members and program directors work together to implement the accreditation process.**

Parks and Recreation Ontario (PRO)
dedicated to promoting the value and benefits of parks and recreation to the public

National Associations in the United States

National School Age Care Alliance (NSACA)

National School Age Care Alliance (NSACA) sets standards that reflect the best practices for children between the ages of 5 and 14 in group settings where children attend on a regular basis.

NSACA also believes that there is a need for a system that raises public awareness of the importance of out-of-school care and has developed guidelines for centres to improve quality. The Alliance has established as set of standards in the following areas: human relationships, indoor and outdoor environments, activities, safety, health, nutrition, and administration.

National Association for the Education of Young Children (NAEYC)

The **National Association for the Education of Young Children (NAEYC)** is a large, national, professional association that provides a service for accrediting programs that serve children from birth through the elementary years. The program is administered by the National Academy of Early Childhood Programs. The system is voluntary and involves a three-step process: self-study by the director, program staff, and parents; validation visits by trained professionals; and an accreditation decision by a team of Early Childhood experts. The categories of centre operations that are covered by accreditation are the following: interactions among staff and children, curriculum, staff–parent interactions, staff qualifications and development, administration, physical environment, health and safety, nutrition and food service, and evaluation processes.

National School-Age Care Alliance (NSACA)
develops best practices standards for children aged 5 to 14

National Association for Family Child Care (NAFCC)

According to the **National Association for Family Child Care (NAFCC)**, one million family child care providers care for four million children, some of whom are elementary school age. With the move to professionalize all child care settings, NAFCC felt it important to develop a process for accrediting home-based child care. The Association's quality standards for NAFCC accreditation were developed in conjunction with the Family Child Care Project at Wheelock College, Boston. NAFCC's focus is on relationships, environment, developmentally appropriate activities, health and safety, and ethical professional practices.

Training

Between 1997 and 1999, a group of Canadian researchers conducted a study called the National School-Age Care: Quality Assurance Study/Garde en Milieu Scolaire: GEMS (Jacobs, Mill, & Jennings), funded by Child Care Visions, part of Human Resources Canada. The study of the current state of school-age care in Canada included an assessment of training programs.

School-age-care training refers to both prior and in-service education that staff receive relating to school-age children and programming. Postsecondary training requirements and opportunities vary from province to province. Many provinces do not require any training at all. (In Alberta, some municipalities have specific training for those working in school-age child care; see Table 16-2.) In the study, program staff were reported to have a variety of types of certification including certificates, diplomas (ECE or Recreation), and degrees (Social Sciences or Education). Eighty-five percent of respondents came from colleges and CEGEPs (Quebec). The kind of training they received depended on what was offered by the institution. Some staff received training from a complete, self-contained school-age care program of study; others took a school-age programs option within a larger program, such as in ECE. Other staff took a few courses related to school-age child care. Courses of study usually included topics such as child development, behaviour guidance, curriculum planning, recreation, and field placement. Some staff received recognition for prior work experience either for a field-placement course credit in a diploma program or through the process of Prior Learning Assessment (PLA). Some provinces, such as Alberta, offer in-service training courses in out-of-school care that focus on program planning, cross-cultural understanding, administration, and behaviour guidance.

The report concluded that there are gaps between needs and availability of training opportunities across Canada. The lack of training requirements for school-age program staff in many provinces contributes to problems such as low salaries and status.

A reconceptualist movement in ECE around the world is worthy of discussion at this point with respect to the training of those who want to work with children in kindergarten programs and in school-age child care/extended-day programs. The emergence of a reconceptualist movement in ECE began in the early 1990s through a series of conferences and publications that challenged current practices. Some of the issues addressed include critiques about developmentally appropriate practice (DAP) and mainstream definitions of "quality" early childhood services; along with perspectives of children, childhood, and diversity. The reconceptualist movement asks ECE professionals to do some deeper thinking about the meaning behind what they value and believe, and then consider how they will put this into practice in their daily work with children and families. This movement has brought forth much reflective thinking about the best approaches to program planning and curriculum development. Some of this change has been stimulated by interest in particular approaches such as emergent curriculum and Reggio Emilia, which then culminate in the establishment of meaningful and thoughtful program philosophies. (Pacini-Ketchabaw & Pence, n.d.).

Report Recommendations: A Model School-Age Child Care Program

Jacobs (2000) identifies a model school-age program. As in some European communities, services for children and families are grouped together in one area. Within this approach, children can move freely between school, after-school care, recreation programs, and other related facilities (pool, library, park, skating rink). This is a model outlined in the Profile at the beginning of this chapter. This approach reduces stresses associated with transportation and provides an opportunity to create a seamless day for school-age children. Communication between teachers and staff in the child care centre regarding program planning, curriculum development, and individual children's needs is facilitated as they work together in the same building. Sharing space, materials, and equipment would provide for better working conditions and lower costs. Staff schedules might be less fragmented by split shifts, giving them a better salary and benefits when they work full-time.

Jacobs's report also recommended more research in the following areas:

- more specific regulations for school-age programs
- the most appropriate and effective training
- types of in-service training
- the needs of children aged 9–12
- staff working conditions: schedules, salaries, benefits
- use of emergent curriculum in school-age programs
- types of parent–staff communication
- evaluation processes of quality (SACERS)

Evaluation

School-Age Care Environmental Rating Scale (SACERS)

Developed by Harms, Jacobs, and White (1996), the **School-Age Care Environmental Scale (SACERS)** grew out of a need to have a method of rating programs that serve the 5-to-12-year age range. Harms, Jacobs, and White drew from a number of sources, including Harms's earlier rating scale, and developed criteria for developmentally appropriate practice. The authors also used research studies done in Canada and the United States (Galambos & Garbarino, 1983; Vandell & Corasanti, 1988; Vandell, Henderson, & Wilson, 1988).

School-Age Care Environmental Scale (SACERS)
a method of rating programs that serve children 5 to 12 years of age

Using SACERS, specially trained observers follow a numerical scale to assess seven categories on a scale of one to seven based on written criteria for each item. The following is a brief description of the items listed in each category.

Figure 16-4 ■ Trained observers use the School-Age Care Environmental Scale to determine whether a program is meeting standards for developmental appropriateness.

Space and Furnishings, Indoor Space

The scale assesses whether there is sufficient space for gross-motor activities as well as space for privacy. The room arrangement should have adequate space for all activities: homework, routine care, learning, and recreation. Furnishings should allow for children's relaxation and comfort and gross-motor activities. There should be easy access to the host facility and space for staff.

Health and Safety

This section examines health policies and practices. Emergency and safety procedures must be in place, attendance monitored, and departures managed to bring about maximum safety for the children. Meal times are planned as a learning experience, and personal hygiene is part of the educational program.

Activities

Eight types of activities are described in this section: arts and crafts, music and movement, blocks and construction, drama/theatre, language/reading, math/reasoning, science/nature, and cultural awareness. Assessment is made on the basis of frequency, variety of materials and equipment available, and age-level appropriateness. The cultural-awareness category includes ways that staff encourage an acceptance of differences.

Interactions

Interactions refers to staff interactions with children, parents, and one another. Interactions with children should support autonomous behaviour and convey feelings of respect and interest. Staff should also talk to children about ideas related to play activities, helping children to extend their ideas. Parents are informed about policies concerning discipline and also receive information on parenting, health care, sports, and cultural activities for families. Parents are included in decision making as well. The program should promote positive interactions among staff members and classroom teachers.

Program Structure

The schedule of the day should allow smooth transitions and time for children to make choices of activities. Community resources should be used to plan field trips or special-occasion activities. The director/key staff member meets on a regular basis with the host of the program to discuss and resolve any problems.

Staff Development

There should be opportunities and support for staff to attend professional conferences or workshops. Staff meetings include planned opportunities for participants to share new ideas and materials. Self-evaluation by staff is an ongoing process.

Special Needs Supplementary Items

This section is used in conjunction with the preceding items when children with special needs are included in the program. Items address objectives to bring about individualization, appropriate learning opportunities, efforts to promote peer interactions, and ways that staff promote communication.

The full text of this rating scale can be obtained from municipal and provincial community social service and child care departments or from:

Teachers College Press
Columbia University
1234 Amsterdam Avenue
New York, NY 10027
http://www.teacherscollegepress.com

Summary

The perception of school-age care has changed from being simply a safe place for children to one that is a place for growth, nurturing, and the development of life skills. The 1960s in Canada brought about some regulatory changes by adding school-age programs to existing child care systems in Ontario and in some individual municipalities in Alberta. In the 1980s and 1990s, more provinces set up school-age programs, either in association with child care centres or under the jurisdiction of school boards, like those in Quebec. In Ontario, new schools were built with attached child care centres that provided school-age programs. Research reports identified the effects of being latch-key children on emotional and social well-being, and the benefits of supervised out-of-school programs. Other models of the seamless day and differential staffing were piloted for kindergarten programs in schools and child care centres.

In the June 2004 election, the federal Liberal Party made a commitment to develop a pan-Canadian universal child care system for children from infancy to age 12 based on four principles: Quality, Universality, Accessibility, and Developmentally Appropriate Programming, with the addition of Inclusion.

In Ontario a document entitled "Early Learning for Every Child Today: A Framework for Ontario Early Childhood Settings" was developed by the Best Start Expert Panel on Early Learning in 2006. As a result of this report and much research about the value and importance of early learning, the seamless-day, and quality programs for children in their early years, full-day kindergarten programs have been implemented in Ontario and British Columbia. Prince Edward Island began this process in 2008 and other provinces are beginning to look at similar models.

The Child Care Advocacy Association of Canada and the Canadian Child Care Federation continue to work together to support the five key principles of quality, universality, accessibility, developmentally appropriate programming, and inclusion. Quality child care serves the best interests of children and families and requires the partnership of parents; professional associations; federal, provincial/territorial, and municipal governments; training institutions; and child care professionals.

The Ontario Coalition for Better Child Care and Dr. Ellen Jacobs identify important components of a quality school-age program including low ratios, qualified and trained staff, well-compensated staff, an appropriate physical environment, nonprofit delivery, curriculum guidelines, communication, preadolescent programming, and regulatory standards.

Standards and regulations for child care in general and the governing bodies that supervise these programs are different in each province and territory. The Canadian Child Care Federation supports the need for reviewing the policies for school-age child care across Canada. Many provinces have amended their legislation to include some requirements for school-age care. Unregulated care exists in many types of school-age arrangements, including family child care, recreation centres, and parks programs. School-age programs in schools in the province of Quebec are run by the school boards and fall under very minimal regulations of the Ministry of Education. Ontario has also moved child care to the Ministry of Education and school boards offer extended day programs in schools or in with third-party child care centres. Research reports by Lero, Pence, and Jacobs have indicated that regulated care is more likely to produce higher-quality child care.

Various associations across Canada are developing accreditation processes in all sectors of child care and recreation, including school-age care. The Canadian Child Care Federation developed an accreditation process for operators of child care centres; the College of Early Childhood Educators in Ontario is a self-regulatory body that has established a set of standards of professional practice for ECEs; the Association for the Accreditation of Early Learning and Care Services in Alberta has set up an accreditation program for child care centres; and local municipal and community agencies are implementing effective models of accreditation for professionals working in child care centres.

Professional associations such as the Child and Youth Care Association of Alberta (CYCAA) and the School Age Child Care Association of British Columbia (SACCA B.C.) have established standards and guidelines for professional practice and provide a network for sharing knowledge, expertise, experience, and resources on the topic of school-age programming.

The Canadian Parks and Recreation Association (CPRA), Parks and Recreation Ontario (PRO), and American associations such as the National School Age Care Alliance (NSACA), the National Association for the Education of Young Children (NAEYC), and the National Association for Family Child Care (NAFCC) also provide guidelines for quality school-age care and support various accreditation initiatives.

Staff with postsecondary training are reported to have the most appropriate credentials for working with school-age children. They tend to be more responsive to children, prepare more developmentally appropriate activities, and communicate with others more effectively. Many provinces and territories do not have requirements for their staff to have any postsecondary education or do not have specific training requirements for those working in school-age programs, except for some municipalities in Alberta.

Those staff who do have training may have a certificate, diploma, or degree. Most diplomas are from college Early Childhood Education programs and some Recreation Leadership programs. Graduates have usually had one or more courses in school-age programming that includes topics such as child development, curriculum planning, and behaviour guidance.

Jacobs specifies a number of areas that need further research, including in-service training for staff, the best current practice in training, staffing conditions, regulations specific to school-age programs, emergent curriculum, types of parent-staff communication, the needs of 9- to 12-year-olds, quality issues, and program evaluation.

The last method of upgrading quality discussed in this chapter is evaluation. Harms, Jacobs, and White developed the School-Age Care Environmental Scale (SACERS), in which evaluators use seven categories to rate programs: space, indoors and outdoors; health and safety; activities; interactions; program structure; and staff development. (A supplementary section applies to programs that include children with special needs.)

Key Terms

latch-key children

seamless day

Organisation for Economic Co-operation and Development (OECD)

Child Care Advocacy Association of Canada (CCAAC)

Canadian Child Care Federation (CCCF)

accreditation

College of Early Childhood Educators

Association of Early Childhood Educators in Ontario (AECEO)

Child and Youth Care Association of Alberta (CYCAA)

Association for the Accreditation of Early Learning and Care Services (AELCS)

School-Age Child Care Association of British Columbia (SACCA B.C.)

Canadian Parks and Recreation Association (CPRA)

Parks and Recreation Ontario (PRO)

National School-Age Care Alliance (NSACA)

National Association for the Education of Young Children (NAEYC)

National Association for Family Child Care (NAFCC)

School-Age Care Environmental Scale (SACERS)

Student Activities

1. Copy pages 288 and 289, which list the components of a quality school-age program as determined by the Ontario Coalition for Better Child Care and Dr. Ellen Jacobs. Work in small groups to discuss one of the sections. Describe how school-age child care professionals could advocate for improved quality in each of these areas:

   - regulations, standards, ratios
   - staffing and training
   - physical environment
   - curriculum
   - preadolescent needs
   - communication

2. Find out which centres in your community have used a system of program evaluation such as the SACERS. Assign small groups to interview selected centre directors. Ask the following:

   - How difficult was it to go through the process?
   - How did you get staff interested in it?
   - How long did it take?
   - What are the results?
   - Was the effort worth it?

   Report to the class on your findings.

Review Questions

1. Discuss the progress of school-age care from the early 1900s to the present day.
2. What were the results of the pilot study done by the Ottawa–Carleton District School Board about differentiated staffing for kindergarten children?
3. How have full-day kindergarten and extended-day programs developed in Ontario?
4. What are the components of quality school-age care identified by the Ontario Coalition for Better Child Care and Dr. Ellen Jacobs in her 2000 *Directions for Further Research* report?
5. How do regulations differ between provinces/territories regarding staff/child ratios?
6. How are CCCF, College of ECEs, CYCAA, and SACCA working toward increasing quality in school-age care?
7. Describe the basic training needs of someone working in school-age programs.
8. List the seven categories Harms, Jacobs, and White use in SACERS.

Case Study

Athina, the director/owner of the Little Oaks Child Care Centre, has already used the Early Childhood Environmental Rating Scale (ECERS) in her preschool program. Athina is very proud of this fact; she believes it has helped to improve the quality of her program and has helped parents to see the importance and value of child care experiences. She has just returned from a local conference where she heard about the School-Age Care Environmental Rating Scale. She learned that the SACERS is similar to the ECERS and that it includes instructions for use and rating scale items, and a training guide. Workshops are being offered by child care resource services in her community to train staff in the use of the rating scale. Athina wants very much for her school staff members to review the standards and start the process for SACERS training. Most of the staff are eager to start, but several are resistant, saying they don't think they need to assess the quality of their program. They think it is good enough.

1. Why do you think some school-age child care professionals are resistant to the idea of starting the SACERS training?
2. What would you do about the attitude of the resistors?
3. How can Athina help them to be more positive toward the process?

References

Alberta Association for the Accreditation of Early Learning and Care Services (n.d.). *Background Information on the Development of the Accreditation of ELCS in Alberta*. Retrieved June 2004 from http://www.abccaccred.ca

Alberta Teachers Association. (2010). *Who is offering full-day kindergarten in Canada*. Retrieved June 25, 2012, from http://www.teachers.ab.ca/Publications/ATA%20News/Volume%2044% 202009-10/Number%2014/In%20the%20News/Pages/Who%20is%20offering% 20full-day%20kindergarten%20in%20Canada.aspx

Andrew, C. (2002, Fall). Parents' corner: Intergenerational programming. *Education Today*. Retrieved April 26, 2005, from http://www.opsba.org/pubs/et/articles/Fall_2002_Andrew.html

ARA Consulting Group. (1990). *A survey of licensed school-age programs in Ontario, 1989*. Toronto: Child Care Branch, Ontario Ministry of Community and Social Services.

Archambault, D. (1997). *Les services de garde en milieu scolaire: Enquete dans les commissions scolaires et dans les ecoles primaries*. In E. Jacobs and D. Mill (Eds.), *Directions for further research in Canadian school-age child care*. Ottawa: Child Care Visions, Human Resources Canada.

Best Start (2006). *Early learning for every child today: A framework for Ontario early childhood settings*. Ontario Ministry of Children and Youth Services. Retrieved June 25, 2012, from http://www.cfcollaborative.ca/wp-content/uploads/2010/10/ELECT.pdf

British Columbia Ministry of Education. (2010) *Full school day kindergarten*. Retrieved June 25, 2012, from http://www.bced.gov.bc.ca/early_learning/fdk

Cadden, V. (1993, April). How kids benefit from child care. *Working Mother*.

California Department of Education. (1996). *School-age care in California*. Sacramento, CA: Child Development Division.

Canadian Broadcasting Corporation (2004, October 25). Canada's child care will improve, Dryden insists. Retrieved April 8, 2005, from www.cbc.ca/story/canada/national/2004/10/25/childcare_041025.html

Canadian Child Care Federation. (2006). Policy brief on school-age child care. Retrieved June 25, 2012, from http://ruralteammanitoba.cimnet.ca/cim/dbf/CanadianChildCareSchoolAgeChild.pdf?im_id=237&si_id=170

Canadian Parks and Recreation Association (n.d.). *About CPRA*. Retrieved June 2004 from http://www.cpra.ca/cpra-new/About%20CPRA/About_CPRA.htm

Child and Family Canada (1994). *Assuring Quality in Child Care*, Brief submitted to the Standing Committee on Human Resources Development, Part II. P. 4, http://www.cfc-efc.ca/docs/cccf/0000035.htm retrieved Jan. 2, 2004.

Child and Youth Care Association of Alberta (n.d.)). *History*. Retrieved July 2004 from http://www.cycaa.com/history.htm

Child Care Advocacy Association of Canada. (n.d). Retrieved April 8, 2005, from http://action.web.ca/home/ccaac/alerts.shtml?x=73935&AA_EX_Session=62114cf4ae107a3cb7c63810817c0150

College of Early Childhood Educators. (2012). *Purpose and mandate*. Retrieved June 25, 2012, from http://collegeofece.on.ca/en/AboutUs/Pages/Purpose-and-Mandate.aspx

Coplan, J. Ottawa–Carleton district school board. *Junior kindergarten differentiated—Staffing pilot project evaluation report of findings—Year II: 1997–1999*. Ottawa: Carleton University, Department of Psychology.

De Vaal, N. (1998, Spring). Recreation and healthy child development—Everybody's business. *Exploring Environments*, 8(1), 8.

Doherty, G. (1991). *Quality matters in child care*. Mississauga, ON: Jesmond Publishing.

Elora Partnership. (n.d.). *The Elora Partnership home child care accreditation initiative*. Retrieved April 25, 2005, from http://www.familydaycare.com/elora/accred.html

Ferguson, D. (1995). *Child care becoming visible*. Retrieved July 2004 from http://www.cfc-efc.ca/docs/cccns/00000288.htm

Galambos, N. & Garbarino, J. (1983). Identifying the missing links in the study of latchkey children. *Children Today, 13,* 2–4.

Harms, T. Jacobs, E., & White, D. (1996). *School-age care environmental scale*. New York: Teachers College Press.

Jacobs, E. & Mill, D. (2000). *Directions for further research in Canadian school-age child care*. Ottawa, ON: Child Care Visions, Human Resources Canada.

Jacobs, E., Mill, D., & Jennings, M. (1997–1999). *Quality assurance and school-age care*. National School-Age Care Research Project. Ottawa: Child Care Visions Program of the Employability and Social Partnership Division of Human Resources Development Canada.

Lero, D., Pence, A., Shields, M. Brockman, L., & Goelman, H. (1992). *Canadian national child care study: Introductory report*. Ottawa, ON: Statistics Canada and Health and Welfare Canada.

Long, T. & Long, L. (1982). *Latchkey children: The child's view of self care*. ERIC Document Reproduction Service No. Ed 211 229.

Ontario Coalition for Better Child Care. (2000). School-age care: A question of quality. Retrieved April 9, 2005, from http://www.cfc-efc.ca/docs/ocbcc/00000068.htm

Ontario Ministry of Education. (2010). Memorandum—legislative changes under Bill 242—Early learning program plan. Retrieved June 25, 2012, from http://cal2.edu.gov.on.ca/may2010/2010EL6_Bill242.pdf

Ontario Ministry of Education & Ministry of Community Services. (1988–1989). *Child care for school-aged children.* Toronto: Ministry of Education & Ministry of Community Services, pp. 1–4.

Pacini-Ketchabaw, V. & Pence. A. (n.d.) Contextualizing the reconceptualist movement in Canadian early childhood education. Research Connections Canada. Retrieved June 25, 2012, from http://www.cyc.uvic.ca/uccr/pubs/01.Pacini_Pence_Contextualizing_2005.pdf

Park, N. (1993). *School-age child care: Examining patterns of care and parental attitude.* Toronto: The Policy Research Centre on Children, Youth and Families.

Philip, M. (2004, Nov. 24). "Ontario to unveil school child-care plan." *The Globe and Mail.*

Posner, J. K. & Vandell, D. L. (1994). Low-income children's after-school care: Are there beneficial effects of after-school programs? *Child Development,* 65(2), 440–456.

Rodman, H., Pratto, D.J., & Nelson, R. S. (1988). Child care arrangements and children's functioning: A comparison of self-care and adult-care children. *Developmental Psychology,* 21, 413–418.

School-Age Child Care Association of British Columbia. (n.d.). Home page. Retrieved June 2004 from http://www.wstcoast.org/affiliates/sacca/index.html

Toronto District School Board. (n.d.). Parkdale Public School home page. Retrieved June 2004 from http://schools.tdsb.on.ca/parkdaleps/PPS_PAGE.HTM

Vandell, D. L. & Corasaniti, M. A. (1988). The relations between third-graders' after-school care and social, academic, and emotional functioning. *Child Development,* 59(4), 868–875.

Vandell, D. L., Henderson, V. K., & Wilson, K. S. (1988). A longitudinal study of children with day-care experiences of varying quality. *Child Development,* 59(5), 1286–1292.

Young, N. (1994). *Caring for play: The school and child care connection.* Oshawa, ON: Exploring Environments Publications.

Websites

Child Care/Early Learning and Recreation Sites

Child Care Advocacy Association of Canada
http://www.childcareadvocacy.ca

Childcare Resource and Research Unit
http://www.childcareCanada.org

Canadian Child Care Federation
http://www.cccf-fcsge.ca/home_en.html

Canadian Parks and Recreation Association
http://www.cpsionline.ca

Parks and Recreation Ontario
http://www.prontario.org

National After School Association
http://www.naaweb.org

National Association for the Education of Young Children
http://www.naeyc.org

National Association for Family Child Care
http://www.nafcc.org

National Institute on Out-of-School Time
http://www.niost.org

National School-Age Care Alliance (NAACA)
http://sparkaction.org/node/32181

Ministry of Education—Child Care Licensing
http://www.edu.gov.on.ca/eng/parents/orientation-package-en.pdf

Child and Youth Care Association of Alberta
http://cycaa.com

School Age Child Care Association of British Columbia
http://www.saccabc.org

Further Resources

University of Toronto/Ontario Institute for Studies in Education/Atkinson Centre.
Resources—Seamless Day
http://www.oise.utoronto.ca/atkinson/Resources/Videos/index.html

Ontario Ministry of Education
http://www.edu.gov.on.ca/eng

Day Nurseries Act—Ontario
http://www.e-laws.gov.on.ca/html/regs/english/elaws_regs_900262_e.htm

Education Act—Ontario
http://www.e-laws.gov.on.ca/html/statutes/english/elaws_statutes_90e02_e.htm

Ontario Ministry of Education—Extended Day and Third Party Programs
Regulations
**http://www.e-laws.gov.on.ca/html/source/regs/english/2011/elaws_src_regs_
r11221_e.htm**

Kindergarten GAINS (resources to support implementation of full-day early learning–
kindergarten programs)
http://www.edugains.ca/newsite/fulldaykinder/index.html

Ontario Ministry of Education—Webinar on Full Day Kindergarten/Third Party
Programs Regulations/ Extended Day Guidelines
http://events.digitalmedia.telus.com/ontarioeducationeld/061411/index.php

Child and Family Collaborative—Webinar Serious Occurrence Notification Form
http://www.cfcollaborative.ca/webinar-serious-occurrence-notification-form/

British Columbia Early Learning Framework
http://www.bced.gov.bc.ca/early_learning/pdfs/early_learning_framework.pdf

College of Early Childhood Educators
http://collegeofece.on.ca

Childcare Resource and Research Unit
http://www.childcarecanada.org

OECD Directorate for Education—Early Childhood Education and Care Policy:
Canada
http://www.oecd.org/dataoecd/42/34/33850725.pdf

All About Me:

Name:

Full name: _____

I want to be called: _____

Parent(s): _____

Address: _____

_____

Phone number: _____

Vital Statistics!

Then:

Date of birth/arrival to my family: _____

Place of birth: _____

_____ (city, province)

_____

_____ (hospital)

Weight at birth: _____ kg or lb, _____ g or oz.   Length at birth: _____ cm or in. _____

Hair colour at birth: _____

Eye colour at birth: _____

Now:

Height now: _____ m or ft. _____ cm or in. _____

Hair colour now: _____ Eye color now: _____ _____

About My Family:

Members of my family include:

_____

_____

_____

Here are some pictures of:

ME   MY FAMILY

My Friends:

The person I consider my best friend is: _____

My newest friend is: _____

The qualities that I admire in friends are: _____

My Memories:

My first memory of my childhood was: _____

_____

The first birthday that I remember was: _____

_____

My first memories of school include: _____

_____

Some of the things that I would like you to know about me are: _____

_____

_____

I think I am: _____

_____

_____

Thoughts About School:

My favourite school subject is: _____

My least favourite subject is: _____

I like to read (yes or no). Why or why not? _____

_____

I like to read: _____

_____

The best book I ever read or had read to me: _____

I usually have homework assignments every day (yes or no): _____

I usually need to spend this much time completing my homework: _____

I occasionally need help with some subjects, such as: _____

_____

I have some special interests or things I like to do, such as: _____

_____

_____

If I could plan a day in the school-age program, I would include: _____

_____

_____

If I could invite two famous people to join our class for a day, they would be:

_____ and _____

Favourite Things:

Favourite food: _____

Favourite meal: _____

Favourite colour: _____

Second-favourite colour: _____

Favourite group (musical): _____

Favourite song: _____

Favourite board game: _____

Favourite sport to play: _____

Favourite sport to watch: _____

Favourite TV show: _____

Second-favourite TV show: _____

Favourite hobby: _____

Favourite season: _____

My Goals:

This year I want to be able to: _____

_____

For Parents

Some things that I would like you to know about my child include: _____

_____

He/She has the following talents: _____

He/She has the following strengths as a student: _____

He/She enjoyed the following subject(s) in school: _____

_____

My child learns best by: _____

My thoughts on homework are: _____

_____

Other information you should know about my child: _____

_____

A funny/amusing anecdote I would like to share about my child would be the time that: _____

_____

_____

I would be willing to share my talents/skills with the class for the purpose of enrichment. My talents/skills include: _____

_____

I would like to get involved with my child's school-age program experience in the following way(s): _____

_____

_____

The most convenient time(s) for me to do so are: _____

Should a problem arise with my child, I would like you to handle it in the following manner: _____

_____

_____

If you need to contact me, the best time to do so would be: _____

_____ at work _____- _____-_____ between _____ and _____ _____

_____ at home _____- _____-_____ after _____ no later than _____

I'd prefer contact by email: _____ or cellphone _____

(signature) _____

(date) _____

Appendix B

The Inquiry Process in Early Learning–Kindergarten Classrooms

Initial Engagement
notice, wonder, play, observe, listen, question

Communication
share findings, discuss ideas, connect to prior knowledge

Inquiry Process

Exploration
play, facilitate, observe, work together, question

Investigation
gather, compare, sort, classify, interpret, describe, notice patterns, draw conclusions, plan, reflect

Adapted from Ontario Ministry of Education, "Teaching/Learning Approaches," The Full-Day Early Learning-Kindergarten Program, Draft Version, 2010–11, p. 15.

Guidelines for Planning a Successful Field Trip

Field Trip Planning Form

Destination: _____

Host's name: _____ Telephone: _____

Date of trip: _____ Time: _____

Trip objectives:

_____

_____

_____

Previsit date: _____ Time: _____

Information to share: _____

_____

_____

_____

Findings during pre-visit (bathroom locations, accommodations for special needs, arrangements for lunch or snack): _____

_____

_____

_____

Parents informed:

Newsletter and permission forms date: _____

Request for volunteers: _____

Bulletin board posting date: _____

Transportation arrangements: _____

_____

Mode: _____

Payment: _____

Safety factors: _____

_____

_____

_____

Plans for preparing the children (discussions, books, pictures): _____

_____

_____

_____

_____

Safety rules: _____

_____

_____

Plans for things to do and collect during the trip: _____

_____

_____

Items to take along on the trip (cellphone, first aid kit, emergency information cards for each child): _____

_____

_____

Follow-up: Thank-you notes sent to host and volunteers: _____

Activities and discussion with the children: _____

_____

_____

_____

Evaluation of the trip:

Positive and negative aspects: _____

_____

_____

How were objectives met: _____

_____

_____

Field Trip Permission Form

Dear Parent/Guardian,

I give permission for my child, _____ to go on

a field trip to _____. We will be travelling

by _____.

Cost, _____, to be paid to the school-age program by

_____.

Child's Name: _____

Program: _____

_____   _____
           Parent's Signature   (Date)

Possible Causes of Conflict in a School-Age Program

- ❑ Lack of age-appropriate toys and materials
- ❑ Limited availability of open-ended materials that are engaging
- ❑ Lack of suitable space
- ❑ Inability for staff to allow for flexibility in use of space
- ❑ Long waiting periods during transitions
- ❑ Too many transitions
- ❑ Not enough uninterrupted play time
- ❑ Poor atmosphere of cooperation, communication, and community
- ❑ Little opportunity for children to express their feelings in appropriate ways
- ❑ Poor communication between staff and children and between children
- ❑ Misuse of power by staff—expectations too high or too authoritarian
- ❑ Lack of clarity about expectations, limits, and boundaries
- ❑ Too many rules; lack of child involvement in coming up with rules and understanding what they mean
- ❑ Intolerant and unfriendly atmosphere: bullying and little acceptance of differences
- ❑ Absence of problem-solving and conflict resolution skills
- ❑ Limited observation skills; not meeting children's needs and interests
- ❑ Inability to recognize that children have different personalities and temperaments
- ❑ Overdependence on praise vs. encouragement; always expecting external rewards
- ❑ Lack of understanding of children's intentions, reasons for their behaviours

Permission Form for the Exchange of Information

Communication between school-age child care professionals in the program and personnel from the school that the child attends is essential in order to meet each child's individual needs. Communication between school-age child care professionals and the school is intended to benefit the child, and is related to developmental and behavioural aspects. Information shared will be treated as strictly confidential.

School-Age Program: _____

Supervisor: _____

School: _____

Teacher: _____

I grant permission for the communication of information about my child, _____, to be shared as described above.

_____   _____
Parent signature   (Date)

Individual Contract

Here's what I plan to do next!

_____

_____

_____

_____

I will have it done by:

_____

_____

When I do, I'll be able to:

_____

_____

| _____ | _____ | _____ | _____ |
| Date | Student | Witness | Teacher |

Patent Registration Form, My Invention

Patent Registration Form

My Invention _____

Inventors: _____

Name of Contraption: _____

Description: _____

Date: _____

Signatures: _____

Glossary

accreditation   process by which a representative body recognized by the service community and the community in general establishes standards that are above minimum regulatory requirements of the government; programs apply for evaluation and receive a certificate when they meet the standards (p. 308)

active physical play   opportunities for children to plan their activities, experiment with new skills, and learn by trial and error, benefiting all areas of development (p. 278)

anti-bias curriculum   policies and practices that acknowledge the development of children's positive self-worth, identity, and well-being; addressing the impact of stereotyping, bias, and discriminatory behaviour (p. 142)

antisocial behaviour   disruptive behaviour, bothering others, fighting and other forms of physical and verbal aggression (name calling and excluding others from a group) (p. 92)

Association for the Accreditation of Early Learning and Care Services (AELCS)   manages the accreditation process in child care centres and contracted family child care agencies in Alberta (p. 310)

Association of Early Childhood Educators in Ontario (AECEO)   professional organization of individuals who work in early childhood and child care settings; who advocates for quality programs; provides leadership between professionals (p. 310)

authentic feedback   a description of a child's real accomplishments (p. 187)

autonomy vs. shame and doubt   Erikson's second stage, in which the focus is to become independent by gaining control over bodily functions (p. 80)

bias   point of view, belief, or attitude that can be demonstrated verbally, nonverbally, or physically; areas of potential bias include ability, age, appearance, beliefs, class, culture, family composition, gender, race, and sexuality (p. 142)

biodegradable   objects that disintegrate over time (p. 260)

blended family   These are families where there is at least one child from one or both previous relationships plus one child from the current union (p. 31)

body mass index (BMI)   a measure of the ratio of weight to height (p. 51)

bullying   violent behaviour imposed by individuals who wish to intimidate, harass, alienate, and isolate others they perceive as weaker, vulnerable, and easy targets (p. 112)

Eating Well with Canada's Food Guide   guideline for planning healthy, nutritionally balanced snacks and meals based on four food groups, including cultural adaptations (p. 267)

Canadian Association for Health, Physical Education, Recreation, and Dance (CAHPERD)   advocates daily physical activity and more extensive physical education in schools (p. 275)

Canadian Child Care Federation (CCCF)   professional organization that promotes the recognition of quality care for children from infancy to age 12; CCCF advocates for professionals in the field of child care, building credibility through an accreditation system (p. 308)

Canadian Parks and Recreation Association (CPRA)   national voice for a network of people who are in partnership with communities to build a healthy, active quality of life and support social-recreation programs out of school hours (p. 310)

Canadian Standards Association (CSA)   sets standards for safe planning of equipment and design of outdoor play space for children in public playgrounds and child care centres (p. 164)

centring   Piaget's observation that young children focus on only one dimension of a form at a time (p. 62)

Child and Youth Care Association of Alberta (CYCAA)   organization of child care professionals who have common interests, concerns, and objectives in providing quality services to children and youth (p. 310)

Child Care Advocacy Association of Canada (CCAAC)   advocates for strong federal and provincial/territorial policies that entitle all families in Canada to a publicly funded, nonprofit, quality, inclusive child care system (p. 302)

child care practitioner   an individual whose profession is working in child care (p. 3)

childhood education and care   term that denotes higher recognition and value for both care and education of children in formal schooling and in child care (p. 3)

citizenship   being part of a community; being responsible for one's own property; respecting the property of others;

caring for others and doing good deeds for them; following rules and valuing oneself and the environment (p. 254)

classical conditioning conditioning brought about by proximity of stimulus and response (p. 64)

clique a group of children who have similar characteristics and interests (p. 20)

code switching a complete change of language form when addressing adults and when talking to other children (p. 72)

common-law family two individuals of the opposite sex who are not legally married to each other but live together as husband and wife in the same dwelling and have one or more children (p. 31)

communication ways that individuals respond verbally and nonverbally to each other (p. 104)

community rural, urban, suburban settings; buildings; diversity of people, families and cultures; citizenship and caring for the environment (p. 248)

compassion respect of differences and unique personalities, and understanding the feelings of others (p. 101)

concrete operations ability to think symbolically and to reverse processes when information is presented concretely (p. 62)

conflict resolution process of mediating between arguing children in a way that helps them to think situations through for themselves, make decisions, and solve problems (p. 105)

constructing knowledge developing one's own theories about how the world works (p. 219)

constructivism based on a belief that children are curious, capable and interested in learning; allowing for opportunities to build on their interests and ideas that extend on their current knowledge (p. 128)

conventional Kohlberg's second stage of moral development, in which there is an emphasis on social rules of the individual's family, group, or nation (p. 84)

convergent thinking a process of thought that narrows down many ideas into a single focused point (p. 197)

cooperation ability to work together to achieve a common goal (p. 101)

cooperative games games that do not have a definite winner or loser; these games often involve many levels of strategy, effective communication, and working together to solve a problem (p. 182)

culture way of living, shared with other members of the same group, which includes ways of thinking, beliefs, languages spoken, holidays, celebrations, and customs (p. 252)

developmentally responsive planning programs are responsive to individual growth and changes that occur on a continuum of development (p. 127)

differing abilities/special needs individuals with different physical and cognitive limitations (p. 256)

divergent questions questions that have no specific answer and require a child to think critically (p. 222)

divergent thinking a process of thought or perception that involves considering alternatives and taking a line of thought that is different from the usual (p. 197)

documentation means of recording children's learning processes through written, verbal, or visual methods such as a web drawing, thus providing validation of their play and work (p. 132)

early childhood educator trained professional who works with children primarily from birth to age 8 and up to age 12 (p. 3)

early learning and care professional registered early childhood educator working in a full-day early learning and care and extended day program in an elementary school (p. 4)

ecology study of life forms (living and nonliving) as they relate to each other and their environment (p. 258)

ego in psychoanalytic theory, the rational aspect of personality (p. 79)

elaborated code a communication that uses a more extensive vocabulary, is correct grammatically, and is longer (p. 72)

emergent curriculum method of curriculum planning that evolves through continuous observations, dialogue, and documentation as children devise and engage in projects (p. 136)

environment preservation of animals and their habitats; sustainable use of natural resources and the reduction of pollution and waste (p. 258)

ethics a study of right, wrong, duty, and obligation (p. 11)

fitness physical state of well-being that allows people to perform daily tasks with vigor, reduces risks of health problems, and establishes a performance base of physical activity (p. 274)

formal operations ability to consider hypothetical problems without concrete examples (p. 62)

friendship relationship between people that involves qualities of fairness, honesty, trust, respect, compassion, integrity, and caring (p. 254)

gang a group of children who gather together to be out of the realm of adults but also to be antisocial (p. 20)

High/Scope program child-centred approach that involves the children in planning and reviewing their day along with active "doing," which involves workshop time (p. 138)

id in psychoanalytic theory, the part of the personality that is the source of pleasure-seeking drives (p. 79)

identity vs. role confusion Erikson's fifth stage, in which adolescents search for their identity as individuals in a society (p. 80)

inclusion sense of belonging with a blending of differences; not leaving anyone out and helping everyone to feel part of an activity or situation (p. 143)

industry vs. inferiority Erikson's fourth stage, in which children expend all their energies on mastering new skills at home, in school, on the playground, and in their neighbourhood (p. 80)

initiative vs. guilt Erikson's third stage, in which children attempt new activities that can result in either pride (initiative) or guilt when unsuccessful (p. 80)

inquiry learning a process of exploring, observing, gathering information, and engaging in a sense of wonder (p. 198)

integrated learning using interrelated disciplines such as language, math, or science to achieve a goal (p. 191)

lateralization specialization in function of the two hemispheres of the brain (p. 197)

intergenerational program planned, intentional interaction between different age groups in a variety of situations at a level that provides close communication, sharing of feelings and ideas, and cooperative activity (p. 286)

kindergarten programs child-centred, developmentally appropriate, integrated, core day and extended-day programs of play-based learning for 4- and 5-year-old children (p. 140)

latch-key children children who let themselves into their homes with a key and are unsupervised during out-of-school time until their parent(s) or guardian comes home (p. 301)

learning processes by which environmental influences and experiences bring about permanent changes in thinking, feeling, and behaviour (p. 48)

logical consequences a tool for changing behaviour in which the result of a child's misbehaviour is related to the behaviour (p. 102)

lone-parent family family led by a father or mother with one or more children (p. 31)

married-couple family family led by a mother and father who have registered a legal marriage and who have one or more children (p. 31)

mathematical knowledge includes number, geometry, measurement, algebra, and data analysis (p. 223)

maturation progression of changes that takes place as one ages (p. 48)

mediation process in which a person who is not involved in the conflict (the mediator) helps those who are in a conflict to come up with their own solutions (p. 105)

modelling exhibit the behaviours that are expected of children (p. 64)

Montessori programs a prepared environment that supports each child's independence and ability to plan his or her own activities after school (p. 139)

moral realism a stage of moral development in which children believe that rules are determined by an authority figure and they are not to be changed (p. 83)

moral relativism a stage of moral development in which children view punishments as fair or unfair, are more flexible in their thinking, and can discuss moral issues (p. 83)

morality of caring Gilligan's theory that girls are socialized to be caring and nurturing and reluctant to judge right and wrong in absolutes (p. 85)

morality of justice Gilligan's theory that boys will determine what is right or wrong and then follow it with a clear solution when faced with making choices (p. 85)

morality our perception of what is good or right (p. 11)

multiple intelligences eight different ways that children learn: interpersonal, intrapersonal, linguistic, logical-mathematical, spatial, bodily-kinesthetic, musical, and naturalistic (p. 127)

multipurpose equipment equipment that has many possibilities for play activities (p. 165)

National Association for Family Child Care (NAFCC) develops quality standards for accreditation in home-based child care (p. 312)

National Association for the Education of Young Children (NAEYC) a large professional organization that accredits programs for children from birth through the elementary years (p. 312)

National School-Age Care Alliance (NSACA) develops best practices standards for children aged 5 to 14 (p. 311)

natural consequences results of one's behaviour that have an implicit effect on another's reaction; allows children to learn from their actions (p. 101)

nature a variety of characteristics that are inherited from parents (p. 48)

negotiating strategy that involves ongoing discussions about thoughts, ideas, and feelings and emphasizes cooperative problem solving to assist in resolving differences (p. 105)

nonbiodegradable objects that will not disintegrate over time (p. 260)

nurture all the experiences and influences one is exposed to from the moment of conception on throughout a lifetime (p. 48)

observation means of gathering information about children's interests, needs, and developmental abilities through recorded methods to further relevant learning opportunities (p. 132)

operant conditioning the process by which children act upon their environment and are reinforced for their behaviours (p. 64)

Organisation for Economic Co-operation and Development (OECD) a forum in which governments can work together to solve social, economic, and environmental issues (p. 302)

Parks and Recreation Ontario (PRO) dedicated to promoting the value and benefits of parks and recreation to the public (p. 311)

peacemaking a program approach that is used to promote a healthy emotional, social, and nonviolent climate (p. 98)

physical knowledge how objects behave as a result of their characteristics (p. 223)

play self-motivated, pleasurable, and process-oriented aspect of children's daily life that is vital to their social, emotional, cognitive, and physical development (p. 129)

positive self-image good image of oneself as well as good feelings based on perceptions conveyed by others (p. 98)

postconventional Kohlberg's third stage of moral development, in which there is an emphasis on moral values and principles (p. 84)

power appropriate ways for children to feel that they have some say about activities and practices in their program (p. 97)

preconventional Kohlberg's first stage of moral development, in which there is an emphasis on punishment and rewards (p. 84)

preoperational period ability to begin to think symbolically and to remember experiences and objects independently of the immediate encounter (p. 62)

problem solving the ability to focus on more than one aspect of a situation at a time, to consider more than one point of view, to generate and agree on solutions and implement them (p. 99)

project-based curriculum approach that involves the investigation of a real-world topic based on children's interest or initiated by school-age child care professionals (p. 136)

recreation leader adult in a school-age program where the emphasis is on recreational aspects (p. 3)

Reggio Emilia programs programs that incorporate elements of emergent curriculum and project-based approaches, focusing on an integration of graphic arts as tools for cognitive, linguistic, and social development (p. 137)

respect treating individuals with kindness and understanding regardless of size, age, gender, or ethnic or cultural background, plus taking care of toys, equipment, and the physical environment (p. 94)

responsibility professional duty of school-age child care professionals to promote and improve the quality of the social environment; also the children's ability to regulate their own behaviour, to recognize the impact of their behaviour on others, to practise strategies of self-control, and to take care of their physical environment (p. 93)

restricted code communications that are more limited and may rely on gestures and voice intonation to convey meaning (p. 72)

rights to be oneself, to be listened to, to express one's feelings in appropriate ways, to be treated with compassion, and to enjoy a general sense of happiness (p. 93)

risk taking being able to challenge oneself and make appropriate decisions, with adult support (p. 86)

rules a simple set of guidelines that are developed with input from the children in order for everyone to feel safe and secure in their social setting (p. 94)

safety checklist survey of all playground structures in comparison to standards, guidelines, and laws set by municipal, provincial/ territorial, and federal agencies (p. 165)

same-sex-parent family composed of lesbian couples, gay male partners, or singles from this group with one or more children (p. 32)

scaffold system that supports children as they move from one intellectual level to the next (p. 66)

scaffolding the process of acquiring new skills and knowledge through interactions with peers and/or adults (p. 223)

School-Age Care Environmental Scale (SACERS) a method of rating programs that serve children 5 to 12 years of age (p. 313)

school-age care worker adult working in child care or recreation-oriented school-age program (p. 3)

School-Age Child Care Association of British Columbia (SACCA B.C.) province-wide nonprofit organization that is open to professionals and students working or studying in the school-age child care field; its goal is to improve the availability, quality, and affordability of school-age child care (p. 310)

school-age child care professional individual working in a licensed school-age program in child care or with a recreational focus (p. 3)

seamless day concept that provides a link between junior and senior kindergarten and before and after kindergarten in child care; allows for the coordination of services, resources, and curriculum planning between qualified professionals, and ensures limited transitions for the children (p. 301)

Second Step Violence Prevention Program behaviour-intervention program that focuses on developing prosocial behaviours and reducing impulsive and aggressive behaviours of children (p. 118)

self-concept perception of one's self and perceptions conveyed by others (p. 17)

self-esteem children's view of themselves in relation to their ability to accomplish their goals and expand their skills (p. 16)

self-regulation ability to recognize how one's own emotional and cognitive abilities can facilitate positive relationships (p. 92)

sensorimotor period Piaget's first period, in which infants use all their senses to explore and learn about the world around them (p. 61)

single-purpose equipment play equipment that can be used for only one kind of play (p. 165)

social competence getting along with others, listening to other viewpoints, understanding the importance of establishing and following rules, and using empathy (p. 92)

social knowledge information children cannot construct for themselves (p. 223)

stepfamily two-parent family where one parent is not the biological or adoptive parent of the child(ren) (p. 31)

storage strategies methods used to increase memory (p. 61)

superego in psychoanalytic theory, the part of the personality that controls behaviour through the development of conscience (p. 79)

trust vs. mistrust Erikson's first stage, in which babies learn to trust that others will take care of their basic needs and that others can be depended upon (p. 80)

values the qualities we believe to be intrinsically desirable and that we strive to achieve in ourselves (p. 10)

Waldorf programs child focused; develops attributes of a well-rounded person to think creatively, be socially responsive, and have a strong sense of emotional and physical well-being (p. 139)

zero tolerance policy used for discipline procedures in elementary and secondary schools to curb violence (p. 118)

zone of proximal development the hypothetical environment in which learning and development take place (p. 66)

Text Credits

p. 11, Eight Ethical Principles. © Canadian Childcare Federation. Reprinted with permission.

pp. 15–16, *National Post,* September 9, 2000, pp. E1–E6.

p. 60, List of Quality Issues. *Quality Assurance and School Age Care 1997–1999,* Social Development Canada. Reproduced with the permission of the Minister of Public Works and Government Services, 2012.

p. 92, DAS Code of Behaviour. Reprinted by permission of the Downtown Alternative School.

pp. 94–95, Guidelines for Establishing and Reinforcing Appropriate Behaviour. Adapted from Todd, C. M. (1992). Establishing rules. In Todd, C. M. (Ed.), *School-age connections,* 1(6), pp. 3–5. Urbana-Champaign, IL: University of Illinois Cooperative Extension Service. Used by permission of Christine M. Todd, University of Georgia.

p. 97, Adapted from *Teaching young children in violent times, building a peaceable classroom,* 2nd ed. (p. 142), by D. Levin, 2003, Washington DC: NAEYC.

p. 105, *Webster's Encyclopedic Dictionary of the English Language, Canadian Edition.* (1988). New York: Lexicon Publications, Inc.

p. 114, *Bullying: A crisis in our schools and our communities,* by R. Chodzinski, 2004, Welland, ON: Soleil Publishing; and *Bullying: A crisis in our schools and our communities,* by National Strategy on Community Safety and Crime Prevention (n.d.), retrieved April 25, 2005, from http://www.prevention.gc.ca/en/library/publications/fact_sheets/bullying.

pp. 126–127, "A school-age program with a difference," by E. Lowe, 2000, *Interaction,* CCCF, Winter, pp. 30–34.

p. 128, IPA Declaration on the Child's Right to Play. International Play Association, http://www.ipaworld.org/ipa_declaration.html

p. 130, Canadian Child Care Federation (2001). Resource sheet #23: Developmentally appropriate practices in school-age child care. Ottawa, ON: CCCF.

p. 142, Wolpert, E. (1999). *Start seeing diversity—The basic guide to an anti-bias classroom.* St. Paul, MN: Redleaf Press. Page 13.

p. 143, Blisson, J. (1997). *Celebrate! An anti-bias guide to enjoying holidays.* St. Paul, MN: Redleaf Press. Page 27.

p. 144, *Include me too! Human diversity in early childhood,* by K. Murphy Kilbride, 1997, Toronto: Harcourt Brace & Co., Canada, p. 216.

p. 165, Canadian Paediatric Society. (1996). *Well beings* (2nd. ed.). Ottawa: Canadian Paediatric Society, pp. 971–997. (Weekly, Monthly, and Yearly Safety Checklists)

p. 179, Based on "Hoist Your Sails," submitted by Miss Ella Des Brisay from Halifax in *Children's Games from Many Lands,* ed. N. Millen; Friendship Press, New York, 1943.

p. 185, Nim Game. From *THE MULTICULTURAL GAME BOOK: MORE THAN 70 TRADITIONAL GAMES FROM 30 COUNTRIES* by Louise Orlando. Scholastic Inc./Teaching Resources. Copyright © 1993 by Louise Orlando. Reprinted by permission.

pp. 246–247, From "Celebrating the diversity of Mother Earth: First Nations child care project, Bkejwanong Children's Centre," by T. Perron & J. Woehl, 1998, *Interaction,* CCCF, pp. 32–34.

pp. 264–265, From Nova Scotia Agriculture and Fisheries (2004). *What is 4-H? The basics.* Retrieved April 25, 2005, from http://www.gov.ns.ca/nsaf/4h/awareness/whatis4h.htm

pp. 268–269, Eating Well with Canada's Food Guide Excerpts. *Canada's Food Guide.* Health Canada, 2011. Reproduced with the permission of the Minister of Health, 2012.

pp. 298–299, Note: From Toronto District School Board, (n.d.), retrieved October 2004, from http://schools.tdsb.on.ca/parkdaleps.

pp. 306–307, Governance for ECE by province/territory. Reprinted with permission from the Early Years Study/Margaret Wallace and McCain Family Foundation. www.earlyyearsstudy.ca.

p. 310, Child and Youth Care Association of Alberta.

p. 310, School-Age Child Care Association of British Columbia.

p. 327, © Queen's Printer for Ontario, 2010. Reproduced with permission.

Photo Credits

p. 164, Morgan Lane Photography/Shutterstock

p. 174, © Royalty-Free/Corbis

p. 176, © D. Berry/PhotoLink/Getty Images

p. 177, © Nicola Sutton/Life File/Getty Images

p. 257, © Photodisc Collection/Getty Images

p. 259, © Russell Illig/Getty Images

p. 301, © PhotoLink/Getty Images

Index

Thematic-based approach, 135–36
Thingamajigs projects, 228
Thinking
  concrete, 220, 221
  convergent, 197–98
  critical, 222
  developmental stages and, 23, 24, 25
  divergent, 197
  See also Cognitive development
Tic-Tac-Toe Dice, 185–86
Time management, 133, 147–48
Time-out, 110–11
Toothpicks, for construction projects, 201
Tornado in a jar, 238
Torso exercises, 277–78
Towers and castles, construction of, 202
Toys, 189
Training, school-age care, 301, 304, 312–13
Transitions, 147
  planning, 134
  preparing, 111
Trivial Pursuit®, 176, 288
Trust *vs.* mistrust stage, in psychosocial
    theory, 80
Trust walk, 257
T-shirt chromatography, 230
Turiel, E., 83
Tutoring, 288
Twenty Pairs (game), 184–85
Twig architecture, 249

UNICEF, 129
United Generations Ontario (UGO),
    286–87

Universal principles stage, of moral
    development, 84
Upset the Fruit Basket (game), 182
Upside-down face painting, 213

Values, personal, 10–12
Vandell, D.L., 301
Velocity, 229
Violence
  CDs, 207
  in settling disputes, 104
  video games, 189
  zero tolerance policy, 118
  See also Bullying
Visual arts
  collage, 202
  construction activities, 201–202
  discussion, 206
  equipment, 205–206
  large masks, 204–205
  modelling activities, 199–201
  painting and drawing, 204–205
  paper quilt, 203
  sewing projects, 203
  weaving projects, 202
Visualize, ability to, 71
Vocabulary, language development and, 70,
    71–72
Volunteer Grandparents Society, 286
Volunteers, 286–87
  activities, 287–91
  guidelines for using, 292–93
Vygotsky, L.S., 66–67, 127–28, 129

Walking sticks, 257
Walpole Island First Nation, 246
Warm-up exercises, 275
Watson, J.B., 64
Weather, charting, 237
Weaving projects, 202
Webbing, 132
White, D., 313
Wicking, 231
Wildlife Refuge, 292
Wilson, C., 135
Windmill project, 228
Withdrawn child, 114–16
Wolpert, E., 142
Women, and divorce, 33–34
Wood, for construction projects, 201
Word processing, 191
Worm environment, 234

Yahtzee®, 176
Yashima, Taro, 142
Yoga, 278
Young, N., 299, 311
Young school-age children, and cross-
    gender fraternization, 19

Zero tolerance, of violence, 118
Zipper, invention of, 227
Zone of proximal development,
    66–67
Zwerling, Mat, 176